A haunting theme of *State Capture in South Africa* is that South Africa is no different from most of the postcolonial world. It jars with the psyche of South Africans because so many of us did believe we would be different with our Constitution and the towering figure of Madiba. *State Capture in South Africa* also tells us why we are no different. It juxtaposes the structural explanations that direct us to historical processes, to deflection analyses that solely blame elites of the preceding racist and colonial society, to descriptive studies that explain the state capture underpinnings and finally, to comparative cases where similar processes play out and may even have been challenged. A must-read for all who are interested in the failed promise and future of this tragic land.

– Adam Habib, Director,
School of Oriental and African Studies (SOAS), University of London

In *State Capture in South Africa*, Buthelezi and Vale have curated an important academic and theoretical context to understand how this phenomenon manifested in South Africa. The book unravels the disparate elements of state capture and unpacks its political economy dimensions. The various actors and elite networks that enabled the capture of the South African state are identified, and their roles in undermining our constitutional democracy clearly expounded. This adds significantly to the discourse on re-establishing the democratic state.

– Lawson Naidoo, Executive Secretary,
Council for the Advancement of the South African Constitution (CASAC)

STATE CAPTURE IN SOUTH AFRICA

HOW AND WHY IT HAPPENED

EDITED BY
MBONGISENI BUTHELEZI AND PETER VALE

WITS UNIVERSITY PRESS

Published in South Africa by:
Wits University Press
1 Jan Smuts Avenue
Johannesburg 2001

www.witspress.co.za

First published 2023

http://dx.doi.org.10.18772/22023068318

978-1-77614-831-8 (Paperback)
978-1-77614-832-5 (Hardback)
978-1-77614-833-2 (Web PDF)
978-1-77614-834-9 (EPUB)

This publication is peer reviewed following international best practice standards for academic and scholarly books.

Project manager: Catherine Damerell
Copy editor: Sally Hines
Proofreader: Lisa Compton
Indexer: Margaret Ramsay
Cover design: Hybrid Creative
Typeset in 10 point Minion Pro

Dedicated to Fanyana 'Pelepele' Buthelezi, 1951–2022

CONTENTS

LIST OF FIGURES AND TABLE   ix
ACKNOWLEDGEMENTS   xi
ABBREVIATIONS AND ACRONYMS   xiii

INTRODUCTION   Understanding and Explaining State Capture   1
Mbongiseni Buthelezi and Peter Vale

SECTION 1   FRAMING THE ISSUE

CHAPTER 1   Elite Formation, Factions and Violence in the Political
Economy of Corruption   19
Karl von Holdt

CHAPTER 2   State Capture, the Racket and Predatory Power   39
Robyn Foley

CHAPTER 3   The Foundations of Corruption in South Africa   65
Ryan Brunette

SECTION 2   STATE CAPTURE IN ACTION

CHAPTER 4   Legal Mobilisation against State Capture   89
Jonathan Klaaren

CHAPTER 5   How Professionals Enabled State Capture   109
Cherese Thakur and Devi Pillay

CHAPTER 6   Civil Society in the Face of State Capture: Solidarity and Disharmony   130
Luke Spiropoulos

CHAPTER 7   Media Capture, the Mirror of State Capture   151
Reg Rumney

SECTION 3   PAST AND FUTURE

CHAPTER 8   State Capture and the Popular Imagination: Narrowing the Narrative   175
Sizwe Mpofu-Walsh

CHAPTER 9   Cycles of State Capture: Bringing Profiteers and Enablers to Account   197
Hennie van Vuuren and Michael Marchant

CHAPTER 10 Old Ways and New Days: An Interview with Barney Pityana   217
            Mbongiseni Buthelezi and Peter Vale

CHAPTER 11 Can Democracy Bind the State? Comparative Thoughts from
            Brazil, India and South Africa   234
            Patrick Heller

CONTRIBUTORS   257
INDEX   261

FIGURES AND TABLE

FIGURE 2.1   The racket of predatory power in South Africa's state capture.
              Graphic by Robin Foley.   44

FIGURE 2.2   The shape of state capture: roles and functions in the shadow
              state. Graphic by Robin Foley.   47

TABLE 2.1   Types of rackets that enabled state capture in South Africa.   48

FIGURE 8.1   *Lenin Lived, Lenin Lives, Lenin Will Live Forever!* Soviet
              propaganda poster by Viktor Ivanov and inspiration for Brett
              Murray's *The Spear* (2010). Courtesy of Alamy.   179

FIGURE 8.2   *The Spear* by Brett Murray (2010). Image reproduced courtesy
              of Brett Murray/Everard Read Gallery.   180

ACKNOWLEDGEMENTS

This collection has been long in the making. Our initial thanks must go to the authors of these compelling chapters who have made the almost four-year-long journey with us.

We are grateful to Jill Weintroub for her work on the initial edit and proofing of the draft manuscript. What a joy it was to work with her; at an earlier stage, Lweendo Hamukoma helpfully commented on the chapters.

Publisher Veronica Klipp, commissioning editor Roshan Cader, Corina van der Spoel, Andrew Joseph and Kirsten Perkins showed us why Wits University Press is a national treasure.

Among other instruments, edited books are the public face of academic and policy work. However, those who do the backroom labour necessary for this work to succeed are seldom acknowledged. So, and with much enthusiasm, this is a shout-out to the secretarial, administrative, cleaning and gardening staff at the Public Affairs Research Institute. Thank you for your selfless support.

The Editors

ABBREVIATIONS AND ACRONYMS

ANC	African National Congress
BBBEE	Broad-Based Black Economic Empowerment
BJP	Bharatiya Janata Party
CASAC	Council for the Advancement of the South African Constitution
CIPC	Companies and Intellectual Property Commission
Cosatu	Congress of South African Trade Unions
CPS	Cash Paymaster Services
EFF	Economic Freedom Fighters
GEAR	Growth, Employment and Redistribution
HDW	Howaldtswerke-Deutsche Werft
IFP	Inkatha Freedom Party
IKL	Ingenieurkontor Lübeck
IRBA	Independent Regulatory Board for Auditors
JSE	Johannesburg Stock Exchange
KBL	Kredit Bank Luxembourg
MK	uMkhonto we Sizwe
NDPP	National Director of Public Prosecutions
NGO	non-governmental organisation
NPA	National Prosecuting Authority
Numsa	National Union of Metalworkers of South Africa
OCCRP	Organized Crime and Corruption Reporting Project
OUTA	Opposition to Urban Tolling Alliance (Organisation Undoing Tax Abuse from 2016)
PARI	Public Affairs Research Institute
PRCA	Public Relations and Communications Association
PT	Partido dos Trabalhadores
PwC	PricewaterhouseCoopers
R2K	Right2Know

RDP	Reconstruction and Development Programme
RET	radical economic transformation
SAA	South African Airways
SABC	South African Broadcasting Corporation
SACP	South African Communist Party
Saftu	South African Federation of Trade Unions
SAPS	South African Police Service
SARS	South African Revenue Service
SASSA	South African Social Security Agency
SCA	Supreme Court of Appeal
SCRP	State Capacity Research Project
SOE	state-owned enterprise
TRC	Truth and Reconciliation Commission
UDF	United Democratic Front
UN	United Nations
Unisa	University of South Africa
WMC	white monopoly capital

Introduction

Understanding and Explaining State Capture

Mbongiseni Buthelezi and Peter Vale

LIFE MIRRORING FICTION

'From the day a few years before when I had left Parliament depressed and aggrieved, I had felt, like so many other educated citizens of our country, that things were going seriously wrong without being able to say just how' (Achebe [1966] 2001, 35). These words are spoken by Odili Samalu, the narrator of Chinua Achebe's novel *A Man of the People*, who tells the story of his country's postcolonial transition. After studying in the capital city, Odili has chosen to return to teach in a small village in his home region rather than work in an office in the capital, because he is disillusioned by the mismanagement of the country and the corruption he sees taking hold.

Later, in the same passage, he observes: 'We complained about our country's lack of dynamism ... We listened to whispers of scandalous deals in high places – sometimes involving sums of money that I for one didn't believe existed in the country ... But sitting at Chief Nanga's feet I received enlightenment; many things began to crystallize out of the mist – some of the emergent forms were not nearly as ugly as I had suspected but many seemed much worse' (Achebe [1966] 2001, 35).

The year is 1960. Chief Nanga is Odili's former teacher who has become a corrupt, philandering minister in the national government. The country is led by the

People's Organisation Party, which, it is revealed later, takes a 10 per cent cut off state contracts for its coffers (Achebe [1966] 2001, 106–107). The opposition Progressive Alliance Party offers no alternative as some of its members defect to the People's Organisation Party as soon as they are elected in order to access positions of power and opportunities to 'chop' – the colloquial phrase used for personal enrichment.

Odili eventually joins a group to launch a new party that runs for election against the People's Organisation Party and contests Nanga's seat. But the group is swiftly crushed through the deployment of private armies, thugs and state power, including the police and the revenue authority. As he infiltrates Nanga's election rally, Odili thinks to himself that if he were to climb to the podium and tell the crowd that the great man they have come to hear is an 'Honourable Thief' (Achebe [1966] 2001, 127), they would simply laugh at him and say, 'What a fool! Whose son is he? Was he not here when white men were eating; what did he do about it? Where was he when Chief Nanga fought and drove the white men away? Why is he envious now that the warrior is eating the reward of his courage?'

With small adjustments from fiction to fact, the foregoing account might well be a description of South Africa since the advent of democracy in 1994: the sense of things going wrong and being unable for a long time to understand with clarity; sums of money many thought did not exist being siphoned out of the state and its institutions; and leaders using liberation credentials to place themselves in positions of power, from which they claim to be acting in the interest of the formerly oppressed while looting public resources. This is indeed what has come to pass in South Africa in a reprise of what has taken place in earlier times in other postcolonial African countries, the most glaring example being South Africa's neighbour, Zimbabwe. That this should have come to pass in post-apartheid South Africa is especially irksome, given the towering figure cut by the country's first democratically elected president, Nelson Mandela, and the accompanying boast that citizens of the 'new South Africa' lived under 'the best Constitution in the world'. Put in Tocquevillian terms, South Africa was – or would be – an exception to the postcolonial experience in Africa. The focus of this book is the saga of why this has not been the case. Because the state itself was captured for the gain of a few at the expense of the many, this book, in part, is the story of the undoing of the country's sense of exceptionalism.

Using various points of entry, the chapters in this volume lean towards what the French theorist Jean-François Bayart called 'the politics of the belly' – a phrase that is tapped from the Cameroonian expression *la politique du ventre* (Bayart 1993). Perhaps because it is positioned outside the limiting categories of social scientists, Bayart's notion helpfully captures the interplay between patrimonialism, clientelism, corruption, misuse of political and economic power, and inept government. Such an outcome involves overturning a postcolonial social order to serve the interests of a small but powerful elite. Revealingly, Bayart's shorthand explanation was passed over in South Africa, notwithstanding that the achievements of the long struggle against apartheid were at great risk. In no small part, this is because 'understanding' and 'knowing', as philosophers of language tell us, are not always in sync. This was especially so in South Africa, where the thrall of the idea that apartheid had ended crowded out an understanding that the issues that faced the country were not only about race and apartheid but also involved far deeper legacies of colonialism. In what follows, we return to Bayart and place him alongside other thinkers on the postcolonial African state in order to position this book among its intellectual forebears.

This is not the occasion to delve into the complexities of the philosophy of language, but the full extent of how the state and the democratic order were being corroded was not plain until a vocabulary emerged that made it comprehensible. Like Odili and the citizens of Achebe's fictional country that references actual countries, for several years South Africans seemed to have a growing sense that something was going wrong in their country, without being able to say with certainty what it was.

How did this change?

WHAT DO WE UNDERSTAND BY STATE CAPTURE?

It was the publication in 2016 of a report by the Public Protector called 'State of Capture' that first helped to bring the message home that something was seriously amiss in post-apartheid South Africa (Public Protector 2016). In the report, Thuli Madonsela singled out the relationship between President Jacob Zuma and a particular family of Indian émigrés, the Guptas. Her intervention came after denial by Zuma's government that anything untoward was underway, even in the face of increasing evidence. Mostly assembled by investigative journalists, the evidence pointed to three central issues: irregularity in the awarding of public contracts; illegality in the appointments of board members and executives to some state-owned corporations; and the repurposing of public institutions. The mounting evidence sparked opposition to the Zuma presidency from disparate voices in civil society and the press; by then, too, several motions of no confidence in parliament had been brought against the president – each of these was to fail. Increasingly, too, the courts were used to seek out governmental accountability under the Constitution, while, behind closed doors, business organisations engaged the emerging issue of malfeasance within the corridors of power. Finally, the public took to the streets, led by the movement that boldly branded itself #ZumaMustFall (Runciman, Nkuna and Frassinelli 2017).

But if the notion of what was underway was gradually being understood, it still had to be named.

In May 2017, the Public Affairs Research Institute (PARI) published an analysis of how the affairs of state institutions were being conducted under Zuma's presidency (PARI 2017). The report, 'Betrayal of the Promise: How South Africa Is Being Stolen', brought the issues into clear focus. A few days later, the contents of an email dump – dubbed the GuptaLeaks – were released by the mass-circulation *Sunday Times*. This offered a trail of evidence to the claims made in the PARI report. Taken together, the report and the leaks offered an increasingly coherent analysis of what was underway. Put in idiomatic language, the dots were being joined together and, as they were, the extent of corruption was progressively being revealed. Also revealed was that the destruction of the investigation and prosecution capabilities of both the South African Police Service and the National Prosecuting Authority was part of the same project of state capture.

The unfolding drama that led to these breakthroughs is further described in the riveting 2018 account, *Shadow State: The Politics of State Capture* (Chipkin and Swilling 2018).

UNDERSTANDING STATE CAPTURE WITHIN THE AFRICAN STORY

From its origins in the 'State of Capture' report, the term 'state capture' has gained wide currency – indeed, within the local political lexicon, it has become a signifier for a particular form of political behaviour. In this way, it loosely resembles in a local setting the catch-all nature of the term 'Watergate', which is associated with the web of scandals that plagued the United States presidency from 1972 and ended in Richard Nixon's 1974 resignation from that office. It is certainly so that the term 'Watergate' has been exported beyond the US, where the suffix 'gate' has been attached to various local political scandals. To be sure, the term 'Guptagate' was used in the earliest days of state capture in South Africa, but its use quickly faded – as a result, the term 'state capture' in political rhetoric is pervasive. This said, it often confuses rather than enlightens. Because this is so, some elucidation of its use is necessary.

The term 'state capture' has been used in entirely opposite political directions: each deals with alleged wrongdoing by one side of a divide or by the other. For one group, state capture is the seizure – or attempted seizure – of key institutions of the state by a criminal network associated with Zuma's presidency. This is the sense in which the term is used in this book. This position directly links state capture to the Zumas – specifically former president Jacob and his son Duduzane – and the three Gupta brothers, Atul, Ajay and Rajesh. It also describes the myriad networks – primary, secondary and tertiary – that have extracted rents from the country's public purse. In this form, state capture is invariably presented as a Manichean struggle between good and evil.

In another use of the term, state capture is diversionary: this pins the blame for mounting setbacks in the country on 'white monopoly capital'. The latter phrase is coded language for the centuries-old white elite, which, so the logic runs, 'captured' the state from the arrival of the first Europeans in 1652 (see Friedman 2021). On the level of street politics, the diversionary use places the responsibility for the 'capture of the state' on white-owned businesses, with a special place reserved for wealthy families such as the Ruperts and the Oppenheimers. Used in this way, the term 'state capture' is an insult reserved particularly for whites who are said to have enriched themselves through the exploitation of black people under colonial domination and/or apartheid.

It should be noted, too, that there are several ancillary uses of the term, such as when some analysts signal that the phenomenon of 'capturing' parts of the state is replicated at a provincial and local level (see Olver 2017). Another example is as a blanket call-out against untoward actions similar to how the term 'corruption' calls out anything ranging from collusion in tender processing to any form of unfair treatment by a person in an official position.

The term 'state capture' is occasionally used to signal the political drama that has gripped South Africa since what has been called the 'Polokwane Moment' – the fraught 2007 transition from the presidency of Thabo Mbeki to that of Jacob Zuma. The latter figure was, and continues to be, at the very centre of intrigue – a strand in popular culture, even – rather than of politics. To appreciate why this is so, we need some background. The incoming president Zuma came to the position with two contrasting public images. On the one hand, he was seen as a unifying figure who promised to smooth the relations between the ruling party and its Alliance partners, the South African Communist Party and the Congress of South African Trade Unions. It was hoped, too, that he would change the tone of the relationship between the government and the populace by listening to what people wanted, unlike his remote predecessor. He was helped in these endeavours by his mastery of cultural repertoires, including a willingness to engage the public through the use of indigenous languages. On the other hand, he was patently deeply flawed: Zuma faced allegations of corruption stemming from the infamous post-apartheid Arms Deal; he had been charged, but acquitted, on charges of rape; and he was prone to making patriarchal, sexist and homophobic statements.

Notwithstanding the latter, Zuma succeeded in gathering around him a group of fervent supporters and financial backers. Large crowds marched in support of him at his numerous court appearances, and many leaders in the African National Congress (ANC) openly came out in his support. Importantly, too, influential names in the business world had thrown their weight behind the Friends of Jacob Zuma Trust, which was established, among other reasons, to raise funds in his support (Zungu 2018). Unsurprisingly, several of these supporters have subsequently been cited in corruption cases, which suggests that they were cosying up to Zuma to buy political protection. Indeed, the relationship between sections of business, state officials and hangers-on of Zuma and his family helped to create a soap opera-like atmosphere around his succession to the presidency of both the ruling party and the country. Initially, the resulting spectacle seemed as important as the politics around the new president. This has left a long trail of popular interest – ongoing theatrics, perhaps – associated with the notion of state capture.

On assuming the presidency, Zuma's leadership was marked by an accelerated use of state power to advance the interests – business and other – of his own family and his circle of supporters. The most significant of these was the co-optation of Zuma's family by the Guptas – so much so that another shorthand term, 'Zupta', briefly entered local political nomenclature. And the closeness – indeed, intimacy – of the association became clear when it emerged that Duduzane Zuma was a director of several Gupta-owned companies.

The full extent of the process that was underway and its position within the politics of both transformation and governance were set out by Ivor Chipkin and Mark Swilling:

> Corruption normally refers to a condition where public officials pursue private ends using public means. While indeed corruption is widespread at all levels and is undermining development, state capture is a far greater, systemic threat. It is akin to a silent coup and must, therefore, be understood as a political project that is given a cover of legitimacy by the vision of radical economic transformation. The March 2017 Cabinet reshuffle was confirmation of this silent coup; it was the first Cabinet reshuffle that took place without the full prior support of the governing party. This moves the symbiotic relationship between the constitutional state and the shadow state that emerged after the ANC Polokwane conference in 2007 into a new phase (2018, 30).

Chipkin and Swilling then set down some of the challenges that these shifts presented both to the country's Constitution and its democratic order:

> While it is obvious that the highly unequal South African economy needs to be thoroughly transformed, the task now is to expose and analyse how a Zuma-centred power elite has managed to capture key state institutions to repurpose them in ways that subvert the constitutional and legal framework established after 1994 … It is now clear that the nature of the state that is emerging … will be incapable of driving genuine development programmes … The need for radical economic transformation must be rescued from a political project that uses it to mask the narrow ambitions of a powerful elite that is only really interested in controlling access to rents and retaining political power (2018, 30).

As the depredations of Zuma and his associates and the repurposing of state institutions were brought to light, there were many attempts to dislodge him from the presidency. Yet, as noted, he managed to survive no less than eight motions of no confidence in parliament. Throughout these, he maintained a vice-like grip on the ruling party: this was achieved, in part, by building a coalition that comprised many who similarly faced troubles with the law, or who nursed grievances against the previous leadership of the ANC and the state, especially under his predecessor Thabo Mbeki.

JUST ANOTHER AFRICAN POSTCOLONIAL STATE?

The Zuma-Gupta project is a chapter in the longer story of South Africa since the end of apartheid in 1994. From the heady days of the negotiations at the Congress for a Democratic South Africa and the first democratic election of 27 April 1994, the hopes and dreams of the country's people have been dashed. Repeated promises by the ANC of 'a better life for all' in its election slogans have come to naught, especially for impoverished people who have seen little improvement in their circumstances since apartheid ended.

In retrospect, the hopes of South Africa's people and everyday dreams of individuals rested on three closely linked expectations:

- In the democratic era, the ANC would use political power to transform the state from its racial (and racist) basis that it obtained during apartheid.
- The ANC would use the state to build an inclusive economy, transforming it from the racial capitalism of the preceding century and a half.

- Governance under the ANC would not descend into corrupt free-for-alls for those holding political and state power, and for those with proximity to authority.

These expectations depended, in turn, on the assumption that, having lived in foreign places, ANC members had learned the lessons of Nigeria, Kenya, Zaire/Congo, Mozambique and, latterly, Zimbabwe. Such faith in democracy hinged on the promise that the country's leaders would not turn into the Chief Nangas and Chief Kokos of Achebe's novel, and that their parties would not turn into a People's Organisation Party and the Progressive Alliance Party of Achebe's account of post-colonial politics on the continent.

It is surprising that the abundant failures of independent African states as a result of patrimonial politics and the clinging to power of former freedom fighters, infused with a generous dose of neocolonial interference, seem to have taught the ANC so little. At the same time, it is not surprising that South Africa followed the same well-worn path for two interconnected reasons. First, the ANC's economic policy is rooted in 'a petty-bourgeois aspiration for upward social mobility' through capitalism (McKinley 1997, 1). The latter was preferred over the possibility of making any deep changes to the country's economic structure. Moreover, this lack of change authorised corrupt wealth accumulation at the very inception of democratic South Africa by creating pathways for politically connected entrepreneurs to become Black Economic Empowerment partners of white-owned firms under the affirmative action legislation that was ostensibly intended to transform the economy but made little more than cosmetic change. Second, the party (and so, ultimately, the state over which it had presided) absorbed a variety of contradictory ideological leanings, political moralities and social values into its programme. As a result of these, the post-apartheid state rests on two central problems:

- The continuity of a strain of capitalism that characterised apartheid. One result has been to encourage competition – rather than cooperation – among black elites (see Levy et al. 2021, 34). This has yielded a decided turn to state coffers as the central source of accumulation.
- An absorption into the governing structures of the 'new South Africa' of people from across all the bureaucracies that existed when apartheid ended. This has included those from the corrupt Bantustan system and those who had served elsewhere within the apparatus of the apartheid state. This incorporation has left an indelible stain on the theory and practice of public administration in the post-1996 years (Chipkin 2021).

The inevitable tensions these have wrought were compounded by sidebar agreements made during the negotiation process itself. The most significant of these was the series of concessions made to regional formations, in particular the one made to the Inkatha Freedom Party (IFP) in KwaZulu-Natal. Although the IFP won provincial elections in 1994 and 1999, it lost control of the province to the ANC in 2004. But the die was cast, and the IFP left its mark of exceptionalism on the political culture and administration of the region – and, indeed, on the entire country.

It should be no surprise, then, that the ANC and the state are riddled with contradictions: these have been drawn to the surface over time and have broken out into obvious factional warfare since Cyril Ramaphosa became its leader. On the face of this, party discipline has frayed: so much so that branches, regions and entire provinces have become the fiefdoms for competing factions, many of which use both corruption and violence to sustain their respective holds on power. In this way, the modus operandi of the Zuma-Gupta strain of political behaviour is replicated at all tiers of state administration.

While the ANC and state institutions have both made – and faced – these hurdles, the transformation of the economy has been slower than expected. As already noted, this can be attributed to choices made about economic policy, although a recent paper explains how ideas, institutions and endemic inequality can produce the very cycle of toxic underdevelopment that has been the fate of post-apartheid South Africa: 'Reflecting in the mid-1970s on his experience as a scholar-practitioner in Latin America, [the acclaimed Development theorist Albert] Hirschman summarized the previous quarter-century as characterized by a "changing tolerance for inequality". The earlier part of the period was characterized by optimism … But over time, rising polarization, civic conflict, and military rule spread across the continent. Growth, underpinned by hope, had transmuted into anger' (Levy et al. 2021, 8–9).

The paper points out that ideas – 'specifically, the role of expectations about the future' – play a key role in development (Levy et al. 2021, 10). In South Africa, the central (though unstated) idea behind the settlement was that 'a thriving future could be built around cooperation and thus create the possibility of win-win outcomes with shared benefits' to all the country's citizens (11). Moreover, the institutions, namely, the 'rules of the game … humanly devised constraints for governing human interactions', that provided a controlling governance framework for the white minority were strong and were extended to the entire population in the transition to democratic governance in 1994 (12). The 1996 Constitution became the focal institutional mechanism for advancing claims to socio-economic, political and other rights. The bargain among elites and the mode of incorporating non-elites into these held true, but this was only for a while. At its zenith, economic expansion – which was characterised by social cash transfers and employment growth – reached as high as 5 per cent per annum between 2005 and 2008. As a result, an anticipated win-win outcome managed to hold the country together at times when the social order was under severe strain.

However, things began to unravel when (1) the tacit understanding between old (white) economic elites and new (black) economic elites failed to hold (Levy et al. 2021), and (2) competition within the ANC thrust Jacob Zuma into the leadership of the party in 2007 and, two years later, into the presidency of the country. This is when Zuma and his cohort seized on the brewing dissatisfaction with the settlement of 1994 to pursue a project of plundering the state on the pretext of driving change through the slogan 'radical economic transformation'.

What made it possible for the Zumaites – to use a term that has been used to describe the Zuma faction within the ANC – to undertake their project in full view of watchdog bodies of the state and civil society and the public at large? The answer to this question is to be found in the oldest predicament of South African politics: white wealth and black poverty. The ending of apartheid and subsequent policy choices have ensured that race-based inequality has remained (and is likely to remain) intact. Black people – even those who slowly were ascending to the middle class – felt that their lives were not changing fast enough. Put differently, the social ordering around the category of 'race', which was the essence of colonialism, and which was supercharged under apartheid, was not dismantled fast enough. In some instances, it was not dismantled at all. Disappointment then turned to what Albert Hirschman dubbed 'anger' (Levy et al. 2021, 8); what Levy and colleagues revealingly call 'becoming furious' (4). Among the country's students, this rage poured out on university campuses, beginning with the #RhodesMustFall protests at the University of Cape Town in 2015.

The cumulative outcome provided the backdrop for state capture – it was tapped from what literary theorist Raymond Williams, in his discussion of modern tragedy, described as 'the loss of hope; the slowly settling loss of any acceptable future' (1966, 2). It is against the backdrop of this 'loss of hope' that the idea of state capture and the ideas of this book must be understood.

In enduring this episode, South Africa became just another unremarkable postcolonial African state that faces grief. A great deal of the literature on the nature of the African state has defined it as neo-patrimonial (Erdmann and Engel 2006). It is said to be such because the state is weakly autonomous from society; hence social relations such as kinship easily penetrate what should be a domain of depersonalised professional interaction (Mann 1984; Bayart 1993; Ake 1996). Bayart goes further and calls the African state the 'rhizome state', in which the informal and the illegal form an integral part of state practice (1993). It is this character of the post-colonial African state, according to this literature, that yields states that are unable to provide for the needs of their populations due to weak sovereignty and hence neo-patrimonialism. While much of this literature has been criticised for making grand generalisations about Africa (Wai 2012), its usefulness for our purposes here is that it names some of key features of many states in postcolonial Africa that have become obvious in the post-apartheid South African state as well, and pointedly so in the Zuma era of state capture that this volume attempts to make sense of.

INTRODUCING THE COLLECTION

When Zuma resigned from the presidency in mid-February 2018, it was clear that his leadership had been characterised by wholesale corruption and maladministration, and that these, with other malfeasance, had not only enriched the country's first family but also the president's cronies, both within and without state structures. It was also plain that important state-owned enterprises, which were responsible for the operation, maintenance and development of public infrastructure, had also been corroded by state capture.

Eight months later, PARI hosted an international conference called 'State Capture and Its Aftermath: Building Responsiveness through State Reform'. The intention was to examine the implications of the capture of the state by political and business elites. By this time, the Judicial Commission of Inquiry into Allegations of State Capture, Corruption and Fraud in the Public Sector including Organs of State, known as the Zondo Commission, had commenced its work. The central recommendation of the report released by Public Protector Thuli Madonsela was the establishment of an inquiry into state capture to be headed by a judge to be chosen not by the country's president, as is the practice, but by the Chief Justice. Although this made judicial sense – given that the incumbent president would, in all probability, become a focus of the exercise – it was resisted by the Presidency. In the end, however, Zuma established the commission under the relevant legislation, but its chair was appointed by the then Chief Justice Mogoeng Mogoeng, whose chose his deputy, Raymond Zondo.

Given the centrality of the Zondo Commission to state capture, it seems necessary to pause and consider its relevance to PARI's particular interest in the issue. Three points stand out. The first is a sceptical point that was linked to a truism: avoid political unpleasantness, call for a commission of inquiry. Unsurprisingly, then, history is littered with the detritus and other fallouts from public commissions of inquiry. Indeed, the very birth of the 'new South Africa' was wrapped around the country's Truth and Reconciliation Commission (TRC), which was established to investigate the gross human rights violations committed under apartheid. This fact feeds into the second point: the overloaded public expectations that invariably accompany the establishment of commissions of inquiry. The long tail of the expectations that surrounded the TRC continues to haunt South Africa's political life. Much of this arises from the fact it was expected that the TRC could dissolve – absolve, perhaps – the myriad sins of apartheid and deliver reconciliation within the country. The Zondo Commission has likewise been burdened with exposing the scope and nature of state capture and, some have even hoped, of prosecuting those who were responsible. Finally, and this is linked to the foregoing point, the legalistic ambience of commissions of inquiry often fogs up – rather than clears up – constitutional and political issues.

The idea of this edited collection emerged from the October 2018 PARI conference, which aimed to understand how things had gone awry in the country's governance. But given PARI's mission of engaging the public in civic affairs, as the title suggested, it also hoped to stimulate further discussion about how to prevent future recurrence of what was then quite openly being called state capture. However, as Patrick Heller's contribution to this book illustrates, the gathering also sought to see South Africa's experience through a comparative frame. Drawing three countries closer – each born in the crucible of deep categorical inequality – Heller uses political sociology to explain the relationship between civil society and political society in India, Brazil and South Africa.

The 2018 conference was to be followed by another. In October 2019, PARI and the Ahmed Kathrada Foundation conferred on the topic of 'Defeating State Capture and Rebuilding the State'. A further conference, 'Understanding the Findings and Recommendations of the Zondo Commission', was hosted in 2022 by PARI and the Council for the Advancement of the South African Constitution, following the release of the Zondo Commission report. It will become clear that the chapters in this volume touch only in passing on the Zondo Commission, their main focus being on the period before its establishment.

The volume is organised into three sections: the first section offers diverse conceptualisations of corruption in South Africa. Karl von Holdt takes up Karl Polanyi's theorisation of capitalism as a 'movement' that introduced a dynamic of marketisation and commodification, which brought more and more social processes into market processes and removed them from social uses. Land, labour and money were the key commodities that fell into this process. Such a historical movement is reversed through a counter-movement by society when it resists its effects and re-embeds these commodities in society, subordinating the economy to social ends. Von Holdt argues that corruption in South Africa (and, by extension, elsewhere in the postcolonial world) is a counter-movement to colonial accumulation, which was a global process of disembedding economic processes from social life as land and labour were commodified. In his analysis, corrupt accumulation thus emerges as a process of forming a black elite that predates Zuma and will continue in different forms well after a presidency during which corruption took a particularly extreme form in what has come to be dubbed 'state capture'.

Where Von Holdt places the Zuma years in a longer historical trajectory, Robyn Foley defines state capture as very much part of the Zuma era by linking the financial dimension of corruption to a political project in the way that the first analyses led by Chipkin and Swilling did. Foley goes on to explain how this economic-political project is operationalised by turning to older notions of 'rackets', 'racket society' and 'racketeering' developed on the edges of the Frankfurt School of Critical Theory. She shows how the racket included a combination of state-owned companies, international and local private companies, government departments and law enforcement institutions.

In a different take, Ryan Brunette delineates three tendencies in South African anti-corruption discourse – moralist, neoliberal and Marxist-Fanonist. He critiques all of them as being unable to explain fully the structural features of South African society and thus the drivers of corruption. His theorisation and explanation identify syndicates that cut across political and administrative lines in public institutions to coordinate corrupt activities. He sees syndicates as having a symbiotic relationship with political machines that mobilise to bring their members into public office and, in turn, politicise processes of appointing officials into bureaucracies in order to pursue corrupt ends through the state.

The second section moves on to a closer description of how state capture unfolded in some sectors, and what forms its exposure and resistance took. Jonathan Klaaren traces civil society mobilisation against Zuma's government and extra-governmental networks. He places particular focus on legal action to account for how the broader movement took place partly through litigation.

Cherese Thakur and Devi Pillay examine how professionals, including auditors, management consultants and lawyers, facilitated malfeasance. The authors point to the failure of regulatory institutions to detect and act against members of these professions before going on to reflect on some of the ways in which the regulators can improve the accountability of professionals.

Luke Spiropoulos examines why it took until late in Zuma's presidency for civil society to develop a coherent analysis of state capture and the coordinated response that eventually yielded the mobilisation of the #ZumaMustFall movement. He concludes that action was at first dispersed because it came from different ideological places and was undertaken by disparate organisations. It was as media exposés, analyses and legal cases built up over time that cohesion was assembled, with the nature of the problem of state capture becoming clearer.

Reg Rumney delves into the media's role in exposing state capture and the counter by the Zuma-Gupta network, using both traditional media – a daily newspaper and a television station – as well as social media, to tarnish those who were exposing and opposing wrongdoing, as well attempting to launder the reputation of their enterprise.

The final section of the book expands the frame of state capture in terms of genre, time scale and international comparative perspective. Sizwe Mpofu-Walsh focuses on how state capture was taken up in some popular cultural forms. He reads how state capture was represented and reacted to in a selection of paintings, films and rap songs produced between 2012 and 2019. Mpofu-Walsh's criticism of these popular art forms is that they offered a narrow reading of state capture as exceptional, aberrant behaviour by a few in the late Zuma period, rather than showing the deeper economic, political and historical roots of the phenomenon.

Hennie van Vuuren and Michael Marchant demonstrate the continuities of corruption networks from the apartheid era to the present. They show how the arms traders who were busting sanctions by selling weapons to the apartheid government, and the banks, consultancies and lawyers who enabled them historically, continue to undertake the same unethical actions with impunity.

In the same vein of tracing historical precedents, Mbongiseni Buthelezi and Peter Vale conduct an interview with Barney Pityana, a scholar and anti-apartheid activist. Pityana offers a reading of some of the discontinuities in the ANC as it moved from being a liberation movement to a governing party, and in the change of political power from the Afrikaner minority government to the ANC. These discontinuities have led to political, professional and personal cultures that are permissive of wrongdoing in the state.

The book closes with Heller's comparative reading of democratic deepening in India, Brazil and South Africa to answer the question, 'Can democracy bind the state?' He outlines how relations between political elites, the state and civil society have evolved in each place to result in very different outcomes: Brazil is the clearest case of democratic deepening, where civil society has been able to penetrate the political sphere so completely; India is the opposite with civil society subordinated by the political class; and South Africa is the in-between case.

Debate will undoubtedly continue for a long time to come on the meanings of state capture, the Zuma years, the post-apartheid trajectory of the South African state and society, as well as the roles of institutions and individuals in what has transpired. This volume is one of the initial contributions to slowly making sense of a phase that has caused great harm to the social fabric of South Africa and to the country's standing in the world. It sits alongside many popular titles published in the recent past, explaining various episodes, locations and actors in the drama that continues to unfold. It aims to open up lines of enquiry that we hope other scholars will pursue further.

REFERENCES

Achebe, Chinua. [1966] 2001. *A Man of the People*. London: Penguin.
Ake, Claude. 1996. *Democracy and Development in Africa*. Washington, DC: Brookings Institution.
Bayart, Jean-François. 1993. *The State in Africa: The Politics of the Belly*. London: Longman.
Chipkin, Ivor. 2021. 'From Democracy as a Political System to Democracy as Government: A Contribution to Democratic Theory from Public Administration'. *Transformation* 105: 1–25. https://muse.jhu.edu/article/793954.
Chipkin, Ivor and Mark Swilling. 2018. *Shadow State: The Politics of State Capture*. Johannesburg: Wits University Press.
Erdmann, Gero and Ulf Engel. 2006. 'Neopatrimonialism Revisited: Beyond a Catch-All Concept'. Working Paper No. 16, German Institute of Global and Area Studies. https://papers.ssrn.com/sol3/papers.cfm?abstract_id=909183.
Friedman, Steven. 2021. *Prisoners of the Past: South African Democracy and the Legacy of Minority Rule*. Johannesburg: Wits University Press.
Levy, Brian, Alan Hirsch, Vinothan Naidoo and Musa Nxele. 2021. 'South Africa: When Strong Institutions and Massive Inequalities Collide'. Research Paper, 18 March 2021, Carnegie Endowment for International Peace.
Mann, Michael. 1984. 'The Autonomous Power of the State: Its Origins, Mechanisms and Results'. *European Journal of Sociology* 25, no. 2: 185–213. https://www.cambridge.org/core/journals/european-journal-of-sociology-archives-europeennes-de-sociologie/article/abs/autonomous-power-of-the-state-its-origins-mechanisms-and-results/338F971178F06BCD3ABC9C573E67B2D8.
McKinley, Dale. 1997. *The ANC and the Liberation Struggle: A Critical Political Biography*. London: Pluto Press.
Olver, Crispian. 2017. *How to Steal a City: The Battle for Nelson Mandela Bay*. Johannesburg: Jonathan Ball.
PARI. 2017. 'Betrayal of the Promise: How South Africa Is Being Stolen'. State Capacity Research Project Report, Public Affairs Research Institute, Johannesburg. https://pari.org.za/betrayal-promise-report/.
Public Protector. 2016. 'State of Capture'. Report No. 6, 14 October 2016. http://www.saflii.org/images/329756472-State-of-Capture.pdf.

Runciman, Carin, Linah Nkuna and Pier Paolo Frassinelli. 2017. 'Survey Sheds Light on Who Marched against President Zuma and Why'. *The Conversation*, 20 April 2017. https://theconversation.com/survey-sheds-light-on-who-marched-against-president-zuma-and-why-76271.

Wai, Zubairu. 2012. 'Neo-Patrimonialism and the Discourse of State Failure in Africa'. *Review of African Political Economy* 39, no. 131: 27–43. https://www.tandfonline.com/doi/abs/10.1080/03056244.2012.658719.

Williams, Raymond. 1966. *Modern Tragedy and the Affective Life of Politics*. London: Chatto and Windus.

Zungu, Lungani. 2018. 'Where Are the Friends of Jacob Zuma Now?' *Sunday Tribune*, 5 April 2018. https://www.iol.co.za/sunday-tribune/opinion/where-are-the-friends-of-jacob-zuma-now-14264181.

SECTION 1

FRAMING THE ISSUE

1

Elite Formation, Factions and Violence in the Political Economy of Corruption

Karl von Holdt

In May 2017, South African president Jacob Zuma fired minister of finance Pravin Gordhan from cabinet – and unleashed a storm of protest and mobilisation.[1] This move was widely seen as the final onslaught in a campaign to 'capture' the state for corrupt networks stretching across South Africa and far beyond – to Russia, China, India and Dubai. Opposition political parties and broad social movements calling themselves 'civil society' began to organise a campaign to remove Zuma. A split emerged within the African National Congress (ANC) as Gordhan and a network of prominent ANC leaders and veterans launched a struggle to 'reclaim' it. The two key Alliance partners of the ANC, the South African Communist Party (SACP) and the Congress of South African Trade Unions (Cosatu), also spoke out against Zuma's move and joined the campaign to remove him – ironically, as until then they had been castigating Gordhan for following the same 'neoliberal' policies as his predecessors.

Protests, public meetings and well-supported marches took place. The biggest demonstration of the post-apartheid period was estimated to have mobilised tens of thousands in a march to the Presidency in Pretoria, led by opposition political parties, with the Economic Freedom Fighters (EFF) in the lead. Political rivals, such as the EFF, the liberal opposition Democratic Alliance, the SACP, and some social movements and NGOs, joined hands in what came to be seen as a national crisis. In parliament, opposition parties served notice of a motion of no confidence in the president – the fourth such motion over the previous two years. However, this time it attracted unprecedented interest because of speculation that a number of ANC MPs would support it. Few did, and for a few months, Zuma survived.

Ultimately, however, the turbulence led to the election in December by a narrow margin of Cyril Ramaphosa as president of the ANC, the recall by the ANC of Jacob Zuma as president of South Africa, his replacement in January 2018 by Ramaphosa, and the latter's announcement of a 'New Dawn' for South Africa.

The transition from Thabo Mbeki to Jacob Zuma as ANC president in Polokwane in 2007 and the subsequent recall of Mbeki as South African president in 2008 likewise had been accompanied by intense internal struggles and mobilisations. Still, the 2017 contestation was more public, bitter and unpredictable. After Polokwane, Zuma was able to move methodically to assert his dominance of the ANC, purging Mbeki allies from positions of power and precipitating the breakaway of the Congress of the People. Ramaphosa had to move much more cautiously to establish his authority and adopted a strategy of 'unifying' the ANC, while facing powerful resistance from within.

The narratives in the media and the public domain regarding state capture under Zuma tend to depict this as a breakdown of morality and law enforcement. This is unconvincing, though superficially plausible. Indeed, a much deeper set of social forces and processes underlies and shapes the struggles within the ANC. More broadly, political struggles are inseparable from struggles over the shape of the economy, specifically over class formation.

This chapter explores the political economy of corruption and (briefly) anti-corruption in South Africa in order to develop an analysis of current challenges and future prospects.

In order to grasp the significance of the struggles over elite formation, I use Karl Polanyi's concept of movement and counter-movement revolving around struggles over the disembedding and re-embedding of the economy in society (Polanyi [1944] 1957). This reveals a contradictory process of disembedding and re-embedding, rather than a linear trajectory, which in turn shapes the form of political struggle.

I use this framing to analyse the political dynamics of the Zuma regime, the fightback by Gordhan and his allies centred on the Treasury, contestation for control of the ANC and the post-Zuma presidency of Ramaphosa. Finally, I discuss the constraints on and possible future of the Ramaphosa project in the ANC.

DISEMBEDDING AND RE-EMBEDDING THE ECONOMY IN SOCIAL LIFE

Neoliberalism has become the dominant critical frame for understanding development in South Africa. Yet, as Gillian Hart argues, it remains inadequate to the task of grasping the 'turbulent, shifting forces taking shape in the arenas of everyday life' (2013, 6). Hart is concerned with the important processes of hegemony and nationalism but tends to ignore class formation and particularly its material base. In contrast, I argue that the processes through which emerging elite classes are being forged are critical for understanding politics in South Africa, particularly the sharp contestations.

Polanyi argues that capitalism brought into existence a dynamic of marketisation and commodification through which a broader range of social and productive activities are ensnared in market processes and abstracted from social use. Ultimately, even the three fictitious commodities that are essential for human life and society – land, labour and money – are commodified, destroying the basis of society. These are *fictional* commodities precisely because they cannot be turned into commodities without destroying their social and life-giving function. Polanyi argues that this marketisation process constitutes a historical *movement*, which society resists in the form of a *counter-movement* to re-embed land, labour and money in society and to subordinate the economy to social ends.

Polanyi barely mentions colonialism ([1944] 1957). Yet, colonial dispossession itself was an element in the global disembedding of economic processes from social life, through which primarily land and labour were commodified. Struggles of national liberation constituted a counter-movement for reclaiming land and labour, and re-embedding the people in their own territory and in their own 'nation' – although the newly independent regimes routinely intensified dispossession and marketisation, while seeking to establish their economic base. The kind of analysis suggested here points to the material dimensions of nationalism, particularly to the fierce struggle of indigenous elites to come into existence and gain possession of the sources of wealth in Africa in general, and not least in South Africa. It was this process that exercised Frantz Fanon's mind in *The Wretched of the Earth*, despite his aversion to it (Fanon [1961] 1967).

This process of national class formation is ignored, or dismissed with a moralism, by most critical left analysis, including that of Hart (2013), despite its absolute centrality to the understanding of politics in South Africa and of decolonisation more broadly. To understand how this has played out in the politics of the ANC, it is essential to grasp the distinctiveness of the moment when the ANC was at last able to establish itself in government.

The 1980s and 1990s were a moment of globalisation and the ascendancy of neoliberalism cemented by the collapse of the communist regimes – the allies of the ANC – across the Soviet Union and Eastern Europe. It was, in Polanyian terms, a period of heightened marketisation and, in particular, of accelerated financial-isation, which consolidated the abstraction of that fictional commodity, money, from any social use. Accumulation is disembedded from production and territory, becoming a process insulated from national policy intervention. The earlier wave of post-Second World War anti-colonial movements came to power in a different period when the developmental state and national strategies for industrialisation were commonly adopted by newly independent regimes (as well as by entrenched reactionary regimes, such as apartheid South Africa), representing in some cases a Polanyian counter-movement seeking to re-embed development nationally against the domination of Western capitalism at the time.

In the 1990s, by contrast, the emerging global regime of globalised and finan-cialised accumulation and the prevailing geopolitical order tended to preclude such strategies for newly independent or democratising regimes, including that of South Africa. This provides the essential global context for understanding the politics of the ANC. And the local balance of forces were also not favourable to more radical policies on the part of the ANC. Apartheid military forces remained strong, many state institutions and some sectors of the population were potentially resistant to the ANC government and had already been oriented towards neoliberal policies by the apartheid regime, and the ANC had no governing experience (Marais 1998).

DISEMBEDDING ACCUMULATION: THE THABO MBEKI REGIME

Drawing on the theoretical argument outlined above, let us turn briefly to char-acterise the strategic tensions that marked the Mbeki regime, understood to have included the Nelson Mandela period when Mbeki was effectively running the gov-ernment (1994–2007). In doing this, I draw on Hart's presentation of the dynamics of denationalisation and renationalisation but reframe this in terms of the Polanyian dynamic. The first phase of this regime was chiefly characterised by dramatic pro-cesses of disembedding accumulation. During this time, capital controls were lifted, allowing a massive flight of South African capital, the listing offshore and globali-sation of what had been powerful South African corporations, the sharp reduction of import tariffs and the consequent de-industrialisation of many manufacturing sectors, as well as fiscal austerity, privatisation and other aspects of a typical neolib-eral economic reform agenda (Ashman, Fine and Newman 2011). At a political level, this period saw heightened conflict between the ANC and its Alliance partners as it attempted to roll back and limit the power of Cosatu and the SACP.

Hart highlights the fact that the Mbeki regime was characterised not solely by neoliberalism, but also by specific and important processes of renationalisation: specifically, reconceptualising the national democratic revolution – the core strategic concept of the ANC – as a narrow, disciplined technocratic project centred on the formation of a new 'patriotic' black bourgeoisie, which was threatened by the 'ultra-left' posturing of his critics. In 2003, the ideological perspective of the Mbeki government shifted again with the articulation of a robust concept of the developmental state, abandoning the commitment to privatisation in favour of a decisive role for state-owned enterprises (SOEs) to foster and shape economic growth, as well as the adoption of broader welfare policies to tackle the problems of the marginalised masses occupying the 'second economy' (Hart 2013, 199).

For Hart, these shifts remain gestures towards renationalisation operating at the level of ideology and designed to contain working-class challenges rather than fundamental shifts reflecting material goals. This is where it becomes useful to introduce a material analysis of struggles to re-embed accumulation in the national territory of South Africa. Thus, the focus on creating the conditions for the emergence of a black bourgeoisie is not just a sign of Mbeki's conservative orientation; it is instead an attempt to address a very real, very material and burning aspiration. Settler colonialism and apartheid had worked explicitly to prevent the emergence of black middle classes and particularly entrepreneurs, whether on the land, in commerce or in manufacturing.

The result is that one glaring dimension of racial inequality in South Africa – usually considered only in terms of inequality between the bottom and top of society – is between black business and white business and between black and white middle classes more broadly. This dimension of inequality requires redress as long as business remains a significant class in South Africa. Moreover, the biggest and most competitive white-owned and white-managed corporations have demonstrated scant commitment to the development of South Africa, globalising and shifting capital at the earliest opportunity. Hence, the question of a *patriotic* black bourgeoisie with national commitment, which so exercised Mbeki's mind. These are inherently political dynamics with real material content *and place the political economy of a rising class at the centre of ANC politics.*

Likewise, the new emphasis on a developmental state and the SOEs signalled an assertive stance concerning the forces of disembedded marketisation, combined with re-embedding control of critical elements of the economy, however half-heartedly these shifts may have been implemented, rather than relying on the neoliberal illusion of foreign investment. Nevertheless, they point to the very real dynamics of a counter-movement focused on re-embedding finance, production and class formation in the national territory of South Africa and asserting the state's sovereignty in attempting to address the conditions of the people, against the logic of globalisation.

Unfortunately for Mbeki, these shifts were too limited, contradictory and late. He relied on Broad-Based Black Economic Empowerment (BBBEE), a legislated and negotiated process for the transfer of assets from existing corporations to new black business partners. This did not consist of an unfettered transfer of assets; share transfers are financed through a range of mechanisms that entail substantial debt financing for new black owners. These transactions tended to establish black capitalists as junior partners and simultaneously constitute a new source of profit for (white) financial capital. Few of these rentier capitalists have any involvement in business operations or production. While, in some cases, BBBEE may have created the basis for an elite coalition between black and white businesses, the minority stakeholding and high financial gearing of black partners have made the constraints of this model increasingly clear. This 'empowerment' elite remains small, economically weak, politically dependent on the ANC and politically compromised by the rise in inequality at the same time as they were being empowered. The result, Martin Plaut and Paul Holden argue, is that 'the power of the BEE elite remains precarious' (2012, 213–238).

THE RISE OF THE INFORMAL POLITICAL-ECONOMIC SYSTEM

Many black entrepreneurs and aspirant elites were unable to access these opportunities, either because of political gatekeeping or because they lacked the capital or skills. Already, during the Mbeki period as well as the presidency of Mandela, an alternative political-economic system was emerging at national, provincial and local levels, through which networks of state officials, ambitious entrepreneurs as well as small-time operators were rigging tenders or engaging in other kinds of fraud to use revenue flows from the state to sustain or establish businesses or simply to finance self-enrichment. Given the property clause in the Constitution, as well as the conservative strategies adopted by the ANC government, and in the context of economic domination by large corporations and white-owned businesses, there was little alternative for channelling the aspirations and burning sense of injustice of black elites and would-be elites in post-apartheid South Africa. The state – newly 'renationalised' by the liberation struggle – had become the only channel for the emergence of these aspirant classes, given the scope of its resources and activities (Von Holdt 2013). At the same time, the narrow scope and precarious status of Mbeki's official black empowerment elite were some of the factors behind his political isolation and his overthrow by the Jacob Zuma 'tsunami'.

Given the prevailing focus on Zuma and the Gupta family as the architects of 'corruption', it is essential to note that an informal political-economic system, including its intersection with violence, was already emerging in South Africa prior to and outside the emergence of the Zuma network. Research into the intersection between community protests and ANC politics revealed how, already in 2008 to 2009, local government had become the locus of intense struggles over access to tenders, budgets and jobs between different ANC factions in many towns and townships. Outsider factions positioned themselves as leaders in community protests against incumbent factions so as to access the resources at the disposal of local government. When they were successful, they constituted new patronage networks to reward their followers. Violence was frequently deployed in these struggles, involving the burning down of homes and municipal facilities, assault and, increasingly, assassination. In addition, local factional networks were linked into regional and provincial ANC structures and networks, where similar struggles took place over the control of ANC structures and so of access to provincial government and resources (Dawson 2014, 2017; Langa and Von Holdt 2012; Mukwedeya and Ndlovu 2017; Ndletyana, Makhalemele and Mathekga 2013; Von Holdt 2013, 2014; Von Holdt et al. 2011).

At the national level, the first significant scandal to gain public attention was that of the Arms Deal under Mbeki, which involved many big and small kickbacks. The key aim of this appears to have been to secure substantial funding for the ANC. Still, in the process, several ANC-linked businesspeople, frontmen and political figures – including, allegedly, Zuma – were able to enrich themselves.

The existence of a broader informal political-economic system is revealed by several narratives and news reports, including the recent publication of an insider account of the functioning of such a regime in the City Council of Nelson Mandela Bay. This illustrates how successive factions of the ANC in the Eastern Cape used their control of the council to build patronage networks, foster murky business operations, fund the ANC and enrich themselves (Olver 2017), without, it seems, any interaction with the Gupta networks and surrogates that were so central to the Zuma project. Continuing revelations about VBS Mutual Bank, and Bosasa, the private security company owned by the ANC-rooted Watson brothers, show how long-standing and widespread these practices were, sufficient to constitute what I call *a patronage-violence complex*.

A 2012 interview with a trade union national office bearer, who was also an ANC and SACP activist, gives a sense of the scale of the involvement in diverting state resources and of the collective understanding that this was a widely acceptable and familiar set of practices:

> It's about the kind of lifestyle they live, the cars they drive, and including what we drink when we are socialising. When you ask, 'But comrades, why are we doing things like this?' They say, 'You live in the past.' And when it comes to tenders, the first thing they want to know is how much they are going to get from the tender. When you ask them, 'How can you do such a thing?' They ask you, 'What's wrong with you? This is how things are done.' They really laugh their lungs out when you ask them about these things.
>
> It is the issue about our value system and what our struggle is about that is crucial to me, things such as selflessness, serving people. So our cadres look for one of us who seems to be doing better, and they follow in their footsteps and become dominant values that overshadow the old values.
>
> The younger ones have been communicated this message that this is the way of doing things; so you don't need to be good at school; you don't need to work hard; you can find shortcuts; you have got to be connected. There are just too many people who are trapped in corruption now. You cannot deal comprehensively with it because the problem is at the top. People know this will collapse the ANC or the state if it is dealt with in a serious way. I am afraid, comrade, I am very afraid.[2]

This 'way of doing things' constitutes a system of practices and understandings that pervade the ANC and the state, embedded in a local moral order that provides legitimacy and rationale for such practices. This is a kind of counter-movement to the dis-embedding processes of globalisation and 'good governance' championed by the Mbeki government and its technocrats, working to re-embed economic agency and wealth formation in the emergence of a local elite – a counter-movement of local processes to appropriate wealth from the circuits of finance. And it was in this pervasive informal political-economic system, the patronage-violence complex, that Zuma and his networks were able to locate themselves, which also provided the basis for the emergence of the formal discourse of 'radical economic transformation' within the ANC.

I argue that this system of practices constitutes an informal patronage-violence complex. By a system, I do not mean a centrally coordinated or planned structure, but a pervasive and decentralised *set of interlocking networks that reinforce and compete with each other* in mutually understood ways and are increasingly structured by the use of violence.

RE-EMBEDDING CLASS FORMATION: THE ZUMA REGIME

The Zuma campaign to replace Mbeki took the form of a populist challenge in which Zuma as a figure came to represent 'a point of condensation for multiple, pre-existing tensions, anger and discontents that until recently were contained within the hegemonic project of the ruling bloc in the ANC' (Hart 2013, 97–98), which, in Hart's analysis, represented a strategy for mobilising and simultaneously containing popular antagonisms. Zuma was able to embody rural authority, patriarchal respectability and family commitment, militant insurgency and deep ANC history, as well as familiarity with popular cultural repertoires, and thus emerge as the 'authoritative other' to the remote and intellectual Mbeki (Hart 2013). Thus, Zuma kindled SACP and Cosatu hopes of a counter-movement towards a much stronger developmental state capable of re-embedding the economy in society and addressing the crisis of social reproduction experienced by the working class and the poor. The Zuma slate of candidates won a decisive victory at the 2007 ANC conference. A year later, Mbeki was removed as president of South Africa, and Zuma became president in 2009.

In retrospect, it is clear that the Zuma project was focused less on a left turn than on strengthening and deepening the patronage-violence complex and locating himself and his close allies at its centre. Zuma himself had been caught up in the Arms Deal scandal under Mbeki. It had become apparent that Mbeki was alarmed when it emerged that his deputy would run for the presidency of the ANC, and he was keen to see Zuma prosecuted for corruption. Indeed, in the interminable court disputes over whether Zuma should be charged or not, it emerged that there had been attempts to interfere in the case by prosecutors close to Mbeki. Accordingly, as president, Zuma moved to build a network of supporters in the South African Police Service (SAPS) and the National Prosecuting Authority (NPA) to protect himself and his allies against any further attempt at investigation or prosecution. Analysis of these dynamics made it clear that control of the coercive institutions of the state (police, intelligence, prosecution authority, prisons and ultimately the judiciary) would be the logical outcome of the consolidation of this patronage-violence complex (Von Holdt 2013, 2014).

Rapidly, any sign of populist mobilisation disappeared. On the face of things, Zuma was proceeding along the same policy lines as his predecessor. The centres of global connection and neoliberal management in the Treasury, the South African Revenue Service (SARS) and the Reserve Bank remained intact. In reality, though, the Zuma regime – and this included his key allies in the provinces and their associates located in ANC branches and regions and in local government – was opening up the channels for the informal political-economic system to expand and incorporate new networks, including members of his family. At the same time, he and his collaborators were moving to gain control of key positions in the NPA and the SAPS, in the first instance protecting Zuma from prosecution for his involvement in the Arms Deal procurement scandal under Mbeki, but ultimately aimed at heading off investigation or prosecution of anyone in the rising networks.

The pace and scale of this project increased exponentially after the first three or four years, in which Zuma networks were consolidating their power at all levels of the ANC and government. At about the same time an explicit formal political discourse was emerging, with an emphasis on radical economic transformation (PARI 2017). This centred initially on the idea of aggressively using state procurement to foster the development of black businesses, which then expanded to include direct funding for the formation of black industrialists. The State Capacity Research Project has argued that the Presidency and newly appointed officials in the state were 'increasingly prepared to play fast and loose with the law and the Constitution, not simply out of self-interest, but out of political conviction' (PARI 2017, 47). Increasingly, black management and business forums articulated the conviction that, in the words of the head of the Black Management Forum, the 'rules of the game' were rigged against black business, making it virtually impossible 'to penetrate the private sector because of long-established relationships, over and above the deliberate bias towards white-owned companies' (PARI 2017, 48).

While the Treasury and its networks of technocrats believed that fair procedures, international standards of governance and rigorous competition could be reconciled with Black Economic Empowerment in accordance with the Constitution, its opponents progressively saw not only the Treasury but also the government's financial laws and regulations as well as the Constitution as an obstacle to rapid racial transformation. One proponent of this perspective has argued that white monopoly capital and a credit-based black capitalist class – formed through the official BBBEE policies – were fighting back against the rise of an independent tender-based capitalist class, which, together with the leadership of the ANC, was engaged in a struggle to overcome the colonial class structure (Malikane 2017, quoted in PARI 2017, 48). This argument demonstrates the ways in which the project of re-embedding class formation, both rhetorically and in material practice, significantly exceeds the ideological mobilisations identified by Hart, involving a project to wrest economic power from technocratic, globalised black and white elites committed to global marketisation, and re-embed it in processes of aggressively forging a new black elite.

It should be clear that this formal set of policy positions drew from and reinforced the patronage-violence complex and gave it an ideological cover under the Zuma government. It is imperative for an understanding of the Ramaphosa regime, though, to grasp that this complex extends way beyond the projects of Zuma and his circles.

THE ZUMA-GUPTA NEXUS AND STATE CAPTURE

The Zuma project, dubbed 'state capture' by the first attempt to synthesise and provide a coherent analysis of the information revealed through the multitude of journalistic investigations and large-scale email leaks, centred on the relationship between a family of Indian businessmen, the Gupta brothers, and President Zuma and members of his family (PARI 2017). This analysis presented state capture as highly centralised. It focused on two goals: the enrichment of the Guptas and the Zuma family; and the provision of a constant flow of cash to political allies and government officials, with the aim of maintaining a solid political base for the Zuma faction, as well as a network of compliant functionaries who would facilitate further corrupt deals. It suggested a rather narrowly based project, in which case it could be relatively easy to shut down by cauterising the infection with prosecutions and renewed emphasis on the proper regulation of government operations and contracts – as the report recommended. However, it was unable to explain the political durability of Zuma's control of the ANC, nor could it predict the depth of resistance to the reinforcement of the rule of law.

As argued above, the patronage-violence complex was always more extensive and decentralised, consisting of multiple networks and centres of power at national, provincial and local levels, which overlapped, collaborated or competed, as a number of studies by journalists and disaffected officials have shown. I draw on a sample of these, in addition to PARI (2017), to establish some of the characteristics of this informal political-economic system (Hofstatter 2018; Maseko 2021; Mothepu 2021; Myburgh 2019; Olver 2017).

(1) The Zuma-Gupta project, narrowly defined, focused on the extensive SOEs, particularly the two most significant, Eskom and Transnet, establishing compliant boards and collaborators at senior management levels, who could ensure that a group of front companies were inserted as intermediaries between the SOE and the suppliers of services, equipment and capital

projects. Inflated contracts allowed for millions and even billions of rand to be paid as kickbacks into these and other front companies. The money was then recycled into building the Gupta business empire and into political funds that could be used to strengthen the Zuma faction in the ANC, enriching a variety of officials and managers en route (PARI 2017; Hofstatter 2018; Maseko 2021; Mothepu 2021).

(2) The power of Zuma and his allies at a national level was sustained by provincial political barons, each of whom presided over provincial regimes of corruption. These provincial regimes had their own autonomous histories and established reciprocal relations with the Zuma circle at various points. In the Free State, for example, Ace Magashule had established a network of corruption across the northern region of the province as a base from which to establish his control of the provincial ANC. While this was successful, Thabo Mbeki, as president of the ANC and aware of Magashule's corrupt practices, repeatedly prevented his appointment as premier. However, Magashule swung the support of the Free State ANC behind Zuma at the 2009 ANC elective conference in which Zuma ousted Mbeki. Magashule was subsequently appointed as premier. From then on, Magashule rapidly escalated the scale of corruption across the province, while collaborating with Zuma and the Guptas on various projects, including the infamous Estina dairy case (Myburgh 2019). On the other hand, an autonomous regime of corruption was established in the Eastern Cape ANC, which seems to have had little or nothing to do with the corruption regime at the national level (Olver 2017). The provincial barons in the North West Province and Mpumalanga were strong supporters of the Zuma circle, but their histories have not yet been fully documented (but see Rousseau 2020).

(3) The power of the provincial barons rested on a series of local regimes of corruption established in local governments across the provinces. Like the provincial regimes, these too had autonomous histories characterised by a series of struggles at local and regional levels within the ANC. They were characterised by shifting alliances, with some local bosses more autonomous than others (Myburgh 2019; Von Holdt et al. 2011).

(4) The network of beneficiaries at the provincial and local levels was extensive. For example, the corrupt housing programme in the Free State benefited several hundred businesses, including local politicians, business associates, government officials, friends and family of Magashule and his allies (Myburgh 2019). Many of these were legitimate businesses, but many were flimsy operations or shell companies, leaving a multitude of projects incomplete

or uninhabitable. Moreover, even legitimate businesses were drawn into the patronage-violence complex since they would be required to make donations to individuals and the ANC or be frozen out of future contracts (Myburgh 2019). Similar practices were evident in the Eastern Cape (Olver 2017).

(5) The patronage-violence complex operated not only to enrich networks and individuals but also to fund the ANC. Indeed, the first big corruption scandal to attract public attention, the Arms Deal, appears to have had directing funds to the party as its primary purpose. There is a symbiotic relationship between the imperatives of financing the ANC and informal factions as well as the individual accumulation of wealth, most clearly illustrated by Crispian Olver (2017).

(6) The patronage-violence complex subverted and worked towards the destruction of state institutions. The deployment of corrupt individuals to strategic positions, and the sidelining of technical professionals and experts, the subversion of proper procedures and record-keeping, in addition to the siphoning off of substantial amounts of cash, led to the decline of SOEs and government departments. Eskom remains unable to maintain a reliable power supply and is burdened with unsustainable debt, which constitutes a dangerous risk for the national economy. South African Airways was forced into business rescue and partial privatisation. Other SOEs, such as Transnet, Prasa and Denel, have been left deeply compromised or bankrupt. The Department of Water Affairs has lost billions, while allowing critical infrastructure to decay; it remains unable to fund rehabilitative projects. Most local governments are effectively dysfunctional. The NPA was gutted in order to protect Zuma and his allies. SARS was broken, again to protect a range of interests, including Zuma and his allies. The reality sharply contradicts the claims of the radical economic transformation enthusiasts that their strategy will improve the developmental trajectory of South Africa.

(7) The workings of the patronage-violence complex were facilitated by a plethora of global corporations, from the most prominent global consulting and auditing firms to state corporations of the former communist regimes of China and Russia. Both KPMG and Bain produced consultancy reports for SARS, which facilitated its capture by a Zuma-linked group and made a series of spurious attempts to smear, harass or arrest minister of finance Pravin Gordhan. In addition, KPMG and McKinsey played essential roles in the looting of SOEs. As for the former communist regimes, China North Rail, China South Rail and Dongfang Electric Corporation were the beneficiaries of substantial supply contracts to Transnet and Eskom, including

hefty kickbacks to Gupta-linked accounts. At the same time, Rosatom, the Russian power company, was involved in the failed attempt to drive through an enormous nuclear power station tender, opposition to which cost two finance ministers their positions (PARI 2017; Hofstatter 2018).

(8) Violence is integral to the dynamics of the patronage-violence complex, whether deployed against whistleblowers, competitors or citizens who resist or demand justice. A selection of four cases from many more illustrates some dimensions of this. Olver (2017) describes the assassination of Buyis-ile Mkavu, a high-profile councillor aligned with the dominant faction of the ANC in Nelson Mandela Bay, who was investigating extensive corruption in housing contracts. This led to widespread fear and uncertainty, as 'we don't know who will be next' (Olver 2017, 3). In the Free State, Noby Ngombane, an SACP activist who worked in the premier's office, attempted to curtail maladministration, making enemies of both factions of the ANC. He was gunned down in his driveway in 2005. The provincial police were complicit in diverting the investigation into a cul-de-sac and attempting to implicate Ngombane's wife (Myburgh 2019). Ignatius 'Igo' Mpambani, an associate of Magashule's who had been involved in several episodes of state looting, was shot dead in his car in Johannesburg in 2017. Bundles of cash worth over a million rand were found in his car. Again, investigations into his death were ineffectual (Myburgh 2019). In Limpopo Province, one ANC councillor and two trade unionists were assassinated for calling for the arrest of political fig-ures involved in the looting of the VBS Mutual Bank, which siphoned off the substantial deposits of municipal councils as well as pensioners from poor communities, collapsing the bank (Sadiki and Ledwaba 2020). Violence emerges as a significant resource in regulating relationships in this informal system when other forms of regulation fail (Von Holdt 2013, 2014).

(9) Elite formation through wealth accumulation is intrinsic to the workings of the patronage-violence complex. Government officials and politicians are intent on enriching themselves and their families. Many businesses seek pref-erential treatment when it comes to tenders and contracts, and many among them collude in inflating the contracts, paying kickbacks or funding the ANC. A large number of these businesses are shell companies that are estab-lished in complex networks of front companies for the purposes of cycling and recycling cash between different parties. In contrast, others are flimsy operations designed to at least partially fulfil tenders. Still others are substan-tial businesses seeking rapid growth or having no alternative but to negotiate the corruption game. Thus, elite formation can be described as a broad pro-

cess through which several different classes are emerging – a wealthy political elite, a parasitic comprador class feeding off the state and a black capitalist class engaged in a serious endeavour to build businesses. Little, if any, research has been conducted to understand these processes and particularly what the beneficiaries of corruption, tender rigging and kickbacks are actually doing with their wealth, in order to assess whether a genuine black capitalist class is forming, to establish what proportion of wealth is recycled into productive investment and accumulation, or to what extent it is squandered in maintaining patronage and in conspicuous consumption. Moreover, such processes play out over time and include questions of intergenerational transfer.

The strengthening and deepening of the informal patronage-violence complex through the Zuma-Gupta state capture project further reinforced the struggle to re-embed elite formation through the appropriation of wealth from the disembedded formal circuits of capital. Thus, the appropriation of finance through inflated tenders and fraudulent contracts, and its recirculation through Gupta- and Zuma-linked companies, and back into political patronage networks, contributed to the emergence of new elites in a convergence of political power and economic power. In turn, strengthening this elite contributed to buttressing broader networks at the national, provincial and local levels, each with their own mechanisms for siphoning off wealth at different state levels, whether in Nelson Mandela Bay, North West Province, Mpumalanga or Gauteng.

All these practices of the patronage-violence complex flouted the rules and laws of so-called best-practice governance in the financialised global order. It is these systems of governance that tend to render financial circuits inaccessible to aspirant local elites, being designed in the broadest sense to buttress and facilitate the disembedding processes of marketisation. Hence, the logic of the informal system made it necessary to attempt the capture of the Treasury and the tax agency. The irony of this subversive project was that it was facilitated by some of the global paragons of 'good governance' and 'best practice', which signifies that no opportunity for profit-making is too filthy for the guardians of marketisation.

THE GORDHAN-RAMAPHOSA FIGHTBACK: A NEW DAWN FOR DISEMBEDDING ACCUMULATION?

The victory of Ramaphosa at the ANC conference at the end of 2017 was widely seen as a victory for the rule of law, democracy, investment and growth, and there is much truth in this when compared with the Zuma regime. This is why the working-class wing of the ANC Alliance supported the Gordhan-Ramaphosa campaign. The campaign was also supported by big business, most of the press and international institutions. At the same time, regulatory institutions in the US and South Africa started to investigate the complicity of US-based auditing and consulting companies in corruption. South African companies began terminating their contracts with them as a result. KPMG and Bain suffered serious reputational damage. The UK-based public relations company Bell Pottinger, which was contracted by the Guptas to launch fake news and social media attacks on the emerging opposition to the Zuma-Gupta project, was investigated and has since closed. This pattern of sanctions against those who facilitated state looting, together with the Gordhan-Ramaphosa campaign, constituted a fightback by the forces of globalisation and marketisation against the illicit re-embedding project of the Zuma networks and those who facilitated this project.

In the four years that he has been president, Ramaphosa has moved slowly to establish new leadership in the NPA, SARS and the SOEs, and to infuse new blood into his cabinet. The ANC leadership on his watch has gradually put in place important policies designed to clean up the ANC image, culminating in the 'step-aside' rule preventing anyone charged with serious crime from occupying or standing for elective positions. However, nothing particularly new or innovative has been visible on the economic front, beyond attempts to staunch the haemorrhaging of cash in state corporations. At the centre of economic policy seems to be the campaign to increase direct foreign investment, signalling a return to the failed policies of the Mbeki presidency. There are no significant answers for the crisis of poverty and inequality – indeed, government moved gradually in the opposite direction as it implemented an austerity programme as a result of the economic impacts of the Covid-19 pandemic coming on top of the crisis of looting, patronage and destruction of capacity, which characterised the state capture project.

Ramaphosa was elected ANC president in December 2017 with the slenderest of majorities, with two provincial barons implicated in corruption also elected to powerful positions (secretary general and deputy president). His election probably owed more to internal anxiety about the tarnished ANC image and loss of electoral support under Zuma than to anti-corruption sentiment; electoral decline means fewer seats in national, provincial and municipal legislatures and fewer opportunities for party members. Hence, the new party president did not have a clear or uncontested mandate to tackle corruption.

Tested by never-ending crises – the pandemic, economic slowdown, the July 2021 looting, rioting and destruction, ever-increasing electricity load shedding, corruption scandals and electoral decline – Ramaphosa has emerged as inde-cisive and out of touch, seemingly unable to grasp the necessity for urgency in addressing the upheaval. He is endlessly consulting or calling for new summits in an attempt to ensure buy-in and to overcome resistance to controversial policies. His progress in solidifying his position in the ANC has rested on a chimerical attempt to 'build unity', indicating his discomfort with making hard decisions or confronting resistance. In all of this, he seems to be the perfect president for the contemporary ANC, which is paralysed by opposing factions and riddled with corruption – one who can be relied upon to make vaguely promising pronounce-ments, while avoiding rocking any boats or provoking resistance from his ene-mies; in a word, ineffectual.

Ramaphosa's natural inclination to avoid making difficult decisions is reinforced by the tenuousness of his position in the ANC, split as it is on the issue of cor-ruption and stepping aside. It was clear from the beginning that he would have to include corrupt figures in his coalition of support (Von Holdt and Naidoo 2019). Indeed, halfway through the Covid-19 pandemic, his administration was rocked by allegations of massive and widespread corruption in relation to accelerated ten-dering for protective clothing and equipment for the health department and other state institutions. Several of Ramaphosa's allies and supporters were implicated, including his spokesperson, the Gauteng MEC for health, and his health minister, who had appeared to be the most dynamic minister in his cabinet and was effective in engaging the public and managing the pandemic response. All were forced to resign. These events only reinforce the analysis presented above about the perva-siveness of the patronage-violence complex, and the extent to which it penetrates the ANC, the government and Ramaphosa's administration. Indeed, Ramaphosa himself has been implicated in a bizarre scandal involving the unreported theft of stashes of US dollars, worth millions of rand, from one of his farms, and the alleged attempt to buy the silence of the thieves, strengthening the view that corruption is pervasive in the ANC and deepening public cynicism.

In an earlier article, I argued that Ramaphosa would need to establish a stable coalition in order to achieve his stated goals of ending corruption and attracting international investment. But this would require him to incorporate figures involved in corruption, which, in turn, would strengthen resistance to his anti-corruption measures and ultimately generate new instability (Von Holdt and Naidoo 2019). He has, however, succeeded in overseeing important elements of his anti-corruption drive, including the Zondo Commission into what I have argued here should be seen as a limited notion of state capture, the process of rebuilding the prosecutions and tax authorities, and the step-aside rule in the ANC.

But, as the spectre of prosecutions crept closer, with charges being laid against Magashule and the contempt of court order against former president Zuma, resistance culminated in the July 2021 uprisings, orchestrated in the first instance by networks of Zuma supporters and their allies, but decisively expanded by the participation of criminal syndicates as well as crowds of ordinary citizens – mostly the poor and excluded, but including middle-class elements. Those eight days in July demonstrated the power of networks within the patronage-violence complex to mobilise extensively, as well as their potential populist appeal in the context of intractable poverty and inequality. While the eight days were shaped by multiple different groups with a variety of agendas, to the extent that it had a political goal it seems to have been to weaken Ramaphosa's presidency or even to force his removal by showing that he was incapable of bringing the widespread rioting and instability to a rapid end. While this may have backfired to some extent by demonstrating the limited reach of the Zuma-supporting faction – the unrest was confined to two provinces only (those with a significant Zulu-speaking population, and particularly migrant worker hostels) – as well as taking a significant economic toll on the Zuma-supporting province of KwaZulu-Natal, in particular, it nonetheless deepened the sense of crisis and drift in the Ramaphosa administration.

The tension between the small cohort of political leaders and senior technocrats untainted by allegations of corruption or association with corrupt figures, and the agents of the patronage-violence complex, will persist and continue to define the future trajectory of the ANC. A pervasive weakness of the anti-corruption faction is their adherence to orthodox and unimaginative neoliberal policies, which pre-empts any possibility of transforming the socio-economic plight of the majority of citizens. Moreover, their neoliberal policy orientation renders Ramaphosa and his faction vulnerable to a populist mobilisation, corresponding with the one that brought about Mbeki's downfall.

Clearly, the patronage-violence complex is so entrenched and pervasive within the ANC that a full-frontal attack on it, even if this is conceivable, would be less likely to cleanse it than to tear it to pieces – as suggested in 2012 by the trade unionist interviewed above. And, indeed, perhaps the contradictions at the heart of the ANC will lead to a split or series of splits in the organisation. However, it seems unlikely that this will occur until the ANC loses electoral power.

The two central problems confronting South Africa are the barriers thwarting the emergence of a stable black elite in general and a business class in particular, coupled with the profound legacy of poverty, marginalisation and inequality left by apartheid. The fundamental source of these problems is the failure to significantly redistribute the massive concentration of wealth in white hands, which was produced by three centuries of colonialism and apartheid. Until this is addressed, the patronage-violence complex is likely to remain deeply rooted and extensive in South Africa's political economy, and to command as well a degree of popular support, no matter which political party is in power. Though with profoundly perverse consequences, it is the only project presently on the horizon that attempts to re-embed elements of economic life in the realities of South African society.

NOTES

1 This chapter is a substantially revised, refocused and updated version of 'The Political Economy of Corruption: Elite-Formation, Factions and Violence', Working Paper 10, SWOP, Johannesburg. https://www.swop.org.za/post/2019/02/18/working-paper-10-the-political-economy-of-corruption-open-access.
2 Interview, trade union office bearer, 2012.

REFERENCES

Ashman, Sam, Ben Fine and Susan Newman. 2011. 'Amnesty International? The Nature, Scale and Impact of Capital Flight from South Africa'. *Journal of Southern African Studies* 37, no. 1: 7–25. https://www.tandfonline.com/doi/abs/10.1080/03057070.2011.555155.

Dawson, Hannah. 2014. 'Patronage from Below: Political Unrest in an Informal Settlement in South Africa'. *African Affairs* 113, no. 453: 518–539. https://academic.oup.com/afraf/article-abstract/113/453/518/91103?redirectedFrom=fulltext.

Dawson, Hannah. 2017. 'Protests, Party Politics and Patronage: A View from Zandspruit Informal Settlement, Johannesburg'. In *Southern Resistance in Critical Perspective: The Politics of Protest in South Africa's Contentious Democracy*, edited by Marcel Paret, Carin Runciman and Luke Sinwell, 118–134. London: Routledge.

Fanon, Frantz. [1961] 1967. *The Wretched of the Earth*. London: Penguin.

Hart, Gillian. 2013. *Rethinking the South African Crisis: Nationalism, Populism, Hegemony*. Pietermaritzburg: University of KwaZulu-Natal Press.

Hofstatter, Stephan. 2018. *Licence to Loot: How the Plunder of Eskom and Other Parastatals Almost Sank South Africa*. Cape Town: Penguin Books.

Langa, Malose and Karl von Holdt. 2012. 'Insurgent Citizenship, Class Formation and the Dual Nature of Community Protest: A Case Study of "Kungcatsha"'. In *Contesting Transformation: Popular Resistance in Twenty-First Century South Africa*, edited by Marcelle C. Dawson and Luke Sinwell, 80–100. London: Pluto Press.

Marais, Hein. 1998. *South Africa: Limits to Change: The Political Economy of Transition*. London: Zed Books.

Maseko, Themba. 2021. *For My Country: Why I Blew the Whistle on Zuma and the Guptas*. Johannesburg: Jonathan Ball.

Mothepu, Mosilo. 2021. *Uncaptured: The True Account of the Nenegate/Trillian Whistleblower*. Cape Town: Penguin Books.

Mukwedeya, Tatenda G. and Hlengiwe Ndlovu. 2017. 'Party Politics and Community Mobilisation in Buffalo City, East London'. In *Southern Resistance in Critical Perspective:*

The Politics of Protest in South Africa's Contentious Democracy, edited by Marcel Paret, Carin Runciman and Luke Sinwell, 107–117. London: Routledge.

Myburgh, Pieter-Louis. 2019. *Gangster State: Unravelling Ace Magashule's Web of Capture.* Cape Town: Penguin Books.

Ndletyana, Mcebisi, Pholoane Makhalemele and Ralph Mathekga, eds. 2013. *Patronage Politics Divides Us: A Study of Poverty, Patronage and Inequality in South Africa.* Johannesburg: Mapungubwe Institute for Strategic Reflection.

Olver, Crispian. 2017. *How to Steal a City: The Battle for Nelson Mandela Bay.* Johannesburg: Jonathan Ball.

PARI. 2017. 'Betrayal of the Promise: How South Africa Is Being Stolen'. State Capacity Research Project Report, Public Affairs Research Institute, Johannesburg. https://pari. org.za/betrayal-promise-report/.

Plaut, Martin and Paul Holden. 2012. *Who Rules South Africa? Pulling the Strings in the Battle for Power.* Johannesburg: Jonathan Ball.

Polanyi, Karl. [1944] 1957. *The Great Transformation: The Political and Economic Origins of Our Time.* Boston: Beacon Press.

Rossouw, Rehana. 2020. *Predator Politics: Mabuza, Fred Daniel and the Great Land Scam.* Johannesburg: Jacana.

Sadiki, Rolivhuwa and Lucas Ledwaba. 2020. 'Fear Rules in Affected Communities as Prosecutors Zoom in on Suspected VBS Killings'. *Daily Maverick*, 26 June 2020. https:// www.dailymaverick.co.za/article/2020-06-26-fear-rules-in-affected-communities-as-prosecutors-zoom-in-on-suspected-vbs-killings/.

Von Holdt, Karl. 2013. 'South Africa: The Transition to Violent Democracy'. *Review of African Political Economy* 40, no. 138: 589–604. https://www.tandfonline.com/doi/abs /10.1080/03056244.2013.854040.

Von Holdt, Karl. 2014. 'On Violent Democracy'. *The Sociological Review* 62, no. 2: 129–151. https://journals.sagepub.com/doi/abs/10.1111/1467-954X.12196.

Von Holdt, Karl, Malose Langa, Sepetla Molapo, Nomfundo Mogapi, Kindiza Ngubeni, Jacob Dlamini and Adèle Kirsten. 2011. 'The Smoke That Calls: Insurgent Citizenship, Collective Violence and the Struggle for a Place in the New South Africa'. Centre for the Study of Violence and Reconciliation and SWOP, Johannesburg. https://www.csvr.org. za/docs/thesmokethatcalls.pdf.

Von Holdt, Karl and Prishani Naidoo. 2019. 'Mapping Movement Landscapes in South Africa'. *Globalizations* 16, no. 2: 170–185. https://www.tandfonline.com/doi/abs/10.10 80/14747731.2018.1479019.

State Capture, the Racket and Predatory Power

Robyn Foley

The term 'state capture' was the South African Word of the Year 2017 (Pijoos 2017), ascending in the public consciousness following the release of the Public Protector's 'State of Capture' report in the closing months of the previous year (Public Protector 2016). It detailed the findings of an investigation into an alleged corrupt relationship between senior government officials and the Gupta family, who were personally connected to the country's then president, Jacob Zuma. Running to 355 pages, the report suggested that the Guptas had leveraged political influence to irregularly (sometimes illegally) extract rent from the state.

Since the release of the report, South Africans have been inundated with revelations of corruption, maladministration and an array of abuse by those in power. Although the capture of the state has been slowed, the systems that enabled it have not been fully explained. Appreciating why this is so is a secondary interest of this chapter. The primary interest is to draw the South African experience closer to definitions and analytical tools and so to explain the underlying 'logics' and patterns of behaviour that fuelled ways in which legitimate authority can be captured.

SETTING THE SCENE

A turning point in the unfolding saga was 7 April 2017, when the post-apart-heid state witnessed its largest protests (Business Day 2017). In an extraordinary show of unity, people from various South African communities united behind #ZumaMustFall. The month of mass protests that followed was a direct response to the firing of minister of finance Pravin Gordhan and his deputy, Mcebisi Jonas. The latter's public revelations of an attempted R600-million bribe by the Guptas triggered the Public Protector's initial investigation into the Guptas and their links to the president's family and their cronies.

The alleged bribe was facilitated by the president's son Duduzane Zuma in August 2015 (Jonas 2018). Importantly for our purposes, the bribe was linked to the prediction – by the Guptas – that Jonas was to become the country's next finance minister. Indeed, a few months later, Zuma announced the removal of Nhlanhla Nene, who at the time held the finance portfolio, replacing him with an unknown African National Congress (ANC) backbencher, Des van Rooyen. This was the first of several late-night cabinet shuffles, in which the president moved – or replaced – members of his cabinet without explanation and seemingly without policy logic. It later emerged that there were several reasons for the removal of Nene, but none of them could reasonably be considered to be in the interests of South Africa's people. Instead, each seemed only to serve the president's interests, or those of his family and his cronies. In the Nene case, this was confirmed by a whistleblower employed at the Gupta company Trillian. In testimony before the Zondo Commission in 2020, Msilo Mothepu pointed out that there were a dozen projects that the Zuma-Gupta network was seeking to implement at the time – this included a nuclear deal with Russia with a projected cost of a trillion rand (Zondo Commission 2020c).

But Van Rooyen's tenure as finance minister was short-lived: Nene's firing had sent a shock wave through the markets, resulting in at least R378 billion in value being wiped off the Johannesburg Stock Exchange and, in its wake, an estimated loss of some 148 000 jobs (Merten 2019). Within days and following an outcry from inside and outside the ANC, Zuma reappointed the previous holder of the same office, Pravin Gordhan (Areff 2015). Because he was aware of the shenani-gans of the Guptas, Gordhan posed an obstacle to the project of capturing the state. After unsuccessful attempts to squeeze him out, Zuma would later remove Gordhan (together with Deputy Minister Mcebesi Jonas) from office in yet another late-night reshuffle on 30 March 2017 (Chirume et al. 2017). This capricious decision – seem-ingly made irrationally – again shook the markets (Merten 2019). These are but a few examples in a growing list of moves that appeared to serve the interests of a closed group rather than the national interest. Other notorious incidents were the violation of the integrity of a South African Air Force base, and 'security' upgrades to the president's private homestead (Public Protector 2014).

In the months that followed, pressure mounted to remove Zuma from office. Opposition parties, working together with dissenting members in the ANC, pressed parliament to formally inquire into the allegations contained within, or linked to, the Public Protector's report on state capture. Civil society and religious organisations built public awareness of the extent of corruption in the country, while the business community voiced anxiety at the Zuma presidency's damage to the country. In parallel to these developments, a collective of academics – the State Capacity Research Project – issued a groundbreaking study titled 'Betrayal of the Promise: How South Africa Is Being Stolen' (PARI 2017).

The Public Protector's report did not contain definitive findings of guilt against specific individuals, nor did it provide for remedial actions to be taken concerning any of the allegations in the public domain. It recommended, instead, that a judicial commission of inquiry be established to investigate the entire matter. But, in a significant departure, the Public Protector suggested that the presiding judge would be determined not – as is the practice – by the president but rather by the country's Chief Justice. In another departure, it was recommended that the proposed judicial commission should be afforded the same investigative powers as those enjoyed by the Public Protector's office. So it was that in January 2018, more than a year after the release of the Public Protector's report, Zuma promulgated the establishment of the Judicial Commission of Inquiry into Allegations of State Capture, Corruption and Fraud in the Public Sector including Organs of State, to be chaired by Deputy Chief Justice Raymond Zondo, hereafter and in the public domain referred to as the Zondo Commission.

STATE CAPTURE, THE SHADOW STATE AND THE RACKET

A working definition might suggest that state capture – note the lower case – is a form of 'grand corruption'. This suggests evidence of 'firms shaping and affecting formulation of the rules of the [bureaucratic] game through private payments to public officials and politicians' (Hellman, Jones and Kaufmann 2000, 'Summary'). But this explanation is limited: it covers a particular type of corruption implying specific directionality in terms of the instigating agent and the intended target. Additionally, it limits the idea of state capture to one dimension only – so, as Pieter Labuschagne puts it, 'discussions around state capture are principally done from an economic context, not from a political perspective' (2017, 51).

The 'Betrayal of the Promise' report (PARI 2017) addressed these gaps in the utilisation of the concept by linking the transactional acts of visible corruption with the blurred and informal power dynamics that have enabled the South African state to become captured. Using the idea of State Capture – note the upper case – the report drew together the corruption and the actors, activities and factors that have characterised the uniqueness of misgovernance in South Africa. So, in this sense, state capture is the formation of a 'shadow state' directed by a power elite, which operates within – but parallel to – the constitutional state. Its objective is to repurpose the state (and its governance) to extract benefits aligned with the power elite's narrow financial and/or political interests (Chipkin and Swilling 2018; PARI 2017).

The latter understanding addresses some of the limitations of viewing the issue purely in economic terms. Firstly, there is no separation between public and private domains: those involved in state capture do not distinguish between a constitutional state and a shadow state. Indeed, it turns on actors colluding within and outside government, both legally and illegally, by employing formal and informal modes of engagement. Secondly, the broader definition does not relate to the act of corruption only. Instead, it 'refers to the organised process of reconfiguring the way[s] in which … [state institutions are] structured, governed, managed and funded so that [they come to serve] a purpose different to [their] formal mandate[s]' (PARI 2017, 5). So, state capture embraces a range of acts, actions and activities that do not necessarily meet the strict definition of corruption. Thirdly, state capture is not a single event, nor is it confined to a few select individuals: its success depends on a range of persons operating within different institutions. Finally, to succeed, it requires large collectives to cooperate in repurposing state institutions. But most of those involved are unlikely to realise any form of substantive benefit.

To explain how state capture manifests itself, it is essential to understand the logic behind the formation of a shadow state. Here, the concept of the 'racket' is instructive, and it is to this issue we now turn. The notion of 'rackets' and the 'racket society' evolved at the edges of the Frankfurt School of Critical Theory.[1] Informed by that work, we learn that rackets are comprised of and operationalised by 'cliques, gangs and other established groups that act protectively towards their own members, while externally they attempt to circumvent the market process by misappropriating economic income and by deceiving the public' (Adorno and Horkheimer, quoted in Granter 2017). Although useful conceptually, this abstraction of the racket does not address how they operate, however.

For this understanding, we must turn to the psychoanalytical field of transactional analysis, which refers to the 'coercive feelings' that trigger people to participate in the process of racketeering (Ernst 1973). The latter is a pattern of manipulative behaviour that enables the racketeer – usually an individual – to enrol others into acting out an untruth that is masked by a seemingly credible story. Both the idea and the theory, which underpins the notion, recognise racketeering as self-perpetuating and self-reinforcing (Christoph-Lemke 1999; Ernst 1973; Erskine and Zalcman 1979; Granter 2017; Klein and Regatieri 2018; Scheit and Fischer 2018). Taken together, this logic and the resulting underlying manipulation – through extortion, say – drive the racket forward. So, if an individual racket proves effective, it will continue to be repeated and even replicated elsewhere.

On the other hand, if rackets are sanctioned or ignored, they can become accepted behaviour within what is called a 'racket society'. Thus, for example, the 'normalisation' of state ministers informally meeting with businesspeople, or (to draw closer to our immediate interest) President Zuma asking directors general of state departments to 'help' the Guptas' *New Age* newspaper to gain access to the state's advertising budget.[2] This makes such behaviour seem routine, so that it becomes gradually accepted as regular by broader society. The result is that social norms and democratic practice are corroded.

THE RACKET AND PREDATORY POWER

South Africa's democracy is cast in the Weberian notion of formal legal-rational governance – power is defined, limited and distributed in terms of practical institutions that make, adjudicate and enforce the Constitution in a legally binding form. But, like all human-centred organisations, the functioning of this system does not depend on the written word alone but on the manner in which laws and bureaucracy are manifest in the daily lives of the country's citizens. Thus, enacting the values and principles from which the country's laws are conceived requires continuous reflection, refinement and reinforcement (Le Roux and Davis 2019; Rosenfeld 2000).

State capture occurs when formal-legal structures are subverted and eroded by the informal structures that prey on the citizenry and their understandings of democracy. Unfortunately, these have been self-perpetuating and reinforcing, and so state capture in the country must be understood as the outcome of the racket of predatory power, as outlined in figure 2.1.

THE SHAPE OF STATE CAPTURE

By the end of 2020, the Zondo Commission had heard testimony from more than 278 witnesses and summoned 2 736 individuals to testify (Chabalala 2020).

The Racket of Predatory Power

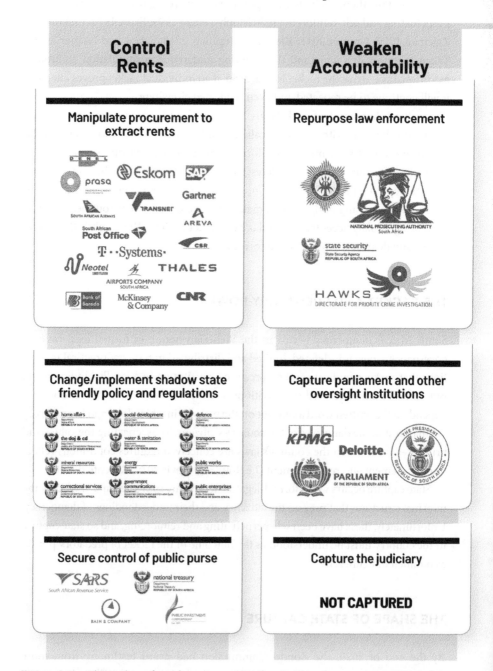

Figure 2.1: The racket of predatory power in South Africa's state capture. Graphic by Robin Foley.

Maintain Legitimacy

Enable and protect patronage networks

Control the message through the media and drive misinformation

Curtail transparency and discredit opposition to the shadow state

NOT CAPTURED

Although the Gupta network was the central focus of interest, investigations by the commission revealed several other networks entangled in state capture. These sometimes operate semi-independently, but they are interconnected by political affiliation and formal and informal relationships with those in power. Determining precisely who the members of these various networks are has not been easy, but it is clear that individuals can be involved in multiple state capture projects simultaneously. Unlike instances of 'petty' corruption, where a direct link can be established between the actions of the official and the illicit payment by the benefiting party, in the racket, an individual can be a facilitator in one project and the beneficiary of an entirely separate project.

Moreover, members of clandestine networks can take on different roles required to achieve the same state capture objective. These are not fixed, nor are they defined by any prescripts. This confirms that the shadow state operates without fixed rules. Figure 2.2 outlines the various broad functions and roles that different individuals carry out in the projects of state capture.

It is essential to point out that individuals – even organisations – might unknowingly or unwillingly be integrated into the actions of the shadow state. As suggested, the motivations and intentions behind each individual's participation in the shadow state can vary greatly. Deception and manipulation also occur within the shadow state. As a result, individuals may not have full knowledge of the actual objectives of another party. What distinguishes the 'power elite'[3] from the broader shadow state is that the networks of the former are aware of – in fact, must fully support and drive towards – the objectives of state capture. Indeed, these are the racketeers.

Drawing on the literature on rackets (Ernst 1973; Granter 2017; Klein and Regatieri 2018), table 2.1 presents the typologies of rackets that comprised state capture in South Africa.

THE EXTENT

There have been some 28 major investigations, inquiries and commissions related to state capture in the country. This includes the three parliamentary inquiries launched following the release of the 'State of Capture' report (Public Protector 2014) and by the GuptaLeaks (2017a); investigations surrounding Eskom and Transnet (National Treasury 2018a, 2018b; Portfolio Committee on Public

Elites

Often used because of their political influence and allegiance, these individuals are deployed to positions of exclusive and administrative power within the constitutional state. Their function is to oversee the enactment of the shadow state agenda and to help change the rules of the constitutional state or to bypass them when necessary.

Brokers

Act as coordinators and distributors of the gains plundered from the state. These actors are generally never directly involved in the transactions and activities of corruption. In South Africa, this group includes the Guptas, the Watson brothers and other politically connected individuals who act as brokers in this way.

Internal Fixers

Involved at an administrative or operational level, they are the technocrats and bureaucrats that oversee the subverting or breaking of the rules. Their function is to 'rig' the game by tender fixing, to facilitate 'insider trading' on knowledge of business opportunities and 'regularising' of processes after the fact.

External Fixers

Can operate formally or informally, both within and outside the constitutional state. Informally, they are the dealers and handlers who, among other activities, launder money and pay bribes. Formally, they are the consultants-financial, legal and auditing professionals that facilitate and enable legitimisation of the extraction of rents and authoritatively enable the 'legitimatising' of illegal/immoral behaviour.

Middlemen

Are involved directly in the transactions and generally have more formal exchanges. Examples include 'business development partners', advisers and BBBEE front companies. Their function is to bridge big-business interests and the shadow state. They often only take a small percentage of the contract value and pass the rest on to the brokers for distribution (but they can also be brokers).

Corrupt Corporates

These are the companies and corporates that pay the bribes and work with the middlemen/brokers to attain lucrative government contracts, extracting rents and distributing benefits back to the broader network.

Formal Exchanges
Legal and professional type relations

Informal Exchanges
Private and personal type relations

Figure 2.2: The shape of state capture: roles and functions in the shadow state. Graphic by Robin Foley.

Table 2.1: Types of rackets that enabled state capture in South Africa.

Type	Description	Example
Conspiracy	All parties have the same goal and aligned strategy to be implemented (enrol each other for purposes of mutual benefit). The deception is directed outwards to the public.	Zuma and the Guptas conspired to establish *New Age* newspaper and the ANN7 24-hour news channel. At his first appearance at the Zondo Commission, Zuma openly admitted that it was his idea, for the purpose of celebrating what he deemed the positive developments and achievements of the state (Zondo Commission 2019b).
Collusion	A racketeer enrols a less powerful party into an action that operates for the benefit of both parties. The goals for each party are different, but the strategy is aligned. The deception is directed outwards to the public but can also be within the racket.	Tom Moyane and consultancy company Bain colluded in pre-planning the restructuring of SARS. As noted by the Nugent Commission: 'We think what occurred can fairly be described as a premeditated offensive against SARS, strategised by the local office of Bain & Company Inc, located in Boston, for Mr Moyane to seize SARS, each in pursuit of their own interests that were symbiotic but not altogether the same. Mr Moyane's interest was to take control of SARS. Bain's interest was to make money' (Nugent Commission 2018, 27).
Coercion	A racketeer uses various direct and indirect threats to compel a reluctant party to actively participate in a scheme. Threats might range from being sacked, to physical violence directed against the individual or those close to them, blackmail or exclusion from being considered as a contractor.	Several individuals testifying at the Zondo Commission have done so in camera, using pseudonyms to hide their identities for fear of reprisals and threats to their lives. Several witnesses have testified to their enrolment in corrupt projects for fear of losing their livelihoods. For example, a former head of the Free State housing department, Mpho Mokoena, was instructed by then MEC Mosebenzi Zwane that if he did not sign off on an unlawful procurement process Mokoena should 'resign' (Zondo Commission 2020b). Perhaps the most emblematic example is provided in an interview on 19 March 2016, where in response to the revelations by Mcebisi Jonas, Bathabile Dlamini cautioned members of the ANC against airing the party's dirty laundry in the media, saying: 'All of us in the NEC [National Executive Committee] have our smallanyana skeletons and we don't want to take out skeletons because all hell will break loose' (SABC 2016).
Complicity	The racketeer aims to silence someone who knows that a racket is going on but is compelled to say and do nothing. The coercive feelings deployed are confusion, fear and shame.	In 2011, Riaz 'Mo' Shaik and other senior officials of the State Security Agency decided to halt all investigations into the Guptas, after it became clear that Jacob Zuma was not pleased to hear about the investigation (Shaik 2019).
Con	The racketeer enrols others under false pretences. The deception lies within the racket, where the strategy is enacted, but goals are divergent, and the only benefit derived is for the racketeer.	Benny Jiyane became the BEE partner of VR Laser and facilitated the sale of the remaining shares in the company to Salim Essa, without knowing that the latter was in cahoots with the Guptas. Jiyane believed Essa's story of partnership but, after VR Laser secured lucrative contracts with Denel, the Guptas moved in, forcefully ejected Jiyane from the business and took it over (Corruption Watch 2019).

Enterprises 2018); the Mokgoro inquiry into the fitness of officials at the National Prosecuting Authority (NPA) (The Presidency 2019); the high-level panel review of the State Security Agency (High-Level Review Panel on the SSA 2018); the Nugent Commission into the South African Revenue Service (SARS) (Nugent Commission 2018); and the Zondo Commission.

From the various reports, public hearings, court cases and collective investigative journalism, it is plain that state capture is not, as Jacob Zuma has asserted, '[just] people who did things to others in one form or the other, and you can call it any other name … [but] not this big name "state capture"' (Deklerk 2018). By contrast, state capture was multi-levelled, multi-layered, multi-nodal and (as we have seen) multi-targeted. Moreover, the phenomenon is spread across the country. It reaches beyond the borders, too. Within South Africa, seven out of the nine provinces have been directly implicated, reaching down to the lowest level of government. The Estina dairy farm scandal provides a good example of the extent of the reach of state capture. Money meant for the development of local farmers in the Free State Province was looted to pay for a lavish Gupta wedding (GuptaLeaks 2017b; Shadow World Investigations 2019).

Thirteen national-level ministries and more than 15 state-owned enterprises (SOEs) have been central to the project. In addition, strategic institutions, which provided critical economic services (energy, transportation and infrastructure development), and various law enforcement agencies and government entities that provide vital social services have been affected. Each of these was repurposed to serve one or more of the objectives, which are analysed in what follows.

Objective 1: Extraction of Rents

This, the most readily visible form of repurposing, occurs through the manipulation of government procurement processes. As capital-intensive entities with large operating budgets, SOEs like Eskom, Transnet, South African Airways and defence contractor Denel were targets. In addition, there are cases where established policies were reformulated to facilitate the extraction of rent. For example, in 2016, minister of public enterprises Malusi Gigaba insisted that coal-supply contracts to Eskom be awarded to mines with 50 per cent-plus black ownership by 2018/2019 (Eskom 2016; Godinho and Hermanus 2018). However, rent extraction involved manipulation and subversion of the processes that underlie public-funded procurement programmes. This included prior knowledge of, or even a hand in, the development of bid specifications, influence in the evaluation or adjudication committees, or influencing the authorising party (at the executive or board level) to favour a particular (read corrupt) endeavour. There were many instances in which the procurement processes, guided by the Public Finance Management Act, were manipulated to enable the looting of public institutions.

Undoubtedly, the oversight role played by the National Treasury provided a significant impediment to greater rent extraction. In hindsight, it is apparent that the ministerial reshuffles discussed earlier took place moments after the Treasury refused to sign off on large deals or was resisting rent-seeking initiatives of the shadow state. But government institutions were only one side of the corrupt and clandestine transactions. The roles played in state capture by private sector companies require greater scrutiny. Indeed, as the evidence shows, large international firms were deeply involved in kickback schemes, inflating costs and, in some instances, participating directly in theft from the public purse. The likes of SAP, T-Systems, China South Rail, Net1, Bain & Company, McKinsey & Company, and so on (all internationally based) have derived significant financial benefit, with little to no consequences for their involvement.

Objective 2: Weakening of Accountability

The second objective was to 'capture' the criminal justice system. For state capture to flourish, law enforcement and the entities responsible for state security are required to shield the shadow state from criminal prosecution and to target opponents. To succeed, complicity within the South African Police Service, the Directorate for Priority Crime Investigation (the Hawks), the NPA and the intelligence community was necessary. The effective hollowing-out of these institutions undoubtedly compromised the enforcement of the rule of law. This outcome explains why white-collar criminal elements related to state capture have managed to escape prosecution (Business Insider SA 2020; BusinessTech 2019).[4]

It is essential to understand that the notion of 'accountability' extends beyond what can be considered criminal. As a result, there are several state institutions other than those in the legal cluster that play a role in holding those in power to account. This is one of the primary responsibilities of parliament and of the Chapter Nine institutions,[5] which includes the Office of the Public Protector. In the same vein, the extent to which the ANC-dominated National Assembly was 'captured' is debatable. However, it is instructive to recall that Zuma emerged unscathed from several votes of no confidence throughout his presidency (Wilkinson and Africa Check, 2017). It is also informative to recall the Constitutional Court's rebuke relating to parliament's whitewash 'fire pool report',[6] which justified the R245-million 'security upgrades' to Zuma's homestead. The ruling argues:

> There was everything wrong with the National Assembly stepping into the shoes of the Public Protector by passing a resolution that purported effectively to nullify the findings made and remedial action taken by the Public Protector and replacing them with its findings and 'remedial action' … It is another way of taking the law into one's hands … The failure by the National Assembly to hold the president accountable by ensuring that he complies with the remedial action taken against him is inconsistent with its obligations to scrutinise and oversee executive action and to maintain oversight of the exercise of executive powers by the president (Economic Freedom Fighters v Speaker of the National Assembly and Others 2016).

Certain private sector professional firms also played roles in weakening accountability and facilitating the extraction of rents. These were the auditors, consultants, lawyers and bankers who provided a veil of legitimacy that facilitated the movement of monies and turned a blind eye to dirty dealings and financial irregularities. At least three of the 'Big Four' international auditing firms – KPMG, Deloitte and PwC – were implicated in malfeasance (Abedian and Mantell 2017; Cameron 2019).

Objective 3: Maintaining Legitimacy

There are three elements to maintaining legitimacy within a democratic state, and the media, together with civil society, must vigilantly monitor these.

The first seeks to weaken the institutions that would hold those in power to account and control what informs public opinion. An example is when the chief operations officer of the national broadcaster, the South African Broadcasting Corporation, instructed news teams not to show the destruction of property during service delivery protests in mid-2016 (Ad Hoc Committee on the SABC Board Inquiry 2017; Zondo Commission 2019c). Here, the intention was to impair the public's ability to grasp the extent of the protest and downplay – or deny – the country's levels of anger and dissatisfaction. Another example was when the Gupta-owned media outlets, *New Age* and ANN7, published 'sunshine' stories about the Zuma administration.

Like others across the world, South Africans are challenged by the rise of populism and an onslaught of 'fake news' aiming to create division. This use of the media (particularly social media) was glaringly seen in the propaganda crafted by the London-based public relations company Bell Pottinger to influence public perception and shape opinion (GuptaLeaks 2017c). At the behest of the Guptas, the Bell Pottinger campaign attempted to mitigate the negative exposure of the family and legitimise its dealings in South Africa as fighting 'white monopoly capital' and promoting 'radical economic transformation'. As noted in the 'Betrayal of the Promise':

> It is now clear that while the ideological focus of the ANC is 'radical economic transformation', in practice, Jacob Zuma's presidency is aimed at repurposing state institutions to consolidate the Zuma-centred power elite. Whereas the former appears to be a legitimate long-term vision to structurally transform South Africa's economy to eradicate poverty and reduce inequality and unemployment, the latter – popularly referred to as 'state capture' – threatens the viability of the state institutions that need to deliver on this long-term vision (PARI 2017, 2).

The use of propaganda is tightly connected with the second element of maintaining legitimacy, namely, to delegitimise – or remove – individuals or instances that expose the abuses of power and acts of corruption. Various forms of clandestine campaigning were used in state capture, including leaking salacious stories that – often through intimidation – remove obstacles and promote alternative narratives. The most startling of these was the evidence that the State Security Agency was used to infiltrate protest movements and that it spied on non-governmental organisations (NGOs) in order to protect the political interests of Zuma's government (High-Level Review Panel on the SSA 2018).

The final element in maintaining legitimacy lies in the patronage and clientelism embedded in the political system itself (Anciano 2018; Van de Walle 2007). A sufficient number of individuals need to benefit from state capture to ensure there is sufficient support to justify its continued existence and counter negative exposure. Those that benefit from its windfalls need to funnel resources into justifying the actions of the shadow state. This, in turn, provides protection from scrutiny and prosecution – thus effecting a 'protection racket'. The underlying logic of predatory power was famously stated by the two-time former Brazilian president, Getúlio Vargas: 'For my friends, everything; for my enemies, the law' (O'Donnell 2004, 40).

CURTAILING STATE CAPTURE

The power of civil society and the courts were instrumental in minimising the damage caused by the shadow state. Many of the state capture cases had been reported in the media long before being revealed at the Zondo Commission. Whistleblowers and tenacious investigative journalists revealed the dubious wrongdoing throughout the Zuma years. And it is because of the intentional features of democratic design in South Africa's Constitution, mandating transparency, participation and fairness in government functioning, that civil society was enabled to approach courts and Chapter Nine institutions to intervene. For example, in March 2017, the Black Sash Trust brought an action to the Constitutional Court to ensure that 17 million beneficiaries would continue to receive their social grants.[7] The case saw then minister for social development Bathabile Dlamini reprimanded for placing the country's most vulnerable at risk of not receiving the means of survival (Pijoos 2018). And, in another instance, Earthlife Africa and the Southern African Faith Communities' Environment Institute jointly challenged the government's plan to push through the nuclear deal with Russia, which would have cost the country an estimated R1 trillion (Gosling 2018).[8]

Another standout case before the Constitutional Court was brought by Corruption Watch, Freedom Under Law and the Council for the Advancement of the South African Constitution.[9] This challenged the appointment of Shaun Abrahams as National Director of Public Prosecutions (NDPP), following the coerced departure of his predecessor, Mxolisi Nxasana. The court position was confirmed in the following extract from the judgment:

> Former President Zuma appointed Advocate Abrahams following his unlawful removal of Mr Nxasana. That removal was an abuse of power. Advocate Abrahams benefited from this abuse of power. It matters not that he may have been unaware of the abuse of power; the rule of law dictates that the office of the NDPP be cleansed of all the ills that have plagued it for the past few years (Corruption Watch NPC and Others v President of the Republic of South Africa and Others 2018).

THE FIGHTBACK

Civil society protests in April 2017 played a decisive role in 'recapturing' the state by amplifying a call for Zuma to go. This only happened ten months later at the ANC's national conference, which brought Cyril Ramaphosa to the presidency of the ANC. The latter ran on an anti-state capture platform and narrowly beat the radical economic transformation faction nominee Nkosazana Dlamini-Zuma. This outcome has been viewed as a compromise, with individuals from both factions within the ANC equally deployed into top leadership (Mail & Guardian 2018a). At the time, Ace Magashule, who was implicated as being a part of the Gupta network

(Myburgh 2019), was elected as the party's secretary general. (He was suspended from this position in May 2021.) However, perhaps the most unexpected outcome was the election of David Mabuza as the ANC's deputy president. As the premier of Mpumalanga, Mabuza held sway on how the branches in his province would vote and unexpectedly shifted support to Ramaphosa. Both Magashule and Mabuza were long-time Zuma allies, forming part of the so-called Premier League that provided the political support that enabled state capture (Friedman 2019a).

On 14 February 2018, Zuma finally announced his resignation as president of South Africa. However, it was plain from the performance that it was a reluctant step (CNBC Africa 2018; Lowman 2018). Presenting himself as a hapless victim, he called 'state capture' a 'politically decorated expression' – 'a fake political tool' of his purported enemies (Deklerk 2018).

The Ramaphosa presidency has made steps towards 'recapturing' the state. At the forefront have been unambiguous support of the Zondo Commission and the establishment of three other commissions of inquiry. In one of these, the commission investigating SARS resulted in Commissioner Tom Moyane being fired, while two key senior officials, alleged to be Zuma allies, were fired from the NPA (Landman 2019). Moreover, there has been transparency in presidential appointments: a respected and experienced prosecutor, Shamila Batohi, was appointed to head the NPA, and Edward Kieswetter was appointed as Moyane's successor at SARS (Mabuza 2019; Mail & Guardian 2018b). Other institutions weakened during the Zuma presidency have experienced an exodus of complicit staff, and, notably, many of the suspect contracts have been cancelled. In addition, several of the provincial and local-level shadow state networks have unravelled. One example concerns VBS Mutual Bank: this entailed looting some R2 billion from a mutual bank that held the savings of residents in the impoverished Limpopo Province. Fifteen local municipalities made irregular deposits into the bank in contravention of the Municipal Finance Management Act. At the time of writing, eight individuals faced criminal charges, and the many implicated municipal officials were removed from office (Motau 2018; Nicolaides, Ngatane and Zulu 2020; Wicks 2020).

In response to the dismantling of the state capture networks, there has been a realignment of political forces. Without unified support within the ANC, the Ramaphosa presidency has been precarious (Brkic 2018), with limited space for bold, sweeping change. Political trade-offs have enabled remnants of Zuma's regime to enjoy continued access to the state and its resources. Indeed, efforts to contain this have often been thwarted. However, without significant control over key institutions, the shadow state has transitioned to coordinating operations outside of government. This has resulted in several structures within the ANC and leaders in the organisation aligned with the former president collaborating with numerous newly formed organisations that continue to advance a pro-Zuma narrative. Their primary objective is to sabotage efforts to hold power elites accountable, keep those implicated in state capture out of jail and ultimately regain political control of the ANC and, in turn, the state. Thus, much of their energy appears to be directed towards delegitimising the primary opponents of state capture, namely the judiciary, the media and civil society (Corder 2019; Haffajee 2018, 2019; Ngqakamba 2019).

The 'fightback campaign' has attempted to muddy the country's public discourse and create an environment of political paralysis. Cyril Ramaphosa has been caught up in the crosswinds, particularly in a controversy around the funding of his ANC presidential campaign (Cowan 2019). A probe by Public Protector Busisiwe Mkhwebane (successor to Thuli Madonsela) questioned whether or not Ramaphosa had lied to parliament about having received a donation from the controversial ANC-linked company Bosasa (Rabkin 2019). The report's findings were taken on review, and the courts were scathing in their rebuke of the new Public Protector's conduct (Mailovich 2020). But leaked financial records exposed the exorbitant monetary value attached to presidential political campaigning. As damaging as this was, an associated list of political funders laid bare the embedded power relations between corporate and political elites – arguably, this is the most pervasive racket of all (Davis 2019; Friedman 2019b). Testimony at the Zondo Commission has outlined how businesses such as Bosasa participated in election campaigns and donated to the ANC in exchange for continued access to lucrative government contracts (Zondo Commission 2019a).

BEYOND STATE CAPTURE

The cost of state capture under the Zuma presidency is a matter for speculation, although some alarming figures are in circulation. In 2017, Pravin Gordhan estimated an amount of R250 billion (The Citizen 2017), but by 2019 the amount was estimated (by President Ramaphosa) to be at least twice that amount (Omarjee 2019). These figures appear to reflect only direct costs, however. Marianne Merten has detailed that the indirect cost could be an estimated 'R1.5-trillion over the second term of the Jacob Zuma administration' (2019). Arguably, cost-based calculations are insignificant when weighed against other issues. Consider, as an example, the 'opportunity cost' lost through unproductive investment, crude rent extraction and the cumulative impact on the country's development. An economist at the South African Reserve Bank noted that 'in a normally functioning economy, growth should be over 4 per cent [given South Africa's level of investment], and there certainly hasn't been growth … This is the evidence of what state capture looks like … [it's] where you have major investment and no growth' (Magubane 2019).

Undoubtedly, state capture eroded the government's ability to meet the basic service delivery objectives and fulfil its constitutional obligations. At the local level, the struggle for access and control over state resources witnessed increased social violence, leaving unanticipated levels of tragedy. So, the Life Esidimeni catastrophe (Mitchley 2019; Moseneke 2018) and the spiral in political killings in KwaZulu-Natal, as detailed by the Moerane Commission (Moerane Commission Investigating Political Killings in KZN 2018), were not isolated from the political and economic fallout fostered by state capture (Von Holdt 2019).

State capture has still to play itself out entirely, and the extent of corrosion within various legislative bodies remains to be understood. However, the underlying patterns of behaviour that enabled state capture to occur in these sites have been recognised for some time. For example, in 2010, an (ANC) National General Council discussion document entitled 'Leadership Renewal Discipline and Organisational Culture' recognised 'objective factors contributing to organisational decay'. These included the rise in 'patronage and neo-patrimonialism … The bureaucratisation of political movements … Statist approaches to social transformation … Corruption … [and the] erosion of progressive values and organisational culture' (ANC 2010, 6–7). Even with this candid acknowledgement, the party has been unable to rise to the challenge of addressing the behaviour that clearly drives its decay.

Though some would seek to reduce the damage caused to merely being 'nine wasted years' for development, it is clear from the above that the broader impact of state capture has been the derailing of South Africa's democratic promise of 'a better life for all'. The patterns of predatory behaviour identified in this chapter preceded the Zuma administration and will continue with impunity, as long as those implicated have not been held accountable. Ironically, in this, state capture is readily comparable with and arguably a continuum of the racket of predatory power embedded in apartheid.

Appreciating a 'logic' behind how the institutional form of state capture has been experienced in South Africa differentiates it from being merely a species of grand-scale corruption. This is one reason why this chapter has argued that state capture was an encompassing project and not just a collective of one-off events orchestrated by a few individuals. The corruption that underpinned state capture is not a stand-alone problem in and of itself: it is a symptom of the corrosion of democratic principles of justice, equality and the rule of law. A reformist position on the issues often draws from a medical metaphor by arguing that state capture can be 'cured', or, more drastically, 'cut away'. But – to continue with the metaphor – this is a misdiagnosis.

Corruption is a social phenomenon derived from underlying social, economic or political conditions. Ending corruption will require a broader perspective that acknowledges South Africa's troubled past and its complex present. Viewing state capture through the framework of rackets and racketeering, as we have done in this chapter, gives both shape and form to an issue which – regrettably – looks certain to plague South African people for decades to come.

NOTES

1   The Frankfurt School of Critical Theory was a movement originally based in Frankfurt, Germany, from the 1920s. It was established by a group of intellectuals and political dissidents who were dissatisfied with the inability of social theory to explain the reactionary politics of the early twentieth century and sought alternative routes to understand the social development of societies (see https://plato.stanford.edu/entries/critical-theory/).

2   When questioned during his testimony at the Zondo Commission on whether it was 'okay' for a president to ask a director general of a department to 'please help' the Guptas' *New Age* newspaper to access the state's advertising budget, former president Zuma responded: '… if such a call is made, would that call have moved away from the normal procedures, would it be trying to compel the DG to do a wrong thing or whatever, even if the call was made or not made?' (Zondo Commission 2019b).

3   The definition of 'power elite' followed in this chapter is offered by the authors of 'Betrayal of the Promise', as 'a relatively well-structured network of people located in government, state institutions, SOEs, private businesses, security agencies, traditional leaders, family networks and the governing party. The defining feature of membership of this group is direct (and even indirect) access (either consistently or intermittently) to the inner sanctum of power to influence decisions. It is not a ruling class per se, although it can see itself as acting in the interests of an existing class or, as in the South African case, a new black business class in the making. Nor is it just the political-bureaucratic leadership of the state, which is too fragmented to reliably mount a political project. The power elite is not necessarily directed by a strong strategic centre, and it includes groups that are to some extent competing for access to the inner sanctum and the opportunity to control rents. The power elite exercises its influence both through formal and informal means' (PARI 2017, 5–6).

4   In late 2017, when reports of the large-scale fraud of Steinhoff financial records began to emerge, the company's share price plummeted, wiping an estimated R20 billion off the value of government pensions (Ensor 2018; Gerber 2019). Pensioners and investors lost billions and, to date, not a single executive has been arrested or held accountable.

5   Chapter Nine institutions, so called because they are established by Chapter 9 of the South African Constitution, are intended to support the strengthening of constitutional democracy.

6   The rebuke came after an ad hoc committee of parliament had adopted a report endorsing then minister of police Nathi Nhleko's report on upgrades to Zuma's homestead, including a swimming pool that was passed off as intended for firefighting purposes, as security upgrades (see Davis 2015).

7   The Black Sash Trust is a social justice NGO that focuses on South Africa's social assistance system and government's administration of social grants (see http://www.blacksash.org.za/).

8   EarthLife Africa and the Southern African Faith Communities' Environment Institute are NGOs focusing on issues of environmental justice (see https://earthlife.org.za/; https://safcei.org/).

9   Corruption Watch, Freedom Under Law and the Council for the Advancement of the South African Constitution are three NGOs involved in several litigative actions against the Zuma administration and the state-capture project (see https://www.corruptionwatch.org.za/; https://www.freedomunderlaw.org/; https://casac.org.za/).

REFERENCES

Abedian, Iraj and Simon Mantell. 2017. 'Analysis: Unpacking KPMG International's Mea Culpa Media Statement Brings More Questions than Answers'. *Daily Maverick*, 3 October 2017. https://www.dailymaverick.co.za/article/2017-10-03-analysis-unpacking-kpmg-internationals-mea-culpa-media-statement-brings-more-questions-than-answers/.

Ad Hoc Committee on the SABC Board Inquiry. 2017. 'Interim Report of the Ad Hoc Committee on the SABC Board Inquiry into the Fitness of the SABC Board, Dated 27 January 2017'. Parliament of the Republic of South Africa, Cape Town. https://static.pmg.org.za/SABC-Ad-Hoc-Committee-Interim-Report-27-Jan-2017.pdf.

ANC. 2010. 'Anatomy of Organisational Decay'. National General Council discussion document. *Politicsweb*, 29 July 2010. https://www.politicsweb.co.za/documents/anatomy-of-organisational-decay--anc.

Anciano, Fiona. 2018. 'Decolonising Clientelism: "Re-Centring" Analyses of Local State-Society Relations in South Africa'. *Politikon* 45, no. 1: 94–111. https://www.tandfonline.com/doi/full/10.1080/02589346.2018.1418214.

Areff, Ahmed. 2015. 'Timeline: How South Africa Got Three Finance Ministers in Four Days'. *News24*, 14 December 2015. https://www.news24.com/SouthAfrica/News/timeline-how-south-africa-got-three-finance-ministers-in-four-days-20151214.

Brkic, Branko. 2018. 'President Cyril Ramaphosa (and His Team): What a Difference 179 Votes Make'. *Daily Maverick*, 19 December 2018. https://www.dailymaverick.co.za/article/2018-12-19-president-cyril-ramaphosa-and-his-team-what-a-difference-179-votes-make/.

Business Day. 2017. 'Tens of Thousands Take to the Streets to Denounce Zuma'. *Business Day*, 7 April 2017. https://www.businesslive.co.za/bd/national/2017-04-07-south-africans-march-in-protest-against-zuma/.

Business Insider SA. 2020. 'The Biggest South African Business Scandals over the Past Decade'. *Business Insider*, 11 January 2020. https://www.businessinsider.co.za/the-top-south-african-business-scandals-the-past-decade-2020-1.

BusinessTech. 2019. 'How Fraud at Some of South Africa's Biggest Companies Flew under the Radar'. *BusinessTech*, 28 July 2019. https://businesstech.co.za/news/business/331341/how-fraud-at-some-of-south-africas-biggest-companies-flew-under-the-radar/.

Cameron, Jackie. 2019. 'Eskom Attacks Deloitte as Fresh Corruption Scandal Erupts: Pay Back the Money!' *BizNews*, 22 October 2019. https://www.biznews.com/sa-investing/2019/10/22/eskom-deloitte-corruption-scandal.

Chabalala, Jeanette. 2020. 'Zondo: State Capture Commission Will Ask High Court for Another Extension'. *News24*, 21 December 2020. https://www.news24.com/news24/southafrica/news/just-in-state-capture-commission-will-ask-high-court-for-another-extension-justice-zondo-20201221.

Chipkin, Ivor and Mark Swilling. 2018. *Shadow State: The Politics of State Capture*. Johannesburg: Wits University Press.

Chirume, Joseph, Ashraf Hendricks, Ashleigh Furlong and Nombulelo Damba-Hendrik. 2017. 'Zuma Cabinet Reshuffle: What People Are Saying'. *GroundUp*, 31 March 2017. https://www.groundup.org.za/article/zuma-cabinet-reshuffle-what-people-are-saying/.

Christoph-Lemke, Charlotte. 1999. 'The Contributions of Transactional Analysis to Integrative Psychotherapy'. *Transactional Analysis Journal* 29, no. 3: 198–214. https://journals.sagepub.com/doi/abs/10.1177/036215379902900305.

The Citizen. 2017. 'R250bn Lost to State Capture in the Last Three Years, Says Gordhan'. *The Citizen*, 12 September 2017. https://citizen.co.za/news/south-africa/1651069/r250bn-lost-to-state-capture-in-the-last-three-years-says-gordhan/.

CNBC Africa. 2018. 'Jacob Zuma Resigns as President of South Africa'. *YouTube*, 15 February 2018. https://www.youtube.com/watch?v=Eoz0dlM0gZU.

Corder, Hugh. 2019. 'Critics of South Africa's Judges Are Raising the Temperature: Legitimate, or Dangerous?' *The Conversation*, 22 August 2019. https://theconversation.com/critics-of-south-africas-judges-are-raising-the-temperature-legitimate-or-dangerous-122209.

Corruption Watch. 2019. 'Zondo Commission – VR Laser's Jiyane Swiftly and Sneakily Forced out by Gupta Cronies'. *Corruption Watch*, 20 March 2019. https://www.corruptionwatch.org.za/wp-content/uploads/2019/03/Zondo-Commission-%E2%80%93-VR-Laser%E2%80%99s-Jiyane-swiftly-and-sneakily-forced-out-by-Gupta-cronies.pdf.

Corruption Watch NPC and Others v President of the Republic of South Africa and Others; Nxasana v Corruption Watch NPC and Others (CCT 333/17; CCT 13/18) [2018] ZACC 23; 2018 (10) BCLR 1179 (CC); 2018 (2) SACR 442 (CC) (13 August 2018).

Cowan, Kyle. 2019. 'Exclusive: Inside the CR17 Leaks and the Conflict between Ramaphosa's Man and Security Head'. *News24*, 13 September 2019. https://www.news24.com/SouthAfrica/News/exclusive-inside-the-cr17-leaks-and-the-conflict-between-ramaphosas-man-and-security-head-20190913.

Davis, Rebecca. 2015. 'Parliamentary Diary: As ANC MPs Vote "Yes", Nkandla Report Now Truly Secure in Comfort'. *Daily Maverick*, 19 August 2015. https://www.dailymaverick.co.za/article/2015-08-19-parliament-diary-as-anc-mps-vote-yes-nkandla-report-now-truly-secure-in-comfort/.

Davis, Rebecca. 2019. '#CR17 Email Leaks: Separating the Myths from the Facts, Part Two'. *Daily Maverick*, 21 August 2019. https://www.dailymaverick.co.za/article/2019-08-21-cr17-email-leaks-separating-the-myths-from-the-facts-part-two/.

Deklerk, Aphiwe. 2018. '"There Is No State That Was Captured" – Zuma'. *Timeslive*, 12 September 2018. https://www.timeslive.co.za/news/south-africa/2018-09-12-there-is-no-state-that-was-captured-zuma/.

Economic Freedom Fighters v Speaker of the National Assembly and Others; Democratic Alliance v Speaker of the National Assembly and Others (CCT 143/15; CCT 171/15) [2016] ZACC 11; 2016 (5) BCLR 618 (CC); 2016 (3) SA 580 (CC) (31 March 2016).

Ensor, Linda. 2018. 'Pension Funds Lost Billions over Steinhoff'. *Business Day*, 31 January 2018. https://www.timeslive.co.za/sunday-times/business/2018-01-31-pension-funds-lost-billions-over-steinhoff/.

Ernst, Franklin H., Jr. 1973. 'Psychological Rackets in the Ok Corral'. *Transactional Analysis Journal* 3, no. 2: 19–23. https://www.tandfonline.com/doi/abs/10.1177/036215377300300211.

Erskine, Richard G. and Marilyn J. Zalcman. 1979. 'The Racket System: A Model for Racket Analysis'. *Transactional Analysis Journal* 9, no. 1: 51–59. https://journals.sagepub.com/doi/10.1177/036215377900900112.

Eskom. 2016. 'Eskom Will Continue to Insist on Procuring Coal from 50%-plus Black-Owned Coal Miners'. *Politicsweb*, 5 December 2016. https://www.politicsweb.co.za/politics/we-insist-on-procuring-coal-from-50plus-blackowned.

Friedman, Steven. 2019a. 'Cabinet Picks Show Ramaphosa and Allies Believe They're Firmly in Control'. *The Conversation*, 30 May 2019. https://theconversation.com/cabinet-picks-show-ramaphosa-and-allies-believe-theyre-firmly-in-control-118083.

Friedman, Steven. 2019b. 'Why New South African Law Won't End the Toxic Mix of Money and Politics'. *The Conversation*, 5 August 2019. https://theconversation.com/why-new-south-african-law-wont-end-the-toxic-mix-of-money-and-politics-121461.

Gerber, Jan. 2019. 'Steinhoff: To Go for Low-Hanging Fruit or Big Fish, Asks Batohi'. *News24*, 15 October 2019. https://www.news24.com/SouthAfrica/News/steinhoff-to-go-for-low-hanging-fruit-or-big-fish-asks-batohi-20191015.

Godinho, Catrina and Lauren Hermanus. 2018. 'Reconceptualising State Capture: With a Case Study of South African Power Company Eskom'. Conference paper delivered at 'State Capture and Its Aftermath: Building Responsiveness through State Reform', 22–23 October 2018. Public Affairs Research Institute, Johannesburg.

Gosling, Melanie. 2018. 'Another Victory for Environmental Duo Who Put a Halt to SA's Nuclear Deal'. *Daily Maverick*, 24 April 2018. https://www.dailymaverick.co.za/article/2018-04-24-another-victory-for-environmental-duo-who-put-a-halt-to-sas-nuclear-deal/.

Granter, Edward. 2017. 'Strictly Business: Critical Theory and the Society of Rackets'. *Competition & Change* 21, no. 2: 94–113. https://journals.sagepub.com/doi/10.1177/1024529417690716.

GuptaLeaks. 2017a. '#GuptaLeaks'. https://www.gupta-leaks.com/.

GuptaLeaks. 2017b. '#GuptaLeaks: The Dubai Laundromat – How Millions from Dairy Paid for Sun City Wedding'. https://www.gupta-leaks.com/atul-gupta/guptaleaks-the-dubai-laundromat-how-millions-from-dairy-paid-for-sun-city-wedding/.

GuptaLeaks. 2017c. '#GuptaLeaks: How Bell Pottinger Sought to Package SA Economics Message'. https://www.gupta-leaks.com/category/bell-pottinger/page/3/.

Haffajee, Ferial. 2018. 'How the EFF Dominates the Disinformation Market'. *Daily Maverick*, 12 December 2018. https://www.dailymaverick.co.za/article/2018-12-12-how-the-eff-dominates-the-disinformation-market/.

Haffajee, Ferial. 2019. 'The Fightback: Is the Resistance Julius Malema's Path to the Presidency?' *Daily Maverick*, 26 June 2019. https://www.dailymaverick.co.za/opinionista/2019-07-26-the-fightback-is-the-resistance-julius-malemas-path-to-the-presidency/.

Hellman, Joel S., Geraint Jones and Daniel Kaufmann. 2000. '"Seize the State, Seize the Day": State Capture, Corruption, and Influence in Transition'. World Bank Policy Research Working Paper, Washington, DC. https://openknowledge.worldbank.org/handle/10986/19784.

High-Level Review Panel on the SSA. 2018. 'High-Level Review Panel Report on the State Security Agency'. December 2018. https://www.gov.za/sites/default/files/gcis_document/201903/high-level-review-panel-state-security-agency.pdf.

Jonas, Mcebisi. 2018. Statement and Documents Submitted by Mcebisi Jonas. Commission of Inquiry into State Capture. https://sastatecapture.org.za/site/documents.

Klein, Stefan and Ricardo Pagliuso Regatieri. 2018. 'Unfettered Capitalism: On Rackets, Cronies and Mafiosi'. *Tempo Social* 30, no. 3: 67–84. https://www.scielo.br/j/ts/a/tyrbJ WzbQjwgqBYWdY84H9y/?lang=en.

Labuschagne, Pieter. 2017. 'Patronage, State Capture and Oligopolistic Monopoly in South Africa: The Slide from a Weak to a Dysfunctional State?' *Acta Academica* 49, no. 2: 51–67. https://journals.ufs.ac.za/index.php/aa/article/view/3351/3213.

Landman, J.P. 2019. 'It's Not All Doom and Gloom. How the Ramaphosa Presidency Is Reclaiming the State'. *News24*, 22 August 2019. https://www.news24.com/Columnists/ GuestColumn/jp-landman-its-not-all-doom-and-gloom-how-the-ramaphosa-pres-idency-is-reclaiming-the-state-20190822?hootPostID=756fe0003b7b20282b02b6d-9dead1e01.

Le Roux, Michelle and Dennis Davis. 2019. *Lawfare: Judging Politics in South Africa*. Johannesburg: Jonathan Ball.

Lowman, Stuart. 2018. 'Word for Word: Jacob Zuma's Resignation Speech, Late as Ever'. *BizNews*, 15 February 2018. https://www.biznews.com/sa-investing/2018/02/15/jacob-zuma-late-resignation-speech.

Mabuza, Ernest. 2019. 'Panel Appointed to Recommend New Sars Commissioner'. *Timeslive*, 7 February 2019. https://www.timeslive.co.za/politics/2019-02-07-panel-appointed-to-recommend-new-sars-commissioner/.

Magubane, Khulekani. 2019. 'Damage from State Capture "Worse than Suspected" – SARB'. *Fin24*, 6 June 2019. https://www.fin24.com/Economy/damage-from-state-capture-worse-than-suspected-sarb-20190606.

Mail & Guardian. 2018a. 'Cyril's Compromised Compromise Cabinet'. *Mail & Guardian*, 26 February 2018. https://mg.co.za/article/2018-02-26-cyril-ramaphosa-cabinet-reshuffle-reaction-anc-da-eff-ifp/.

Mail & Guardian. 2018b. 'NDPP Appointment Process a Step in the Right Direction – Pikoli'. *Mail & Guardian*, 23 October 2018. https://mg.co.za/article/2018-10-23-ndpp-appointment-process-a-step-in-the-right-direction-pikoli/.

Mailovich, Claudi. 2020. 'Busisiwe Mkhwebane Roasted as Court Finds for Cyril Ramaphosa in Bosasa Matter'. *Timeslive*, 10 March 2020. https://www.timeslive.co.za/news/south-africa/2020-03-10-high-court-sets-aside-mkhwebanes-findings-against-ramaphosa/.

Merten, Marianne. 2019. 'State Capture Wipes Out Third of SA's R4.9-Trillion GDP – Never Mind Lost Trust, Confidence, Opportunity'. *Daily Maverick*, 1 March 2019. https:// www.dailymaverick.co.za/article/2019-03-01-state-capture-wipes-out-third-of-sas-r4-9-trillion-gdp-never-mind-lost-trust-confidence-opportunity/.

Mitchley, Alex. 2019. 'Life Esidimeni Tragedy: Another NGO Ordered to Pay Back the Money'. *News24*, 25 October 2019. https://www.news24.com/SouthAfrica/News/life-esidimeni-tragedy-another-ngo-ordered-to-pay-back-the-money-20191025.

Moerane Commission Investigating Political Killings in KZN. 2018. 'Report of the Moerane Commission of Enquiry into the Underlying Causes of the Murder of Politicians in KwaZulu-Natal'. http://www.kznonline.gov.za/images/Downloads/Publications/ MOERANE%20COMMISSION%20OF%20INQUIRY%20REPORT.pdf.

Moseneke, Dikgang. 2018. 'Life Esidimeni Arbitration Report'. http://section27.org.za/ wp-content/uploads/2018/05/Life-Esidimeni-arbitration-award-by-retired-Deputy-Chief-Justice-Dikgang-Mosenke.pdf.

Motau, Terry. 2018. 'VBS Mutual Bank: The Great Bank Heist: Investigator's Report to the Prudential Authority'. *South African Reserve Bank*, 10 October 2018. https://www.resbank.co.za/Lists/News and Publications/Attachments/8830/VBS Mutual Bank - The Great Bank Heist.pdf.

Myburgh, Pieter-Louis. 2019. *Gangster State: Unravelling Ace Magashule's Web of Capture*. Cape Town: Penguin Books.

National Treasury. 2018a. 'Chapter I: Final Report: Forensic Investigation into Various Allegations at Transnet'. November 2018. http://www.treasury.gov.za/comm_media/press/2018/Final%20Report%20-%20National%20Treasury%20-%20Procurement%20of%20Locomotives%2015112018.pdf.

National Treasury. 2018b. 'Chapter III: Final Report: Forensic Investigation into Various Allegations at Eskom'. November 2018. http://www.treasury.gov.za/comm_media/press/2018/Final%20Report%20-%20Fundudzi%20-%20Eskom%2015112018.pdf.

Ngqakamba, Sesona. 2019. '"Bring It on! Let's Meet on the Streets": Malema Challenges SACP, Civil Society Groups'. *News24*, 18 July 2019. https://www.news24.com/SouthAfrica/News/bring-it-on-lets-meet-on-the-streets-malema-challenges-sacp-civil-society-groups-20190718.

Nicolaides, Gia, Nthakoana Ngatane and Sifiso Zulu. 2020. 'From Bank Heist to Arrests: A Timeline of the VBS Scandal'. *Eyewitness News*, 17 June 2020. https://ewn.co.za/2020/06/17/from-bank-heist-to-arrests-a-timeline-of-the-vbs-scandal.

Nugent Commission. 2018. 'Commission of Inquiry into Tax Administration and Governance by SARS: Final Report'. 11 December 2018. http://www.inqcomm.co.za/Docs/media/SARS Commission Final Report.pdf.

O'Donnell, Guillermo. 2004. 'The Quality of Democracy: Why the Rule of Law Matters'. *Journal of Democracy* 15, no. 4: 32–46. https://www.journalofdemocracy.org/articles/the-quality-of-democracy-why-the-rule-of-law-matters/.

Omarjee, Lameez. 2019. 'Ramaphosa Says State Capture Cost SA More than R500bn, Overseas Criminals Will Be Brought to Book'. *Fin24*, 14 October 2019. https://www.fin24.com/Economy/South-Africa/ramaphosa-says-state-capture-cost-sa-more-than-r500bn-overseas-criminals-will-be-brought-to-book-20191014.

PARI. 2017. 'Betrayal of the Promise: How South Africa Is Being Stolen'. State Capacity Research Project, Public Affairs Research Institute, Johannesburg. https://pari.org.za/betrayal-promise-report/.

Pijoos, Iavan. 2017. 'State Capture Named SA Word of the Year'. *News24*, 16 October 2017. https://www.news24.com/SouthAfrica/News/state-capture-named-sa-word-of-the-year-20171016.

Pijoos, Iavan. 2018. 'ConCourt Ruling on Dlamini, Sassa Debacle a Victory – Black Sash, FUL'. *News24*, 27 September 2018. https://www.news24.com/SouthAfrica/News/concourt-ruling-on-dlamini-sassa-debacle-a-victory-black-sash-ful-20180927.

Portfolio Committee on Public Enterprises. 2018. 'Report of the Portfolio Committee on Public Enterprises on the Inquiry into Governance, Procurement and the Financial Sustainability of Eskom'. 28 November 2018. https://www.parliament.gov.za/storage/app/media/Links/2018/November 2018/28-11-2018/Final Report - Eskom Inquiry 28 NOV.pdf.

The Presidency. 2019. 'Enquiry in Terms of Section 12(6) of the National Prosecuting Authority Act 32 of 1998: Unabridged Version'. 1 April 2019. http://www.thepresidency.gov.za/sites/default/files/Section 12%286%29 Enquiry report - unabridged version.pdf.

Public Protector. 2014. 'Secure in Comfort'. Report No. 25 of 2013/14, March 2014. http://www.pprotect.org/sites/default/files/Legislation_report/Final%20Report%2019%20March%202014%20.pdf.

Public Protector. 2016. 'State of Capture'. Report No. 6 of 2016/17, 14 October 2016. http://www.pprotect.org/sites/default/files/legislation_report/State_Capture_14October2016.pdf.

Rabkin, Franny. 2019. 'Ramaphosa Launches Court Review of Public Protector's Bosasa Report'. *Mail & Guardian*, 31 July 2019. https://mg.co.za/article/2019-07-31-ramaphosa-launches-court-review-of-public-protectors-bosasa-report/.

Rosenfeld, Michel. 2000. 'The Rule of Law and the Legitimacy of Constitutional Democracy'. *Southern California Law Review* 74, no. 5: 1307–1352. https://heinonline.org/HOL/Page?public=true&handle=hein.journals/scal74&div=55&start_page=1307&collection=journals&set_as_cursor=3&men_tab=srchresults.

SABC. 2016. 'Dlamini Warns on Wrong Channels to Raise Issues within ANC'. *YouTube*, 19 March 2016. https://www.youtube.com/watch?v=YiZ_-gd2Cb8.

Scheit, Gerhard and Lars Fischer. 2018. 'Rackets'. In *The Sage Handbook of Frankfurt School Critical Theory*, edited by Beverley Best, Werner Bonefeld and Chris O'Kane, 1551–1566. Thousand Oaks, CA: Sage Publications.

Shadow World Investigations. 2019. 'First Submission to the Commission of Inquiry into Allegations of State Capture Regarding the Estina/Vrede Integrated Dairy Project'. https://shadowworldinvestigations.org/wp-content/uploads/2019/12/SWI-Submission-to-the-Zondo-Commission-Estina-and-the-Gupta-Enterprise.pdf.

Shaik, Riaz. 2019. Statement and Documents Submitted by Riaz Shaik. Commission of Inquiry into State Capture. https://sastatecapture.org.za/site/documents.

Van de Walle, Nicolas. 2007. 'The Path from Neopatrimonialism: Democracy and Clientelism in Africa Today'. Working Paper No. 3-07, Mario Einaudi Center for International Studies. https://ecommons.cornell.edu/bitstream/handle/1813/55028/2007_WP3_vandeWalle.pdf?sequence=1&isAllowed=y.

Von Holdt, Karl. 2019. 'The Political Economy of Corruption: Elite-Formation, Factions and Violence'. SWOP Working Paper No. 10, Johannesburg. https://www.swop.org.za/post/2019/02/18/working-paper-10-the-political-economy-of-corruption-open-access.

Wicks, Bernadette. 2020. 'More Charges and More Accused in the Dock Soon for VBS Scandal'. *The Citizen*, 8 October 2020. https://citizen.co.za/news/south-africa/courts/2367937/more-charges-and-more-accused-in-the-dock-soon-for-vbs-scandal/.

Wilkinson, Kate and Africa Check. 2017. 'Fact Sheet: How Many Motions of No Confidence Has Zuma Faced?' *Eyewitness News*, 29 June 2017. https://ewn.co.za/2017/06/29/fact-sheet-how-many-motions-of-no-confidence-has-zuma-faced.

Zondo Commission. 2019a. Transcript from Inquiry into State Capture: Day 075 (28 March 2019) – Testimony of Angelo Agrizzi. Commission of Inquiry into State Capture. https://www.statecapture.org.za/site/hearings/date/2019/3/28.

Zondo Commission. 2019b. Transcript from Inquiry into State Capture: Day 133 (15 July 2019) – Testimony of Jacob Zuma. Commission of Inquiry into State Capture. https://www.statecapture.org.za/site/hearings/date/2019/7/15.

Zondo Commission. 2019c. Transcript from Inquiry into State Capture: Day 157 (5 September 2019) – Testimony of Krivani Pillay, Mwaba Phiri and Thandeka Gqubule-Mbeki. Commission of Inquiry into State Capture. https://www.statecapture.org.za/site/hearings/date/2019/9/5.

Zondo Commission. 2020a. Transcript from Inquiry into State Capture: Day 260 (3 September 2020) – Testimony of Nomvula Mokonyane. Commission of Inquiry into State Capture. https://www.youtube.com/watch?v=KeWClgfYasQ.

Zondo Commission. 2020b. Transcript from Inquiry into State Capture: Day 269 (22 September 2020) – Testimony of Nthimotse Mokhesi and Mpho Mokoena. Commission of Inquiry into State Capture. https://www.statecapture.org.za/site/hearings/date/2020/9/22.

Zondo Commission. 2020c. Transcript from Inquiry into State Capture: Day 322 (10 December 2020) – Testimony of Msilo Mothepu. Commission of Inquiry into State Capture. https://www.statecapture.org.za/site/files/transcript/327/DAY_322_TRANSCRIPT_DD_2020-12-10.pdf.

3

The Foundations of Corruption in South Africa

Ryan Brunette

This chapter is concerned with three key protagonists in South Africa's debate about not only state capture but corruption generally. I will call these protagonists the 'Moralists', the 'Neoliberals' and the 'Marxists-Fanonists'. These labels do not encompass everyone in the debate. There are people who cross between, mediate and even sometimes move beyond them. But Moralism, Neoliberalism and Marxism-Fanonism have prominence. They arise out of the country's great and enduring sociopolitical tendencies and ideological traditions. Each systematically elides important features of the problem of corruption, and that they do so is both self-defeating and obstructive of South Africa's progress.

THE DEBATE ABOUT CORRUPTION IN SOUTH AFRICA

The articulation of a concept of corruption is ordinarily already an act of anti-corruption. At its core, the concept asserts certain standards of political conduct, which are seen as in some sense vital to the viability of a political community. It simultaneously identifies, denounces and announces a desire to curtail excessively self-regarding behaviour that violates those standards and, therefore, threatens the community. The concept of corruption is among the oldest and most widely used concepts in the lexicon of human politics. It appears in the extant texts of dynastic Sumeria and Egypt (Westbrook 2003), in the laws of classical Rome and China, and across the canon of political thought in such diversity as Plato, Kautilya, Ibn Khaldun, Niccolò Machiavelli, Jeremy Bentham, Mikhail Bakunin and W.E.B. Du Bois.

Those who hope to talk sensibly about corruption must have answers to questions having to do with what standards of conduct, what roles these apply to, how these roles relate to the broader institutional architecture of societies, how these institutions are wrecked and what changes are needed to prevent that. Consequently, the concept is mobilised by diverse social interests into elaborate discourses of corruption and campaigns of anti-corruption. In this process, it has often launched from narrow attacks on individual deviance, into expansive warnings about entire societies hurtling towards collapse, along with utopian visions of course correction.

In this context, the debate about corruption in South Africa is exemplary. First, it forestalls the common complaint that corruption talk is in some sense beneath intelligent political discussion – 'not in the realm of ideation, nor is it visionary' (Dangor 2020) – and that it distracts from more important things. This complaint is inept. The idea of corruption is ancient. It concerns the fundaments of political order and change. It casts a profound influence over all of humanity's political enquiries, such that Plato's account of the corruptions of oligarchy and democracy is the fountain from which flow the theories of contemporary history of Karl Marx, Friedrich Hayek and Frantz Fanon.

Second, the context sets up two distinctions that will help illuminate the omissions of the contemporary South African debate. The first is between formal and substantive accounts of corruption, where a purely formal account is concerned solely with upholding established standards of conduct, while substantive accounts bring into contention much thicker partisan programmes. The second distinction is between individualising and structural accounts of corruption, the former locating the cause of corruption in the character and motivations of persons, and the latter explaining corrupt behaviour as a consequence of overarching social arrangements. The Moralists, Neoliberals and Marxists-Fanonists elide the formal-structural axis of these distinctions, which means that in important ways they miss the causal reality of corruption.

The Moralist Approach

Much of South Africa's debate about corruption occurs under the construct of Moralism (Fogel 2020). The approach is embedded in the folk wisdom that since corruption denotes bad behaviour, it is a problem of bad people, which tends to reduce anti-corruption to efforts at education, monitoring and punishment. The hard core of Moralism is South Africa's liberation establishment and the more moderate, constitutionalist elements of the African National Congress (ANC), together with its network of alliances and influence in the centres of governmental, economic and ideological power. These categories include deployees to the higher reaches of the state bureaucracy, political stalwarts who have since moved into corporates and their allies, along with a broad contingent in academia, the media, the struggle legacy foundations, the old churches and the non-governmental sector.

An early organised expression of Moralism in post-apartheid South Africa was the ANC's moral regeneration movement. In Nelson Mandela's words, it identified a deep 'spiritual malaise' in society, the symptoms of which included 'the extent of corruption both in the public and private sector' (Rauch 2005, 13). The movement would address this by mobilising civil society in a manner reminiscent of the struggle against apartheid, in a diffuse campaign of moral education and action. The discourse of moral regeneration became a constant theme of government-sponsored anti-corruption summits going into the 2010s. A Moralist thread continues in President Cyril Ramaphosa's contemporary speeches. These routinely 'reinforce commitment' to 'ethical leadership' by calling for 'investigating and prosecuting any and all acts of corruption' (Ramaphosa 2018). The Moralist litany can be found across the party's public pronouncements, for example, in talk of promoting 'revolutionary morality' through the 'political education' of a new generation of 'disciplined cadres'. It diffuses outwards in widespread laments about the passing of the 'moral giants' of the liberation movement, the associated loss of 'moral compass' and the obsession with imprisonment as South Africa's primary weapon against corruption (McKaiser 2021).

Raymond Guess (2009, 42) notes that 'ethics is usually dead politics: the hand of the victor in some past conflict reaching out to try to extend its grip to the present and the future'. Indeed, Moralism's formalist strictures – its confinement of the discussion to specific standards of conduct and its emphasis on education and policing – hides a substantive partisan logic. In social terms, the tendency arises from those strata that have been integrated most comfortably into the intellectual and material practices of the post-apartheid hegemonic project. For these strata, it is convenient for anti-corruption strategy to taper towards mobilising the 'political will' to identify, punish and deter deviance, an ultimately regime-maintaining move often revealingly couched in terms of reviving the best of the anti-apartheid struggle and the so-called 'Mandela moment'.

Moralism constitutes the discursive centre of much of South Africa's organised anti-corruption movement. In the state capture crisis, the approach offered in significant part the mobilising logic of efforts to oust Jacob Zuma from the presidency of the country. It enjoys the popular appeal of a folk psychology and alignment with an existing, if diminished, hegemony. The recognition of some need to enforce standards of political conduct is definitional to anti-corruption, including for Neoliberals and Marxists-Fanonists. The Moralists, therefore, can mobilise quickly, widely and, to some extent, across ideological divisions. The label Moralist, however, points to the substitution of a moral judgement, an attribution of personal fault, for structural causal understanding. In this essentially conservative move, Moralism detracts from an analysis of how the broader arrangements of society might create conditions for corruption, because this might mean that these arrangements should change.

The Neoliberal Approach

The Neoliberals come from a less satisfied social position, one inhabited by people who have felt threatened by the post-apartheid project. Their arguments aim for substantive structural reform of the South African political economy, precisely in ways that are thought to foreclose that threat. The approach is advocated by the leading faction of the official opposition, the Democratic Alliance, along with a sympathetic network of supporters across more conservative liberal academia, media and advocacy, including the South African Institute of Race Relations, the Free Market Foundation and Politicsweb. Neoliberal anti-corruption's broader social base is primarily white, including a significant part of South Africa's old and established professional-managerial and capitalist classes.

The Neoliberals often argue that the ANC's single-party dominance loosens the constraints of electoral accountability, giving freer rein to corruption (Giliomee and Simkins 1999). The corruption of South Africa's politics is understood to be a product of the ruling party's Leninist organisational doctrine, which sets out a policy of unconstrained control of state functions and partiality in favour of specific social interests (Leon 2022). The ANC's 'racial nationalist' approach to redistribution, elaborated as Black Economic Empowerment, is often given a significant role (Zille 2017). In the more coherent expressions of Neoliberal thought, these concerns often arise out of a more general worry about state intervention in markets. The ANC government is considered to be influenced by Marxist political-economic dogma, obliged by the ANC's Alliance partners, the South African Communist Party (SACP) and the Congress of South African Trade Unions (Cosatu). These ensure that the South African state has retained extensive control of major economic sectors, in such areas as electricity supply, ports and rail, telecommunications and natural resources. State control, the argument continues, serves to widen public official discretion over economic processes, creating opportunities for political and bureaucratic rent-seeking and corruption. These opportunities encourage the formation of new interests, pursued by new organised groups, that set about promoting wider intervention in the economy, generating more opportunities for rent-seeking and culminating in an ever-expanding problem of corruption (Louw 2014; Myburgh 2019).

The term 'Neoliberal' is used advisedly. The antagonism with nationalist and communist 'collectivism', the account of these tendencies as essentially runaway rent-seeking coalitions, echoes the concerns of the first neoliberals, including Ludwig von Mises, Walter Lippmann and Hayek. The Neoliberal approach to anti-corruption tends to a strategy of reasserting state neutrality against partisan social interests. The Neoliberals work to loosen the political hold of these interests on the state, to eliminate criteria of racial redress and redistribution in public policy, and ultimately to retrench public power towards the limited role of guarantor, arbiter and facilitator of people as entrepreneurs in markets.

The Marxist-Fanonist Approach

The Marxist-Fanonist left seeks radical transformation in an opposed direction. We treat the Marxist and Fanonist positions together as a convenient simplification, but one that is justified by the fact that Fanon's writings on such matters were significantly influenced by Marx, Marxist writings on postcolonial Africa were extensively influenced by Fanon, and, in South Africa, there is a strong convergence between Marxist and Fanonist analyses of corruption. These theorisations are influential along the left flank of the ANC, and in ideologically committed quarters of the SACP and Cosatu, along with its offshoot, the South African Federation of Trade Unions. The approach has been elaborated by intellectuals in these organisations, but more influentially those across the independent left, with a foothold in academia, the media and community organising.

In the Marxist-Fanonist account, the ANC is a cross-class, national coalition of the black bourgeoisie, the working class and the poor. In this coalition, the bourgeoisie is the leading element. Its location in the social formation and its accompanying sense of historical mission are seen as decisive for the process of corruption. Specifically, South Africa's black bourgeoisie aspires to the values, status and wealth of the white upper classes. What this entails, first, is an interest in maintaining the basic framework of South African capitalism, but the black bourgeoisie was historically stunted by white supremacist racial restrictions on accumulation, so this opens up the question of how to compete in the still often racially exclusive and oligopolistic corporate economy. It follows that, second, the black bourgeoisie has an interest in using the state to promote black business and, ultimately, to assert black dominance of the economy as the unfinished work of national liberation (Marais 2011; South African Communist Party 2006).

These imperatives, with the rise of the Washington Consensus in the 1990s, explain the ANC government's 'betrayal' of a socialist developmentalist line, its co-optation by white capital, and its turn to the Growth, Employment and Redistribution programme (Bond 1998). The party's consequent failure to pursue an egalitarian process of development has further constricted channels for black economic advancement, generating escalating pressures on the state as a site of original accumulation and corruption. These tendencies have been expressed as a deviation of a fraction of the aspirant black capitalist class into a 'radicalised', more aggressive and illicit accumulation strategy. Jacob Zuma's late presidency and the social forces that coalesced around it are seen as the archetypical expression of this trend (Ashman 2019; Modiri 2017; Von Holdt 2019; see also Von Holdt in chapter 1 of this volume).

The Marxist-Fanonist approach is inclined towards understanding South Africa's corruption problem as an inevitable outcome of the country's failure to break with a colonial and capitalist development path. Alexander Beresford has argued, representatively, that the 'proliferation of patronage-dependent accumulation in South Africa' is 'a central feature of the development of capitalism … inexorably bound up with the processes of class formation that accompany it' (2015, 229). The problem of corruption is thereby reduced to the left's predetermined antagonism with colonialism and capitalism. The strategy for addressing the problem is thus collapsed into a project of decolonisation and socialism. The black working class and poor must be mobilised into hegemony, capital disciplined or abolished, and productive relations reconstituted in a process of democratically led, socialistic and redistributive development.

The Elision of a Formal-Structural Approach

The Moralist approach, formal and individualising, fixates on the relationship between standards of conduct, motivation and punishment. It avoids considerations of structure. Neoliberalism and Marxism-Fanonism bring structure into the analysis, but their substantive partisan programmes overwhelm sustained consideration of the structural determinants of formally defined corruption. In this nexus, between formal and structural moments of corruption, the most serious omission is how the specific structural arrangement of the framework of government is itself implicated in the problem.

This omission is significant. Human motivation, pace the Moralists, is powerfully determined by how individuals are positioned within the structure of social relations. Social position defines the sorts of standards of conduct one is socialised into, the interactions one might enjoy or suffer, the resources and opportunities that are available and foreclosed, the actions that are enabled and constrained, and so on. Like all human conduct, corruption happens within such a structure, and the Moralist focus on individuals is unlikely to be effective inasmuch as efforts at education, monitoring and enforcement leave this structure intact. In Italy in the early 1990s, for instance, the Mani Pulite scandal led to the arrest of more than 3 000 politicians, officials and associates, the conviction of more than 1 000 others and several suicides. It contributed to the collapse of Italy's post-war party system. However, the longer-term effect of this effort on the level of corruption was negligible. The broader structure within which corruption thrived was simply repopulated and reorganised, and a new generation of political leaders set about passing laws that made corruption easier and prosecution more difficult (Della Porta and Vannucci 2012).

The Neoliberals and Marxists-Fanonists, sensing the limitations of Moralism, offer structural explanations in response. These explanations, however, come out as seriously incomplete; they leave a great deal of unexplained variation, because the actual problem of corruption gets wholly submerged by substantive programmatic objectives. So, to move through the explanations they give, the claim is made that single-party dominance causes corruption. But how does this proposition account for the fact that in the twentieth century Sweden's Social Democrats were long dominant and clean, while the competitive French and American systems exhibited significant problems of corruption? In statistical work on this relationship, which generally relies on perception measures of corruption, the number of effective parties in a system is in some analyses associated with higher levels of corruption (Chang and Golden 2006); in other analyses with lower levels of corruption (Tavits 2007); and in still other analyses the relationship between the variables is U-shaped, such that corruption initially declines and then rises again as we move from a small number of effective parties to larger numbers (Schleiter and Voznaya 2014). Clearly, there is no straightforward relationship between single-party dominance and corruption.

Moving on, the ANC's Leninist organisational doctrine is said to be the cause of corruption in South Africa. Yet, in Italy and India, the evidence is that the communist parties governed more cleanly, albeit only at regional and local levels, than did the Christian Democrats and Congress respectively. The argument is put that state intervention in the economy generates corruption. In reality, the countries with the largest states, say those in northern Europe among the rich countries, or the rich countries among the others, are among the least corrupt in the world. Statistically, bigger government is robustly associated with less corruption (Elliott 1997; Montinola and Jackman 2002). There are, to be fair, tentative statistical grounds for concluding that restrictive regulations generate higher levels of corruption, but this would suggest that the issue is not to what extent government intervenes but rather how it intervenes (Gerring and Thacker 2005; Hopkin and Rodríguez-Pose 2007). The claim is made that the ANC's project of racial-nationalist redistribution or black capitalist class formation drives corruption. The causal relationship here may be in the hypothesised direction, but similar processes in the so-called minority-majority cities of the US, and in Malaysia, while certainly not free of corruption, have evidently produced far less extensive and debilitating episodes.

A similar incompleteness afflicts the solutions proposed by Neoliberals and Marxists-Fanonists. The term 'state capture' was actually coined by World Bank economists working on the former USSR in the 1990s, precisely while disproving the then prevalent view that neoliberal reforms would themselves address corruption (Hellman and Schankerman 2000). Systematic state withdrawal from economic activities is disruptive of existing economic processes. It generates personal insecurity by dislocating established careers. It also opens opportunities for officials and emerging businesspeople to sell state assets to themselves and to write market regulations in ways that serve their own interests. So the evidence suggests that liberalisation may actually exacerbate corruption, as has been evidenced not only in the former Soviet bloc (Stiglitz 2002) but also in China (Sun 2004), in the broader East Asian region (Painter 2005), in Latin America (Manzetti and Blake 1995) and in Africa (Mwenda and Tangri 2005). The process of global, post-Second World War decolonisation gave rise to dozens of wide-ranging projects of state-led and often socialist development, but these, more often than not, were accompanied by debilitating problems of corruption (Kohli 2004; Sandbrook 1985). The Marxists-Fanonists can respond, as they often do, that with sufficient vision, political will and popular mobilisation, they themselves can avoid this. But this is pure voluntarism. It elides the structural determinants of corruption, reprises 'revolutionary morality' as the motor of anti-corruption and so, in the end, says nothing more than the Moralists do.

THE ARCHITECTURE OF CORRUPTION IN SOUTH AFRICA

A simple strategic lapse underlies the denouement of the foregoing section. The substantive partisan programmes in question require a fairly uncorrupted state to implement them. The South African state is increasingly corrupted, but the Neoliberals and Marxists-Fanonists offer these same programmes as solutions to the problem. The outcome of this contorted reasoning is a sort of utopian ideologism: a politics that asserts its ideals while neglecting their real conditions, one that therefore allows crippling obstacles to accumulate in the way of its own ends. In South Africa, corruption occurs within a politics of corrupt syndicates and political machines. These organisations have emerged within a governmental framework defined by the extensive politicisation of public administration personnel practices. They have formed over and work to govern and entrench a society characterised by widespread impoverishment.

Corrupt Syndicates

A corrupt syndicate is a group of people who come together to manipulate public administrative processes, in ways that violate recognised standards of conduct, in order to generate personal benefits for its members. Revelations of state capture in South Africa amount to illuminations of a series of corrupt syndicates. In modern societies generally, corruption at any appreciable scale is typically operationalised by syndicates. These tend to cross the boundary between political office – in which we include broader political associations such as parties and labour unions – and administrative office. They typically extend across relevant regulatory and operational functions, such as rule-making, licensing, policing, investigation, prosecution and service delivery. Syndicates ordinarily reach out to include private businesses, but this is not always the case.

This architecture of syndicates can be accounted for by certain features of modern states. Firstly, in these states, the most remunerative opportunities for corruption are embedded in extensive and complex processes, which can only be operationalised by groups of people. Second, the offices responsible for these processes are organised into checks and balances, which include regulatory and operational roles arrayed across both political and administrative layers of the state. To succeed, corrupt actors must cast networks of associates across these checks and balances, because a failure to do so opens them up to resistance, stalled authorisations and whistleblowing, public scandals and investigations, prosecutions and imprisonment. Third, in some circumstances, syndicates generate revenue without the participation of private businesses. They can, for instance, simply embezzle. They can assess recruitment fees and tithes on public jobs. They can solicit bribes from individuals for benefits like official documentation, the forgiveness of fines and the avoidance of criminal charges. In other public functions, such as the allocation of business licences, subsidies and contracts, the formal process, along with its revenue-generating opportunities, extends into the business sector, and so in such cases syndicates require a business arm.

The single most important condition for syndicate formation has to do with the checks and balances. Just about everything a state can do to regulate and close down corruption, including prosecutions, ultimately rests on them. In South Africa, public debate often raises the importance of controlling corruption by strengthening checks and balances, especially between the executive and legislative branches through a process of electoral reform. In modern times, however, the practical scope for constructing effective checks and balances at this level has narrowed considerably. Political parties are efficient vehicles for accumulating and employing the resources that politicians need to mobilise voters, take power and realise goals. They have everywhere assumed an important and dominant role in the selection of candidates and the control of incumbents across the executive and legislative branches. What this means is that they are also often efficient vehicles for socialising politicians into corrupt practices, enforcing corrupt bargains between them and protecting corrupt leaders from broader efforts at accountability (Della Porta and Vannucci 2016).

The extent to which electoral reform can address this dynamic is today evidently limited. There are countries that have attempted to loosen the hold of parties, introducing direct election of presidents, dividing legislatures into two chambers, and ensuring that representatives in each are themselves elected directly, from differently proportioned constituencies and at staggered intervals. The US more or less entrenched these premises in its constitution from the start, but in the course of the nineteenth century it also built the world's first modern mass parties, and it did so on the back of extraordinary levels of corruption. A feature of Italy's fight against corruption in the 1990s was the expansion of direct election of legislators, but, although this may have played a role in reconfiguring the party system, it achieved little by way of tangible gains against the problem of corruption (Della Porta and Vannucci 2012; Donovan 1995). South Africa's own parliamentary closed-list proportional representation system brings the executive and the legislature closer together and likely strengthens the bonds of parties. Statistically, there are international comparative grounds for arguing that this is associated with higher levels of corruption (Kunicová and Rose-Ackerman 2005), but this association is weak and it collapses in the presence of suitable controls. As shown by the cases of the US, Italy, other countries like Belize, Kenya and even South African local government, alternative electoral systems offer no panacea for corruption (Treisman 2007).

There are, fortunately, other strategies with greater promise. If the significance of executive-legislative checks and balances has been eroded by the rise of modern parties, the concomitant expansion of modern state bureaucracies has brought into greater prominence the relationship between parties and public administrations. At issue is the degree to which politicians are empowered or constrained in the appointment and removal of public administrators. Where politicians exercise broad powers in these respects, they can position associates across the regulatory authorities and administrative segregations of duties that control the largest and most important expenditures and operations of the state. In the South African debate, it is often suggested that this high degree of political control over public administration personnel practices is ordinary and inevitable, but this is simply not the case. Political powers of appointment and removal are often effectively checked by introducing independent civil service commissions, specialised examination, qualification and training requirements, and closed career recruitment and promotion systems. These are bolstered by the mobilisation of powerful constituencies for bureaucratic autonomy, which bring professional public administrators together with broader societal groups to resist problematic political interference.

Where these constraints hold, the tendency is to constitute politicians and public administrators as distinct groupings, their members following divided career paths, where they are held accountable in accordance with different principles, such as popular electability or reputation for technical competence. As a result, the potential for syndicate formation fractures. Politicians are more likely to check administrative malfeasance in which they have no stake. Public administrators are more likely to check political interference, to refuse authorisations and to blow the whistle if politicians cannot unilaterally determine their employment prospects. Politicians and public administrators are still able to strike corrupt bargains, but it is more difficult to do so and corruption is likely to be restrained.

A wealth of world-historical experience bears out these propositions. Countries that established modern, politically insulated civil service systems before the arrival of mass parties, such as Germany, the Scandinavian countries (Ertman 1997), Japan (Johnson 1982) and Botswana (Lange 2009; Stedman 1992), experienced long and consequential episodes of relatively corruption-free and capable government thereafter. The construction of such civil service systems after the arrival of mass politics was central to the generally successful fight against spoils-era corruption in the US (Skowronek 1982), but also in countries like Australia (Curnow 2003) and Iceland (Kristinsson 2001). The processes of racial capitalist advancement in the US and Malaysia were significantly less corrupt and more developmental than in South Africa, arguably because they occurred after the construction of powerful professional administrative strata able to check and balance political interference (Puthucheary 1978; Stone 1989). To reinforce the point statistically, higher levels of insulation of personnel processes from political arbitrariness are repeatedly robustly associated with lower levels of corruption (Bersch, Praça and Taylor 2017; Dahlström, Lapuente and Teorell 2011; Meyer-Sahling and Mikkelsen 2016; Oliveros and Schuster 2017).

In South Africa, political parties – and also powerful factions and cliques within them – have assumed largely unconstrained powers of appointment and removal in the public administration. This outcome is not satisfactorily explained, as the Neoliberals suggest, as a consequence of the ANC's Leninist doctrine of cadre deployment. Instead, more material imperatives are operative. Across the world, the assertion of political control over personnel practices is a common response to perceived programmatic and social dissonance and distrust between politicians and an existing administrative class, such as prevailed between the liberation movement and old apartheid administrators in the transition to democracy. More enduringly, the politicisation of personnel practices expresses the political usefulness of expanding the number and variety of official posts, along with associated benefits, which can be offered as inducements to the energies of party activists. The Leninist doctrine does not originate so much as establish in party policy and systematise these material logics of political control and mobilisation.

The factor that will continue to enable these logics, especially as the ANC loses its grip on the state and other parties come into power, is South African law as it applies to public administration personnel matters. The rules around appointment and removal vary between the national and provincial public service and municipalities. They also differ between departments, components, and the diverse public and municipal entities. Beyond the courts and some constitutional institutions, however, the norm is that politicians from the incumbent party decide who sits on recommendatory selection committees and the self-same politicians will make the appointment. There is no effective check and balance in such a process. In some state organisations, by operation of statute or by delegations, administrative heads are given powers to appoint their subordinates, but the politicians still appoint the heads. It follows that they can ensure that their choice is loyal and open to cascading political preferences in appointment down the hierarchy. Where politicians encounter recalcitrant permanent public administrators, they can dislodge them by using broad political powers of suspension and dismissal.

The resulting system offers vast opportunities for the construction of corrupt syndicates, and so corrupt syndicates have become ubiquitous. The most prominent and expansive example was the so-called 'Zupta' syndicate. Former president Jacob Zuma and the Gupta family appointed associates to key public offices, across regulatory and operational functions, then manipulated official powers to accumulate billions of rand. The subject of the Zondo Commission of Inquiry into State Capture, the extent and variety of evidence in the public domain, in the commission, through other judicial processes, news media, and so on, suggests that these arrangements are widespread. They have been described in detail not only in national (Myburgh 2017) but also in provincial (Myburgh 2019) and local spheres of government (Olver 2017).

Political Machines

In democracies, there is always fierce competition for public office. This can be for policy objectives or for personal gain. It can be as factionalism within parties, or between parties in general elections. In any case, to face down competition, syndicates must establish a more imposing edifice, what in political science is often called a 'political machine'. A political machine is headed by a single authoritative leader, in the parlance referred to as a 'boss', or a committee of such leaders. Bosses use syndicates to centralise under their control the relevant regulatory and operational functions. The powers and resources drawn from these functions are then applied to the construction of a much larger political organisation. A political machine has a characteristic pyramidic architecture, with bosses dispensing the fruits of their syndicates through a series of intermediary brokers into an expansive grassroots base. When Zuma's arrest provoked mass riots in KwaZulu-Natal and Gauteng in July of 2021, what we were seeing was his political machine in action (Brunette 2021; Wicks, Singh and Hunter 2021).

The regulatory powers of the state take on a new orientation when in the hands of such an organisation. The exercise of these powers is redirected away from impartial oversight and correction, towards the tasks of policing defection from the ranks of the machine and attacking political competitors. Regulatory agencies gather damaging information for blackmail, they generate public scandals through leaks, and they unleash investigations and prosecutions not so much against the corrupt as against opponents. In a machine, resources like jobs, contracts and public services are not distributed on an impersonal basis, but rather as patronage, with an eye to compensating machine operatives, cultivating broad support, and enticing divisions within and desertions from opposition. Machines provoke mass protests and riots to promote internal cohesion, encourage supporters, and intimidate and disrupt enemies. Because the operations of machines are often unlawful, they have no recourse to courts to enforce their agreements and expectations. They may face defecting insiders or intransigent competitors who refuse to be dissuaded by formal regulatory action or patronage. Machines, therefore, usually maintain their own extra-legal enforcement capacities. Corrupt police units, gangs and hitmen are used to generate a climate of fear, a regimen of submission, and to draw a line through threats with physical violence and assassination.

There are two basic conditions that account for the rise of political machines. The first of these conditions, already discussed, is for politicians to have wide powers of appointment and removal in public administrations, which allows them to construct corrupt syndicates to gather the powers and resources that keep the machine in working order. The second condition is an environment consisting of a sufficiently large number of impoverished people. The qualitative literature strongly suggests that political machines are more prevalent in the politics of poor countries (Stokes 2007). Quantitative studies have found robust positive associations between measurements of economic development and measurements of the ubiquity of patronage, covering long periods of time, large numbers of countries, and different regions and populations within countries (Stokes et al. 2013). Sociologically, political machines almost always assert the dominance of a small number of wealthy notables over much larger and poorer communities.

The basic reason for these findings is that people who have access to political and economic rights, and to alternative avenues for generating an income, tend to be less open to the appeals and coercions of machine politics. They become less reliant on patronage to sustain their livelihoods. They have less time available to solicit it. They receive less benefit from a given increment of new income, in terms of the economic law of diminishing marginal utility. So, as people gain access to wider economic opportunities and become wealthier, the cost of maintaining their political acquiescence and support rises and is more difficult for machines to sustain (Calvo and Murillo 2004; Dixit and Londregan 1996). Moreover, where people earn their incomes from rights-based public distributions, from private businesses competing in markets and from growth-oriented productive economies, they will tend to be sensitive to the policy, administrative and economic costs associated with corruption and patronage (Kitschelt and Wilkinson 2007). These observations explain the success of political machines as an organisational framework for politics in South Africa. The majority of the country's citizens live on less than R1 227 per month, which means they are officially below the poverty line. On the narrow definition of unemployment, a third of the country's populace have no job.

It is unsurprising, then, that studies of community politics in South Africa now regularly highlight the importance of patronage (Bénit-Gbaffou 2011; Von Holdt et al. 2011). A survey of broader evidence, including book-length exposés, news media reports, policy documents and a familiarity with politics on the ground will show that this patronage moves through a fairly typical machine system. The bosses of the political machines can ordinarily be found in the leading structures of the ANC, in the national, provincial and local executive committees. They are often leaders in government, the president or ministers, premiers or MECs, mayors or chairs of council committees. In some cases, they have assumed permanent positions within public administrations, which insulates them from the churn of electoral politics. In other cases, they prefer to remain outside of government, in the offices of parties, unions and other political formations, acting at a distance from state power and so relatively hidden from public scrutiny. The intermediary operatives of the machines, managing the dispensation of patronage and violence into voting publics, are chiefly ward-level politicians, such as councillors, branch chairpersons and secretaries, along with their armies of community liaison officers and party members. They include traditional authorities, hostel and shack lords, so-called tenderpreneurs, racketeering 'business forums', taxi bosses and assassins.

The organisational roles of political machines describe a hierarchy of income-generating occupations. The benefits derived therefrom can be consumed or put to further capital accumulation. They are often the only avenue of upward mobility for large, impoverished constituencies. It is frequently true, for these reasons, that machines are perceived by constituents as vehicles of aspiration and attainment. They often explicitly promote projects of ethnic, racial or popular advancement, but theorising the emergence of political machines as a process of, say, black capitalist class formation is ultimately reductive and inadequate. The theory is teleological. It tends to narrow causation to the realisation of an intention. It constructs a coherence of class consciousness and interests that is not established in the present, by predicting its attainment in a future that has not yet come to pass. The reality is more structurally conditioned, various, fluid and contingent. The positions available in machines are diverse and for the most part not helpfully described as capitalist. The boss, associated businesspersons, the various kinds of operatives and grassroots clients – these categories all describe roles with distinct competencies and incomes, incentives and disincentives, opportunities and constraints. These diverse roles serve to construct divergent political and economic interests, and to create potential for tension and conflict.

A machine's boss, for instance, is primarily a politician concerned with maintaining control over the means of administration and, therefore, with ruling. They do so to generate various informal and illicit income streams, but these can be viewed as a benefit of office additional to a salary: plainly, this does not in itself make the boss an emergent capitalist. It is not obvious, moreover, that bosses will be oriented towards fostering a broader capitalist class from within their social base. Firstly, bosses have an interest in fostering dependent constituents. They may see the formation of a powerful new capitalist class from among these constituents as a source of competitors and a threat to their position. In Senegal, for instance, politicians have historically moved actively to prevent such a development (Boone 1990). Secondly, bosses are concerned to disperse resources widely enough to assemble a winning coalition at the polls. This often means building machines that are 'bottom-heavy', with low-paying, short-term and insecure occupations, which runs against the concentration of resource flows needed to foster viable capitalists. It may actually positively inhibit upward mobility by trapping machine clients in career cul-de-sacs, which offer short-term gains that are smaller than the long-term prospects available through other avenues. A process like this helps to explain, for example, why the historically machine-bound Irish upwardly mobilised more slowly than other white immigrant ethnic groups in America (Erie 1988).

Thirdly, bosses may decide to side with established capital against emerging black capitalist contenders. After all, established capitalists are by definition economically dominant, they are the main source of economic growth and revenue for the state, and this economic growth and revenue is a key source of income to bosses. Finally, where politicians do decide to promote a new black capitalist class, there are open strategic questions about whether the best way to do so is through competition or alliance with old capitalists, which involves a choice between economic disruption and shared growth. There are other questions about whether it is best to promote a new black capitalist class through formal policies implemented by effective, rule-bound bureaucracies, or through corrupt syndicates and political machines. The examples of those minority-majority cities in the US and the Bumiputera advance in Malaysia offer different and arguably more successful answers to those questions.

In South Africa, the keen observer of politics on the ground will be familiar with accounts of how small black businesses often chafe at the impositions of politicians, including from irregular and often unsustainable requests for monetary contributions as a condition for continued access to public contracts. The keen observer will also be aware of the prevalence of schemes for breaking up, rotating and dispersing jobs and contracts across broad constituencies, without clear regard for sustained economic mobility and capacity-building. Finally, arguably much of the fight between the Zuma and Ramaphosa tendencies in the ANC, both of which agree on the imperative of black capitalist class formation, is about divergent orientations towards white capital, growth and corruption. In these various relations, the teleology of black capitalist class formation becomes uncertain, the theory emerges as seriously incomplete, and it may simply amount to an ideological contrivance for forcing the new problem of corruption into a pre-existing Marxist-Fanonist framework.

WHEN WILL CORRUPTION END?

Corrupt syndicates and political machines have proliferated in South Africa because the country's public administrations are not appropriately insulated from politicisation, and its citizenry is widely impoverished. These issues must be addressed by appropriately motivated, informed and powerful political coalitions. The Moralists, Neoliberals and Marxists-Fanonists, however, tend to the belief that they can simply continue with old partisan projects regardless of corruption. They often appear to be unconcerned with generating reliable knowledge of the problem. Their political ability to face up to the syndicates and machines has repeatedly been brought into question. In other countries, successful movements against corruption have emerged on the back of major political, social and economic developments. These developments have brought new social and economic groups into politics. They have forged new forms of collaboration across stubborn divides of nation, race and class. They have given rise to new substantive visions and forces, which succeed in shattering and reconstituting the patterns of commitments and alliances across which syndicates and machines have come to preside (Mann 2012; Skowronek 1982). In comparison, the Moralists, Neoliberals and Marxists-Fanonists are stagnant. They spend their time rehashing ancient programmes, while the underlying governmental conditions of their politics break down.

REFERENCES

Ashman, Sam. 2019. 'Financialised Accumulation and the Political Economy of State Capture'. *New Agenda* 75: 6–11. https://www.ajol.info/index.php/na/article/view/192692.

Bénit-Gbaffou, Claire. 2011. '"Up Close and Personal": How Does Local Democracy Help the Poor Access the State? Stories of Accountability and Clientelism in Johannesburg'. *Journal of Asian and African Studies* 46, no. 5: 453–465. https://journals.sagepub.com/doi/10.1177/0021909611415998.

Beresford, Alexander. 2015. 'Power, Patronage, and Gatekeeper Politics in South Africa'. *African Affairs* 114, no. 455: 226–248. https://www.jstor.org/stable/43817167#metadata_info_tab_contents.

Bersch, Katherine, Sérgio Praça and Matthew M. Taylor. 2017. 'State Capacity, Bureaucratic Politicization, and Corruption in the Brazilian State'. *Governance* 30, no. 1: 105–124. https://onlinelibrary.wiley.com/doi/abs/10.1111/gove.12196.

Bond, Patrick. 1998. *Elite Transition: From Apartheid to Neoliberalism in South Africa.* Pietermaritzburg: University of Natal Press.

Boone, Catherine. 1990. 'The Making of a Rentier Class: Wealth Accumulation and Political Control in Senegal'. *Journal of Development Studies* 26, no. 3: 425–449. https://www.tandfonline.com/doi/abs/10.1080/00220389008422163.

Brunette, Ryan. 2021. 'No Two Elephants Are Alike'. *Africa Is a Country*, 4 August 2021. https://africasacountry.com/2021/08/no-elephants-are-alike.

Calvo, Ernesto and Maria V. Murillo. 2004. 'Who Delivers? Partisan Clients in the Argentine Electoral Market'. *American Journal of Political Science* 48, no. 4: 742–757. https://www.jstor.org/stable/1519931#metadata_info_tab_contents.

Chang, Eric C.C. and Miriam A. Golden. 2006. 'Electoral Systems, District Magnitude and Corruption'. *British Journal of Political Science* 37, no. 1: 115–137. https://www.jstor.org/stable/4497282#metadata_info_tab_contents.

Curnow, Ross. 2003. 'What's Past Is Prologue: Administrative Corruption in Australia'. In *The History of Corruption in Central Government*, edited by Seppo Tiihonen, 37–64. Amsterdam: IOS Press.

Dahlström, Carl, Victor Lapuente and Jan Teorell. 2011. 'The Merit of Meritocratization: Politics, Bureaucracy, and the Institutional Deterrents of Corruption'. *Political Research Quarterly* 65, no. 3: 656–668. https://journals.sagepub.com/doi/abs/10.1177/1065912911408109.

Dangor, Zane. 2020. 'Beware the Anti-Corruption Trojan Horse'. *Daily Maverick*, 13 August 2020. https://www.dailymaverick.co.za/opinionista/2020-08-13-beware-the-anti-corruption-trojan-horse/.

Della Porta, Donatella and Alberto Vannucci. 2012. 'When Anti-Corruption Policy Fails: The Italian Case Eighteen Years after the Mani Pulite Investigations'. In *The Social Construction of Corruption in Europe*, edited by Dirk Tänzler, Konstadinos Maras and Angelos Giannakopoulos, 133–164. Farnham: Ashgate.

Della Porta, Donatella and Alberto Vannucci. 2016. *The Hidden Order of Corruption: An Institutional Approach*. Farnham: Ashgate.

Dixit, Avinash and John Londregan. 1996. 'The Determinants of Success of Special Interests in Redistributive Politics'. *The Journal of Politics* 58, no. 4: 1132–1155. https://www.journals.uchicago.edu/doi/10.2307/2960152.

Donovan, Mark. 1995. 'The Politics of Electoral Reform in Italy'. *International Political Science Review* 16, no. 1: 47–64. https://www.jstor.org/stable/1601168#metadata_info_tab_contents.

Elliott, Kimberly Ann. 1997. 'Corruption as an International Policy Problem: Overview and Recommendations'. In *Corruption and the Global Economy*, edited by Kimberly Ann Elliott, 175–236. Washington, DC: Institute for International Economics.

Erie, Steven P. 1988. *Rainbow's End: Irish-Americans and the Dilemmas of Urban Machine Politics, 1840–1985*. Berkeley: University of California Press.

Ertman, Thomas. 1997. *The Birth of Leviathan: Building States and Regimes in Medieval and Early Modern Europe*. Cambridge: Cambridge University Press.

Fogel, Benjamin. 2020. 'A Cycle of Diminishing Expectations'. *Africa Is a Country*, November 2020. https://africasacountry.com/2020/11/a-cycle-of-diminishing-expectations.

Gerring, John and Strom C. Thacker. 2005. 'Do Neoliberal Policies Deter Political Corruption?' *International Organization* 59, no. 1: 233–254. https://www.jstor.org/stable/3877884#metadata_info_tab_contents.

Giliomee, Hermann and Charles Simkins, eds. 1999. *The Awkward Embrace: One-Party Domination and Democracy*. Cape Town: Tafelberg.

Guess, Raymond. 2009. *Politics and the Imagination*. Princeton: Princeton University Press.

Hellman, Joel and Mark Schankerman. 2000. 'Intervention, Corruption, and Capture: The Nexus between Enterprises and the State'. *Economics of Transition* 8, no. 3: 545–576. https://onlinelibrary.wiley.com/doi/abs/10.1111/1468-0351.00055.

Hopkin, Jonathan and Andrés Rodríguez-Pose. 2007. '"Grabbing Hand" or "Helping Hand"? Corruption and the Economic Role of the State'. *Governance* 20, no. 2: 187–208. http://eprints.lse.ac.uk/3526/1/Grabbing_hand_or_helping_hand(LSERO).pdf.

Johnson, Chalmers. 1982. *MITI and the Japanese Miracle: The Growth of Industrial Policy, 1925–1975*. Stanford: Stanford University Press.

Kitschelt, Herbert and Steven I. Wilkinson, eds. 2007. *Patrons, Clients and Policies: Patterns of Democratic Accountability and Political Competition*. Cambridge: Cambridge University Press.

Kohli, Atul. 2004. *State-Directed Development: Political Power and Industrialization in the Global Periphery*. Cambridge: Cambridge University Press.

Kristinsson, Gunnar Helgi. 2001. 'Clientelism in a Cold Climate: The Case of Iceland'. In *Clientelism, Interests, and Democratic Representation: The European Experience in Historical and Comparative Perspective*, edited by Simona Piattoni, 172–192. Cambridge: Cambridge University Press.

Kunicová, Jana and Susan Rose-Ackerman. 2005. 'Electoral Rules and Constitutional Structures as Constraints on Corruption'. *British Journal of Political Science* 35, no. 4: 573–606. https://www.cambridge.org/core/journals/british-journal-of-political-science/article/abs/electoral-rules-and-constitutional-structures-as-constraints-on-corruption/946C36EC533FFEF6277E40EC7135013C.

Lange, Matthew. 2009. *Lineages of Despotism and Development: British Colonialism and State Power*. Chicago: University of Chicago Press.

Leon, Tony. 2022. 'As Cadre Deployment Took Root Civil Society Failed to See Writing on Wall'. *Business Day*, 16 January 2022. https://www.businesslive.co.za/bd/opinion/columnists/2022-01-16-tony-leon-as-cadre-deployment-took-root-civil-society-failed-to-see-writing-on-wall/.

Louw, Leon. 2014. 'Corruption Flourishes in Hothouse of Bureaucracy'. *Businesslive*, 3 September 2014. https://www.businesslive.co.za/archive/2014-09-03-corruption-flourishes-in-hothouse-of-bureaucracy/.

Mann, Michael. 2012. *The Sources of Social Power*. Vol. 2. Cambridge: Cambridge University Press.

Manzetti, Luigi and Charles H. Blake. 1995. 'Market Reforms and Corruption in Latin America: New Means for Old Ways'. *Review of International Political Economy* 3, no. 4: 662–697. https://www.jstor.org/stable/4177207#metadata_info_tab_contents.

Marais, Hein. 2011. *South Africa Pushed to the Limit: The Political Economy of Change*. London: Zed Books.

McKaiser, Eusebius. 2021. 'Without Tutu and Mandela, Is South African Moral Exceptionalism Dead?' *Foreign Policy*, 27 December 2021. https://foreignpolicy.com/2021/12/27/tutu-mandela-south-africa-moral-exceptionalism-dead/.

Meyer-Sahling, Jan-Hinrik and Kim Sass Mikkelsen. 2016. 'Civil Service Laws, Merit, Politicization, and Corruption: The Perspective of Public Officials from Five East European Countries'. *Public Administration* 94, no. 4: 1105–1123. https://nottingham-repository.worktribe.com/output/836298/civil-service-laws-merit-politicization-and-corruption-the-perspective-of-public-officials-from-five-east-european-countries.

Modiri, Joel. 2017. 'Captured States, Captured Imaginations'. *Daily Maverick*, 3 August 2017. https://www.dailymaverick.co.za/opinionista/2017-08-03-captured-states-captured-imaginations/.

Montinola, Gabriella R. and Robert W. Jackman. 2002. 'Sources of Corruption: A Cross-Country Study'. *British Journal of Political Science* 32, no. 1: 147–170. https://www.cambridge.org/core/journals/british-journal-of-political-science/article/abs/sources-of-corruption-a-crosscountry-study/C9D3C5EE50868B75F18365870834E4AB.

Mwenda, Andrew M. and Roger Tangri. 2005. 'Patronage Politics, Donor Reforms, and Regime Consolidation in Uganda'. *African Affairs* 104, no. 416: 449–467. https://academic.oup.com/afraf/article-abstract/104/416/449/85340?redirectedFrom=PDF.

Myburgh, James. 2020. *The Last Jacobins of Africa: The ANC and the Making of Modern South Africa*. Johannesburg: Politicsweb Publishing.

Myburgh, Peter-Louis. 2017. *The Republic of Gupta: A Story of State Capture*. Cape Town: Penguin Books.

Myburgh, Peter-Louis. 2019. *Gangster State: Unravelling Ace Magashule's Web of Capture*. Cape Town: Penguin Books.

Oliveros, Virginia and Christian Schuster. 2017. 'Merit, Tenure and Bureaucratic Behavior: Evidence from a Conjoint Experiment in the Dominican Republic'. *Comparative Political Studies* 51, no. 6: 759–792. https://journals.sagepub.com/doi/abs/10.1177/0010414017710268.

Olver, Crispian. 2017. *How to Steal a City: The Battle for Nelson Mandela Bay*. Cape Town: Jonathan Ball.

Painter, Martin. 2005. 'The Politics of State Sector Reforms in Vietnam: Contested Agendas and Uncertain Trajectories'. *Journal of Development Studies* 41, no. 2: 261–283. https://www.tandfonline.com/doi/abs/10.1080/0022038042000309241.

Puthucheary, Mavis. 1978. *The Politics of Administration: The Malaysian Experience*. Kuala Lumpur: Oxford University Press.

Ramaphosa, Cyril. 2018. 'State of the Nation Address'. 16 February 2018. https://www.gov.za/speeches/president-cyril-ramaphosa-2018-state-nation-address-16-feb-2018-0000.

Rauch, Janine. 2005. 'Linking Crime and Morality: Reviewing the Moral Regeneration Movement'. *South African Crime Quarterly* 11: 9–13. https://journals.assaf.org.za/index.php/sacq/article/view/1021.

Sandbrook, Richard. 1985. *The Politics of Africa's Economic Stagnation*. Cambridge: Cambridge University Press.

Schleiter, Petra and Alisa M. Voznaya. 2014. 'Party System Competitiveness and Corruption'. *Party Politics* 20, no. 5: 675–686. https://journals.sagepub.com/doi/abs/10.1177/1354068812448690.

Skowronek, Stephen. 1982. *Building a New American State: The Expansion of National Administrative Capacities, 1877–1920*. Cambridge: Cambridge University Press.

South African Communist Party. 2006. 'State Power'. Discussion document. https://www.marxists.org/history/international/comintern/sections/sacp/2006/komanisi.htm.

Stedman, Stephen J., ed. 1992. *Botswana: The Political Economy of Democratic Development*. Boulder, CO: Lynne Rienner.

Stiglitz, Joseph. 2002. *Globalisation and Its Discontents*. New York: W.W. Norton and Company.

Stokes, Susan. 2007. 'Political Clientelism'. In *The Oxford Handbook of Comparative Politics*, edited by Carles Boix and Susan Stokes, 604–627. Oxford: Oxford University Press.

Stokes, Susan, Thad Dunning, Marcelo Nazareno and Valeria Brusco. 2013. *Brokers, Voters, and Clientelism: The Puzzle of Distributive Politics*. Cambridge: Cambridge University Press.

Stone, Clarence. 1989. *Regime Politics: Governing Atlanta, 1946–1988*. Lawrence, KA: University Press of Kansas.

Sun, Yan. 2004. *Corruption and Market in Contemporary China*. Ithaca, NY: Cornell University Press.

Tavits, Margit. 2007. 'Clarity of Responsibility and Corruption'. *American Journal of Political Science* 51, no. 1: 218–229. https://www.jstor.org/stable/4122915#metadata_info_tab_contents.

Treisman, Daniel. 2007. 'What Have We Learned about the Causes of Corruption from Ten Years of Cross-National Empirical Research?' *Annual Review of Political Science* 10: 211–244. https://www.annualreviews.org/doi/abs/10.1146/annurev.polisci.10.081205.095418.

Von Holdt, Karl. 2019. 'The Political Economy of Corruption: Elite-Formation, Factions and Violence'. SWOP Working Paper No. 10, Johannesburg. https://www.swop.org.za/post/2019/02/18/working-paper-10-the-political-economy-of-corruption-open-access.

Von Holdt, Karl, Malose Langa, Sepetla Molapo, Nomfundo Mogapi, Kindiza Ngubeni, Jacob Dlamini and Adèle Kirsten. 2011. 'The Smoke That Calls: Insurgent Citizenship, Collective Violence and the Struggle for a Place in the New South Africa'. Centre for the Study of Violence and Reconciliation and SWOP, Johannesburg. https://www.csvr.org.za/docs/thesmokethatcalls.pdf.

Westbrook, Raymond, ed. 2003. *A History of Ancient Near Eastern Law*. 2 vols. Boston: Brill.

Wicks, Jeff, Kaveel Singh and Qaanitah Hunter. 2021. *Eight Days in July: Inside the Zuma Unrest That Set South Africa Alight*. Cape Town: Tafelberg.

Zille, Helen. 2017. 'What I Learnt in Singapore'. *Politicsweb*, 20 March 2017. https://www.politicsweb.co.za/opinion/what-i-learnt-in-singapore/.

SECTION 2

STATE CAPTURE IN ACTION

4

Legal Mobilisation against State Capture

Jonathan Klaaren

With the election of Cyril Ramaphosa to the presidency of the African National Congress (ANC) in December 2017 and his replacement of Jacob Zuma as president of the country a couple of months later amid persistent allegations of Zuma's corruption, South Africa was reported to be entering a 'New Dawn'.[1] This chapter analyses the legal and organisational aspects of mobilisation against state capture. It argues that the power of the law in its action against state capture consisted not only in the institutional strength of the courts, but was also significantly constituted in the impact that the legal profession and policy organisations working with the courts and other legal institutions were able to jointly produce.

The Judicial Commission of Inquiry into Allegations of State Capture, Corruption and Fraud in the Public Sector including Organs of State began hearing testimony in mid-2018; by July 2019, the Zondo Commission had heard testimonies from more than 80 persons over 130 days (Swilling 2019).

TOWARDS AN ANALYSIS AND DEFINITION OF STATE CAPTURE

In April 2017, the Open Society Foundation funded the State Capacity Research Project (SCRP), in which a number of academics collaborated to craft a response to President Jacob Zuma's continued attempts to establish control over the National Treasury (Foley and Swilling 2018). As noted elsewhere in this volume, the first outcome of the SCRP was the 'Betrayal of the Promise' report (PARI 2017), which later appeared in book form as *Shadow State: The Politics of State Capture* (Chipkin and Swilling 2018). The second outcome was a case study of state capture at the South African Social Security Agency (SASSA) (Foley and Swilling 2018). While the primary purpose of the 'Betrayal of the Promise' report was 'to provide an academic framework in which to better understand the social, political, and economic moment in South Africa', it was additionally a purposeful intervention in the politics of the moment (Foley and Swilling 2018, 1).

In the SCRP's view, state capture is a project reaching beyond simple corruption and is different from other instances of grand corruption in its political nature (Foley and Swilling 2018, 1). In its mode of operation, state capture engages in a set of network activities that run counter to the intentions, objectives and rules of the Constitution. The SCRP is careful to distinguish the phenomenon of state capture from simple corruption. It argues:

> If we are to expand our understanding of state capture from merely the typical activities of bribery and corruption to being a broader political project, we have to extend our enquiry beyond just the financial flows of ill-gotten gains and definitively criminal activities, to include the currency of power, the bartering of political favours by manipulation of state institutions (trading of fear and favours) and determine the cost this places on all South Africans (Foley and Swilling 2018, 1–2).

The SCRP views state capture as grand corruption but as more than such (see Foley in chapter 2 of this volume). Indeed, while it has been convincingly argued that the state capture experience has crystallised and brought to light an anti-corruption principle in South African constitutional jurisprudence, when we appreciate its political dimensions, state capture cannot be fully identified as equivalent to corruption, whether in its simple or grand or combined manifestations (Cachalia 2019). Rather, the state capture episode falls in line with instances of South African state and non-state action, for which accountability has not yet been established. These instances include most prominently the unfinished business of the Truth and Reconciliation Commission, including its failure to examine economic crimes and the post-apartheid Arms Deal.

To a notable degree, both the political project of state capture and the response to it have operated within the field of South African constitutionalism. It is perhaps easiest to see the place of state capture from within what one might term South African constitutionalist public discourse. The term 'state capture' had become part of the public discourse in South Africa from as early as 2015. The unexpected firing of minister of finance Nhlanhla Nene in December of that year negatively affected the financial markets and the value of the country's currency. Thousands of middle class and other citizens marched in the streets to protest against 'state capture' (Chipkin 2018). With only a slight grammatical nuance, the term was used several months later in the report of the Public Protector (one of the constitutionally established Chapter Nine institutions), which was released in late 2016 (Public Protector 2016). This report identified prima facie evidence of extensive corruption by, among others, the Gupta brothers, Jacob Zuma and his son Duduzane Zuma.

As Karl von Holdt has noted in chapter 1 of this volume, both corruption and anti-corruption are a form of politics. In order to identify the constitutionalist dimension of the state capture political project, it is useful to first ask whether state capture was identified solely with the Zuma and Gupta families or whether it was broader. The July 2018 SCRP report on 'SASSA-gate' argues that state capture was broader, encompassing an episode of politics – the near non-payment of social grants – in which neither the Gupta family, nor its associates, nor Zuma and his were directly involved. Instead, then minister of social development Bathabile Dlamini – responsible for SASSA – was at the centre of this controversy. A tender involving the largest state contract in South Africa's history was manipulated, and the monies paid to the country's social grants recipients were subjected to illegal and unethical deductions. To resolve the crisis, assure payment and halt the corruption, the Constitutional Court had to publicly identify the private firm distributing the grants and subject it to strict monitoring and accounting requirements (Klaaren 2020b). The SCRP report argues that the SASSA case demonstrates that state capture is not contained in or limited to only a closed circle of connected individuals but is part of a much larger network of political players (Foley and Swilling 2018). Still, the report is at pains to point out that Jacob Zuma was indirectly involved, at the very least, through the actions of his close political allies, including Dlamini.

Read together with the 'Betrayal of the Promise' report, the account of SASSA-gate is illustrative of the constitutionalist dimension of state capture in at least two aspects. First, the state capture project is shown as involving at its centre not the Guptas but Jacob Zuma, a person occupying the presidency of the country and the governing party. The character of the state capture project thus cannot be delinked from its exercise of at least a portion of the power of the holder of the most powerful office in the land. This overlap with formal state power is a consistent theme in the

SCRP literature. Linking to a long-standing conflict over the nature of transparency in democratic South Africa, the state capture project is sourced as beginning with the parliamentary passage of the 2010 version of the Protection of State Information Bill in 2011 (Chipkin and Swilling 2018). The literature uses the term 'shadow state' – a concept that appears as the obverse of the constitutional state. The two are zero-sum. In its terms, the SCRP states that 'the political project, which is state capture, extends beyond just looting of the state – it is also about the corruption of collective values and the mutating of political ideals ... cannot be read directly from the printed letters in the pages of the Constitution, but are discovered by reading between the lines and reside in the spirit and principles on which this document is founded' (Foley and Swilling 2018, 1).

Second, the 2017/2018 SCRP accounts are noteworthy for showing that the state capture political project was dominantly undertaken through network instruments and techniques. As such, state capture involved techniques of governance more than institutions of government. This parallels one form of the SCRP definition of state capture. The SCRP identifies seven key forms of activities undertaken within the state capture project. While not all activities need to be present, these are typical state capture activities and include (1) securing control over the public service; (2) securing access to rent-seeking opportunities by exploiting regulations, in particular manipulating tender processes; (3) securing control over strategic procurement opportunities by intentionally weakening key technical institutions and formal executive processes; (4) securing parallel political, governmental and decision-making structures that undermine the functional operation of government institutions; (5) securing control over state-owned enterprises by chronically weakening their governance and operational structures; (6) securing control over the country's fiscal sovereignty; and (7) securing the loyalty of the security and intelligence services by appointing loyalists (PARI 2017). Identifying in this way a set of typical, even if not necessary, activities constitutive of the state capture phenomenon is helpful towards constructing the outlines of that political project.

Taking advantage of new techniques of outsourced government such as public/private partnerships, the state capture operation unfolded as one of networks rather than of hierarchies, bureaucracies or command and control. Mark Swilling has described state capture as 'the formation of a shadow state directed by a power elite. This shadow state operates within – and parallel to – the constitutional state in formal and informal ways' (Swilling 2019). In this sense, state capture was not only a shadow state but also a shadow of the state.

TWO LITIGATION FORAYS AGAINST STATE CAPTURE

This section outlines two examples of litigation against state capture: the fight against partiality within the National Director of Public Prosecutions (NDPP) and the lawsuits against corruption and maladministration in the payment of social grants. Singling these out does not suggest that they were necessarily more significant than other legal campaigns, although the two were central and broadly representative of the litigation undertaken.

The first litigation is associated with the Council for the Advancement of the South African Constitution (CASAC), which describes itself as 'a project of progressive people who seek to advance the South African Constitution as the platform for democratic politics and the transformation of society' (CASAC 2018). It embraces the contestation of ideas and encourages debate on how best to build a just and equal society in which people can live securely and with dignity.

In July 2013, CASAC embarked upon what would turn out to be a long-running case against state capture. The organisation filed papers in the Constitutional Court, asking it to declare that then president Jacob Zuma had failed in his constitutional obligation to appoint a prosecutions chief 'diligently and without delay'. This case was eventually decided in mid-2018 in CASAC's favour, with an order that current president Ramaphosa appoint a national director of the National Prosecuting Authority (NPA) within 90 days of 13 August 2018 (Corruption Watch NPC and Others v President of the Republic of South Africa and Others 13 August 2018). The case had four of the five 'new' public interest law organisations participating, with applicants Corruption Watch and Freedom Under Law, and CASAC and the Helen Suzman Foundation as amici curiae.

The case had at least two significant institutional dimensions that went beyond the immediate consequence that Shaun Abrahams, the NDPP appointed by Jacob Zuma, had to vacate the position. First, the Constitutional Court struck down two important aspects of the statutory framework structuring the NPA. The court voided the section of the Act providing for an NDPP in terms of the president's discretion to continue to serve past retirement age. This action bolstered the institutional independence of the NPA. Further, parliament was ordered to make changes to the framework, allowing the president to suspend an NDPP for an indefinite period with no pay, again enhancing NPA autonomy. These are consequential changes to the Act; more changes to the appointment and removal provisions may follow as part of the legislative consideration needed (Belvedere 2020; Breytenbach 2018).

President Ramaphosa's implementation of the order in this case created another arguably even more significant second institutional consequence. While not required to do so, Ramaphosa opted to set up a panel of persons to recommend three to five candidates for the role of NDPP. This mechanism parallels that set up in the Constitution to propose judges for the Constitutional Court, subject to the final choice of the president from the four candidates identified by the Judicial Service Commission. While this mechanism cannot yet be said to be an institution (as it could be reversed or abandoned at the next NDPP vacancy), it is an interesting consequence that would not likely have been put into place without the litigation (Maughan 2018).

A second noteworthy instance of a lawsuit against state capture occurs in the social grants payment sector. The SCRP documented this striking attempt to capture SASSA, the state structure responsible for distributing a large portion of the state budget (Foley and Swilling 2018). The report focuses on the 2017 payments crisis at the height of state capture. However, the first strategic lawsuit in this sector may be traced to an action launched nearly a decade earlier by Cash Paymaster Services (CPS), ironically later to be itself the target of several lawsuits. To understand the legal and organisational aspects of mobilisation against state capture, it is necessary to begin some ten years before the non-payments crisis.

At this point in the story, SASSA had been created by legislation in 2006 as a national agency to manage social grant payments. The new institution took over that function from the provinces amid allegations of pervasive corruption and inefficiency. In early 2007, SASSA issued a request for proposals for a national system to pay grants. In late 2008, it was forced to withdraw this tender and issue a narrative report in early 2009 explaining the reasons for the withdrawal. In the meantime, the continuing provincial distribution contracts (to CPS and other payments companies) were extended by SASSA, with the concurrence of the National Treasury. Then minister of social development, the respected Zola Skweyiya, introduced a theme of market competitiveness, where a regulator or state agency applies the principle of competitive policy to attempt to structure a well-functioning and competitive market, aiming to avoid a monopoly by providing opportunities for new entrants into the market (Foley and Swilling 2018). Sadly, this was not the approach followed by Skweyiya's successors.

In this light, it may not be surprising that CPS fired a first legal salvo, attempting to void a letter of agreement between SASSA and the South African Post Office, which recorded an intention to develop an intergovernment agency relationship between these two public entities to develop a public payment system for social grants. CPS appeared happy with the market position it had achieved. The legal basis for the CPS litigation to void this letter was that it violated procurement policies. The case proceeded through the High Court in October 2009, with an interim win for CPS then reversed in the Supreme Court of Appeal (SCA) in March 2011, with a win for SASSA (CEO of the South African Social Security Agency N.O and Other v Cash Paymaster Services 11 March 2011). The reasoning in the 2011 SCA case was a precedent for the reasoning of the Constitutional Court two years later (AllPay Consolidated Investment Holdings (Pty) Ltd and Others v Chief Executive Officer of the South African Social Security Agency and Others 27 March 2013).

Further litigation took place after the next tender – the request for proposals, which had been released in April 2011 and then infamously 'clarified' in a last-minute change that favoured CPS in June 2011 – had been awarded to CPS on 17 January 2012. It was not litigation undertaken in the public interest. A collective of losing bidders, including the other provincial payment service providers, sued the Department of Social Development, SASSA and CPS. This was the beginning of litigation known as AllPay, a case that remains open before the Constitutional Court. In August 2012, the High Court found against CPS but declined to set aside the tender as a matter of remedy, and in March 2013, the SCA upheld the cross-appeal of CPS, making the tender award valid (AllPay Consolidated Investment Holdings (Pty) Ltd and Others v CEO of the South African Social Security Agency and Others 27 March 2013).

At this point, AllPay approached the Constitutional Court, where Corruption Watch and the Centre for Child Law became amici curiae in the case. The Constitutional Court ruled on 29 November 2013 that the tender was invalid (AllPay Consolidated Investment Holdings (Pty) Ltd and Others v Chief Executive Officer of the South African Social Security Agency and Others 29 November 2013). However, on 17 April 2014, the Constitutional Court suspended the order of invalidity (AllPay Consolidated Investment Holdings (Pty) Ltd and Others v Chief Executive Officer of the South African Social Security Agency and Others 17 April 2014). The action of the court was premised on SASSA issuing a new tender within a proper procurement process, with the CPS contract coming to an end in early 2017. The then new minister for social development, Bathabile Dlamini, influenced this procurement process (for the post-CPS 2017 onwards contract) to benefit CPS and the state capture project.

One aspect of the legal contestation in this litigation featured the entrance into the fray of the Black Sash Trust, with the Centre for Applied Legal Studies as its lawyers, to safeguard the data protection and privacy rights of social grant beneficiaries. This was important because they were often subject to coercive financial and other services marketing by CPS-linked companies. In addition to privacy violations, in some instances the deductions resulting from this marketing meant that social grant recipients received no net funds from their social grants. The Black Sash contested the initial request for proposals issued in December 2014, leading to a revised request for proposals after a Constitutional Court order for 24 March 2015 (AllPay Consolidated Investment Holdings (Pty) Ltd and Others v Chief Executive Officer of the South African Social Security Agency and Others 2015).

The continuing influence of state capture led to the third significant Constitutional Court judgment in this legal campaign. The flashpoint was the expiration at the end of March 2017 of the invalid–but temporarily valid–contract for CPS. The court had discharged its initial supervisory jurisdiction over SASSA on 25 November 2015 (Foley and Swilling 2018). Here, in widely televised and compelling proceedings, the Constitutional Court on 17 March 2017 again extended the validity of the CPS contract to secure the delivery of the social grants. Just as significantly, the court held the minister to account, initiating a separate process for determining her personal liability for the crisis and attempting to ensure that CPS did not profit from the further extension (Black Sash Trust v Minister of Social Development and Others 17 March 2017). The public interest law organisation Freedom Under Law intervened in this action. The March 2017 hearing was televised nationwide and undoubtedly turned the tide against state capture.

The dramatic Constitutional Court litigation of March 2017 conceivably overshadows other directly relevant litigation. Two less dramatic cases are significant for understanding the full scope of the legal mobilisation against state capture in the social grant payments sector. First, the Black Sash took the Department of Social Development to court over matters related to the data protection and privacy rights of social grant beneficiaries. Second, Corruption Watch took SASSA to court over an alleged extra payment of about R300 million by SASSA to CPS for the re-registration of beneficiaries. The High Court decided in favour of Corruption Watch in early 2018.

The discussion above focused on two instances that were part of the rising number of anti-corruption legal actions evident before and during the height of state capture. The first was the 'unfit for public office' line of cases driven by CASAC and pursued with the assistance of Corruption Watch and several of the new civil society groups emerging during 2011 and 2012. The second was litigation in the social grants sector that attempted to avoid disruption to the delivery of these grants (socio-economic rights in South Africa in terms of the Bill of Rights) to around 15 million of the country's poorest citizens. The discussion was concerned with the historical precedents of these legal actions and with their political and institutional consequences rather than on the content of the law made or enforced by the two cases.

CIVIL SOCIETY MOBILISATION CONTESTING STATE CAPTURE

Litigation such as the court actions outlined in the previous section both contributed to and were embedded within political mobilisation against state capture. Taking into account the initiating organisations and the support structure for this litigation, there are at least two distinctive elements of this mobilisation in the South African context: an increased level of business participation in such civil society politics and the significant role played by a 'second generation' of organisations wielding the sword of public interest law, and leading to the introduction of a new theme into public discourse, namely, the call for an efficient public administration.

An extraordinary wave of mobilisation against the state capture phenomenon dating from the firing of finance minister Pravin Gordhan and Ramaphosa's narrow victory for the presidency of the ANC in December 2017 resulted in Zuma's forced resignation in February 2018. Even before these events, one crucial initiative of political mobilisation began in August 2016. This was Sipho Pityana's (2016) speech at Makhenkesi Stofile's funeral, regarded by many as the founding event of the campaign SAVE South Africa (Chipkin and Swilling 2018).

Organisations representing the business sector were prominent new members in this wave of civil society activism. One essential actor was Business Leadership South Africa, which represents the country's largest corporations. At the time, other civil society actors thought the entry of the business sector into the political sphere was tardy. Moreover, the direct participation by businesses in collective legal mobilisation was fairly short-lived. From the point at which Ramaphosa emerged as the president of the ANC, the evidence suggests that the business sector had returned to the individualised pursuit of redress for corruption or an accommodative stance in its relationships with state departments and state-owned entities. Once the immediate risk of state capture appeared countered, business organisations no longer initiated funding or, in some cases, withdrew civil society funding already in the pipeline.

While business participation was notable, much of the mobilisation against state capture was facilitated through established organisations, some of which had a history of anti-apartheid protest. For instance, Section27 played an important role in mobilising opposition as well as instituting litigation against the state. It partnered with other groups to organise a protest demonstration at Pretoria's Church Square, following the long-feared move against Gordhan. Section27's tradition of constituency organising against HIV/Aids, itself drawing on anti-apartheid protest traditions (Robins 2008), supplied helpful experience. Nonetheless, some of the organisations facilitating the mobilisation against state capture did not have a direct history of anti-apartheid protest.

A significant portion of activity sounded themes of legal process as well as those of bureaucratic integrity, pushing boundaries for South African civil society. As Ivor Chipkin (2018) noted at the time, this marked a moment where civil society activists were, for the first time, paying attention to issues of state-building and the ethics of public administration. Some of this action took the form of calling for institutional change. The Centre for Accountability proposed an institutional anti-corruption mechanism, the Integrity Commission, to be established at the level of a Chapter Nine institution (Thamm 2018). Arguably, this was mandated by the Glenister litigation and its finding that the Hawks in its initial version lacked the constitutionally requisite degree of institutional independence. Such an innovation would require a constitutional amendment and, pertinently, the South African Human Rights Commission already has constitutional competence in this area (Klaaren 2005). The articulation of these law-heavy themes and proposals and their generally positive public reception added nuance to the public denunciation of corruption, inflecting it with a defence of the values of the Constitution and the institutions and structures it establishes.

The prominent use of law in civil society mobilisation is hardly new in South Africa. A direct link may be made from South Africa's history of legal activism against apartheid to the legal organising against state capture. This tradition includes episodes such as the 1952 'coloured' voting cases, the effective use of the law by the trade union movement from the 1973 Durban Moment onwards (Maree 2019) and mobilisation during the 1980s (Abel 1995). Among early post-apartheid legal actions in this tradition, the most significant may well be the actions focused on corruption in the Arms Deal. Lawyers for Human Rights, an anti-apartheid organisation founded in the late 1970s, was a key organisation promoting this litigation. Overall, the Arms Deal cases were unsuccessful. They were unable to prevent the corruption involved or recover the proceeds. Furthermore, they did not succeed in uncovering the truth of what happened. However, one Arms Deal court case led to a judicial commission of inquiry, the Seriti Commission, being constituted. However, it was widely regarded as a whitewash and was eventually judicially set aside (Feinstein, Holden and Van Vuuren 2014).

The most direct and successful precedent for the legal actions against state capture consists in the three Glenister cases (Glenister v President of the Republic of South Africa and Others 17 March 2011). This litigation was initiated and financed by a businessperson, Bob Glenister. Positioned outside of established civil society and prompted by the dismantling of the Scorpions, an elite and successful post-apartheid police/prosecutions division within the NPA that was replaced by the Hawks in 2009, the action was taken in the wake of the limited mobilisation against the Arms Deal. As legal activist Paul Hoffman observes, 'The Glenister cases … spawned imaginative judicial interventions based on the notion that failure to take appropriate measures to combat corruption is regarded as a violation of human rights in South Africa' (2017). Beyond the business sector, opposition parties drove much of the significant litigation directed against state capture. Perhaps the most prominent was the case launched by the Economic Freedom Fighters against President Zuma over the Nkandla issue (Economic Freedom Fighters v Speaker of the National Assembly and Others 31 March 2016). Another critical case was the legal action taken by the Democratic Alliance against the dropping of corruption charges dating from the Arms Deal against Jacob Zuma (Democratic Alliance v President of South Africa and Others 5 October 2012).

The remainder of this section turns to focus on the organisers of and the support structure for litigation against state capture. Such legal mobilisation was often facilitated by intermediary organisations, including those with links to, or even existing within, the legal sector. These organisations were comprised in part, but by no means exclusively, of law firms and public interest law organisations. Personnel at several of the leading Johannesburg corporate law firms were called upon – or took the initiative – to provide legal arguments that business organisations could undertake against aspects of state capture. This creative and innovative lawyering also took place in intermediary spaces, such as among public interest-oriented advocates at the Bar. Similar activity resulted in the university-based Centre for Applied Legal Studies' engagement in a hybrid litigation partnership with the Black Sash and Corruption Watch in the SASSA litigation described above. The lawyers may come off rather well in this telling, but perhaps only in comparative terms (Marchant et al. 2020). And, of course, this story is not entirely positive for organisations and individual professionals in the legal sector. At least as a footnote, it is necessary to record that at least one law firm – Hogan Lovells – joined the ranks of the captured or even the captors (Van Wyk 2018a, 2018b).

As discussed above, a second generation of post-apartheid public interest law organisations was founded around 2010 or began to engage in litigation in the public interest at that time. This group includes organisations established soon after the end of apartheid, such as the Centre for Constitutional Rights, the Centre for Accountability and the Helen Suzman Foundation, as well as a set of newly minted civil society groups like Corruption Watch, CASAC and Freedom Under Law, mentioned earlier, and the Organisation Undoing Tax Abuse, which were established between 2008 and 2012.

These second-generation public interest law organisations differ in at least three ways from their predecessors. First, the earlier ones – including the Centre for

Applied Legal Studies, Lawyers for Human Rights and the Legal Resources Centre – had walk-in clinics or offered legal services to individual members of the public (Klaaren 2020c). By contrast, the new public interest law organisations do not have client services. Arguably, Corruption Watch is an exception, with outreach programmes and interactive social media portals. Second, the new groups appear to be more closely aligned to the establishment agenda, with a seemingly significant overlap of personnel and funding sources, especially in the business sector. Indeed, several of the new public interest law groups do not have much, if any, staff beyond a single director (as in the case of Freedom Under Law and CASAC). In terms of the political spectrum, while CASAC is a self-avowedly progressive organisation and Corruption Watch is aligned with the broad trade union movement, Freedom Under Law has establishment lawyers, ex-judges and businesspersons on its board, and the Helen Suzman Foundation and the Organisation Undoing Tax Abuse are not aligned with the ANC but operate within mainstream business and Democratic Alliance politics. In December 2017, the Helen Suzman Foundation and Magda Wierzycka, the chief executive officer of a financial services firm, embarked on litigation against President Zuma and 74 other persons for breaches of the Prevention of Corrupt Activities Act (Thamm 2017). Finally, the first generation evinced a socio-economic rights agenda and displayed a set of organisational mandates; the newer groups are firmly mandated to deal with civil and political rights and governance issues located within a rule-of-law agenda.

It is more accurate to term at least some of these new organisations less as human rights or public interest law organisations and more as lobbying groups. In this sense, their appearance and action would fit with the appearance of other lobby groups, including AfriForum, a group aligned with conservative and white racial politics (Friedman 2018). These developments may point to the emergence of a new type of lobbying politics, the opposite of state capture politics. This is because influence is mobilised not to capture state power but rather to influence the holder of state power, without regard to the identity of that holder of state power. This phenomenon within civil society may form part of the emergence of regulatory politics in post-apartheid South Africa (Klaaren 2020a).

THE PLACE OF LAW IN THE MOBILISATION AGAINST STATE CAPTURE

This section uses legal-mobilisation theory to explore in further depth the place of law in the mobilisation against state capture. The prominence of legal themes and legal sector organisations within the South African mobilisation against state capture demands an explanation. Most commonly, the direct employment of law occurs within individualised actions – matters often ending in settlement or the resolution of the dispute upon payment of relatively small amounts (Garth and Cappelletti 1978). Indeed, one might easily argue that law is most often employed to frustrate collective mobilisation. For instance, employment discrimination litigation in the US demonstrates the general phenomenon whereby legal jurisdiction may extend jurisdiction without providing an effective remedy (Nielsen, Nelson and Lancaster 2010). Critical legal studies have long engaged in such analyses of the law's anti-mobilising effect. This observation is relevant to the use of the law against corruption and state capture in South Africa. Many individual cases against fraud and corruption have been opened and processed in South Africa without forming part of a broader social movement (Chipkin and Swilling 2018). The existence of an institution such as the Independent Police Investigative Directorate does not necessarily entail the existence of an effective social movement against police corruption and other abuses. Yet, there are connections as well. Day-to-day action taken by individuals and by organisations against corruption is often facilitated by institutions and mechanisms (Corruption Watch 2018).

Attending to the research of Charles Epp on law reform campaigns is helpful to enhance understandings of the specific legal character of this mobilisation against state capture. A political scientist working in socio-legal or law and society studies, Epp focuses on the classic instances of campaigns for change led by or conducted on behalf of vulnerable, primarily identity-based groups targeting courts (Epp 1998, 2010). Drawing on research conducted in the US context, Epp (2008) has argued that the development of institutional support for social reform litigation and professional networks with an interest in legal responsibility have enhanced the capacity of courts to affect policy changes. In this view, the power of the courts lies not entirely (or perhaps not even primarily) in their institutional strength but instead in the impact that the courts and their surrounding infrastructure (including the legal profession and policy organisations) may jointly produce. Along these lines, Epp notes that 'if classic implementation studies focused on judicial power and bureaucratic evasion, a more recent body of research has focused on more diffuse signals from the judiciary in generating law-related perceptions and norms, and their role in mobilising advocacy coalitions and in generating pressure for normative conformity among other agencies and organisations' (2008, 3).

Legal mobilisation against state capture in South Africa fits the support structure/democratic infrastructure paradigm. Epp argues that 'the more fragmented and porous the institutional structure of a governing system, the greater the incentives for groups to turn to courts to achieve policy goals; the litigation strate-gies of disadvantaged groups, like other groups, reflect these incentives' (Epp 2008, 4). The fragile institutional capacity of the South African state to counter corruption forced – or at least facilitated – the turn to court-based litigation by forces wishing to counter state capture and tackle the problem of corruption.

As shown above, the character of South Africa's collective legal mobilisation against state capture went well beyond the paradigm of strategic or impact litiga-tion (Klaaren, Dugard and Handmaker 2011). The actors in the legal campaigns described in this chapter did not see the state as an obstacle, requiring those actors to adopt the stance of a combatant with the state. Instead, the state was temporar-ily absent or put out of action. Indeed, the actors saw the need (Fowkes 2016) to restore the permanent infrastructure of the state (Von Schnitzler 2016). This com-bination of the temporary and the permanent allowed public interest law organ-isations to readily adopt creative and collaborative strategies to (either tacitly or explicitly) join up with those elements of the bureaucracy able to participate. The collaborations with state officials were critical to the successes in litigation enjoyed by these campaigns. The use of litigation within mobilisation is appropriately understood as collective action beyond impact litigation (Fowkes 2016; Friedman 2019; Klaaren 2020a).

There is support for this legal mobilisation perspective within constitutional legal scholarship as well. The work of South African constitutional scholars focus-ing on building constitutional infrastructures fits with this understanding about the interrelationships among personal action, institutional logics and social movement campaigns. Heinz Klug points out how the existence of a combination of 'integrity institutions' (including the Public Protector) was a significant factor in the ability of individuals, non-governmental organisations and opposition parties to 'temper' the abuse of power that had begun to undermine the post-apartheid democracy (Klug 2019). Aiming at 'self-dealing' by elected public representatives that threatens the republican institutions of democratic self-government, Firoz Cachalia has found a precautionary anti-corruption principle justified on political process grounds in recent decisions of the Constitutional Court (Cachalia 2019). The articulation and validation of such a principle by the highest court in the land can encourage individuals and organisations within civil society. James Fowkes (2016) has theo-rised the crucial role of infrastructures – mechanisms for implementing judicial decisions – in building South Africa's Constitution by the Constitutional Court. In his view, where the 'official institutional infrastructure cannot, for one or other reason, be relied on to some degree, the presence of civil society groups can be vital because they can serve as temporary infrastructure' (Fowkes 2016, 222). Given the situational ascendancy of state capture's shadow state over the official bureaucracy, civil society played a vital and interactive infrastructural role with the courts.

REFLECTIONS

This chapter has noted the increasingly prominent place of business in civil society mobilisation through the law. An extensive review of this exceeds this chapter's ability to track the history of organised business's policy stance towards corruption. One episode within that history would comprise the corruption uncovered by the competition authorities in the construction of football stadiums for South Africa's hosting of the 2010 FIFA World Cup. This research is worth pursuing, given the significance of the business sector within the South African political economy and the dominant narratives constitutive of South African politics (Klaaren 2019). Both the mobilisation against and the state capture phenomenon itself raise questions of public and private division. From both directions, it appears that there is a substantial blurring of this line. This seems to be a feature of the operation of the political economy in the global South (Dubash and Morgan 2013), which may lead to other lines of research, even in fields as distinct as innovation studies. There may be a parallel worth exploring between the (arguably pragmatic) mixing of public and private in development discourse and the horizontal application of human rights in the South African discourse (Knorringa 2010). As South Africa moves away from party pre-eminence, the substance of political coalitions put together in this public/private mode looks more and more like the form of a transaction. Perhaps the work and tools of competition lawyers could be put to good use in engineering powerful and lasting coalitions aiming to fulfil the Constitution (Law and Calland 2018).

A second reflection begins with the observation that traditional public interest law groups were on the sidelines of the state capture fight. A theme of this chapter has been to note the emergence of new civil society actors and their participation in effective coalitions (Bracking 2018). In the fight against state capture, the public interest organisations were the new kids on the block, eclipsing the anti-apartheid stalwarts. This leads to several questions. Has the emergence of public interest law organisations led to a post-apartheid division of labour within the public interest law firm sector? How did the effective hybrid collaborations, such as that between Freedom Under Law, the Centre for Applied Legal Studies and the Black Sash, come together and cohere (Mottiar and Lodge 2020)? There are powerful reasons to answer these questions. On one understanding of the rule-of-law concept – seeing it as a historical complex engendered by the actions of those inside and outside the legal sector – the culture of the rule of law in South Africa may be credited with cat-alysing some of the litigation undertaken against state capture. Does the litigation undertaken by the new entrants to legal mobilisation represent a meaningful new phase in the construction of the rule of law in South Africa?

Finally, it is worth noting that the depiction of the role of law in collective legal mobilisation in this chapter has been optimistic and positive – fostering political mobilisation against corruption. This differs from accounts of the role of law that emphasise their character as negative lawfare – a never-ending slog of expensive and time-consuming litigation leading nowhere. Both accounts can be equally valid. For example, a recent study of instability in a South African municipal-ity has observed that 'actions that advance factional ends are often undertaken through legalistic appeals to legislation, regulations and administrative protocol, seeking to bestow particular courses of action with the legitimacy of an "action of state"' (Phadi, Pearson and Lesaffre 2018, 604). As demonstrated in this chapter, the careful investigation of the role(s) of law in countering and advancing the phenomenon of corruption and the political project of state capture is an impor-tant task.

NOTE

1   An initial version of this chapter was presented in Leiden at the Law and Development Research Network in 2018 and at the Public Affairs Research Institute conference 'State Capture and Its Aftermath: Building Responsiveness through State Reform', 22–24 October 2018. It has benefited from comments from Firoz Cachalia, Rudolph Mastenbroek and others.

REFERENCES

Abel, Richard L. 1995. *Politics by Other Means: Law in the Struggle against Apartheid, 1980–1994*. New York: Routledge.

AllPay Consolidated Investment Holdings (Pty) Ltd and Others v CEO of the South African Social Security Agency and Others (678/12) [2013] ZASCA 29; [2013] 2 All SA 501 (SCA); 2013 (4) SA 557 (SCA). 27 March 2013.

AllPay Consolidated Investment Holdings (Pty) Ltd and Others v Chief Executive Officer of the South African Social Security Agency and Others (CCT 48/13) [2013] ZACC 42; 2014 (1) SA 604 (CC); 2014 (1) BCLR 1 (CC). 29 November 2013.

AllPay Consolidated Investment Holdings (Pty) Ltd and Others v Chief Executive Officer of the South African Social Security Agency and Others (No 2) [2014] ZACC 12; 2014 (6) BCLR 641 (CC); 2014 (4) SA 179 (CC). 17 April 2014.

AllPay Consolidated Investment Holdings (Pty) Ltd and Others v Chief Executive Officer of the South African Social Security Agency and Others [2015] ZACC 7. 2015.

Belvedere, Florencia. 2020. 'Appointments and Removals in Key Criminal Justice System Institutions'. Position Papers on State Reform, Public Affairs Research Institute, Johannesburg.

Black Sash Trust v Minister of Social Development and Others (Freedom Under Law NPC Intervening) (CCT48/17) [2017] ZACC 8. 17 March 2017.

Bracking, Sarah. 2018. 'Corruption & State Capture: What Can Citizens Do?' *Daedalus* 147, no. 3: 169–183. https://direct.mit.edu/daed/article/147/3/169/27204/Corruption-amp-State-Capture-What-Can-Citizens-Do.

Breytenbach, Glynnis. 2018. 'We Should Be Considering Constitutional Amendments to Ensure an Independent NPA'. *Daily Maverick*, 21 August 2018. https://www.dailymaverick.co.za/article/2018-08-21-we-should-be-considering-constitutional-amendments-to-ensure-an-independent-npa/.

Cachalia, Firoz. 2019. 'Precautionary Constitutionalism, Representative Democracy and Political Corruption'. *Constitutional Court Review* 9: 45–79. http://www.saflii.org/za/journals/CCR/2019/3.pdf.

CASAC. 2018. 'About CASAC'. https://www.casac.org.za/about-casac-2/.

CEO of the South African Social Security Agency N.O and Other v Cash Paymaster Services (Pty) Ltd (90/10) [2011] ZASCA 13; [2011] 3 All SA 233 (SCA); 2012 (1) SA 216 (SCA). 11 March 2011.

Chipkin, Ivor. 2018. 'The End of Tyranny: How Civil Society in South Africa Fought Back'. In *Rising to the Populist Challenge: A New Playbook for Human Rights Actors*, edited by César Rodríguez-Garavito and Krizna Gomez, 101–112. Bogotá: Dejusticia.

Chipkin, Ivor and Mark Swilling. 2018. *Shadow State: The Politics of State Capture*. Johannesburg: Wits University Press.

Corruption Watch. 2018. 'National Anti-Corruption Strategy: What's It About?' *Corruption Watch*, 5 July 2018. https://www.corruptionwatch.org.za/national-anti-corruption-strategy-overview/.

Corruption Watch NPC and Others v President of the Republic of South Africa and Others; Nxasana v Corruption Watch NPC and Others (CCT 333/17; CCT 13/18) [2018] ZACC 23. 13 August 2018.

Democratic Alliance v President of South Africa and Others (CCT 122/11) [2012] ZACC 24; 2012 (12) BCLR 1297 (CC); 2013 (1) SA 248 (CC). 5 October 2012.

Dubash, Navroz K. and Bronwen Morgan. 2013. *The Rise of the Regulatory State of the South: Infrastructure and Development in Emerging Economies*. Oxford: Oxford University Press.

Economic Freedom Fighters v Speaker of the National Assembly and Others; Democratic Alliance v Speaker of the National Assembly and Others (CCT 143/15; CCT 171/15) [2016] ZACC 11; 2016 (5) BCLR 618 (CC); 2016 (3) SA 580 (CC). 31 March 2016.

Epp, Charles R. 1998. *The Rights Revolution: Lawyers, Activists, and Supreme Courts in Comparative Perspective*. Chicago: University of Chicago Press.

Epp, Charles R. 2008. 'Law as an Instrument of Social Reform'. In *The Oxford Handbook of Law and Politics*, edited by Keith E. Whittington, R. Daniel Kelemen and Gregory A. Caldeira. Oxford: Oxford University Press.

Epp, Charles R. 2010. *Making Rights Real: Activists, Bureaucrats, and the Creation of the Legalistic State*. Chicago: University of Chicago Press.

Feinstein, Andrew, Paul Holden and Hennie van Vuuren. 2014. 'We're Withdrawing from the Arms Procurement Commission and Here's Why'. *Daily Maverick*, 29 August 2014. https://www.dailymaverick.co.za/article/2014-08-29-op-ed-were-withdrawing-from-the-arms-procurement-commission-and-heres-why/.

Foley, Robyn and Mark Swilling. 2018. 'How One Word Can Change the Game: Case Study of State Capture and the South African Social Security Agency'. State Capacity Research Project, Research Report, Centre for Complex Systems in Transition, Stellenbosch University. https://www0.sun.ac.za/cst/publication/how-one-word-can-change-the-game-a-case-study-of-state-capture-and-the-south-african-social-security-agency-sassa/.

Fowkes, James. 2016. *Building the Constitution*. Cambridge: Cambridge University Press.

Friedman, Steven. 2018. 'Trump's Comment about South Africa Is a Reminder That Race Still Matters'. *The Conversation*, 28 August 2018. http://theconversation.com/trumps-comment-about-south-africa-is-a-reminder-that-race-still-matters-102212.

Friedman, Steven. 2019. *Power in Action: Democracy, Citizenship and Social Justice*. Johannesburg: Wits University Press.

Garth, Bryant G. and Mauro Cappelletti. 1978. 'Access to Justice: The Newest Wave in the Worldwide Movement to Make Rights Effective'. *Buffalo Law Review* 27: 181–292. https://www.repository.law.indiana.edu/facpub/1142/.

Ginwala Commission of Enquiry. 2008. 'Report of the Enquiry into the Fitness of Advocate VP Pikoli to Hold the Office of National Director of Public Prosecutions (Ginwala Report)'. November 2008. https://www.gov.za/sites/default/files/gcis_document/201409/ginwalareport1.pdf.

Glenister v President of the Republic of South Africa and Others (CCT 48/10) [2011] ZACC 6; 2011 (3) SA 347 (CC); 2011 (7) BCLR 651 (CC). 17 March 2011.

Hoffman, Paul. 2017. 'Combating Corruption at the Coalface in the Courts: Jurisprudential Gems Mined in Braamfontein'. Fifth Stellenbosch Annual Seminar on Constitutionalism in Africa, 20 September 2017, Institute for Advanced Study, University of Stellenbosch.

Klaaren, Jonathan. 2005. 'SA Human Rights Commission'. In *Constitutional Law of South Africa*, edited by Stuart Woolman, Michael Bishop and Jason Brickhill, 24C. Cape Town: Juta & Co.

Klaaren, Jonathan. 2019. 'Laying the Table: The Role of Business in Establishing Competition Law and Policy in South Africa'. *International Review of Applied Economics* 33, no. 1: 119–133. https://www.tandfonline.com/doi/full/10.1080/02692171.2019.1524034.

Klaaren, Jonathan. 2020a. 'Regulatory Politics in South Africa 25 Years after Apartheid'. *Journal of Asian and African Studies* 56, no. 1: 79–91. https://journals.sagepub.com/doi/full/10.1177/0021909620946852.

Klaaren, Jonathan. 2020b. 'Social Grant Payments and Regulatory Responses to Corruption in South Africa'. In *Corruption and Constitutionalism in Africa: Revisiting Control Measures and Strategies*, edited by Charles M. Fombad and Nico Steytler, 90–109. Oxford: Oxford University Press.

Klaaren, Jonathan. 2020c. 'South Africa: A Profession in Transformation'. In *Lawyers in 21st-Century Societies: Volume 1: National Reports*, edited by Richard L. Abel, Ole Hammerslev, Hilary Sommerlad and Ulrike Schultz, 535–546. London: Hart Publishing.

Klaaren, Jonathan, Jackie Dugard and Jeff Handmaker. 2011. 'Public Interest Litigation in South Africa: Special Issue Introduction'. *South African Journal on Human Rights* 27, no. 1: 1–7.

Klug, Heinz. 2019. 'Transformative Constitutions and the Role of Integrity Institutions in Tempering Power: The Case of Resistance to State Capture in Post-Apartheid South Africa'. *Buffalo Law Review* 67, no. 3: 701–742. https://digitalcommons.law.buffalo.edu/buffalolawreview/vol67/iss3/15/.

Knorringa, Peter. 2010. 'A Balancing Act: Private Actors in Development Processes'. Inaugural Lecture, International Institute of Social Studies, Erasmus University Rotterdam. https://repub.eur.nl/pub/22268/.

Law, Mike and Richard Calland. 2018. 'South Africa Is Learning the Ropes of Coalition Politics – and Its Inherent Instability'. *The Conversation*, 13 May 2018. http://theconversation.com/south-africa-is-learning-the-ropes-of-coalition-politics-and-its-inherent-instability-96483.

Marchant, Michael, Mamello Mosiana, Paul Holden and Hennie van Vuuren. 2020. 'The Enablers: The Bankers, Accountants and Lawyers That Cashed in on State Capture'. *Open Secrets*, February 2020. https://www.opensecrets.org.za/the-enablers/.

Maree, Johann. 2019. 'The Durban Moment: Turning Temporary Worker Action into a Permanent Democratic Trade Union Movement … and Then …?' *Transformation* 100, no. 1: 53 –77. https://muse.jhu.edu/article/745582/pdf.

Maughan, Karyn. 2018. 'Cyril Ramaphosa in Major Shift Asking Panel to Help Find Shaun Abrahams's Replacement'. *Business Day*, 10 October 2018. https://www.businesslive.co.za/bd/national/2018-10-10-cyril-ramaphosa-in-major-shift-asking-panel-to-help-find-shaun-abrahams-replacement/.

Mottiar, Shauna and Tom Lodge. 2020. '"Living inside the Movement": The Right2Know Campaign, South Africa'. *Transformation* 102, no. 1: 95–120. https://muse.jhu.edu/article/752989.

Nielsen, Laura Beth, Robert L. Nelson and Ryon Lancaster. 2010. 'Individual Justice or Collective Legal Mobilization? Employment Discrimination Litigation in the Post Civil Rights United States'. *Journal of Empirical Legal Studies* 7, no. 2: 175–201. https://www.americanbarfoundation.org/uploads/cms/documents/jels_final.pdf.

PARI. 2017. 'Betrayal of the Promise: How South Africa Is Being Stolen'. State Capacity Research Project Report, Public Affairs Research Institute, Johannesburg. https://pari.org.za/betrayal-promise-report/.

Phadi, Mosa, Joel Pearson and Thomas Lesaffre. 2018. 'The Seeds of Perpetual Instability: The Case of Mogalakwena Local Municipality in South Africa'. *Journal of Southern African Studies* 44, no. 4: 593–611. https://www.tandfonline.com/doi/full/10.1080/03057070.2018.1464301.

Pityana, Sipho. 2016. 'Speech at Stofile Funeral'. *News24*, 26 August 2016. https://www.news24.com/SouthAfrica/News/text-sipho-pityana-speech-at-stofile-funeral-20160826.

Public Protector. 2016. 'State of Capture'. Report No. 6 of 2016/17, 14 October 2016. http://www.pprotect.org/sites/default/files/legislation_report/State_Capture_14October2016.pdf.

Quintal, Genevieve. 2019. 'Jacob Zuma Is Too Sick to Appear at Zondo Inquiry Next Week'. *Business Day*, 5 November 2019. https://www.businesslive.co.za/bd/national/2019-11-05-jacob-zuma-is-too-sick-to-appear-at-zondo-inquiry-next-week/.

Robins, Steven L. 2008. *From Revolution to Rights in South Africa: Social Movements, NGOs and Popular Politics after Apartheid*. Woodbridge: Boydell & Brewer.

Swilling, Mark. 2019. 'State Capture Commission Awaits a Star Witness – Jacob Zuma'. *News24*, 14 July 2019. https://www.news24.com/Analysis/state-capture-commission-awaits-a-star-witness-jacob-zuma-20190714.

Thamm, Marianne. 2017. 'State Capture: Helen Suzman Foundation and Magda Wierzycka Sue President Zuma and 74 Others'. *Daily Maverick*, 15 December 2017. https://www.dailymaverick.co.za/article/2017-12-15-state-capture-helen-suzman-foundation-and-magda-wierzycka-sue-president-zuma-and-74-others/.

Thamm, Marianne. 2018. 'Anti-Corruption Watchdogs Call for Integrity Commission for the Hawks'. *Daily Maverick*, 27 September 2018. https://www.dailymaverick.co.za/article/2018-09-27-anti-corruption-watchdogs-call-for-integrity-commission-for-the-hawks/.

Van Wyk, Pauli. 2018a. 'Hogan Lovells Went out of Their Way Not to Investigate SARS' Jonas Makwakwa, Documents Show'. *Daily Maverick*, 15 May 2018. https://www.dailymaverick.co.za/article/2018-05-15-hogan-lovells-went-out-of-their-way-not-to-investigate-sars-jonas-makwakwa-documents-show/.

Van Wyk, Pauli. 2018b. 'Scorpio Analysis: KPMG and Hogan Lovells Still Have Much SARSplaining to Do'. *Daily Maverick*, 24 May 2018. https://www.dailymaverick.co.za/article/2018-05-24-kpmg-and-hogan-lovells-still-have-much-sarsplaining-to-do/.

Von Schnitzler, Antina. 2016. *Democracy's Infrastructure: Techno-Politics and Protest after Apartheid*. Princeton: Princeton University Press.

5

How Professionals Enabled State Capture

Cherese Thakur and Devi Pillay

Capturing a state is neither simple nor easy. It is an enterprise with many moving parts: deals to be made, illicit funds to be channelled, tracks to be covered, and regulators and watchdogs to be dodged. Such a project needs assistance from people with a special set of attributes: people who possess skills, knowledge and a questionable degree of commitment to integrity and ethics. This is where professional enablers played a role – the lawyers, auditors, consultants and others who used their expertise to oil the wheels of state capture in South Africa.

The average consumer of news media will be familiar with the names of high-ranking public officials implicated in state capture as well as those with whom, it is alleged, they concluded improper deals, including former president Jacob Zuma, former Free State premier Ace Magashule, and businesspeople Gavin Watson and the Gupta brothers Ajay, Atul and Rajesh. Less familiar are the names of those who facilitated such transactions. With a few notable exceptions, they have escaped scrutiny. Some of those exposed for their misdeeds have embarked on reputation rehabilitation campaigns but they have, by and large, avoided any serious dent to their operations.

Any account of state capture would be incomplete without a serious analysis of how professionals were able to ensure that the plans to decimate state institutions for private gain were carried out.

It is helpful to examine these actors through the lens of 'professionalism'. This is because the designation 'professional', though shifting, has acquired a certain lustre. There is a sense – undoubtedly cultivated by professionals themselves – that the established professions, such as law and accounting (and newer ones, such as consulting), are set apart from other occupations (McDonald 1995, 29). This sense of deference can be harmful to the public good.

WHAT IS A PROFESSIONAL?

To understand why it is important to single out professionals when attempting to make sense of state capture, we must consider what is meant by a 'profession' and a 'professional'. Two disclaimers: first, the study of the sociology of professions is vast, diverse and largely rejects neat classifications; and second, it is not possible to provide more than a brief snapshot of what is at issue.

The twentieth century has been described as a 'golden age of professions'. At that time, the term referred almost exclusively to the 'traditional' professions, such as law, medicine, accounting and engineering. They enjoyed benefits such as a higher degree of social status and, to some extent, greater earnings than other workers (Gorman and Sandefur 2011, 277).

It was also an age in which a great deal of study was dedicated to professions (Gorman and Sandefur 2011). Many scholars tried to establish a set of criteria that could be used to distinguish professionals from other occupations. Due to a lack of consensus, they were not wholly successful. The criteria that did emerge included the following: expert knowledge, technical autonomy, a normative orientation towards the service of others, higher social status and greater financial reward (Gorman and Sandefur 2011).

Expert knowledge is obtained through years of (often costly) dedicated study. Professional competence is established through qualifying examinations, which are necessary to gain entry to the profession. Technical autonomy refers to the control that professions exert over knowledge (Gorman and Sandefur 2011), conduct that has been described as 'gatekeeping' and 'monopolistic' (Young and Muller 2014, 4). For instance, while any person with means may access the body of statutes and case law, lawyers claim that they are uniquely placed to find, analyse and draw conclusions about the law, and so solve legal problems. For this service, their clients pay a premium.

Professionals, it is claimed, should execute their duties in the service of others (Pandey 1985). Professionals are required to abide by elevated ethical standards and allow themselves to be governed by codes of conduct. Accordingly, they should be held 'to account' if they fall below prescribed standards of behaviour. Lastly, there is little doubt that the preceding three items have led to a number of professions enjoying prestige – and earning a higher income – in comparison to other occupations. However, these criteria do not unambiguously distinguish professions from other specialist occupations (Young and Muller 2014). They do not capture the structural or institutional features of professions, which includes the establishment and maintenance of collegial formations as reflected in an ongoing commitment to a set of agreed-upon professional norms (Sciulli 2005). Thus, professionals organise and regulate themselves under 'professional bodies', structures that potentially set them apart from other forms of work.

The contested meaning of 'professional' is demonstrated by the continuing debate on whether management consulting falls within the classification. The history of management consulting is deeply intertwined with that of the other traditional professions (McKenna 1995), and many would regard its professional status as a fait accompli. Nevertheless, many business and consulting experts would answer the question with a firm 'not yet' (Greiner and Ennsfellner 2008). In order for management consultants to be considered professionals, the occupation would need to meet certain standards, including additional training and certification beyond on-the-job training and a greater focus on consulting-specific courses. Experts argue that the sole accreditation organisation for consultants – the International Council of Management Consulting Institutes – should take steps to achieve greater legitimisation of its work. Moreover, clients should hold management consultants to account for substandard work, and greater research into consultant effectiveness should be conducted (Greiner and Ennsfellner 2008).

Notwithstanding this arguably weaker claim to the designation of 'a profession' as against lawyers, auditors and accountants, this chapter will include management consultants under the rubric of professional. In the context of state capture, they appear to have played a similar role.

HOW HAVE PROFESSIONALS FURTHERED STATE CAPTURE?

Thanks to whistleblowers, investigative journalists and other individuals concerned with exposing corruption, many irregular actions by auditors, accountants, management consultants and lawyers have come to light. These, however, are likely only to have scratched the surface of the true extent of their involvement in state capture. After all, professionals are skilled at concealing their affairs from public scrutiny, for instance by making sure that staff and suppliers are bound by confidentiality agreements. Those firms that are exposed are well-resourced enough to call on public relations consultants and legal advisers to minimise reputational damage and shield them from adverse consequences.

Nevertheless, some allegations are just too serious to cover up. What follows is a discussion of the various instances where professional services firms drew criticism for their dubious conduct in South Africa.

Auditing and Accounting

Some of the most serious allegations have been levelled against the auditing profession for its involvement in state capture through grand-scale corporate malfeasance. In particular, the 'Big Four' auditing firms – KPMG, PricewaterhouseCoopers (PwC), Deloitte and Ernst & Young – have faced scrutiny. These firms have burnished histories and broad international footprints; their service offerings have expanded over the years to include tax and legal advice, management consulting, entrepreneurial advice, risk consulting and much more. They purportedly recruit the best and the brightest from top universities, and carefully cultivate their reputations as a prestigious addition to the CV of any aspirant professional. All of this has contributed to the great degree of public trust in their professionalism. If it was signed off by one of the Big Four, the thinking goes, it must be above board. This notion has been patently disproven by state capture.

KPMG has sustained the most severe blow to its reputation. In 2019, a KPMG director, Jacques Wessels, was struck off the register of auditors by the Independent Regulatory Board for Auditors (IRBA) after he was found guilty of misconduct (IRBA 2019). This was in relation to his audit work for Linkway Trading, a Gupta-linked company that was accused of diverting money from the Estina dairy project to pay for the R30-million wedding at Sun City hosted by the Gupta family in 2013. Wessels was found guilty of contravening the IRBA's rules in many respects, including failures to investigate unusual transactions, failing to comply with rules aimed at preventing money laundering and dishonestly restating the financial statements of Linkway to characterise wedding expenses as 'cost of sales'. These expenses were erroneously treated as an unspecified tax-deductible, costing the South African Revenue Service (SARS) more than R2 million. Further, Wessels had exercised poor professional judgement in accepting the Guptas' invitation to attend the wedding (IRBA 2019).

KPMG was allegedly involved in the manipulation of the valuation of one of the Gupta-linked companies, Oakbay Resources and Energy Limited, at the time of that company's listing on the Johannesburg Stock Exchange (JSE). This was ostensibly done in order to avoid repaying a massive loan from the Industrial Development Corporation by providing shares in lieu of payment. It was later alleged that the share price was fixed (AmaBhungane and Scorpio 2017). The firm was also responsible for the 'Rogue Unit' report (Open Secrets 2020b), which erroneously claimed that an unauthorised unit was operating within SARS under the control of then minister of finance Pravin Gordhan. Gordhan was later ousted from his position, in part due to this report (Hosken 2017). These events profoundly damaged the institution, especially after a number of SARS executives and investigators were suspended and removed from their positions. KPMG retracted the report and indicated that it would pay 'some kind of reparations' to affected SARS employees (Wicks 2020). In addition, the firm undertook to pay back the R23 million it had received to compile the report (Du Toit and Cowan 2020).

KPMG auditor Sipho Malaba was criminally charged in June 2020 for contraventions of the Prevention of Organised Crime Act of 1998. He is alleged to have concealed fraud at VBS Mutual Bank by issuing an unqualified audit opinion despite patent irregularities. In return, he received soft loans to the tune of R33.9 million, which he spent on luxury cars, properties and settling debt (Van Wyk 2020).

The fallout has been dramatic. The KPMG CEO, Trevor Hoole, resigned. Later, the resignation of the chairperson of the board, Ahmed Jaffer, as well as that of several partners, was announced without explanation, and several clients reviewed and terminated KPMG's services. KPMG 'lost a third of its R3-billion annual revenue in the wake of the scandal', and its 'workforce had shrunk from 3,400 to 2,200' (Heard and Kleyn 2020). Later, the Auditor-General ended its relationship with KPMG, meaning that the firm could no longer conduct audits of government institutions. Even its pledge to donate some R40 million to non-profit organisations has not fully rehabilitated KPMG's reputation (Omarjee 2018).

KPMG is not the only auditing firm implicated in state capture. Deloitte's consulting arm was alleged to have secured lucrative contracts with Eskom worth R207 million outside of prescribed procurement processes. Deloitte later agreed to pay back R150 million after reaching a settlement with Eskom. While they denied involvement in state capture, Deloitte conceded that there were technical irregularities in the procurement process (Open Secrets 2020a).

Deloitte's audit work has been called into question in three prominent private sector scandals. The first, concerning Deloitte's signing-off on an audit of African Bank in 2013, was the subject of a two-year disciplinary hearing by the IRBA that concluded in June 2020. Deloitte was charged with having disregarded its own report flagging concerns about the bank's overestimation of its cash flow forecasts

(Buthelezi 2020). The IRBA argued that this led to material misstatements in the bank's financial statements. This, in turn, misled investors who had taken these statements as evidence of its financial health when the opposite was true (Brown 2020). African Bank collapsed and was placed under curatorship in 2014.

The so-called Steinhoff scandal has also seen Deloitte appear before the IRBA. Its auditors failed to detect accounting irregularities calculated to enrich executives, which resulted in its profits being misrepresented to the tune of R100 billion. Despite this, Deloitte issued unqualified audit opinions (Open Secrets 2020a). The IRBA's investigation into this matter was continuing at the time of writing. Furthermore, Deloitte failed to pick up on Tongaat Hulett's massive overstatement of assets in its 2018 financial statements (Open Secrets 2020a). If shareholders had been alerted to the gross mismanagement taking place, they might have been able to intervene – potentially avoiding a R12-billion write-off in equity (Crotty 2020).

While these lapses concerned private entities, the impact on the public was profound: about 1.7 million current and retired state workers, for instance, were estimated to have lost R11.57 billion in pension fund value following the collapse of Steinhoff (Mahlaka 2019). Investors in Tongaat Hulett would have been prejudiced in a similar way (Open Secrets 2020a).

PwC has also found itself in hot water. In July 2020, PwC was called to testify before the Zondo Commission regarding its irregular provision of services to South African Airways (SAA) for a five-year period after it had initially been appointed for a year alongside Nkonki – an auditing firm acquired by Gupta associate Salim Essa. In addition, there was a significant conflict of interest between PwC and Yakhe Kwinana, a member of the SAA board. PwC and Nkonki gave clean audits to SAA for five consecutive years between 2012 and 2016. During this period, SAA was in a state of dramatic financial decline. The board was engaging in acts of corruption and fraud, and the company's governance structures were in shambles. None of this was detected – or reported – by its auditors.

When the Auditor-General took over the auditing in 2016, it found SAA's records and accounting practices in chaos, with poor internal controls and record-keeping, and severe under-capacitation. Compliance with legislation was critically weak and irregular, and wasteful expenditure was high. In addition, there were no consequences imposed for multiple transgressions of proper processes. These systemic problems should have been apparent to any attentive auditor. If these problems had been identified and reported – as they should have been, according to the Public Audit Act – SAA might be in a better position today.

It bears noting that PwC supplied internal auditors to VBS Mutual Bank during the period when its financials were grossly misstated. PwC denies that its scope of work extended to the detection of fraud (Donnelly 2018). Nonetheless, the IRBA instituted an investigation into the internal auditor at VBS (IRBA 2018).

Law

Perhaps the most prominent law firm implicated in unethical dealings is Hogan Lovells, an international firm with a South Africa-based operation. The firm was commissioned by SARS to produce a report on the conduct of Jonas Makwakwa, the former chief officer for business and individual taxes. Makwakwa was accused of money laundering after R1.7 million in cash deposits into his bank account was flagged as suspicious by the Financial Intelligence Centre. The Hogan Lovells report was used by the then SARS commissioner, Tom Moyane, to clear Makwakwa of wrongdoing and return him to his post. Moyane himself was later removed from office by President Cyril Ramaphosa, following recommendations in the interim report issued by Judge Robert Nugent in his role as chair of the Commission of Inquiry into Tax Administration and Governance by SARS (the Nugent Commission).

Hogan Lovells claimed that it was not mandated to consider any criminal wrongdoing – rather, it was charged with investigating malfeasance in an employment context. This was not enough to prevent vehement criticism of the firm by the British peer Lord Peter Hain. He brought a complaint against the firm with the Solicitors Regulation Authority in the United Kingdom. The Solicitors Regulation Authority decided not to take regulatory action against Hogan Lovells – a result, Hain argued, based on a 'technicality in that it relied on the fact that the UK firm did not "control" the South African firm' (Cameron 2018). Following this decision, the firm alerted the Law Society of the Northern Provinces in South Africa to the issue. A ruling was made clearing it of unprofessional conduct in relation to the report.

Although Hogan Lovells was cleared by two regulatory authorities, its reputation has undoubtedly been coloured by its involvement in compiling the report for SARS. Failures of governance at SARS have had a tangible, real-world effect on South African citizens, most notably through poor tax collection, which was cited as one of the reasons for the first value-added tax increase in 25 years (BusinessTech 2018).

The second scandal concerned the conduct of a lawyer, which came to light after he had left the firm. The partner, Brian Biebuyck, was implicated in corrupt dealings with government officials by former Bosasa chief operating officer Angelo Agrizzi in his testimony before the Zondo Commission. Hogan Lovells expressed its shock following Agrizzi's testimony and vowed to report criminal conduct to the authorities (News24 2019). It bears asking: if Biebuyck's involvement in Bosasa transactions could go undetected at a large, well-resourced, internationally linked firm like Hogan Lovells, what misconduct by lawyers has not come to light?

Lawyers have furthermore been criticised for a practice that is technically legal but hugely damaging to the proper operation of justice: the so-called Stalingrad defence strategy. This strategy aims to interminably drag out court matters by raising procedural and other technical points at every turn (Moyo v Minister of Justice and Constitutional Development and Others 2018). This is regularly used in criminal cases but has also been used to frustrate civil litigation and disciplinary proceedings. These tactics cause legal costs to mount for the plaintiff, further stalling or even preventing outright the merits of the matter from seeing the light of day.

The legal profession could do more to push back against this strategy. One way is for judicial officers to come down strongly against lawyers where it is apparent that challenges are brought to delay rather than to raise a valid legal issue. This can be done through censure in the judge's written reasons and, in extreme cases, adverse costs orders. Another way is for legal practitioners to be held accountable by the Legal Practice Council for contraventions of its code of conduct, which provides that 'a legal practitioner shall not abuse or permit abuse of the process of court or tribunal and shall act in a manner that shall promote and advance the efficacy of the legal process' (Legal Practice Council 2019, 48).

Management Consulting

As we have established, management consulting is arguably a non-traditional member of the professions. By at least one account, management consulting emerged from the activities of other professionals, such as engineers, accountants and lawyers, to provide guidance to businesses (McKenna 1995). While these firms may source their staff from these fields, they have developed far beyond these modest roots, becoming world-shaping behemoths that steer the strategies of large corporations and public institutions.

The prime example of disastrous management consultant intervention in public administration must be the restructuring of SARS by Bain & Company, which took place between 2014 and 2018. The awarding of the tender to Bain was described as a 'procurement sham'. The Nugent Commission report noted that Bain's bid was submitted just one day after the bids were opened. It concluded that Bain 'certainly' had prior knowledge of the bid and indeed was its 'architect'. Top Bain executive Vittorio Massone had cultivated a relationship with Tom Moyane prior to the latter's appointment to the leadership of SARS, an arrangement that served both 'Mr. Moyane's interests in taking control of SARS, and Bain's interest in making money' (Nugent 2018, 46–47).

And then there is McKinsey & Company. According to its website, this global management consulting giant lauds itself as having 'exceptional people in 65 countries' and 'combin[ing] global expertise and local insight to help you turn your ambitious goals into reality'. The two key projects that have compromised McKinsey in South Africa were certainly ambitious but for all the wrong reasons. The first concerned its contract with the embattled power utility Eskom. McKinsey sought to provide advice to develop Eskom's internal project management and engineering capacity – but the tender was awarded in the absence of a competitive bidding process (Bezuidenhout 2019). In addition, the contract was made on a 'no fee, at risk' basis, which meant that McKinsey would be able to claim a cut of savings made by Eskom as a result of its strategies. Eskom did not obtain the required authorisation from the Treasury prior to signing with McKinsey. Of concern was that McKinsey would calculate the savings. Kevin Sneader, global managing partner of McKinsey, later acknowledged that its approach led to a fee that was 'too large' – almost R1 billion – in that it was 'weighted towards recovering our investment rather than being in line with Eskom's situation' (Sneader 2018). The firm has since repaid the fees to Eskom.

The second project was linked to Transnet's acquisition of 1 064 locomotives. The procurement process was beset by irregularities and many of the transactions involved were part of an elaborate kickback scheme. McKinsey established a relationship with controversial Gupta-linked firm Regiments Capital, which was at the centre of state capture at Transnet. McKinsey avers that it withdrew before the tender was awarded and denied involvement with Regiments' rewrite of the business case of the transaction, which resulted in a R16-billion cost escalation. Yet, despite misgivings that McKinsey had about Regiments, it failed to terminate the business relationship until 2016 (Open Secrets 2020c).

Testimony before the Zondo Commission showed that McKinsey secured contracts with Transnet to the value of some R2.1 billion without going through ordinary competitive tender processes. This was enabled by former Transnet CEO Brian Molefe, who created 'a situation of urgency and emergency' to allow for multiple limited tenders (Sokutu 2019), and who parcelled out the mammoth deal into smaller ones to avoid scrutiny (Bezuidenhout 2019).

The reputational damage sustained by both Bain and McKinsey has rippled throughout their operations internationally. (McKinsey, though, has faced a number of scandals in different jurisdictions and emerged relatively unscathed.) The bitter pill for the South African public is that these firms appear to have evaded accountability by public authorities. Unless criminal sanctions are brought – in which case a higher burden of proof will apply – all those consultants who are guilty, at least, of significant lapses of judgement, or of engaging in the wilful decimation of state institutions, at most, will come away with little more than bruised reputations.

Other Professions

While auditors, lawyers and management consultants have faced the brunt of state capture scandals, other 'professionals' across the state and private sector have been implicated. Bankers and financial advisers are professionals with ethical standards in addition to statutory responsibilities. They have to comply with anti-corruption and anti-money laundering legislation and are required to know their customers and perform due diligence. Nedbank, HSBC and the Bank of Baroda have come under fire for their failure to detect suspicious transactions related to state capture – and for their alleged direct involvement in fraud and money laundering (Marchant et al. 2020).

Communications and public relations specialists can also be considered professionals according to some criteria. They have professional associations such as the Public Relations and Communications Association (PRCA), the world's largest public relations body. In 2017, the PRCA terminated the membership of Bell Pottinger, which was at the time one of the largest and most reputable firms in the industry, for its role in state capture in South Africa (PRCA 2017).

WHAT IS TO BE DONE?

For those of the view that professionals should hold themselves to high standards of conduct, the description of this mounting malfeasance is alarming. We should remember there are systemic mechanisms at work that either reward such risk-taking to further the interest of powerful elites or do not deter such behaviour in any sufficient way. The question is: what is to be done to dismantle these mechanisms?

First, the provision of professional services should be grounded in ethics. Here, education, firm commitments and support are key. Professional independence should be safeguarded. Next, hard rules for professional conduct should be established and maintained. Oversight should be provided by an external, recognised body empowered to interpret and apply these rules. Where misconduct is proven, sanction should follow. On a much broader level, the state needs to reconfigure the manner in which it contracts with private sector professional services. We must reckon with the role played by politics in mediating these relationships. The professionalisation of the public administration will play a primary role in protecting state institutions going forward.

Transparency should be woven into all these processes. But it should not stop there: beneficial ownership transparency, whistleblower support and protection, procurement reform and other structural interventions are also critical and urgent areas for reform.

Ethics and Professional Independence

Professionals are often called upon to solve problems and to make judgement calls. This can involve navigating 'grey areas' where a course of action is not immediately apparent. In these circumstances, a firmly grounded understanding of ethics is indispensable. It allows for professionals to appreciate fully the stakes at play and understand the consequences of their actions. Training in ethics is a requirement that must be fulfilled prior to admission to the profession for chartered accountants and lawyers. However, this is not enough. Continued learning and assessment regarding ethical standards should be applied throughout the career of every professional. On a broader level, good leadership that embodies sound ethics in both word and action is essential. Professional firms must create robust internal systems to deter unethical behaviour. When making money is the overriding concern rather than the impact of the firm's actions on the public good, the door is opened to unethical conduct.

It is also important to consider structural and regulatory interventions to limit the opportunities for these grey areas to arise. All-service firms face conflicts of interest inherent in their business practice. These firms – KPMG, PwC and Deloitte – offer an array of services, including auditing, legal and consulting services. Auditors have certain professional standards: they must conduct independent oversight and are mandated to act on irregularities they identify. But they may be disincentivised to do so if their firms are simultaneously engaged in high-paying work for the same client, for fear of compromising those contracts. Furthermore, legal and financial advisers are routinely employed to help clients evade accountability – while the same company conducts their audits.

This is why the UK's Financial Reporting Council has ordered the Big Four accounting firms to break up their audit and non-audit operations by June 2024. South Africa has not issued any such instructions, but as part of its efforts to rehabilitate its image, KPMG South Africa stopped offering non-audit related services to the JSE-listed clients it audits in March 2021 (Buthelezi 2021). Independence is a key facet of professionalism and is indispensable for oversight work like auditing. Splitting the audit functions of large all-service firms could be one way to safeguard that independence.

Oversight by Professional Associations

One of the classic elements that set professions apart from other occupations is membership to professional associations, where admission is restricted to those who have met specified criteria. The association – at least in theory – has a vested interest in maintaining the status of the profession and will therefore monitor and enforce adherence to professional codes and standards. This gives the public reassurance that the professional in question has the requisite qualifications and experience necessary to render the service adequately. The professional consents to the association holding them accountable to that code of conduct, which can be enforced by the imposition of sanctions – including, of course, exclusion.

Historically, these associations emerged as a form of self-regulation (Millerson 1964), but, more recently, they have been regulated by legislation. Since 1 November 2018, the legal profession was brought under the control of a national regulatory body, the Legal Practice Council, which was established in terms of the Legal Practice Act of 2014, with a promulgated code of conduct.

The auditing profession is regulated by the Auditing Profession Act of 2005. The Act also establishes the IRBA, which confers accreditation upon registered auditors and auditing firms – and can terminate it. Compared to other professional bodies, the IRBA has extensive oversight powers. It does not have to wait for complaints to be brought to it – it is empowered to refer matters for investigation where it has a reasonable suspicion of improper conduct. The IRBA is also entitled to inspect or view the practices of registered auditors. Furthermore, auditors of public companies must be inspected at least every three years.

Chartered accountants are required to register with the South African Institute of Chartered Accountants and subject themselves to its code of conduct. Professional accountants are overseen by the South African Institute of Professional Accountants, which enforces its own code of conduct. However, self-styled accountants may operate without membership of any professional association, as long as they do not use specific designations such as a chartered accountant or professional accountant, and they do not deal in matters of taxation.

Management consultants and other 'newer' professions are not subject to professional oversight by an external body. While they may have internal ethics policies and codes of conduct, these are administered internally. Consequently, there is no information or even anonymised statistics regarding the number of complaints and investigations and their outcomes. This is a system conducive to cover-ups rather than accountability.

A relatively new player in the regulatory space that has shown signs of effectiveness is the Companies and Intellectual Property Commission (CIPC), which is responsible for the enforcement of the Companies Act of 2008. In 2018, the CIPC laid criminal complaints against KPMG, McKinsey and the software company SAP, alleging that they had contravened the Companies Act. These complaints are still with the South African Police Service, and CIPC declined to provide further elaboration as to progress on these matters at the time of writing. There has been criticism that CIPC was using its enforcement powers in a 'selective and opportunistic' manner (Mail & Guardian 2018).

Sanctions

Codes of conduct are ineffective unless they are backed by the threat of sanction. Sanctions can have varying degrees of severity, including admonishment, reprimand, the issuing of fines, restitution and exclusion from the profession (temporarily or permanently) or even criminal charges.

Imposing fines is an option available to the Legal Practice Council, the IRBA, the South African Institute of Chartered Accountants and the South African Institute of Professional Accountants. This type of sanction is flexible and can be adjusted to suit the severity of the crime. It offers a middle ground between the lenient sanction of reprimand and the severity of exclusion (Bené 1991). Many of the firms discussed here have been fined in a number of different jurisdictions. However, they are generally so profitable that fines pose no meaningful deterrent to unethical behaviour. Restitution, on the other hand, aims to restore justice rather than to punish. Its basic premise is simple: those who commit wrong should not benefit from their actions. Many believe that restitution is the bare minimum, which is probably why the repayment of fees by KPMG, Bain and McKinsey has not been effective in advancing accountability at these firms.

Exclusion from the profession through mechanisms such as disbarment or withdrawal of accreditation is a severe sanction applied in serious cases. This punishment serves the dual purpose of removing the offending party from further misconduct as well as deterring others from breaking the rules (Bené 1991). While individual professionals are sometimes expelled, firms rarely face this most serious of consequences. The sole example in the realm of state capture is the PRCA's termination of Bell Pottinger's membership, described above. Bell Pottinger collapsed less than a week after its expulsion.

Criminal sanctions are possible where the professional's conduct has extended to fraud, or the contravention of statutory law such as the Prevention of Organised Crime Act of 1998, the Prevention and Combating of Corrupt Activities Act of 2004, the Companies Act of 2008 or any other crime. This requires the collection of evidence by capable investigators and skilled prosecutors to run the matter. It is not an easy method to seek accountability for enabling malfeasance.

An important question is whether sanctions should be applied to individuals or to entire firms. The answer is both. Professional organisations should not be absolved of the responsibility to control and monitor each other's work by scapegoating individuals. In addition, firms should be held vicariously liable where it is not possible to pinpoint who was responsible, particularly since most work is done in teams (Schneyer 1991a, 1). Effective sanctions include fines, public censure (as their continuing success depends on their good reputation) and, in the most extreme cases, where there is a 'chronic and pervasive pattern of intentional wrongdoing', the dissolution of the firm (Schneyer 1991b, 125).

The State and the Private Sector

The state capture saga has made clear just how intimately involved private companies are with the core work of the state.

Evidence before the Zondo Commission has shown that state-owned entities time and again have paid millions for unnecessary advisory services – services for which there was sufficient internal expertise and capacity. This was often deliberate. At Transnet, for example, internal financial controls were sidelined so that work could be outsourced to McKinsey and Regiments. Executives and project leaders were pressured by their superiors to employ consultants they did not need. In other cases, professional companies were contracted and paid for work that had already been competently executed.

In the long run, this leads to institutional decline as skilled professionals leave, thereby stripping state entities of expertise and capacity, reinforcing the need to hire external help and entrenching outsourcing as the norm.

Then there is the matter of the quality of work done by external professional firms. Transnet paid millions to Regiments and Trillian for poor advice that led to costly and harmful business decisions. Their recommendations were based on incorrect facts, poor analysis and significant misrepresentations; these recommendations were adopted wholesale by Transnet executives. This pattern has been repeated across state institutions – Bain's work at SARS is another example. This low-quality work can be incidental, or it can be done deliberately in order to facilitate corruption.

The first problem is that these entities rely on external consultants to make critical decisions, effectively abdicating some of the core responsibilities of the state. The second problem is that state entities lack the capacity (or the willingness) to assess the quality of the professional work that is delivered. Not only is the value of these consulting services never truly scrutinised, but the firms are frequently allowed to assess the success of their own work and claim outsized 'success fees' based on their own calculations.

There is serious work to be done in evaluating the relationship between the state and private professionals. What kind of work should the state hire professionals to do? How do we evaluate the quality of professional work? How do we capacitate state entities to eliminate the need to contract out – and avoid the risks involved?

Much corruption is driven by relationships between private firms and government officials, often mediated through politically connected middlemen. Practices such as audit and legal firm rotation could prevent the formation of cosy, co-dependent relationships between firms and clients. We should also consider that there might be distinct standards for professional work that is conducted in state institutions. For example, testimony before the Zondo Commission concerning PwC's audits of SAA demonstrated a marked difference in the nature of auditing work for private clients as opposed to government clients. Private sector auditors are primarily occupied with confirming the veracity of financial statements. On the other hand, the Public Audit Act charges auditors of public entities with scrutinising compliance matters. Auditors who do not specialise in auditing public entities may not consider this to be a priority and may be ill-equipped to conduct proper oversight in this regard.

Professionals in the State

The acts of corruption and state capture discussed in this book were carried out, in large part, by senior officials in state-owned entities and government departments. These officials are often left out of any analysis of the role of professionals because the discussion tends to focus on the private sector.

In theory, public servants and bureaucrats meet many – if not all – of the classic definitional criteria for professionals. The Constitution envisages a public administration that is professional, effective, impartial and developmentally directed. Yet, despite a number of professional obligations placed on civil servants – such as the

Batho Pele principles and the Public Service Charter, in addition to various codes of conduct and other regulations – there is broad consensus that our public administration has a long way to go before it can be considered truly professional.

The testimonies at the Zondo Commission have shown that many officials lack the expert knowledge, technical autonomy and public service orientation required of professionals. Patronage is regularly exercised through appointments to lucrative positions in the state; the manipulation of appointment processes has been a distinctive feature of state capture. Some of these appointees have been part of the state capture project; others may simply be ill-equipped to fulfil the responsibilities of their role. The state has struggled to attract personnel with professional expertise, while the unfolding of state capture has driven many professionals within the state to leave. Civil servants often have no protection from political interference in their work – and therefore little to no professional autonomy.

Much of the corruption involving private sector professionals is a result of the state's failure to establish a professional public administration. These professionals have not acted in a vacuum; they worked together with government officials for mutual benefit. A public administration that prevents patronage-based appointments, insulates officials from political interference and maintains high professional standards would be less vulnerable to exploitation. Such a public administration would not need to outsource key professional functions and would be better equipped to manage contracts with private sector professionals when it does need to hire them.

Our state institutions should be staffed by civil servants who are considered professionals with all the relevant standards and responsibilities highlighted in this chapter. The National Implementation Framework towards the Professionalisation of the Public Service, published for comment in 2021, could show a way forward if carefully implemented.

Other Structural Interventions

There are other systems and mechanisms that give rise to openings for professionals to breach ethics. The confidentiality and secrecy under which many professionals operate means that improper conduct can go undetected. While confidentiality might be appropriate when dealing with private clients, where public money is involved or there is the potential for a broader public impact, transparency could go a long way to rooting out malfeasance.

Beneficial ownership transparency – a publicly disclosed register of interests – is an important mechanism that undermines the pall of secrecy under which miscreants hide. Open Secrets has pointed out that the Financial Intelligence Centre Amendment Act of 2017 requires accountable institutions to establish information about their clients. This has the potential to expose the use of shell companies and secrecy jurisdictions to launder proceeds of corruption. However, this exercise is performed by potentially conflicted professionals and the outcomes of such investigations are not available to the public (Marchant et al. 2020). There is ongoing advocacy for an amendment to the Companies Act, which provides for a register of beneficial ownership that is accessible to all.

Transparency can be achieved by encouraging those who witness malfeasance to blow the proverbial whistle. Corporates should create environments that are conducive to whistleblowing. This includes establishing a policy and procedures that are communicated to employees – required by the Protected Disclosures Act of 2000 – and ensuring that disclosures are taken seriously. The disastrous outcomes of awarding contracts to McKinsey, Bain and the consulting arm of Deloitte underscore the imperative to overhaul the public procurement system. A Bill to achieve this has been published. However, many scholars, procurement specialists and civil society activists have identified flaws in the initial draft, one of which is insufficient provision for transparency as required by section 217 of the Constitution.

REBUILDING TRUST IN PROFESSIONS

It cannot be that fresh-faced law or accounting students enter universities with the aim of one day using their knowledge to break laws and enable corruption. Many enter their fields to secure a good life for themselves and their families, and to help others. Their career success is a source of pride in their communities.

The malfeasance committed by individuals from venerated professions located in highly regarded firms has been devastating – to the professions, to our state and to the country. The professions have a long way to go to rebuild public trust, especially because there has not been accountability proportionate to the degree of harm caused. The repayment of undeserved fees is small comfort for the destruction of public institutions. In some, albeit limited, cases companies have suffered collateral damage; the retrenchment of 400 KPMG employees is one example (Dludla 2018).

The finest of silver linings is that state capture has prompted renewed interest in the professions. This has given rise to lively public discourse on the power and influence that professionals wield and, most importantly, how such power can be held in check.

At the heart of most of the corruption detailed above is the politicisation of state institutions and the public administration. Our procurement budget is approaching R1 trillion a year; government contracts are extremely lucrative for private companies and individuals. The patronage system embedded in our state governance and ruling party structures ensures that political actors have a significant level of control over the awarding of major contracts. This is why so many professional firms such as Bain and Bosasa have tried – and succeeded – in establishing close ties to ANC politicians, and why so many professional organisations did not hesitate to pay large commissions to middlemen like Salim Essa. This is how the game is played. Training in professional ethics and improved professional regulation will unfortunately do little to change these fundamental incentives. It is therefore critical that we grapple with the nature of our political system and find ways to protect the state from this kind of political interference.

There is one important lesson to be learned: this cannot continue. Companies, individual professionals and their collaborators in government must be held to account for their actions. It is hoped that the professional enablers mentioned here and those who escaped scrutiny will be called to give a full and frank account of their involvement, which will allow a deeper understanding to emerge of the mechanisms that led them to that point. This, in turn, can form the basis for far-reaching – and necessary – reform of the professions.

Where to from here? The answer to that question lies in the hands of regulators, their clients, their business associates and those who teach them – but mostly, it lies in the hands of the professionals themselves, both those within and outside of the state. No person in South Africa has been unscathed by the deleterious effects of state capture. It is up to the professionals to determine for themselves what their legacy in these fraught times will be.

REFERENCES

AmaBhungane and Scorpio. 2017. '#GuptaLeaks: Confidence Game – Or How Professionals Missed Massive Fraud at Oakbay Listing'. *News24*, 15 December 2017. https://www.news24.com/fin24/companies/industrial/guptaleaks-confidence-game-or-how-professionals-missed-massive-fraud-at-oakbay-listing-20171215.

Auditing Profession Act 26 of 2005.

Bené, Stephen G. 1991. 'Why Not Fine Attorneys? An Economic Approach to Lawyer Disciplinary Sanctions'. *Stanford Law Review* 43, no. 4: 907–941. https://www.jstor.org/stable/i252723.

Bezuidenhout, Jessica. 2019. 'Now McKinsey's R2-billion Transnet Bonanza Is in the Spotlight at State Capture Commission'. *Daily Maverick*, 10 May 2019. https://www.dailymaverick.co.za/article/2019-05-10-now-mckinseys-r2-billion-transnet-bonanza-is-in-the-spotlight-at-state-capture-commission/.

Broad-Based Black Economic Empowerment Act 53 of 2003.

Brown, Justin. 2020. 'Audit Watchdog Accuses Deloitte of "Auditing Disaster" at African Bank, Part One'. *Daily Maverick*, 15 June 2020. https://www.dailymaverick.co.za/article/2020-06-15-part-one-audit-watchdog-accuses-deloitte-of-auditing-disaster-at-african-bank/.

BusinessTech. 2018. 'VAT Was Hiked to 15% Because of Mismanagement at SARS – Treasury'. *BusinessTech*, 30 August 2018. https://businesstech.co.za/news/government/268259/vat-was-hiked-to-15-because-of-mismanagement-at-sars-treasury/.

Buthelezi, Londiwe. 2020. 'A Disciplinary Hearing for Deloitte's Auditors of African Bank Took 2 Years, and It's Finally Over'. *News24*, 11 June 2020. https://www.news24.com/fin24/companies/a-disciplinary-hearing-for-deloittes-auditors-of-african-bank-took-2-years-and-its-finally-over-20200611.

Buthelezi, Londiwe. 2021. 'KPMG to Stop Offering Non-Audit Related Services to JSE-Listed Clients It Audits'. *News24*, 15 February 2021. https://www.news24.com/fin24/Companies/Financial-Services/kpmg-to-stop-offering-non-audit-related-services-to-jse-listed-clients-20210215.

Cameron, Jackie. 2018. 'Gupta-Cursed UK Hogan Lovells Lawyers Wriggle out of State Capture Case – on a Technicality!' *BizNews*, 30 July 2018. https://www.biznews.com/global-citizen/2018/07/30/gupta-hogan-lovells-lawyers-state-capture-technicality.

Companies Act 71 of 2008.

Constitution of the Republic of South Africa. Act 108 of 1996.

Crotty, Ann. 2020. 'Tongaat: Deloitte in the Firing Line'. *Moneyweb*, 29 September 2020. https://www.moneyweb.co.za/news/companies-and-deals/deloitte-in-the-firing-line/.

Dludla, Nqobile. 2018. 'KPMG to Lay off 400 Employees in South Africa in Latest Shake-Up after Scandal'. *Reuters*, 4 June 2018. https://www.reuters.com/article/us-kpmg-jobs-idUSKCN1J00W1.

Donnelly, Lynley. 2018. 'PwC's Involvement with VBS under Scrutiny'. *Mail & Guardian*, 20 April 2018. https://www.pressreader.com/south-africa/mail-guardian/20180420/281874414002586.

Du Toit, Pieter and Kyle Cowan. 2020. 'Internal Report Recommends SARS Withdraw Key "Rogue Unit" Reports, Must Apologise to Employees'. *News24*, 8 July 2020. https://www.news24.com/news24/southafrica/investigations/exclusive-internal-report-recommends-sars-withdraw-key-rogue-unit-reports-must-apologise-to-employees-20200708.

Financial Intelligence Centre Act 38 of 2001.

Financial Intelligence Centre Amendment Act 1 of 2017.

Gorman, Elizabeth H. and Rebecca L. Sandefur. 2011. '"Golden Age", Quiescence, and Revival: How the Sociology of Professions Became the Study of Knowledge-Based Work'. *Work and Occupations* 38, no. 3: 275–302. https://journals.sagepub.com/doi/10.1177/0730888411417565.

Greiner, Larry and Ilse Ennsfellner. 2008. 'Management Consultants as Professionals, Or Are They?' CEO Publication T 08-10 (546), Centre for Effective Organisations, University of Southern California. https://ceo.usc.edu/wp-content/uploads/2008/05/2008_10-t08_10-Management_Consultants.pdf.

Heard, Francis and Nicola Kleyn. 2020. 'KPMG: Rogue Reports, Dead Cows and State Capture'. *Daily Maverick*, 22 September 2020. https://www.dailymaverick.co.za/article/2020-09-22-kpmg-rogue-reports-dead-cows-and-state-capture/.

Hosken, Graeme. 2017. 'KPMG Cans SARS "Rogue Unit" Report, Apologises to Gordhan'. *Timeslive*, 15 September 2017. https://www.timeslive.co.za/politics/2017-09-15-kpmg-cans-sars-rogue-unit-report-apologises-to-gordhan/.

IRBA. 2018. 'IRBA Responds Regarding Actions against Auditors of VBS'. *Independent Regulatory Board for Auditors*, 7 November 2018. https://www.irba.co.za/news-headlines/press-releases/irba-responds-regarding-actions-against-auditors-of-vbs.

IRBA. 2019. 'Linkway Trading Auditor Deregistered – Ordered to Contribute to Costs'. *Independent Regulatory Board for Auditors*, 28 March 2019. https://www.irba.co.za/news-headlines/press-releases/linkway-trading-auditor-deregistered-ordered-to-contribute-to-costs.

Legal Practice Act 28 of 2014.

Legal Practice Council. 2019. 'Code of Conduct'. https://lpc.org.za/legal-practitioners/code-of-conduct/.

Mahlaka, Ray. 2019. 'State Worker Pension Fund Could Take a R12bn Hit from Steinhoff Share Collapse'. *Daily Maverick*, 15 August 2019. https://www.dailymaverick.co.za/article/2019-08-15-state-worker-pension-fund-could-take-a-r12bn-hit-from-steinhoff-share-collapse/.

Mail & Guardian. 2018. 'CIPC's Net Should Catch Other Big Fish'. *Mail & Guardian*, 19 January 2018. https://mg.co.za/article/2018-01-19-00-cipcs-net-should-catch-other-big-fish/.

Marchant, Michael, Mamello Mosiana, Paul Holden and Hennie van Vuuren. 2020. 'The Enablers: The Bankers, Accountants and Lawyers That Cashed in on State Capture'. *Open Secrets*, February 2020. https://www.opensecrets.org.za/the-enablers/.

McDonald, Keith M. 1995. *The Sociology of the Professions*. London: Sage Publications.

McKenna, Christopher. 1995. 'The Origins of Modern Management Consulting'. *Business and Economic History* 24, no. 1: 51–58. https://thebhc.org/sites/default/files/beh/BEHprint/v024n1/p0051-p0058.pdf.

Millerson, Geoffery. 1964. *The Qualifying Associations: A Study in Professionalization*. London: Routledge and Kegan Paul.

Moyo v Minister of Justice and Constitutional Development and Others; Sonti v Minister of Justice and Correctional Services and Others (387/2017; 386/2017) [2018] ZASCA 100; 2018 (8) BCLR 972 (SCA); [2018] 3 All SA 342 (SCA); 2018 (2) SACR 313 (SCA). 20 June 2018.

News24. 2019. 'Law Firm "Appalled" That Former Partner Implicated in State Capture Testimony'. *News24*, 18 January 2019. https://www.news24.com/News24/law-firm-appalled-that-former-partner-implicated-in-state-capture-testimony-20190118.

Nugent, Robert. 2018. 'Commission of Inquiry into Tax Administration and Governance by SARS: Final Report'. 11 December 2018. http://www.inqcomm.co.za/Docs/media/SARS%20Commission%20Final%20Report.pdf.

Omarjee, Lameez. 2018. 'State Capture: 4 Companies That Owe SA Millions'. *News24*, 10 September 2018. https://www.news24.com/fin24/economy/state-capture-4-companies-that-owe-sa-millions-20180910/.

Open Secrets. 2020a. 'Deloot: How Deloitte Gets Away With it'. *Daily Maverick*, 12 August 2020. https://www.dailymaverick.co.za/article/2020-08-12-deloot-how-deloitte-gets-away-with-it.

Open Secrets. 2020b. 'KPMG: How a Big Four Auditing Firm Went Rogue in Its Greed for Profit'. *Daily Maverick*, 16 September 2020. https://www.dailymaverick.co.za/article/2020-09-16-kpmg-how-a-big-four-auditing-firm-went-rogue-in-its-greed-for-profit/.

Open Secrets. 2020c. 'McKinsey: Profit over Principle'. *Daily Maverick*, 29 April 2020. https://www.dailymaverick.co.za/article/2020-04-29-mckinsey-profit-over-principle/.

Pandey, Rajendra. 1985. 'Whither Professionalism?' *Sociological Bulletin* 34, no. 1/2: 1–38. https://www.jstor.org/stable/23619768#metadata_info_tab_contents.

PRCA. 2017. 'Bell Pottinger Case Study'. https://www.prca.org.uk/campaigns/ethics/bell-pottinger-case-study.

Prevention and Combating of Corrupt Activities Act 12 of 2004.

Prevention of Organised Crime Act 121 of 1998.

Protected Disclosures Act 26 of 2000.

Public Audit Act 25 of 2004.

Republic of South Africa. 2021. 'National Implementation Framework towards the Professionalisation of the Public Service: Comments Invited'. https://www.gov.za/documents/national-implementation-framework-towards-professionalisation-public-service-comments.

Schneyer, Ted. 1991a. 'Professional Discipline for Law Firms'. *Cornell Law Review* 77, no. 1: 1–46. https://scholarship.law.cornell.edu/clr/vol77/iss1/1/.

Schneyer, Ted. 1991b. 'Professional Discipline in 2050: A Look Back'. *Fordham Law Review* 60, no. 1: 125–131. https://core.ac.uk/download/pdf/144223355.pdf.

Sciulli, David. 2005. 'Continental Sociology of Professions Today: Conceptual Contributions'. *Current Sociology* 53, no. 6: 915–942. https://journals.sagepub.com/doi/10.1177/0011392105057155.

Sokutu, Brian. 2019. 'How Brian Molefe Created "Fake Emergencies" at Transnet to Fill McKinsey and CSR's Coffers'. *The Citizen*, 11 May 2019. https://citizen.co.za/news/south-africa/state-capture/2129448/how-brian-molefe-created-fake-emergencies-at-transnet-to-fill-mckinsey-and-csrs-coffers/.

Sneader, Kevin. 2018. 'Speech by Kevin Sneader, Global Managing Partner of McKinsey & Company, at Gordon Institute of Business Science Seminar, 9 July 2018'. *McKinsey & Company*, 9 June 2018. https://www.mckinsey.com/za/our-work/speech-by-kevin-sneader-at-gordon-institute-of-business-science-seminar.

Tax Administration Act 28 of 2011.

Van Wyk, Pauli. 2020. 'Four VBS Bank, Two PIC Executives, KPMG Auditor and SAPS Lieutenant-General Arrested in R2,7-Billion VBS Robbery'. *Daily Maverick*, 17 June 2020. https://www.dailymaverick.co.za/article/2020-06-17-six-vbs-bank-and-two-kpmg-executives-arrested-in-r27-billion-vbs-robbery/.

Wicks, Bernadette. 2020. 'KPMG "Rogue Unit" Payments "Acceptance of Culpability" – Van Loggerenberg'. *The Citizen*, 21 September 2020. https://citizen.co.za/news/south-africa/government/2360631/kpmg-rogue-unit-payments-acceptance-of-culpability-van-loggerenberg/.

Young, Michael and Johan Muller. 2014. 'From the Sociology of Professions to the Sociology of Professional Knowledge'. In *Knowledge, Expertise and the Professions*, edited by Michael Young and Johan Muller, 3–17. London: Routledge.

6

Civil Society in the Face of State Capture: Solidarity and Disharmony

Luke Spiropoulos

The years 2016 and 2017 witnessed some of the largest anti-government protests in post-apartheid history. They were organised by civil society in response to what was increasingly called 'state capture'. Although the term 'state capture' has been understood in various ways, the protests led to a growing public awareness of high-level corruption in South Africa and contributed to the ongoing effort to push back against it. If we wish to understand this fight, we must first appreciate the strategy, strengths and weaknesses from its beginnings in civil society action.

This chapter uses oral history methods, supported by documents and press reports from the period, to provide an account of civil society's changing tactical and strategic response to state capture over time. The methods have been adapted to take a sample of activists and observers across selected civil society sectors. This involved selecting participants through the prominence of their names in the records of the period or through 'snowballing' approaches. Together these sources suggest three, sometimes overlapping, approaches to the issue – mass communication, legal action and popular mobilisation. While several of the instances of what has come to be known as state capture are described in some detail, this is intended to highlight the strategies and mobilisation of civil society groups rather than to form a history of the state capture phenomenon.

Positioned outside of the state and business, civil society organisations seek to represent and advance the interests of the broader populace. That said, I have excluded traditionally important civil society actors such as newspapers and labour unions from the analysis because the former, at least partially, operate with a profit incentive. At the same time, the latter often partnered with the government or the Tripartite Alliance. Thus, they are different from the groups I deal with – non-governmental organisations (NGOs), non-profit organisations and community-based organisations. While I excluded commercial newspapers, I have included donor-funded investigative journalism NGOs in the survey, as their incentives tend to lie outside those of the corporate media landscapes that they engage with.

CIVIL SOCIETY IN SOUTH AFRICA

During the late apartheid period, labour unions, church groups, civic organisations and what today would be thought of as NGOs – most affiliated with the United Democratic Front (UDF) – developed a powerful force opposing the state. These organisations were thus primed to act as a unified sector, often with overlapping interests.

It should be no surprise then that most of the individuals involved in establishing and running the organisations discussed in this chapter were anti-apartheid activists either in the UDF, the unions or formally within the African National Congress (ANC). The organisations with which they are involved were established, however, after apartheid's ending. This 'explosion of civil society organisations' (McKinley, Interview, 16 March 2020) emerged in part because of the termination of the Reconstruction and Development Programme (RDP) – the post-1994 national socio-economic policy framework aimed at restructuring service provision and a more equitable economy. The RDP is central to understanding South African civil society today: it brought many experienced activists into government, it redirected international donor funding to RDP programmes, and its social democratic promise demobilised organisations on the left wing for a time (Blumenfeld 1997; Feinstein, Interview, 10 February 2020; Pieterse 1997; Roussos, Interview, 12 February 2020). Attracted by the prospect of governing the 'new South Africa', many of the trade union movement leaders in the immediate post-apartheid period were also co-opted into government through this programme (Sikwebu, Interview, 9 April 2020).[1] From 1996, however, the RDP was replaced by the Growth, Employment and Redistribution plan, which was more closely aligned to the Washington Consensus,[2] in sharp distinction to the RDP. In response to an evident neglect of local communities in this period, leading activists began organising outside Tripartite Alliance structures. Thus, many respondents see the origins of their own opposition to state capture as an outgrowth of opposition to what they understood as an increasingly uncaring and eventually authoritarian turn in the post-apartheid state (Bregman, Interview, 3 March 2020; McKinley, Interview, 16 March 2020).

Despite various efforts to reinvigorate civil society in the early 2000s, civil society activism struggled in the post-apartheid era. Broad-based social movements were being replaced by professional NGOs that tended to 'focus on constitutionalism' and were the 'darlings of the funders' (Sikwebu, Interview, 9 April 2020). Thus, according to activist-intellectual Dinga Sikwebu, the most active and popular organisations fighting against the 'neoliberalisation of the state' were the left wing of the Tripartite Alliance: the unions and the South African Communist Party (SACP). Marginalised and struggling, many supported Jacob Zuma at the 2007 ANC elective conference in Polokwane as their last hope to effect 'progressive' change (Sikwebu, Interview, 9 April 2020).

UNDERSTANDING THE PROBLEM

To explain civil society's response to growing corruption, we must look at how it understood state capture as such. As Koketso Moeti of the online advocacy group Amandla.mobi asserts, the definition of the problem of state capture underpinned significant ideological differences in civil society (Interview, 28 April 2020).

On the one hand, there were significant overlaps in the conception of state capture. Informants variously explain it as 'the capture of the highest levels of government by private interests for private interests' (Balton, Interview, 10 February 2020; Feinstein, Interview, 10 February 2020; Smithers, Interview, 17 March 2020; Van Vuuren, Interview, 23 March 2020). Alternatively, it is explained as a plutocracy defined by opacity, opposition to free expression and free association, such that government decisions are made by the political and business elite alone (Bhardwaj, Interview, 19 March 2020). However, there are important differences in civil society's understanding of state capture. For example, Francis Antonie of the Helen Suzman Foundation places the failure of the separation of constitutional powers at the heart of the issue (Interview, 13 March 2020). Dinga Sikwebu, on the other hand, argues that there are certain features of state capture inherent in the capitalist state, and thus 'fighting state capture is an important struggle for the working class' (Interview, 9 April 2020). Similarly, Vinayak Bhardwaj, Andrew Feinstein and Hennie van Vuuren explain state capture as part of a broader global phenomenon, linking political interference to the influence of business (Bhardwaj, Interview, 19 March 2020; Feinstein, Interview, 10 February 2020; Van Vuuren, Interview, 23 March 2020). Neeshan Balton adds that it is important that state capture be understood as systematic, large-scale and high-level government corruption, instead of merely day-to-day corruption. He maintains that there is a strategic benefit in having a tightly defined understanding of state capture lest it is felt that it is beyond anyone's ability to respond to it (Balton, Interview, 10 February 2020). An example of this kind of expansion is Feinstein's argument that the entire apartheid project should be understood as state capture (Feinstein Interview, 10 February 2020).

How civil society leaders explain the origins of state capture in South Africa is also a telling insight into their understanding of the problem. A number of the respondents date its origins earlier than the coming to power of the ANC (Feinstein, Interview, 10 February 2020). Van Vuuren, for example, maintains that the apartheid state created avenues for illicit and illegal global capital flows through local and international financial houses (Interview, 23 March 2020; Van Vuuren 2019).

Drawing from his experience in helping to re-establish the ANC within the country in the early 1990s, Mike Roussos points to the necessity of political parties to establish their own base of funding in order to contest elections against the National Party and the Democratic Party and their long-established funding structures. As a result, investment entities were created within the ANC, and 'comrades' were 'deployed to business', with an understanding that they were raising money for the party (see Robinson and Brümmer 2006, 38; Southall 2008). But, as Roussos suggests, 'there's a fine line between comrades in the state deploying you to business, and [the latter] buying access to the state' (Interview, 12 February 2020). In addition, some respondents note that many, if not most, of the ANC membership returning from exile had no secure sources of income inside the country. It did not take long for businesspeople to take advantage of the nascent fundraising apparatus for self-enrichment. Feinstein points to the presence of international arms dealers at the Convention for a Democratic South Africa talks (Interview, 10 February 2020). Maurice Smithers mentions that insurance magnate Douw Steyn hosted Nelson Mandela as his house guest before the 1994 election, and his concern at witnessing the hotel magnate Sol Kerzner in affable conversation with then deputy president Thabo Mbeki at Nelson Mandela's 1994 inauguration (Interview, 17 March 2020).

To explain the origins of state capture, Dale McKinley argues that the ANC was 'primed for capture' because of its interest in 'wooing capital from its very earliest years' (Interview, 16 March 2020; McKinley 1997). Sikwebu differs, saying that 'the ANC of [its founding in] 1912 and the ANC of the 1980s were not the same entity'

(Interview, 9 April 2020). Instead, Sikwebu argues that the origins of the state capture project lie in the corporatist restructuring of state-owned enterprises (SOEs)
under Mbeki's presidency. Sikwebu expressly refers to the Eskom Conversion Act of
2001, which turned the public power utility into a commercial company under the
Companies Act. This made the minister of public enterprises the sole shareholder,
with control over appointments, and opened space for abuse. Thus, Sikwebu sees
the period from 1999 onwards as a pivotal point from which a distinct form of state
capture emerged that had not been possible before (Interview, 9 April 2020).

Nonetheless, despite differences in defining state capture and its origins, there
was enough consensus for organisations to draw together in the short term to
oppose it. Later, however, divisions would widen, especially as this precarious civil
society coalition tried to decide on the strategy and long-term goals that emerged in
part from their divergent understandings of the nature of state capture.

PUBLIC COMMUNICATION

Civil society's first response to state capture was characterised by mass communication. To overcome the lack of public – or, indeed, state – interest in the issue, it was
necessary to build a framework of information on, and mass interest in, its scale and
extent. For example, in the early 2000s, there was relatively little public attention
paid to corruption.[3] Although there were a few attempts to organise around grand
corruption, the government focused on petty corruption (Van Vuuren, Interview,
23 March 2020). For example, the National Anti-Corruption Forum was established in 2001 as a joint government-business-civil society consultative entity. By
mid-2016, the group had not met for four years (Petersen 2016).

The first substantial efforts to build public awareness around state corruption
took a number of forms, but the exposure of the Arms Deal was a prominent
instance (Feinstein 2007, 2010). Hennie van Vuuren describes the Arms Deal as the
single issue that 'fundamentally corrupted [South African] politics' by redirecting
resources away from the common good – he cites the non-provision of antiretro-
viral drugs – and into private hands (Interview, 23 March 2020). Its exposure led,
for example, to greater interest in the relationship between Jacob Zuma and the
Shaik brothers, which would lead to scrutiny of Zuma's compound in the Nkandla
district, also associated with state capture (Bhardwaj, Interview, 19 March 2020).
The press highlighted several headline-grabbing scandals, including a problematic
2010 cabinet reshuffle, interference in SOE boards, and changes to the leadership
of enforcement agencies such as the Directorate for Priority Crime Investigation

(the Hawks), the Independent Police Investigative Directorate and the National Prosecuting Authority (NPA) (Antonie, Interview, 13 March 2020; Feinstein, Interview, 10 February 2020).

Launched in 2010, the donor-funded, non-profit investigative journalism organisation amaBhungane was central to these communication efforts. Vinayak Bhardwaj, a former journalist at amaBhungane, calls its conceptual underpinning a 'radical view of transparency' – the need for people to know as much as possible, without exception, about what is going on in the country (Interview, 19 March 2020).

Working closely with amaBhungane, the Right2Know (R2K) campaign was founded with a corresponding mandate (Bhardwaj, Interview, 19 March 2020). R2K emerged in 2010 in response to 'the Secrecy Bill' (Minister of State Security 2010) and comparable efforts to securitise the state and 'empower the spooks' (McKinley, Interview, 16 March 2020). As a defender of the free flow of information, R2K was vital to the continued mass media efforts to expose corruption (McKinley, Interview, 16 March 2020).

Supporting amaBhungane and R2K, much of the early reporting on corruption was channelled through established civil society organisations. For example, the Ahmed Kathrada Foundation was among the first to raise (proverbial) red flags about the landing of a private aeroplane at the Waterkloof Air Force Base in violation of National Key Points (1980) legislation. More than any other, this was the event that fully brought the Gupta family to public attention, galvanising civil society (Antonie, Interview, 13 March 2020; McKinley, Interview, 16 March 2020; Roussos, Interview, 12 February 2020; Smithers, Interview, 17 March 2020). As the Ahmed Kathrada Foundation director, Neeshan Balton, later explains, 'We knew that [this] couldn't happen without high-level involvement' (Interview, 10 February 2020). Public demands for accountability on the Waterkloof incident built on already existing rumours about the role of the Gupta family in the affairs of the country. Their intent was made ominous by the government's sponsorship of the 'New Age Business Breakfast' events through which the Gupta-owned *New Age* newspaper promised access to high-ranking politicians at a hefty fee. These were taken up primarily by public entities like the South African Broadcasting Corporation (SABC) and SOEs such as Transnet (Cronje 2020). The Ahmed Kathrada Foundation was concerned about the Guptas' influence over the president's appointments to cabinet and other governing structures. These concerns were compounded when Barbara Hogan, an Ahmed Kathrada Foundation board member, was relieved of her ministerial position in the November 2010 cabinet reshuffle – allegedly because of her opposition to a Gupta-linked airline deal.

The dissemination of this information about the president and the Guptas created support for intensifying direct civil society action on the issue. Dale McKinley refers to this as part of the 'battle of ideas' in building a broad-based campaign (Interview, 16 March 2020). Mike Roussos makes note of information campaigns appealing for a broadened focus from the Opposition to Urban Tolling Alliance (OUTA), which was established around levying tolls on regional highways. The manner in which OUTA presented information to members (and the wider public) allowed it to transform into an effective and expansive anti-corruption movement (Roussos, Interview, 12 February 2020).

While the press was an important site of resistance to state capture, the state increasingly pushed back against what it perceived as a hostile media. This was to have a dramatic effect on a vulnerable sector. Notably, the state shifted much of its advertising spend to *New Age*. While some newspaper houses could absorb these losses, local community papers at the heart of grassroots efforts to communicate information could not. According to Wara Fana of the Eastern Cape Communication Forum, attempts to appeal to ministers and directors to adhere to their mandate to support this type of media had little effect. In the Eastern Cape, 45 of 60 local newspapers have closed since 2012. These included essential staples of local media such as *Isizwe*, which had been running since 1972 and had survived apartheid opposition. Of those which endured this culling, most were radically reduced in size, resulting in layoffs and further hopelessness in the most impoverished communities in the country (Fana, Interview, 17 April 2020).

THE LEGAL ROUTE

In addition to going public on corruption, a range of civil society organisations adopted litigious strategies to highlight the issue. The Helen Suzman Foundation, as we have noted, has a particular interest in questions of the 'rule of law' and the strength of constitutional institutions. The foundation interprets this mandate as requiring particular vigilance over the abuse of 'the coercive institutions of the state' (Antonie, Interview, 13 March 2020). Another NGO with a legal focus, Section27, deals primarily with cases that involve socio-economic rights. R2K focuses legal strategies on developing the 'legal high ground' in order to enforce freedom of information and protest rights: they are concerned that the state's opaqueness is used to hide maladministration and corruption (McKinley, Interview, 16 March 2020).

Cases before the courts helped to build public understanding of the abuse of power and exposed the centralisation of control within the state. The Helen Suzman

Foundation, for example, commenced its response to state capture as amicus curiae – friend of the court – in 2011 in the case known as Glenister II (Glenister v President of the Republic of South Africa and Others 2011). This was a case in opposition to government's disbanding of the Scorpions (formally the Directorate of Special Operations), an investigative unit housed in the NPA, in favour of a unit to be housed in the South African Police Service called the Hawks. The case eventually came before the Constitutional Court, which found that the Hawks were insufficiently independent.

Later, the Helen Suzman Foundation took up the related case of the removal of the head of the Hawks, Anwa Dramat, in order to defend 'the rule of law' by ensuring the institution's independence. At the time of his dismissal, Dramat had pressed forward with investigations of a number of high-profile cases, including the upgrades to Zuma's homestead (Antonie, Interview, 13 March 2020). The success of these legal efforts helped to further strengthen civil society organisations, demonstrating to the public that there was effective legal muscle behind objections against the powerful. Francis Antonie, head of the Helen Suzman Foundation at the time, calls this strategy the 'TAC approach' (Interview, 13 March 2020), referring to the Treatment Action Campaign's efforts at mobilising a base of support around legal action and success in the courts, in turn, to activate further grassroots support.

Seeking and threatening legal action revealed much about the functioning of 'captured' networks within the state. For example, after Jacob Zuma removed minister of finance Nhlanhla Nene from his position in December 2015, it emerged that the board of South African Airways (SAA) had requested that his short-lived replacement, Des van Rooyen, reconsider a deal Nene had already rejected. Responding to this revelation, the Helen Suzman Foundation wrote a letter to the Department of Finance requesting clarification and threatening legal action should the deal go ahead (Antonie, Interview, 13 March 2020). However, the new minister, Pravin Gordhan, eventually approved Nene's version of the deal, rejecting the request from SAA. In response to this, members of the Hawks allegedly threatened the head of the SAA Pilots' Association over accusations that he had leaked information from SAA board meetings (Antonie, Interview, 13 March 2020; Smith 2016; Spicer 2016).

Many other legal cases were initiated only when individuals approached civil society organisations looking for support – or, as Antonie put it, because of the 'files that the fairies [drop] off at the gate' (Interview, 13 March 2020). For example, the Helen Suzman Foundation received files detailing the South African Revenue Service (SARS) investigation into the activities of what the Hawks and others claimed was a 'rogue spying unit' inside SARS. The Helen Suzman Foundation used these files to threaten action against the NPA (Antonie, Interview, 13 March 2020).

Corruption Watch similarly invited tip-offs and then pursued these through the courts (Corruption Watch 2015, 2017).

Civil society organisations also regularly laid complaints about corruption with the Office of the Public Protector and other Chapter Nine institutions. For instance, the Catholic Dominican Order in South Africa lodged the first complaints about the undue influence of the Gupta family on the appointment of cabinet ministers with the Public Protector (Public Protector 2016). This led to the report entitled 'State of Capture', which Public Protector Thuli Madonsela released in the final weeks of her tenure. It recommended the establishment of a judicial commission of inquiry into state capture. Corruption Watch was also involved as amicus curiae in some of the cases in which the Public Protector's powers were called into question (South African Broadcasting Corporation Soc Ltd and Others v Democratic Alliance and Others 2015; Economic Freedom Fighters and Others v Speaker of the National Assembly and Another 2017).

Taken together, these strategies established a legal and evidentiary basis for many of the accusations around state capture that were emerging in the press and elsewhere. They revealed links between particular corruption cases within the state capture project and slowed them down by challenging them legally. Importantly, too, legal action showed members of the public that their voices were not futile and that there were legitimate ways in which the state could be brought to account. Moreover, efforts to intimidate civil society whistleblowers in response often back-fired. An armed robbery at the offices of the Helen Suzman Foundation, for example, blamed on state security agencies, shocked the public and galvanised support for anti-corruption efforts (Thamm 2016). Similarly, there was public outrage at what seemed like the impunity of those implicated in state capture, such as the minister of social development, who effectively ignored court orders (AllPay Consolidated Investment Holdings (Pty) Ltd and Others v Chief Executive Officer of the South African Social Security Agency and Others 2013; GroundUp 2017; South African Social Security Agency and Another v Minister of Social Development and Others 2018), the Hawks for holding SARS whistleblower Vlok Symington hostage, and the chief of operations of the SABC, Hlaudi Motsoeneng, for intimidating staff with-out sanction (Mabuza 2016). Finally, the regular late-notice cabinet reshuffles, re-appointments and dismissals, and the fruitless legal appeals were interpreted by the public as a lack of concern for public accountability by Zuma's allies.

Nevertheless, as Dale McKinley points out, the success of legal strategies 'pre-sumes the continued existence of a free and functioning judiciary' (Interview, 16 March 2020). In such a context, over-reliance on the courts in politically charged cases potentially puts the judiciary at risk of counter-accusations of bias or 'capture'

(Bhardwaj, Interview, 19 March 2020). Further, legal action alone cannot change parliamentary votes or the intra-party politics required to deal with state capture and hold those involved to account. Thus, these informants argue, another approach was needed that could put pressure on parliamentarians and ANC members and potentially change public voting patterns.

PUBLIC MOBILISATION

The building of public knowledge and the deepening of widespread outrage surrounding state capture grew the support bases of civil society organisations, laying the groundwork for later efforts at 'movement-building'. In turn, these efforts helped to provide a 'home' for dissenting voices within the ANC and created room for business leaders in anti-corruption efforts (Balton, Interview, 10 February 2020; Smithers, Interview, 17 March 2020). This came to a head following the market shocks in the wake of the replacement of Nhlanhla Nene with Des van Rooyen in late 2015. As Vinayak Bhardwaj explains, 'Civil society entered a period where Zuma, and getting rid of Zuma, [became] the central preoccupation' (Interview, 19 March 2020).

In early 2016, veteran ANC activist and politician Ahmed Kathrada penned an open letter to Zuma calling on him to resign, following his response to the Public Protector's report on the upgrades to his private property at Nkandla. In the past, Kathrada had tried using networks within the ANC to put pressure on Zuma, but this tactic had failed. Now he appealed to the president through the public and ANC membership. Kathrada's letter led to the establishment of an oppositional 'veterans and stalwarts' group within the ANC. This was built on the earlier 'Sidikwe! Vukani!' (Vote No!) spoilt ballot campaign initiated by former cabinet minister Ronnie Kasrils and former deputy minister Nozizwe Madlala-Routledge (Balton, Interview, 10 February 2020). In addition, influential business leader and ANC member Sipho Pityana made a public appeal to ANC members in a speech at the funeral of veteran activist and former cabinet minister Makhenkesi Stofile (Balton, Interview, 10 February 2020). Pityana was the chair of the board of the mining company AngloGold and would go on to lead efforts to coordinate a broader civil society and public mobilisation from this platform (Balton, Interview, 10 February 2020; Roussos, Interview, 12 February 2020).

One strategy was to put pressure on the ANC – often through civil society structures – by arguing that state capture threatened its future electoral performance. In the past, many ANC members had favoured internal processes of consultation and 'correction' over public displays of dissent. Still, as Kathrada and others found, these efforts were increasingly ineffectual: they appealed, instead, to the feelings of marginalisation of many ANC members. Thus, civil society leaders and their political allies offered a public base of support for dissenting voices within the ANC, especially within the National Executive Committee and among the veterans and stalwarts.

Civil society mobilisation gradually gained momentum as the issue of state capture increasingly impacted the core work of several NGOs. The Social Justice Coalition – formed in 2009 to focus on localised socio-economic rights – became involved in anti-corruption campaigns because state capture undermined service delivery (Bregman, Interview, 3 March 2020). Similarly, R2K emphasised the link between failures in local governance and the capture of government contracts (McKinley, Interview, 16 March 2020). As Dinga Sikwebu argued, many of the 'professional' NGOs, which had been ambivalent about becoming involved in the counter-state capture endeavours, were increasingly aware of their weaknesses in the face of emerging popular and large-scale movements such as #FeesMustFall. As a result, many NGOs joined the anti-corruption efforts to be part of a broader movement (Sikwebu, Interview, 9 April 2020).

The Helen Suzman Foundation and the Ahmed Kathrada Foundation, for their part, were increasingly concerned with the impact state capture was having on the functioning of the state at all levels. For them, the state had been 'hollowed out' to benefit and protect a small set of political actors.[4] This meant that there was little hope of dealing with pressing social issues until the issue of state capture had been addressed (Balton, Interview, 10 February 2020; Van Dalsen, Interview, 13 March 2020). Furthermore, at the grassroots level, organisers found that local councils were operating on a 'my turn to eat' principle (Wrong 2009), in which alternating groups of local businesspeople would capture ANC branches to access municipal spending (Roussos, Interview, 12 February 2020). Similarly, the divided internal ANC politics undermined the leadership of many trade unions and of the dwindling local civic organisations (Roussos, Interview, 12 February 2020). Sikwebu adds that some unions could not adopt anti-state capture positions because they were complicit in it through SOEs and the SABC (Interview, 9 April 2020).

The Awethu! Project, housed at Section27, was involved in mass mobilisation before civil society coalitions were formed. This project had long been trying to produce a network of affiliated community-based organisations that could act as a popular movement in responding to crises like the 2012 Marikana massacre. The prospect of turning this organisation against state capture seemed feasible because meetings at the local community level revealed a great deal of resentment about corruption and the related failures of the state (Smithers, Interview, 17 March 2020).

UNITY AND THE ROOTS OF DIVISION

However, broad-based organising was becoming difficult, as funding was drying up and organisations were increasingly in conflict with each other. At the same time, the National Union of Metalworkers of South Africa (Numsa), which had been drifting away from the Congress of South African Trade Unions and the ANC, decided to initiate a movement focused on broader issues rather than just workers' rights. In 2015, it established the United Front, which was 'a coalition of people fighting for basic services in different communities' in the political spirit of the UDF of the 1980s (Pillay 2014). As a result, many civil society organisations began to consider this group an alternative home for anti-state capture work (Smithers, Interview, 17 March 2020).

The leading grant funders at this point were also becoming part of efforts to bring civil society organisations together to address state capture. For example, the Open Society Foundation established relationships with organisations working to counter state capture and offered to fund projects to facilitate and strengthen these efforts. This was in keeping with the funder's mandate to promote accountability, transparency and representative government, among other aims (Bhardwaj, Interview, 19 March 2020).

The local organisational base of support was thus ready to advance collective mobilisation. Nhlanhla Nene's removal from the finance ministry led to one of the initial efforts at joint mass mobilisation, the #ZumaMustFall movement, which started at the end of 2015. This was organised by an alliance of organisations called Unite Against Corruption, which was made up of NGOs, church groups and labour unions.

While this at first led to several demonstrations, these were relatively small, and there remained little unity among organising groups. Furthermore, the effort was criticised as a predominantly white, middle-class response that was concerned with the effect the situation was having on their investments, despite efforts by organisers to emphasise that it was led by civil society (McKinley, Interview, 16 March 2020; Smithers, Interview, 17 March 2020). It would take some time before the group could shake off this image. The negative public image of anti-corruption movements is something Neeshan Balton describes as a 'tactical error', but one that was not fatal (Interview, 10 February 2020).

Many unions were already suspicious of the concept of state capture on ideological grounds, arguing that a capitalist state is by definition 'captured'. This 'maximalist' view of the situation was compounded by many unions themselves being implicated in the state capture project, according to Sikwebu

(Interview, 9 April 2020). Furthermore, Numsa, some South African Federation of Trade Unions (Saftu) affiliates and the United Front were growing increasingly frustrated with United Against Corruption decisions that did not consider their needs. They put this down to a 'social-democrat' tendency among the organising NGOs, which viewed the working class merely as a means to swell their ranks. As a result, the involvement of the unions in the programme of action was diminished (Sikwebu et al. 2015). Divisions emerged among NGOs, with Francis Antonie pointing to the difficulty of coordinating efforts because 'some organisations, especially [those] from Cape Town, did not want to be too closely associated with us "so-called liberals"' (Interview, 13 March 2020).

Greater collaboration was, however, made possible under the banners of United Against Corruption and the newly formed Save South Africa at a series of meetings arranged by Sipho Pityana. Here, the importance of cohesion was emphasised, as the attacks on Pravin Gordhan became increasingly public in the aftermath of fraud charges being laid against him in late 2016. The charges related to Gordhan's approval of an early retirement claim by the SARS deputy commissioner at the time, Ivan Pillay, who was implicated in the 'Rogue Unit' scandal.[5] This gave the efforts against state capture 'a central message and a face' (Balton, Interview, 10 February 2020). Moreover, this mobilisation gave Gordhan and others in similar positions, such as Minister Derek Hanekom, a base of moral support. According to Balton, 'this alone was a huge contribution' (Interview, 10 February 2020).

In the wake of these attacks on Gordhan, several trade unions and South African Council of Churches affiliates, as well as the SACP, rejoined the anti-corruption efforts (Balton, Interview, 10 February 2020; Roussos, Interview, 12 February 2020). The mobilisation of the churches was particularly significant because some church groups – like the Catholic Bishops' Conference, with whom Mike Roussos worked – had demobilised politically after 1994 and were reticent to re-engage. Even some of those church leaders who had been visible in the anti-apartheid struggle said they 'wanted to pull back from activism once they had made their statement' on state capture, following a meeting with the leadership of the ANC in mid-2016 (Roussos, Interview, 12 February 2020).

Several respondents note rising interest in state capture in academic circles. The publication of a research report, 'Betrayal of the Promise' (PARI 2017), was a significant turning point in further mobilisation. This particular work produced a concrete framework around which to organise and, increasingly, provided a language in which to speak about state capture (Bregman, Interview, 3 March 2020). As Balton reflects, '[We were beginning] to join the dots [in order] to allow us to understand the breadth and extent of this state capture' (Interview, 10 February 2020).

Thus, increased mass mobilisation in 2016 and 2017 helped bridge many ideological differences within civil society. In the words of veteran activist Maurice Smithers, 'eventually we had everyone from the old Trotskyites to OUTA' organising and marching together against state capture (Interview, 17 March 2020). In March 2017, this was further strengthened by a pledge of renewed coordination at the funeral of Ahmed Kathrada. This brought together a new coalition called Future South Africa, led by the Kathrada Foundation.

Yet, not all of civil society was keen on joining forces with these anti-state capture coordinating bodies. Amandla.mobi, for example, deliberately chose not to join the mobilisation efforts. There are a few reasons for this that shed light on the limitations of the effort and the difficulties related to trying to organise collectively in South Africa. For Koketso Moeti, Amandla.mobi's founder, state capture was too narrowly defined. She explained that anti-state capture organisers were overly focused on 'the behaviour of a single-family' – the Guptas – and there was little evidence of a long-term strategy to address corruption. To Moeti, the single-minded focus overlooked earlier, equally important concerns about, for example, local government corruption and the relentless assassination of councillors. Big businesses, such as the sugar companies, reportedly pressuring MPs over a proposed sugar tax, seemed to fall by the wayside too. Further, she explains that anti-corruption organisers too often presumed that the end of state capture would see a 'return' to good governance. Instead, for Moeti, 'good governance' in South Africa has been selective, ignoring the poorest and most marginalised (Interview, 28 April 2020).

Moeti and others are equally concerned that this form of collective organising closed space for a critique of civil society. More specifically, she feels that criticism of any individual or group within the network of solidarity was treated as an attack on anti-state capture efforts as a whole. Thus, she explains, there was little room available to criticise Gordhan's track record as minister for cooperative governance and traditional affairs, especially his deployment of the army in the controversial Operation Fiela, which was seen as a thinly veiled attack on foreign residents (Nicolson 2105).

Echoing the point made by Antonie regarding working with 'the so-called liberals' (Interview, 13 March 2020), Moeti and her colleagues have felt ideologically incompatible with 'the white left' who led the anti-state capture coordination efforts. For example, Moeti feels that underpinning the concerns with state capture and corruption was a distaste for black accumulation while normalising white accumulation (Interview, 28 April 2020). These factors meant that Amandla.mobi decided that working with the solidarity network was at odds with its core responsibility – to provide platforms for communities to access, understand and respond to government policy and legal positions (Moeti, Interview, 28 April 2020). These criticisms resonate with Dinga Sikwebu's concerns about the failure of civil society anti-corruption efforts to build a more extensive 'movement' (Interview, 9 April 2020).

THE END OF ZUMA AND ITS AFTERMATH

The threads of cooperation began to fray reasonably early on. Divides became increasingly apparent in 2017 as the ANC elective conference approached. Neeshan Balton explains that organisations felt increasing pressure to focus on their individual agendas because they began to feel the squeeze on their resources (Interview, 10 February 2020). As Joel Bregman put it, they 'had to explain to funders how resources were being used for [their mandated] projects because of how those projects were linked to state capture' (Interview, 3 March 2020). Thus, the Save South Africa campaign 'basically ended when the money ran out' (Balton, Interview, 10 February 2020). Mike Roussos points out that this was because the corporate entities who were sponsoring some of these efforts felt the work was done when the elective congress ended. Corporates wanted to 'get back to doing business with government' (Roussos, Interview, 12 February 2020).

Maurice Smithers argues that there were too many different approaches among the organisations to allow them to succeed. Moreover, the leaders of civil society movements did not fully commit to a single course of action, and thus it 'never became what it could have been' (Smithers, Interview, 17 March 2020). Dingwa Sikwebu echoes this view, saying that the failure to win large-scale buy-in from labour meant that the coalitions never became 'movements' against state capture. Instead, the initiative enjoyed spurts of collaborated activity coordinated by individual NGOs. He further points to the difficulty of building new 'movements' because they required volunteers. Finally, he argued that under conditions of high unemployment and extreme poverty, people lack the socio-economic stability to commit their time. This is one of his key reasons to explain why civil society turned to 'the constitutional option' and relied on the courts (Sikwebu, Interview, 9 April 2020).

Strategic differences between civil society organisations also hampered the joint anti-corruption efforts and, as Vinayak Bhardwaj suggests, 'public mobilisation was [periodically] undermined by ongoing court action' (Interview, 19 March 2020). In one case, the Economic Freedom Fighters (EFF) and the Democratic Alliance took parliament and the president to court over the failure to follow due process in the attempted impeachment of Zuma (Masondo 2016). The United Democratic

Movement tried to force parliament to allow a secret ballot for an impeachment vote (United Democratic Movement v Speaker of the National Assembly and Others 2017). In both instances, mass action was postponed or cancelled pending the outcome of these cases or because victories were thought to render the action unnecessary (Bhardwaj, Interview, 19 March 2020).

Balton points to deepening differences of opinion on strategy as the ANC's elective congress came closer. Indeed, many organisations put much of their hope and efforts directly into campaigning for the conference. Not only did this mean that their focus was divided, but that many felt they had won with the defeat of Zuma's preferred successor, Nkosazana Dlamini-Zuma. As a result, Saftu, the SACP and the EFF began to pull away and, in some cases, actively oppose coalitions they had previously supported (Balton, Interview, 10 February 2020). Similarly, the UDF veterans' group in Cape Town effectively halted their collective work after the conference (Sikwebu, Interview, 9 April 2020).

Other members of civil society emphasised the importance of commissions of inquiry to investigate the state capture project. This 'procedural approach' could be classified as a fourth type of civil society response to state capture – after mass communication, legal action and mass mobilisation. Non-confrontational commissions relied on public scrutiny and the investigative and remedial procedures of the state. By acting as observers of the Eskom inquiry, a range of civil society organisations committed their resources to ensure proceedings were kept honest and transparent (Bregman, Interview, 3 March 2020).

Many organisations offered support to these commissions in the form of submissions, both individually and as groups. For example, according to the Open Secrets website, the Civil Society Working Group on State Capture is a 'coalition of over 23 civil society organisations ... and has both supported and strengthened the work of the Zondo Commission while maintaining oversight over the commission in the interests of the public'. Bregman points out that for civil society, involvement in procedures like commissions affords them a rare opportunity to make an impact from within a system they are usually fighting (Interview, 3 March 2020).

There have been concerns and limitations in supporting these commissions, however. Bhardwaj, for example, sees it as potentially a distraction from the work that still needs to be done, resulting in an 'abdication of social action and debate' on the part of civil society (Interview, 19 March 2020). While sharing Bhardwaj's concerns, Balton points to further fundamental reservations – the possibility that commissions could damage the public will to keep fighting because it does not provide a limited definition of the concept of state capture. If 'everyday corruption' comes to be associated with state capture, he argues, the sheer volume of the problem will seem insurmountable. A narrower definition can provide a more easily recognised victory, which will bolster public interest in fighting on (Balton, Interview, 10 February 2020).

One way to deal with the state-led format of commissions has been to establish a parallel People's Tribunal on Economic Crimes. This is a collaborative project between Corruption Watch, the Foundation for Human Rights, Open Secrets, the Public Affairs Research Institute and the Right2Know Campaign. The tribunal's panel of legal and activist experts allowed members of the public to submit evidence on 'economic crimes' and released interim findings on the arms trade hearings early in February 2018. This report considered both apartheid-era and post-apartheid economic crimes involving sanctions-busting, arms deals and the later revelations about the state capture project in the late 2000s, linking them in a historical continuum. However, Sikwebu says it was largely about continuities from the apartheid era, and, as a result, its relevance to post-apartheid anti-corruption was limited (Interview, 9 April 2020).

Balton argues for the importance of civil society performing a watchdog role in the country. Thus, the purpose of commissions is to expose as much data as possible to allow structural reforms that reach to the roots of state capture. Balton notes that the 'fightback project' of those who were at the core of capturing the state remains in place (Interview, 10 February 2020), and, as a result, the project is merely on hold. The Ahmed Kathrada Foundation has managed to keep its activities going because it could secure project funding specifically for this issue. The foundation's immediate focus is on trying to organise greater collaboration, particularly at a grassroots level. It has pointed to several necessary reforms for civil society. These include rebuilding the public service, electoral reform and appointment procedure reform (Balton, Interview, 10 February 2020). While several respondents indicate the importance of continued vigilance and influence, only the Ahmed Kathrada Foundation points to the need for a collaborative approach to make this work.

Roussos argues that the future role of civil society is always in question because it is so often co-opted by government and business, as it had been in the 1990s. This is because 'it's very tempting to be involved in actually building something instead of keeping your eye on things from outside' (Roussos, Interview, 12 February 2020). Sikwebu describes this temptation as a kind of naivety about the nature of state structures. He reports joking with those involved in anti-state capture work with a history inside government: 'Welcome back, but don't forget that some of us have been on this side of the trench for a long time. Maybe we didn't have the same illusions about what we could do from inside the state' (Interview, 9 April 2020).

Regarding the outcomes of the commissions, Balton says that failure to secure prosecutions would 'make a mockery of anti-state capture efforts', but that prosecution has been delayed by the 'complexities' of the networks involved (Interview, 10 February 2020). However, Roussos is less optimistic, suggesting that the larger problem is that Zuma's successor, Cyril Ramaphosa, has to protect his fragile leadership (Interview, 12 February 2020).

ONLY CONNECT

Civil society's attempts to respond to state capture began piecemeal, with individual actions of limited scope. However, the work of investigative journalists, legal organisations and NGOs built public knowledge of these abuses over several years. This, in turn, created the conditions for further action through the development of a common language to understand the issue. This was necessary for the eventual coordination of civil society to oppose state capture. Nonetheless, as we have seen, while civil society coordination was possible at various points, South African civil society is not homogeneous, and, over time, the coalition broke down.

The counter-state capture efforts that did emerge were varied and initially uncoordinated because organisations undertook them with different ideological origins, strategic approaches and understandings of why (and how) the South African state was captured. As information about state capture was made public, South Africans' abilities to 'connect the dots', as Pravin Gordhan famously put it (News24 2017), produced a common set of immediate goals around which these groups could rally. This enabled them to overcome ideological differences and coordinate their efforts sufficiently to make a notable impact on the country's political landscape at a crucial moment. The coordination was able to advance the cause of one of the medium-term goals of many of these organisations – the removal from office of President Jacob Zuma. However, at the same time, the removal of Zuma exposed a weakness in the common understanding of the problem of state capture. Several activists argue that state capture was too narrowly centred on the Zuma presidency.

Some civil society organisations now play a watchdog role. But, in contrast, other organisations continue to demand justice, transparency and reform of the political system to help remedy the effects of state capture and eliminate the conditions that allowed it to happen.

NOTES

1 Dinga Sikwebu notes that a tally at the time showed that 80 Numsa leaders had decamped and joined the state. He adds that this meant the RDP's cooperative institutions became captured 'toy telephones' that ensured no accountability (Sikwebu, Interview, 9 April 2020).

2 These were the preconditions for loans or relief established by the International Monetary Fund, the World Bank and the US Treasury, revolving around government austerity, privatisation of enterprises and deregulation of markets.

3 According to Afrobarometer, in 2006 corruption was – alongside HIV – the fastest growing indicator since 1994 (Afrobarometer 2006).

4 As Neeshan Balton points out, good civil servants at various levels were increasingly driven out by frustration (Interview, 10 February 2020). Both Mike Roussos and Francis Antonie indicate that the idea of delivering a service lost importance from the top down (Roussos, Interview, 12 February 2020; Antonie, Interview, 13 March 2020).

5 The scandal involved the removal from their positions of several executives from SARS on the basis of reports that a 'Rogue Unit' existed within the service that investigated certain high-profile taxpayers among other activities. See Pauw (2020).

INTERVIEWS

Antonie, Francis. Helen Suzman Foundation, 13 March 2020.
Balton, Neeshan. Ahmed Kathrada Foundation, 10 February 2020.
Bhardwaj, Vinayak. AmaBhungane and the Open Society Foundation, 19 March 2020.
Bregman, Joel. My Vote Counts, 3 March 2020.
Fana, Wara. Eastern Cape Communication Forum, 17 April 2020.
Feinstein, Andrew. Shadow World Investigations, 10 February 2020.
McKinley, Dale. Right2Know Campaign, 16 March 2020.
Moeti, Koketso. Amandla.mobi, 28 April 2020.
Roussos, Mike. Opposition to Urban Tolling Alliance/Organisation for Undoing Tax Abuse; Southern African Catholic Bishops' Conference, 12 February 2020.
Sikwebu, Dinga. Tshisimani Centre for Activist Education and National Union of Metalworkers of South Africa, 9 April 2020.
Smithers, Maurice. Awethu! A People's Platform for Social Justice, 17 March 2020.
Van Dalsen, Anton. Helen Suzman Foundation, 13 March 2020.
Van Vuuren, Hennie. Open Secrets, 23 March 2020.

REFERENCES

Afrobarometer. 2006. 'The Public Agenda: Change and Stability in South Africans' Ratings of National Priorities'. Briefing Paper No. 45, 6 November 2006. https://www.afrobarometer.org/publication/public-agenda-change-and-stability-south-africans-ratings-national-priorities/.

AllPay Consolidated Investment Holdings (Pty) Ltd and Others v Chief Executive Officer of the South African Social Security Agency and Others (CCT48/13) [2013] ZACC 42; 2014 (1) SA 604 (CC); 2014 (1) BCLR 1 (CC). 29 November 2013.

Blumenfeld, Jesmond. 1997. 'From Icon to Scapegoat: The Experience of South Africa's Reconstruction and Development Programme'. *Development Policy Review* 15, no. 1: 65–91. https://www.researchgate.net/publication/228052399_From_Icon_to_Scapegoat_ The_Experience_of_South_Africa's_Reconstruction_and_Development_Programme.

Corruption Watch. 2015. 'Net1 Responds to CW's Notice of Motion'. *Corruption Watch*, 7 April 2015. https://www.corruptionwatch.org.za/net1-responds-to-cws-notice-of-motion/.

Corruption Watch. 2017. 'Dlamini Not off the Hook Regarding SASSA'. *Corruption Watch*, 15 June 2017. https://www.corruptionwatch.org.za/dlamini-not-off-hook-regarding-sassa/.

Cronje, Jan. 2020. 'Transnet Spent R122m on Sponsorships for New Age Business Briefings'. *Fin24*, 4 February 2020. https://www.news24.com/fin24/Companies/Industrial/ transnet-spent-r122m-on-sponsorships-for-new-age-business-briefings-20200204.

Economic Freedom Fighters and Others v Speaker of the National Assembly and Another (CCT76/17) [2017] ZACC 47; 2018 (3) BCLR 259 (CC); 2018 (2) SA 571 (CC). 29 December 2017.

Feinstein, Andrew. 2007. *After the Party: A Personal and Political Journey inside the ANC*. Johannesburg: Jonathan Ball.

Feinstein, Andrew. 2010. 'An Affront to Justice'. *Mail & Guardian*, 15 February 2010. https:// mg.co.za/article/2010-02-15-an-affront-to-justice/.

Glenister v President of the Republic of South Africa and Others (CCT48/10) [2011] ZACC 6; 2011 (3) SA 347 (CC); 2011 (7) BCLR 651 (CC). 17 March 2011.

GroundUp. 2017. 'Constitutional Court Orders CPS to Carry on Paying Grants, Rejects Fee Increase'. *GroundUp*, 17 March 2017. https://www.groundup.org.za/article/ constitutional-court-orders-cps-carry-paying-grants-rejects-fee-increase/.

Mabuza, Ernest. 2016. 'Conduct of SABC towards Journalists Amounts to Bullying, Court Told'. *Timeslive*, 22 July 2016. https://www.timeslive.co.za/news/2016-07-22-conduct-of-sabc-towards-journalists-amounts-to-bullying-court-told/.

Masondo, Sipho. 2016. 'Constitutional Court's Damning Judgment: Zuma Violated His Oath of Office'. *City Press*, 31 March 2016. https://city-press.news24.com/News/ constitutional-courts-damning-judgment-zuma-violated-his-oath-of-office-20160331.

McKinley, Dale T. 1997. *The African National Congress and the Liberation Struggle*. London: Palgrave Macmillan.

Minister of State Security. 2010. 'Protection of State Information Bill'. http://pmg-assets. s3-website-eu-west-1.amazonaws.com/130423bill06d-2010_2.pdf.

News24. 2017. 'Gordhan Expected in Pretoria for Kathrada Memorial'. *News24*, 5 April 2017. https://www.news24.com/News24/gordhan-expected-in-pretoria-for-kathrada-memorial-20170405.

Nicolson, Greg. 2015. 'Operation Fiela-Reclaim: Xenophobia, Legitimised?' *Daily Maverick*, 13 May 2015. https://www.dailymaverick.co.za/article/2015-05-13-operation-fiela-reclaim-xenophobia-legitimised/.

PARI. 2017. 'Betrayal of the Promise: How South Africa Is Being Stolen'. State Capacity Research Project Report, Public Affairs Research Institute, Johannesburg. https://pari. org.za/betrayal-promise-report/.

Pauw, Jacques. 2020. 'Public Protector & "Rogue Unit": How a Big Lie Became an Even Bigger Lie'. *Daily Maverick*, 8 December 2020. https://www.dailymaverick.co.za/article/2020-12-08-public-protector-rogue-unit-how-a-big-lie-became-a-bigger-and-bigger-lie/.

Petersen, Tammy. 2016. 'PSC Hits Back at DA over Anti-Corruption Forum Meeting Claims'. *News24*, 6 July 2016. https://www.news24.com/SouthAfrica/News/psc-hits-back-at-da-over-anti-corruption-forum-meeting-claims-20160706.

Pieterse, Edgar. 1997. 'South African NGOs and the Trials of Transition'. *Development in Practice* 7, no. 2: 157–166. https://www.tandfonline.com/doi/abs/10.1080/09614529 754620.

Pillay, Verashni. 2014. 'Numsa Maps out Its Brave New World'. *Mail & Guardian*, 30 October 2014. https://mg.co.za/article/2014-10-30-numsa-maps-out-its-brave-new-world/.

Public Protector. 2016. 'State of Capture'. Report No. 6 of 2016/17. http://www.saflii.org/images/329756472-State-of-Capture.pdf.

Robinson, Vicki and Stefaans Brümmer. 2006. 'SA Democracy Incorporated: Corporate Fronts and Political Party Funding'. Institute for Security Studies Paper 129. https://issafrica.org/research/papers/sa-democracy-incorporated-corporate-fronts-and-political-party-funding.

Sikwebu, Dinga, Chris Malikane, Norma Craven and Rehad Desai. 2015. 'Dialogue: Coming Together to Look Outward'. Centre for Civil Society, University of KwaZulu-Natal.

Smith, Carin. 2016. 'SAA Union Forks out R450 000 to Top Pilot – the Potent Backstory'. *BizNews*, 27 December 2016. https://www.biznews.com/undictated/2016/12/27/saa-union-pilot-potent-backstory.

South African Broadcasting Corporation Soc Ltd and Others v Democratic Alliance and Others (393/2015) [2015] ZASCA 156; [2015] 4 All SA 719 (SCA); 2016 (2) SA 522 (SCA). 8 October 2015.

South African Social Security Agency and Another v Minister of Social Development and Others (CCT48/17) [2018] ZACC 26; 2018 (10) BCLR 1291 (CC). 30 August 2018.

Southall, Roger. 2008. 'The ANC for Sale? Money, Morality and Business in South Africa'. *Review of African Political Economy* 35, no. 116: 281–299. https://www.jstor.org/stable/20406509#metadata_info_tab_contents.

Spicer, Michael. 2016. 'The Business Government Relationship: What Has Gone Wrong?' *The Journal of the Helen Suzman Foundation* 78: 3–19. https://hsf.org.za/publications/focus/focus-78-the-economy-1/michael-spicer.pdf.

Thamm, Marianne. 2016. 'Documents and Computers Seized in Armed, Apartheid Military-Style Robbery at Helen Suzman Foundation Offices'. *Daily Maverick*, 20 March 2016. https://www.dailymaverick.co.za/article/2016-03-20-documents-and-computers-seized-in-armed-apartheid-military-style-robbery-at-helen-suzman-foundation-offices/.

United Democratic Movement v Speaker of the National Assembly and Others (CCT89/17) [2017] ZACC 21; 2017 (8) BCLR 1061 (CC); 2017 (5) SA 300 (CC). 22 June 2017.

Van Vuuren, Hennie. 2019. *Apartheid Guns and Money: A Tale of Profit*. Oxford: Oxford University Press.

Wrong, Michela. 2009. *It's Our Turn to Eat: The Story of a Kenyan Whistle-Blower*. New York: Harper Collins.

7

Media Capture, the Mirror of
State Capture

Reg Rumney

In the run-up to the 17 December 2017 election of a new president of the African National Congress (ANC), and therefore president of the country, old-fashioned campaigning was intense. But it was augmented – surpassed even – by a new form of campaigning, at the centre of which was social media. Like all transitions, this was a messy affair displaying that full diversity of 'morbid symptoms' that characterised the interregnum between the 'old' and the 'new' periods, famously identified by Antonio Gramsci in his *Prison Notebooks* (Gramsci 1985, 556). This chapter discusses the symptoms – morbid and other – that emerged in South Africa's press in the state capture years.

In the election itself, the status quo had pinned its hopes on a continuation of (what might be called) a 'Zuma dynasty'. Their candidate was Nkosazana Dlamini-Zuma, a formidable politician with a history of government service; she was also a one-time wife of the outgoing president, Jacob Zuma. Up against Dlamini-Zuma was Cyril Ramaphosa, presented as the great hope of rescuing South Africa from the influence of Zuma, the man dubbed 'a kleptocrat with no interest in the future' by Jonny Steinberg (2020). That Ramaphosa would prevail against those described derisively as the 'Zuptas', the portmanteau word invented to portray the coalescence of the interests of the president and the Gupta family, was by no means assured.

Ramaphosa indeed won the votes of delegates to the ANC elective conference, albeit by a slim margin.

The Zupta social media campaign was not an isolated phenomenon but part of an ambitious project of media capture, which is often seen as complementary to any strain of state capture (Dragomir 2019). Transparency International defines 'state capture' as a form of pervasive corruption that enables private sector actors to 'use corruption to shape a nation's policies, legal environment, and economy to benefit their own private interests' (Martini 2014, 2). In one definition, media capture means the news media become so beholden to vested interests that they lack autonomy (Schiffrin 2017). But this position is contested. So, what degree of autonomy suffices for the media *not* to be captured? In a broad sense, media is always captured, 'subject to less visible, market and political mechanisms that tend to filter the information that is fit to print in a non-conspiratorial way' (Pedro-Carañana, Broudy and Klaehn 2018, 9).

However, this is not the topic of this chapter. This chapter examines the extraordinary efforts of elements within the state to capture traditional news media and to dominate the narrative through social media, and the role of independent media in fighting back against that capture. The underlying argument is that the best defence against media capture is the strong practice of public interest media, the essence of which is 'producing verified and verifiable information' and independence from 'political, commercial or factional interest' (Rumney 2022, 62). The chapter further discusses the role (and place) of the media in the unfolding drama around the Zuma presidency's relationship with the Gupta family. To this end, it is necessary to focus on the changing situation presented by the emerging power of social media; the fading place of the print media in the country; the politics of transformation; and the malfeasance – no, skulduggery – of the Zuma presidency's final years.

THE TWITTER TRENCHES

Whether a campaign by the media helped or hindered Nkosazana Dlamini-Zuma's candidacy remains to be researched. What was apparent was that hundreds of fictitious and anonymous social media accounts and several websites of doubtful provenance allowed smears, defamation and propagation of dubious narratives to benefit the 'Zupta project'. This kind of campaign could not be waged through traditional news media. Although the Gupta-controlled pay-TV news channel ANN7 and *New Age* newspaper were both roped into a campaign for the Zupta ticket, real purchase was delivered by social media.

In the weeks leading up to the elective conference, the anonymously owned website #WMCLeaks ramped up attacks on people said to symbolise the grip that South African whites held on the economy and the media.[1] Primarily journalists were attacked, but Ramaphosa associates were also targeted. Attacks on Ramaphosa were intensified on another anonymous website, dodgysaministers.com.[2] This featured defamatory pieces alongside poorly written defences of the Gupta family and their business interests. A respected *News24* digital journalist, Jean le Roux, considered evidence that the #WMCLeaks website was linked to the Guptas as 'convincing, if not conclusive' (Le Roux 2018). Neither the Guptas nor the Zumas distanced themselves from the messages on those fake news sites, and metadata of those websites and analysis of Twitter accounts and tweets give additional evidence of the link. Several fake news websites and Twitter accounts of the pro-Gupta social media army were traced to a former Gupta employee resident in India, Saurabh Aggarwal (Le Roux and Thamm 2017).

The social media campaign developed its own bizarre features, perhaps because it seemed to have involved non-South Africans working for the Guptas inside or outside the country. The group African Network of Centers for Investigative Reporting has suggested that this campaign was directed from inside South Africa mostly, using DIY social media manipulation software tools rather than being farmed out to professional groups specialising in such campaigns outside the country, although it did indicate there had been some experimentation with this approach (ANCIR 2017). *News24* traced the creator of the websites to India, to a Kapil Garg, CEO of a company based in the region whence the Guptas hailed, Uttar Pradesh (Cronje 2017).

Evidence came to light of further foreign involvement, namely, that of the London-based public relations firm Bell Pottinger. Earlier advice by this outfit to a Gupta subsidiary included a suggestion that what was at issue in the country was the 'economic emancipation' of South Africa's majority. The slogan 'white monopoly capital' (WMC), together with the phrase 'radical economic transformation' (RET), became key slogans associated with the Bell Pottinger operation in South Africa. That the Guptas employed a British company to rescue their reputation in South Africa using social media attracted international coverage. Stories were carried by the *New Yorker* (Caesar 2018), *Vanity Fair* (Mahajan 2019) and the *New York Times* (Onishi and Gebrekidan 2018). For all Bell Pottinger's later claims to innocence, the company's continued involvement in the campaign suggests they should have known the seriousness of the accusations against the family and ended the relationship sooner (Caesar 2018).

The Gupta family suffered further reputational damage by being involved with a firm known for representing dictators. Bell Pottinger stood accused of exacerbating racial tensions in the country (Segal 2018), yet the slogans suggested by the firm, along the lines of #endeconomicapartheid and #growthforall (Dugmore 2018), were not in themselves inflammatory, and while the supporting social media campaign turned out to be abusive and crude, it targeted both black and white journalists and politicians.

The pro-Gupta accounts on Twitter were colloquially known as 'Guptabots'. This is not technically correct. These were sock puppets,[3] which are real people tweeting and retweeting from anonymous accounts, and bots, or bits of software pretending to be people. They were frequently linked to #WMCLeaks and the other attack sites like DodgySAMinisters, amplifying the campaign's poisonous messages, and trolls were employed to attack doubters. Exactly how personalised the attacks became is exemplified by the so-called Cheater Peter sub-campaign. Editor Peter Bruce was accused of adultery, based on what was obviously a surveillance operation conducted by private investigators (Bruce 2017). Respected journalist Ferial Haffajee was also targeted (Haffajee and Davies 2017). Among other targets were Sam Sole, co-founder of the non-profit investigative unit amaBhungane (Pillay 2017), and Adriaan Basson, editor of South Africa's biggest online news platform, *News24* (Du Toit and Cowan 2019).

The #WMCLeaks site had a revealingly phrased definition of white monopoly capital: 'White Monopoly Capital represents the diabolic South African white capitalists who have carried out a long history of slavery & dominance on the native blacks and the nation's economy as a whole. A better South Africa post-apartheid, as envisioned by the black revolutionary Nelson Mandela, still has not seen its first dawn due to the power-hungry and exploitative whites who are unable to assimilate black-white equality in our society' (Wayback Machine 2017).

Like all effective propaganda or statements made to suit some nefarious project, this contained a grain of truth. Like all propaganda, the small truth was used to give birth to bigger lies, not about economic inequality but rather about the corruption occasioned by the particular form of state capture from which the social media campaign was designed to divert attention.

That the campaign fizzled out after the ascendancy of Ramaphosa to the presidency at the beginning of 2018 does not mean it had no effect. The authors of 'Manufacturing Divides: The Gupta-Linked Radical Economic Transformation (RET) Media Network' believe the campaign had been effective in diverting attention away from the Guptas (ANCIR 2017). The seeds of the WMC idea were sown in the fertile soil of widespread South African discontent with the lack of material progress in their lives. Certainly, it contributed to the ugly Twitter environment that has seen *News24* head Adriaan Basson (2020) join a growing group of journalists internationally in quitting the platform or reducing their participation (Liberman 2020).

The RET and WMC campaigns tried to use Facebook to achieve the same objectives as the Twitter campaign but failed in the local setting. Facebook pages that mirrored the fake news websites did not have much traction in South Africa and were not widely shared. Spontaneous comments on those pages reflected a great deal of scepticism about the narratives that were advanced (Fraser 2017). This contrasts with the rest of the world, where anti-journalist social media campaigns have used Facebook with great effect. The best example is that of Maria Ressa, founder and CEO of the Philippines news site Rappler. For years, she has been the target of a well-documented Facebook-facilitated government-sponsored harassment campaign (Posetti 2020). In the Philippines, as in other countries, Facebook is the primary and even the only way many ordinary people use the internet (Wallace 2020); in South Africa, its members far outnumber Twitter users. Facebook has 9.1 million active users and Twitter 4.7 million (Ornico and WorldWideWorx 2020). Twitter was the social media weapon of choice of former US president Donald Trump in his war against the news media, which he dubbed 'fake news'. In South Africa, the same phrase is sometimes used to dismiss criticism or competing narratives or, in one view, to create a moral panic around alternative news or satire, especially those that buttress the traditional gatekeeping function of professional news media (Wasserman 2020).

The Zupta social media campaign ventured beyond the idea of fake news into online assault and included doxing, which is the publication of sensitive private information on the internet with malicious intent. The campaign had a chilling effect on free speech. Twitter users who commented on any of the Twitter attacks on journalists risked diverting a swarm to themselves. The gravest feature of such social media campaigns is their anonymity. Extreme, defamatory, sexist, xenophobic, racist and bigoted commentary thrives on anonymous Twitter accounts and falsely named Facebook accounts, primarily because there is no accountability. AmaBhungane's founder, Sam Sole, has argued that the unaccountable neutrality claimed by social media platforms, such as Facebook and Twitter, clashes with the protections against defamation, hate speech and incitement to violence, and with the right to privacy and dignity that is afforded in South Africa's Constitution. He criticises the anonymising power of the internet, noting that no right exists for anonymous speech – except in journalism, where accountability is the responsibility of the publisher. This recognises that social media platforms have refused to acknowledge their responsibilities as 'publishers'. Moreover, Sole highlights the ability of technology to easily generate 'fake speakers', creating 'the simulacrum of a community of views [which] undermine the very basis of political speech' (Sole 2017). The counterargument is that banning anonymity is a threat to free speech, intensifying surveillance and producing further self-censorship (Phillips and Bartlett 2018).

THE MEDIA VS THE GUPTAS AND THE GUPTAS VS THE MEDIA

Before 2010, not much attention was paid to the Gupta family. They were known as the owners of Sahara Computers, a low-key PC assembly and marketing business, even though their closeness to politicians was hiding in plain sight. Atul, one of the three Gupta brothers, claimed he had a future ANC president (read: Jacob Zuma) 'in his pocket' (Myburgh 2017, 37). They first came to the attention of investigative news media with a 2008 report in *Noseweek* magazine, when they attempted to win an Angolan oil concession under false pretences (Noseweek 2008). Pieter-Louis Myburgh (2017) reveals an earlier scandal, when Sahara Computers, after winning the lion's share of a R1-billion contract to supply PC hardware to Gauteng's schools, failed to fulfil its conditions. Anton Harber (2020) points out that it is surprising how little coverage the latter received and is confounded that the Guptas were allowed to do further business with the government.

The Gupta family's first venture into media was via an intellectual left-leaning magazine called *The Thinker*. This was an unlikely initiative except that it arose from the friendship between ex-minister-in-the-presidency Essop Pahad, known to be one of former president Thabo Mbeki's closest friends and political allies, and the Guptas. There is no evidence linking the Guptas to any editorial input into this publication. Was the Gupta support for Pahad's publication simply friendship or was there a longer game? Whatever the case, that friendship meant the Guptas might have had some influence through Pahad on the Mbeki administration, although it was nothing like the power the family evidently exerted on the presidency when Zuma was in power. Importantly, by the time *The Thinker* was launched, Pahad was no longer a cabinet minister.

As will become clear, the Guptas seemed to see their news media products as instrumental to aims such as pleasing the president, rather than as instruments to build, protect and enhance their reputation.[4] Nevertheless, they betrayed a sense of hubris in relation to their power. Launching a publication or TV channel in South Africa is a sure-fire way to attract attention, as the Guptas would discover when they launched *New Age* in 2010.

The background to this ambition was the ANC's hostility to the established press, which certainly resided in white hands or in corporations perceived to be 'white' and limited in number (MDDA 2009). The biggest print publisher was Media24, a subsidiary of Naspers, the company that had metamorphosed from a modest-sized Afrikaans newspaper group into, first, a multinational pay-TV provider and then into an internet giant. Media24 published books and a wide range of newspapers and magazines, including the country's biggest-circulation daily tabloid *The Sun*. Naspers was – and remains – controlled by a small group of shareholders with preferential voting rights (Crotty 2020). A narrative around questioning media ownership patterns persisting beyond the apartheid era had emerged and was taken up within influential political circles. Early challenges to this state of affairs failed. These included an attempt by New Africa Investments Limited, which was denied by the broadcasting regulator (Fin24 2002), and another (short-lived) by a Nigerian upmarket newspaper called *This Day* (Hadland 2007).

In July 2010, the ANC published a discussion document called 'Media Transformation, Ownership and Diversity' for consideration. This reiterated a call – first made in 2007 – for a Media Appeals Tribunal and attacked the media for, among other things, 'an astonishing degree of dishonesty, lack of professional integrity and lack of independence' (ANC 2010, 8). Yet, the resolution underpinning the document proposed that parliament investigate the 'feasibility' of setting up a tribunal and, in one assessment, this development 'softened many of the more extreme positions [on this issue] taken by some ANC members in the recent past' (Duncan 2010).

By 2011, the pressure on the news media had dwindled and the threat of a press tribunal was off the table (Duncan 2010). The reason for this seeming retreat became clear during the same year: the ANC finally had its own newspaper and so had adopted a new approach to the issue. Critics of this new approach were branded anti-ANC or anti-transformation (Harber 2018b). It was later to become apparent that the ANC had another established media group in its sights as a tool of influence – the South African subsidiary of the Irish-owned Independent News and Media group. In 2009, the company saw the departure of Tony O'Reilly, the man who had overseen the investment in South Africa, and the firm was reported to be facing a 'financial abyss' (Holmwood 2009).

HOPELESS NEW HOPE

The Gupta-owned newspaper *New Age* had an inauspicious beginning. Its launch – originally set for October 2010 – suffered several delays, especially so when the newly appointed editor and other senior staff unexpectedly resigned. A second editor was found, and the newspaper was officially launched on 6 December 2010. The rest of the media may have been sceptical but were initially reticent. After a couple of years, it became apparent that the newcomer expected pro-ANC coverage and would glean large amounts of government advertising from the rest of the news media. Its competitors, *City Press* (City Press 2013), the *Mail & Guardian* (Faull and Evans 2013) and the *Daily Maverick* (De Waal 2013) ran articles on what they considered to be inordinate levels of advertising support from the government.

In carrying out its mission of being pro-ANC and positive towards the government, *New Age* was mediocre rather than innovative. One reason for this was that it had promised to be a national newspaper but, at the same time, undertook to cover news in each of the nine provinces. To effect this, each copy reserved half a page or more, which was devoted to provincial news. Expectedly, the founding proposition that 'local news' sold newspapers was weak. Truly important and interesting news from any province would feature in the national coverage of most newspapers. The result was that most of the provincial coverage in *New Age* was ghettoised and perfunctory. In certain provinces, the paper faced stiff competition from newspapers whose focus was to comprehensively cover provincial affairs, such as East London's *Daily Dispatch*. Importantly, too, *New Age*, as a Zuma-faction mouthpiece, proved how difficult it was to be pro-ANC rather than simply pro a particular (read: Zuma) faction within the ANC itself.

As Anton Harber points out, one lesson from the *New Age* venture was that 'it is tough – if not impossible – to run government-supporting media when the ruling party is fractious and directionless. It is hard to follow your generals when they themselves are not sure where they are headed' (2018b).

Underlying all this was a first-order question: what does 'being pro-ANC' as a news organisation mean? If it meant putting out versions of government or party press releases, this function was defunct in an age of government and party websites. Besides, the government has its own news outlet, *Vuk'uzenzele*, and SAnews. gov.za news service as well as specialist publications such as *Public Sector Manager*.

Perhaps 'being pro-ANC' could be interpreted as not covering controversial news about the governing party, but that approach risked rendering the newspaper irrelevant. Running stories that paint the opposition in a bad light can be construed as pro-ANC, but political scandal usually involves abuse of power, and opposition parties are limited in South Africa to controlling municipalities, and to only one of the provinces. Newspaper stories must have some sensational aspects to attract audiences. Even hyper-partisan newspapers, for example, those representing political parties, must – by definition – carry some news. The hard truth was that *New*

Age appeared not to be well-resourced enough to play a propaganda role or a role in providing different enough coverage to attract readers.

It was not unique in facing the problem of growing a readership without losing money. As an old saying in the news business goes: the way to make a small fortune in newspapers is to start with a big one. Also, the newspaper market has always been distorted by politics, in the sense that competitors may be supported not by advertising or readership revenue but by some entity or individual wanting to buy influence.

As an organ of propaganda, *New Age* was not memorable: as we have established, it failed to capture the provinces and struggled to establish a national profile. Interestingly, too, for an organisation linked to computer hardware and services, its website was slow and cluttered – this at a time when technology was starting to play a vital role in the delivery of news.

Furthermore, it was impossible to verify the newspaper's circulation numbers because this was not measured by the Audit Bureau of Circulation.[5] Instead, it claimed a print run of 100 000 and sold-for copies of 50 000, although an interpretation of the paper's readership from the South African Audience Research Foundation put the paid-copy figure at around 13 000 (Faull and Evans 2013). It was also shown that the paper was bought in bulk by state-owned enterprises. Then, the pretence of providing dedicated provincial coverage made it possible for individual provinces to claim that they were supporting it because it was reporting on their turf. This permitted them to buy advertising space in 'the public interest'. It is clear that the paper's business model relied on indirect funding from the state through various coffers. This was confirmed by evidence given to the Zondo Commission by the former Government Communication and Information System's CEO Themba Maseko (Eyewitness News 2016).

A further hint as to why *New Age* failed is to be found in Rajesh Sundaram's book *Indentured: Behind the Scenes at Gupta TV* (2018), which details the problems the editor – lured from India to launch ANN7 – encountered in the start-up phase of the pay-TV channel. Sundaram's narrative is replete with evidence that illustrates Atul Gupta's lackadaisical approach to news reporting. Sundaram paints a picture of a boorish man more interested in the physical attractiveness of the models the station might employ as presenters than in the quality of journalism. It is clear from Sundaram's account that Atul Gupta despised journalists, spying on them in the workplace to ensure they were not shirking. Moreover, his penny-pinching style of management went beyond good business sense and into illegality, as in employing Indian nationals without proper visas (Sundaram 2018). This portrayal of working for the Guptas squares with other reports – for instance, a description of Atul Gupta trying to get all and any services for free and how he could be 'ruthless' when it came to payment (Myburgh 2017, 39). The totality of the final product spoke volumes: this was especially so in the case of ANN7, which became a byword for poor TV news production and was something of a joke among professional journalists (Davis 2013).

However, the version of news it offered was not a matter of jest, with relentless attacks on perceived enemies of the Guptas and the Zuma presidency as staple items. When, in January 2018, it was announced that ANN7 would lose its slot on the DStv platform, some voices lamented a loss of media diversity, but two of South Africa's most respected media commentators, Anton Harber and veteran anti-apartheid journalist and editor Max du Preez, were united in celebration. The former called ANN7 'dishonest' (Harber 2018a), while Du Preez described it as a 'commercial tool of corrupt interests' undeserving of media freedom activism (Du Preez 2018).

The hostility shown by the mainstream towards both *New Age* and ANN7 raises questions of how to define and understand the issue of media diversity in South Africa's fraught political landscape. The question of diversity and its business twin, sustainability, hangs over all South Africa's media. The best point of entry is to consider the case of the purchase of the Independent Media group by a consortium of black interests, led by the controversial businessperson Iqbal Survé. The news was welcomed by President Jacob Zuma, who was the key speaker at an Independent News & Media SA 'homecoming' celebration event in Cape Town after the purchase (Vecchiato 2014).[6]

The change of ownership was positively received by those working at the newspaper group. They judged the move as rescuing newspapers from a business model that had treated its South African operations as a cash cow: an approach, it was said, that had threatened the future of the group in particular, and media diversity in general (MWASA 2013). That under the new management, the stable might be more sympathetic to the ruling party, and less sympathetic to opposition, was not raised as a problem. The old group was seen to have moved to being 'more pro-ANC', and supporting affirmative action, after the Irish company Independent News & Media bought a controlling stake in 1994 (Carlin 1994). After 1994, 'foreign-owned Independent Newspapers was surprisingly the leader in training and promoting black journalists'; its English-speaking competitor Times Media was not far behind (Berger 1999, 105).

Would these developments mean that the press would become less objective, less professional?

The goal of media is to reach as many members of a potential audience as possible. Some of the processes and procedures of a newspaper are designed to do that, for instance, showing evenhandedness or fairness in reporting, and having a variety of news from sport through weather and business to politics. Traditionally, South African journalists are expected not to identify too closely with any political party. The justification for this practice is the perception of a loss of impartiality that would diminish the credibility of the organisation, be it a newspaper or a website.

The first obligation of journalism, as articulated by Bill Kovach and Tom Rosenstiel in their seminal work on the elements of journalism, is to the truth (2003). The responsibility of the journalist is to tell the best version of the truth that is possible – even while wrapping it in a sensational package to attract a paying readership. The latter, of course, is an element of entertainment that editors neglect at their peril. That this principle may sometimes be more honoured in the breach than in the observance does not make it less important. The hope is that dedication to the truth will be more attractive to audience members than trying to figure out for themselves what is true or what represents vested interest. This does not mean arriving at 'objective truth' or being ideologically neutral. The journalist's job is to ask the right questions and produce an article based on evidence, multi-sourcing, on-location observation and careful analysis.

All of this should entail a serious focus on professionalism, which includes notions of ethics. As we have established, the Guptas did not show much interest in the profession nor in the business of journalism, and this prevented their media outlets from gaining a mass audience.

THE GUPTA MEDIA MONEY MACHINE

All the news media interventions, like other Gupta initiatives, were not what they claimed to be. *New Age* did make some money from government advertising, but much of its revenue was derived from hosting TV business breakfast events, the broadcasting costs of which were borne by the South African Broadcasting Corporation (SABC), while the revenue from them landed in the Gupta coffers (Madisa 2016). Former Gupta employee Rajesh Sundaram says R1.8-million revenue was generated from each business breakfast (Sundaram 2018). This went into the pockets of the Guptas.

Sundaram also claims that ANN7 was originally expected to make most of its money from government advertising; and that for the principals, the quality was unimportant. This was because the advertising was assured by the pressure that would be brought to bear by the station's important politically connected minority shareholder, the president's son Duduzane. This suggests that ANN7's real purpose was to keep Jacob Zuma happy. It is clear that the then president would have had a hand in the shaping of the station at the same time that he benefited from his son's 30 per cent stake in ANN7 (Sundaram 2018).

Another source of accumulation appeared to be extortion, in the form of a direct payment from the MultiChoice pay-TV channel. This was in return for the Guptas using their influence to persuade the SABC and the communications minister to entrench and defend MultiChoice's pay-TV monopoly. In November 2017, *News24* reported that the #GuptaLeaks showed that MultiChoice had made a questionable payment of R25 million to ANN7 and had almost tripled its annual payment to ANN7 from R50 million to R141 million – despite the latter's low audience figures (News24 2017). *News24* linked the ANN7 payments to an intervention by the minister to ignore an ANC decision to require encryption capabilities for the new set-top boxes needed for receiving digital television transmission. This prevented competitors from entering the digital pay-TV market.[7] MultiChoice has denied all these allegations, but there is evidence that MultiChoice created the policy documents that were eventually signed into law (News24 2017). The report – and we must repeat that MultiChoice firmly denied its validity – describes 'regulatory capture', the form of economic capture that inspired the idea of media capture (Schiffrin 2017, 10).

#GUPTALEAKS

On 28 May 2017, the mass-circulation *Sunday Times* ran an article with the headline 'Here they are: The emails that prove the Guptas run South Africa' (Sunday Times 2017). In an editorial on 1 June, the amaBhungane investigation unit agreed with the drift of this claim but revealed that the paper had been given access to only 650 emails from a trove of 100 000 to 200 000 emails – some hundreds of gigabytes worth (amaBhungane 2017, 2020).

Anton Harber details how the #GuptaLeaks found their way from two whistleblowers into the hands of Branko Brkic, the editor-in-chief of *Daily Maverick*, an increasingly influential online newspaper (Harber 2020). Brkic had initially approached businessperson Magda Wierzycka to finance the #GuptaLeaks' project (Harber 2020). He gave her a disk with a copy of the email trove, and she – in Harber's account – prematurely released some of the emails. Harber explains that Wierzycka believed the Guptas would soon find out about the leaks because journalists were not discreet enough and the amaBhungane team were not moving fast enough. Her aim was to circulate the information through WikiLeaks, if possible.

When this failed, she 'distributed 200 copies to people of influence', ensuring the information would soon hit the headlines of local newspapers (Harber 2020, 173–174). Wierzycka also wanted to involve politicians in the revelation of the email contents and had set up a meeting with former minister of finance Pravin Gordhan. The move was resisted by the amaBhungane-*Daily Maverick* team, who believed that this step would taint their journalism (Harber 2020).

AmaBhungane and *Daily Maverick* later explained that the original plan was to 'research thoroughly, for months if need be' to have the important stories ready so that if any attempt was made to halt publication, all the stories could be released at once. Instead of this option, the team had to begin working on publishing the reports immediately (AmaBhungane 2017). They were helped through collaboration with reporters who had been temporarily transferred from *News24*. Newspapers such as *City Press* and *News24*'s website, the biggest in South Africa, considerably broadened the audience for the story – achieving the public interest goals of both amaBhungane and *Daily Maverick*.

The form of this collaboration reveals the changing face of the media landscape in the country. Only one of the three organisations working on the #GuptaLeaks, amaBhungane, is a pure non-profit; the second, *Daily Maverick*, is a hybrid membership organisation with some revenue from members, some from advertising and some from donors. The third, Media24, was and is one the largest commercial news organisations in the country, and one that could afford to devote resources to investigations.

AmaBhungane was a logical choice for exposing the #GuptaLeaks; it had already published reports on the questionable business deals of the Gupta family. On 20 August 2010, amaBhungane reported on an important, though complex, mining and financial story, in which the Guptas were involved in a deal where steel giant ArcelorMittal was about to gain control of strategic iron ore mining rights (Sole 2010). A few stories were devoted to this development, but the pace of amaBhungane reporting involving the Gupta family picked up thereafter. A landmark exposé towards the end of 2016 was amaBhungane's report on the results of a year-long investigation into how the Guptas were transferring out of the country hundreds of millions of rand in kickbacks from companies that were doing business with the state-owned enterprise Transnet (Brümmer, Comrie and Sole 2016).

A regular criticism in reaction to exposés such as those arising from the #GuptaLeaks is that journalists only care about 'government corruption' but are not concerned with corruption in the private sector. The #GuptaLeaks reporting showed that private, often foreign-owned, multinationals turned a blind eye to corruption in South Africa to profit from lucrative contracts. Several multinationals were ensnared in the Gupta web, as an examination of the amaBhungane website shows (AmaBhungane 2020).

In the wake of the #GuptaLeaks, much news coverage has been about the what and the how of state capture and the establishment of commissions of inquiry, raising the prospect of 'scandal fatigue'. What is missing is the deep question: why did all this take place?

In June 2019, Advocate Hermione Cronje, head of the Investigating Directorate at the National Prosecuting Authority, outlined the story or stories that still needed to be done. She referred to a large group of people who were neither whistleblowers nor corrupt actors at compromised institutions and who did nothing about the wrongdoing they saw. She went on to suggest that the deep racial divide in the country continues to plague the body politic and pointed out that economic inequalities in South Africa should not be ignored in explaining how state capture came about (SABC 2019).

Can South Africa's media play a role in this truth-telling?

UNFULFILLED AMBITIONS

The #GuptaLeaks revealed that the Guptas had ambitions beyond that of a single national newspaper and TV channel. They show that Iqbal Survé's Sekunjalo Investment Holdings had negotiated to sell a conditional 50 per cent stake in the company – this would have given the Guptas an effective 27.5 per cent stake in Independent Media. But the deal fell apart. Astonishingly, the sale would have given the Gupta-linked company Oakbay the right to appoint Independent Media's editors (Dugmore 2018). Since the change of ownership of Independent Media in 2013 was not achieved with direct state involvement, it does not fit neatly into a definition of media capture.

Other attempts at media capture by the Guptas included a plan to buy the independent radio broadcaster Primedia and the *Mail & Guardian* newspaper group (Dugmore 2018). Most ambitious of all was the plan to capture the SABC. Sipho Masinga, the SABC's former group executive for technology, testified to a parliamentary hearing that in 2012 he was called to a meeting where the SABC was presented with a Gupta proposal for TNA Media, the holding company of *New Age*, to take over the news function of the SABC (Dugmore 2018).

It seems certain that media plurality makes state capture more difficult. Obviously, then, the decline in plurality is concerning. Print media ownership in South Africa is not ideally diversified, and acquisitions and closures have diminished the number of independent outlets over the years (Rumney 2014). Further rationalisation of print may be inevitable in the wake of the Covid-19 crisis, which has aggravated the problems of print especially, but also of news media in general (Rumney 2020). While radio stations proliferated after the liberalisation of the airwaves and the ending of apartheid, they have not been immune to a decrease in revenue.

Although no longer a monopoly, the SABC has not been exposed to the full force of competition. It owns the important mass-market, indigenous-language radio stations and three of the four free-to-air channels. Because of its powerful position, the SABC is a ready target for state capture or, rather, capture by a faction of the governing party. This could be accomplished through the appointment of unsuitable persons to key positions in its governance or managerial structures. Such vulnerabilities were used to benefit the Guptas financially as well as in attempts to censor news that was hostile to the Zupta regime (Mkentane 2019). Unlike other broadcasters, which are funded by licence fees or directly by the government, the SABC is as vulnerable to declines in advertising as are media houses in the private sector. But the SABC's sole shareholder, the state, can be tapped for funds or guarantees in times of crisis.

MEDIA CAPTURE BY ANOTHER NAME

The significance of investigative journalism, its traditions and its practice have been confirmed through its sensational revelations across several news platforms of wrongdoing by the Guptas. But the ordinary business of news media, in the final analysis, may well have been more important. It was not investigative journalism that brought to public attention the landing at Waterkloof Air Force Base of a private plane from India carrying guests to a Gupta wedding. This was the story that propelled the Gupta family into the spotlight. No, the radio reporter who broke the story chanced upon it in the course of his professional duties. Similarly, the scandal of the state paying for the lavish Zuma compound at Nkandla was uncovered by chance by the late Mandy Rossouw of the *Mail & Guardian* (Harber 2020).

So, more than anything else, the exposure of the Guptas vindicated the craft of journalism in South Africa. Yet, journalists should not bask too long in the reflected warmth of the biggest series of investigations to dominate front pages in the country's history. While civil society and business were spurred to defend the country as the sheer scale of state capture became known, attempts at media capture did not receive the same attention. The diversion of advertising revenue to friendly news outlets, a key feature of media capture elsewhere in the world, was scandalous in intention and should have engendered more outrage in a country that claims to be a democracy. While state ownership, as with the SABC, has traditionally been a key part of media capture, private sector capture is also necessary, and media capture through the allocation of finance to privately owned but state-aligned media outlets merely maintains a veneer of democracy.

Blogs and social media accounts do provide some balance to mainstream media by allowing citizens and groups a voice. But, as outlined at the beginning of this chapter, media capture as it is traditionally envisaged remains important in having the resources to perform professional reporting – or in the case of aggressive media capture, deliberately choosing not to do so. Moreover, the low barriers to entry into the profession have enabled the birth of internet-based news outlets such as *Daily Maverick*. The new non-profit news media model does allow for a greater plurality of news media, but 'in free societies, the bulk of investment has for more than a century come from for-profit media' (Nielsen 2020, 325). Social media platforms threaten the ability of traditional news media to generate revenue as they are forced to migrate online (Dugmore 2018). Their response is to introduce paywalls, subscription models that lock non-subscribers out of all or some content, as *News24* has done, and potentially limit their reach (Uroic 2017).[8]

Social media, as we have seen, can be captured to some extent by malign actors to discredit – or silence – critics and discourage free speech, especially if the state uses trolls, sock puppets and bots against its media enemies. The saga of the Gupta-aligned social media campaigns showed that a new front has been opened up in attempts to aid state capture through media capture, in addition to traditional media.

As the business of media becomes more difficult and further consolidation looms, the threat of traditional media capture, combined with weaponised social media or regulations designed to suppress freedom of speech and new media on the internet, could defuse the impact of the tradition of journalism that helped to push back the state capture of the Zupta years.

In the post-Zupta period, South Africa did not witness the same intense attempt to capture traditional news media in the cause of capturing the state. To be sure, one newspaper group, Independent Media, seemed to be aligned to the RET camp in the sense of being virulently anti-Ramaphosa (Dlamini 2022). But there is emphatically no suggestion that any newspaper or news media organisation was involved in the social media instigation of violence and looting during the violent July 2021 unrest, which President Ramaphosa has described as an 'attempted insurrection' (Sobuwa 2022). Open instigation by Twitter accounts was evident, though closed-messaging app WhatsApp may have been the primary means of organising the looting and rioting (Shapshak 2021). However, the unrest was criminal activity, not narrative manipulation, and social media remains a new terrain in the battle for media capture.

NOTES

1 The archived pages of the WMCLeaks website are available through the Internet Archive's Wayback Machine (https://archive.org/web/). The website is no longer online as a stand-alone site; many of the headlines link to articles that no longer exist.
2 The website is no longer online as a stand-alone site and many of the headlines link to articles that no longer exist. The archived pages of dodgyministers.com can be found at https://web.archive.org/web/20180121180349/http://www.dodgysaministers.com/.
3 A sock puppet can be defined as 'a fictitious online identity created for the purposes of deception' (Kats 2020).
4 This is evident in the descriptions of the interactions of the Guptas with President Zuma around the launch of ANN7 in Rajesh Sundaram's book *Indentured*, including naming the channel the 'Africa News Network', a suggestion by Zuma (Sundaram 2018, 100).
5 The Audit Bureau of Circulation audits the claimed circulation figures of newspapers and magazines so that advertisers can be assured that circulations, the currency of the print news industry, are correct and comparable.
6 The name has since changed to Independent Media.
7 Not allowing eTV or other broadcasters to encrypt channels on the digital TV boxes to be rolled out means that consumers have to have two set-top boxes, a more expensive and unwieldy option. Older TV sets without digital capabilities need set-top boxes to decode the new digital signals. Encryption on the set-top boxes would allow any provider who wants consumers to pay for premium content to block that content to non-payers.
8 News24 operates a 'freemium' model, with most 'breaking news' accessible to non-subscribers but 'premium content' reserved for subscribers (Nevill 2020).

REFERENCES

AmaBhungane. 2017. 'Editorial: The #GuptaLeaks Revealed'. 1 June 2017. https://amabhungane.org/stories/editorial-the-guptaleaks-revealed/.
AmaBhungane. 2020. 'Special Report: The #GuptaLeaks and More – All Our Stories on State Capture'. 10 August 2020. https://amabhungane.org/stories/special-report-the-guptaleaks-and-more-all-our-stories-on-state-capture-2/.
ANC. 2010. 'Media Transformation, Ownership and Diversity'. *Politicsweb*, 29 June 2010. http://www.politicsweb.co.za/documents/the-problem-with-our-press--anc.
ANCIR. 2017. 'Manufacturing Divides: The Gupta-Linked Radical Economic Transformation (RET) Media Network'. African Network of Centers for Investigative Reporting, 27 June 2017. https://s3-eu-west-1.amazonaws.com/s3.sourceafrica.net/documents/118115/Manufacturing-Divides.pdf.
Basson, Adriaan. 2020. 'Adriaan Basson: Why I Will No Longer Tweet'. *News24*, 20 July 2020. https://www.news24.com/news24/columnists/adriaanbasson/adriaan-basson-why-i-will-no-longer-tweet-20200720.

Berger, Guy. 1999. 'Towards an Analysis of the South African Media and Transformation, 1994–1999'. *Transformation* 38: 82–116.

Bruce, Peter. 2017. 'The Price of Writing about the Guptas'. *Business Day*, 29 June 2017. https://www.businesslive.co.za/bd/opinion/columnists/2017-06-29-peter-bruce--the-price-of-writing-about-the-guptas/.

Brümmer, Stefaans, Susan Comrie and Sam Sole. 2016. 'Exclusive: Guptas "Laundered" Kickback Millions – Here's the Evidence'. *AmaBhungane*, 8 December 2016. https://amabhungane.org/stories/exclusive-guptas-laundered-kickback-millions-heres-the-evidence/.

Caesar, Ed. 2018. 'The Reputation-Laundering Firm That Ruined Its Own Reputation'. *New Yorker*, 18 June 2018. https://www.newyorker.com/magazine/2018/06/25/the-reputation-laundering-firm-that-ruined-its-own-reputation.

Carlin, John. 1994. 'O'Reilly Buys 31% of South African Newspaper Group'. *The Independent*, 10 February 1994. https://www.independent.co.uk/news/business/o-reilly-buys-31-south-african-newspaper-group-1393200.html.

City Press. 2013. 'Telkom Splurges R34m on New Age Ads'. *News24*, 10 February 2013. https://www.news24.com/fin24/telkom-splurges-r34m-on-new-age-ads-20130210.

Cronje, Jan. 2017. 'Exclusive: Indian IT Guru Linked to Fake WMC Sites'. *News24*, 26 July 2017. https://www.news24.com/News24/exclusive-indian-it-guru-linked-to-fake-wmc-sites-20170726.

Crotty, Ann. 2020. 'Naspers AGM: The Antithesis of Shareholder Democracy'. *TechCentral*, 24 August 2020. https://techcentral.co.za/naspers-agm-the-antithesis-of-shareholder-democracy/100687/.

Davis, Rebecca. 2013. 'ANN7: Car-Crash Viewing, but No Laughing Matter'. *Daily Maverick*, 25 August 2013. https://www.dailymaverick.co.za/article/2013-08-26-ann7-car-crash-viewing-but-no-laughing-matter/.

De Waal, Mandy. 2013. 'The New Age: A Growing Media Empire, Built with Your Money'. *Daily Maverick*, 19 April 2013. https://www.dailymaverick.co.za/article/2013-04-19-the-new-age-a-growing-media-empire-built-with-your-money/.

Dlamini, Sizwe. 2022. 'Ramaphosa, Gordhan Want to Silence Independent Media Using the Banks'. *IOL*, 19 July 2022. https://www.iol.co.za/news/ramaphosa-gordhan-want-to-silence-independent-media-using-the-banks-c7b1173a-63cc-4b98-a291-8b8f02ccf37b.

Dragomir, Marius. 2019. 'Media Capture in Europe'. Media Development Investment Fund. https://www.mdif.org/wp-content/uploads/2019/07/MDIF-Report-Media-Capture-in-Europe.pdf.

Dugmore, Harry. 2018. 'Paying the Piper: The Sustainability of the News Industry and Journalism in South Africa in a Time of Digital Transformation and Political Uncertainty'. School of Journalism and Media Studies, Rhodes University. https://research.usc.edu.au/esploro/outputs/report/Paying-the-Piper-The-sustainability-of/99450848002621.

Duncan, Jane. 2010. 'Blade Nzimande's Threat to Democracy'. *South African Civil Society Information Service*, 5 October 2010. http://sacsis.org.za/site/article/558.1.

Du Preez, Max. 2018. 'ANN7 Does Not Deserve Our Activism'. *News24*, 6 February 2018. https://www.news24.com/news24/columnists/maxdupreez/ann7-does-not-deserve-our-activism-20180206.

Du Toit, Pieter and Kyle Cowan. 2019. '"I Will Kill You" – Bosasa Operative to Journalist'. *News24*, 5 February 2019. https://www.news24.com/news24/southafrica/news/i-will-kill-you-bosasa-operative-to-journalist-20190205.

Eyewitness News. 2016. 'Gupta Brother to Themba Maseko: You Will Be Sorted Out'. *Eyewitness News*, 3 November 2016. http://ewn.co.za/2016/11/03/gupta-brother-to-themba-maseko-you-will-be-sorted-out.

Faull, Lionel and Sarah Evans. 2013. 'New Age: Dawn of Advertising Riches with No Circulation Figures'. *Mail & Guardian*, 25 January 2013. http://mg.co.za/article/2013-01-25-00-new-age-dawn-of-advertising-riches-with-no-circulation-figures/.

Fin24. 2002. 'Icasa Sinks Nail/Kagiso Deal', *Fin24*, 2 January 2002. https://www.news24.com/Fin24/Icasa-sinks-NailKagiso-deal-20020102.

Fraser, Andrew. 2017. 'We Go inside the Guptabot Fake News Network'. *TechCentral*, 4 September 2017. https://techcentral.co.za/go-inside-guptabot-fake-news-network/76767/.

Gramsci, Antonio. 1985. *Selections from the Prison Notebooks of Antonio Gramsci*. New York: International Publishers.

Hadland, Adrian. 2007. 'The South African Print Media, 1994–2004: An Application and Critique of Comparative Media Systems Theory'. PhD thesis, University of Cape Town. https://open.uct.ac.za/handle/11427/7479.

Haffajee, Ferial and Marc Davies. 2017. 'Ferial Haffajee: The Gupta Fake News Factory and Me'. *Huffington Post*, 2 August 2017. https://www.huffingtonpost.co.uk/2017/06/05/ferial-haffajee-the-gupta-fake-news-factory-and-me_a_22126282/.

Harber, Anton. 2018a. 'South African News Station ANN7 Is on the Skids: Why It Won't Be Missed'. *The Conversation*, 1 February 2018. http://theconversation.com/south-african-news-station-ann7-is-on-the-skids-why-it-wont-be-missed-91085.

Harber, Anton. 2018b. 'The New Age Experiment: Government's Attempt to Control the Media Has Done Industry No Favours'. *The Media Online*, 9 July 2018. https://themediaonline.co.za/2018/07/the-new-age-experiment-governments-attempt-to-control-the-media-has-done-industry-no-favours/.

Harber, Anton. 2020. *So, for the Record: Behind the Headlines in an Era of State Capture*. Johannesburg: Jonathan Ball.

Holmwood, Leigh. 2009. 'Sir Anthony O'Reilly Leaves INM to Be Replaced by His Son Gavin'. *The Guardian*, 13 March 2009. http://www.theguardian.com/media/2009/mar/13/anthony-oreilly-resigns-independent-news-and-media.

Kats, Daniel. 2020. 'Identifying Sockpuppet Accounts on Social Media Platforms'. *NortonLifeLock Research Group*, 29 April 2020. https://www.nortonlifelock.com/blogs/research-group/identifying-sockpuppet-accounts-social-media.

Kovach, Bill and Tom Rosenstiel. 2003. *The Elements of Journalism: What Newspeople Should Know and the Public Should Expect*. London: Atlantic Books.

Le Roux, Jean. 2018. 'The History of WMC'. *News24*, 2 November 2018. https://www.news24.com/news24/analysis/the-history-of-wmc-20181101.

Le Roux, Jean and Marianne Thamm. 2017. 'Scorpio: In the Non-Surprise of the Year, wmcleaks.com Smear Campaign Tracked to a Gupta Associate'. *Daily Maverick*, 21 June 2017. https://www.dailymaverick.co.za/article/2017-06-22-scorpio-in-the-non-surprise-of-the-year-wmcleaks-com-smear-campaign-tracked-to-a-gupta-associate/.

Liberman, Mark. 2020. 'A Growing Group of Journalists Has Cut Back on Twitter, or Abandoned It Entirely'. *Poynter*, 9 October 2020. https://www.poynter.org/reporting-editing/2020/a-growing-group-of-journalists-has-cut-back-on-twitter-or-abandoned-it-entirely/.

Madisa, Kgothatso. 2016. 'SABC Resources Used to Fund ANN7: Vuyo Mvoko'. *Sowetan*, 13 December 2016. https://www.sowetanlive.co.za/news/2016-12-13-sabc-resources-used-to-fund-ann7-vuyo-mvoko/.

Mahajan, Karan. 2019. 'How the Gupta Brothers Hijacked South Africa Using Bribes Instead of Bullets'. *Vanity Fair*, March 2019. https://www.vanityfair.com/news/2019/03/how-the-gupta-brothers-hijacked-south-africa-corruption-bribes.

Martini, Maíra. 2014. 'State Capture: An Overview'. Transparency International, 11 March 2014. https://www.transparency.org/files/content/corruptionqas/State_capture_an_overview_2014.pdf.

MDDA. 2009. 'Trends of Ownership and Control of Media in South Africa'. Media Development and Diversity Agency, 15 June 2009. https://www.yumpu.com/en/document/view/4049053/trends-of-ownership-and-control-of-media-in-south-africa-mdda.

Mkentane, Luyolo. 2019. 'Hlaudi Motsoeneng Defends Controversial SABC "Censorship Policy"'. *Business Day*, 11 September 2019. https://www.businesslive.co.za/bd/national/2019-09-11-hlaudi-motsoeneng-defends-controversial-sabc-censorship-policy/.

MWASA. 2013. 'How INM "Harvested" Independent Newspapers in SA'. *Politicsweb*, 26 February 2013. http://www.politicsweb.co.za/news-and-analysis/how-inm-harvested-independent-newspapers-in-sa?sn=Marketingweb+detail.

Myburgh, Pieter-Louis. 2017. *The Republic of Gupta: A Story of State Capture*. Cape Town: Penguin Books.

Nevill, Glenda. 2020. 'News24.com to Launch "Freemium" Paywall'. *The Media Online*, 13 July 2020. //themediaonline.co.za/2020/07/news24-com-to-launch-freemium-paywall/.

News24. 2017. '#GuptaLeaks: How MultiChoice Paid the Guptas Millions'. *News24*, 24 November 2017. https://www.news24.com/news24/southafrica/news/guptaleaks-how-multichoice-paid-the-guptas-millions-20171124.

Nielsen, Rasmus Kleis. 2020. 'Economic Contexts of Journalism'. In *The Handbook of Journalism Studies*, edited by Karin Wahl-Jorgensen and Thomas Hanitzsch, 324–340. New York: Routledge.

Noseweek. 2008. 'Too Slick Operators'. *Noseweek* 105, 1 July 2008. https://www.noseweek.co.za/article/1739/Too-Slick-Operators.

Onishi, Norimitsu and Selam Gebrekidan. 2018. 'In Gupta Brothers' Rise and Fall, the Tale of a Sullied ANC'. *New York Times*, 22 December 2018. https://www.nytimes.com/2018/12/22/world/africa/gupta-zuma-south-africa-corruption.html.

Ornico and WorldWideWorx. 2020. 'The South African Social Media Landscape 2020'. June 2020. https://website.ornico.co.za/2020/06/10/south-african-social-media-landscape-2020/.

Pedro-Carañana, Joan, Daniel Broudy and Jeffery Klaehn, eds. 2018. *The Propaganda Model Today: Filtering Perception and Awareness*. London: University of Westminster Press.

Phillips, Jess and Jamie Bartlett. 2018. 'Should Anonymous Social Media Accounts Be Banned?' *The Guardian*, 30 September 2018. http://www.theguardian.com/media/2018/sep/30/social-media-anonymity-ban-debate-trolls-abuse--jess-phillips-jamie-bartlett.

Pillay, Verashni. 2017. 'BLF Violently Disrupt amaBhungane Meeting'. *Power 98.7*, 27 July 2017. https://www.power987.co.za/news/blf-violently-disrupt-amabhungane-meeting/.

Posetti, Julie. 2020. 'Journalists Like Maria Ressa Face Death Threats and Jail for Doing Their Jobs: Facebook Must Take Its Share of the Blame'. *CNN*, 2 July 2020. https://www.cnn.com/2020/06/30/opinions/maria-ressa-facebook-intl-hnk/index.html.

Rumney, Reg. 2014. 'Twenty Years of SA Media Ownership (1994–2014)'. In *Media Landscape 2014: Celebrating 20 Years of South Africa's Media*, edited by Department of Communications, 38–57. Pretoria: Department of Communications.

Rumney, Reg. 2020. 'SANEF Covid-19 Impact on Journalism Report (Interim)'. *SANEF*, 1 June 2020. https://sanef.org.za/sanef-launches-covid19-impact-on-journalism-interim-report-2/.

Rumney, Reg. 2022. 'The State of the News Media: An Update to SANEF's 2020 Covid-19 Interim Report and Some Cross-Cutting Issues'. *SANEF*. https://sanef.org.za/wp-content/uploads/2022/08/State-of-the-Media-June-2022-SANEF.pdf.

SABC. 2019. 'Journalists Played Key Role in Exposing Malpractice in SA: Cronje'. *SABC News*, 22 June 2019. https://www.sabcnews.com/sabcnews/journalists-played-key-role-in-exposing-malpractice-in-sa-cronje/.

Schiffrin, Anya, ed. 2017. 'In the Service of Power: Media Capture and the Threat to Democracy'. *CIMA*, 16 August 2017. https://www.cima.ned.org/publication/media-capture-in-the-service-of-power/.

Segal, David. 2018. 'How Bell Pottinger, PR Firm for Despots and Rogues, Met Its End in South Africa'. *New York Times*, 5 February 2018. https://www.nytimes.com/2018/02/04/business/bell-pottinger-guptas-zuma-south-africa.html.

Shapshak, Toby. 2021. 'Fanning the Flames through the Internet'. *Businesslive*, 22 July 2021. https://www.businesslive.co.za/fm/fm-fox/digital/2021-07-22-fanning-the-flames-through-the-internet/.

Sobuwa, Y. 2022. 'July Unrest Was a Deliberate Decision to Instigate, Coordinate and Incite Widespread Destruction – Ramaphosa'. *City Press*, 1 April 2022. https://www.news24.com/citypress/news/july-unrest-was-a-deliberate-decision-to-instigate-coordinate-and-incite-widespread-destruction-ramaphosa-20220401.

Sole, Sam. 2010. 'Guptas Key to ArcelorMittal Deal'. *AmaBhungane*, 20 August 2010. https://amabhungane.org/stories/guptas-key-to-arcelormittal-deal/.

Sole, Sam. 2017. 'Comment: Media, Accountability and Governance'. *AmaBhungane*, 13 September 2017. https://amabhungane.org/stories/comment-media-accountability-governance/.

Steinberg, Jonny. 2020. 'Just Our Luck to Have Got Zuma When We Did'. *Business Day*, 26 November 2020. https://www.businesslive.co.za/bd/opinion/columnists/2020-11-26-jonny-steinberg-just-our-luck-to-have-got-zuma-when-we-did/.

Sundaram, Rajesh. 2018. *Indentured: Behind the Scenes at Gupta TV*. Johannesburg: Jacana Media.

Sunday Times. 2017. 'Here They Are: The Emails That Prove the Guptas Run South Africa'. *Sunday Times*, 28 May 2017. https://www.timeslive.co.za/sunday-times/news/2017-05-28-here-they-are-the-emails-that-prove-the-guptas-run-south-africa/.

Uroic, Igor. 2017. 'Media: The Rise (and Fall?) of Paywalls'. *Alexander Group*, 1 August 2017. https://www.alexandergroup.com/insights/media-the-rise-and-fall-of-paywalls/.

Vecchiato, Paul. 2014. 'SA Media House to "Transform" News Coverage'. *Heraldlive*, 28 February 2014. https://www.heraldlive.co.za/news/2014-02-28-sa-media-house-to-transform-news-coverage/.

Wallace, Savannah. 2020. 'In the Developing World, Facebook Is the Internet'. *Medium*, 7 September 2020. https://medium.com/swlh/in-the-developing-world-facebook-is-the-internet-14075bfd8c5e.

Wasserman, Herman. 2020. 'Fake News from Africa: Panics, Politics and Paradigms'. *Journalism* 21, no. 1: 3–16. https://journals.sagepub.com/doi/pdf/10.1177/146488491 7746861.

Wayback Machine. 2017. 'WMC Leaks: Uncensored Real Stories on White Monopoly Capital'. 9 November 2017. https://web.archive.org/web/20171109015435/https://www.wmcleaks.com/.

SECTION 3

PAST AND FUTURE

8

State Capture and the Popular Imagination: Narrowing the Narrative

Sizwe Mpofu-Walsh

If one is living in an abnormal society, then only abnormal expression can express that society.

— Dambudzo Marechera, *Cemetery of Mind*

Texts – whether films, paintings, poems or songs – always frame a particular picture of the world. They make witting and unwitting choices about which slices of reality to depict, and which slices to omit. On those rare occasions when texts pierce the popular imagination, they can create 'collective social understandings' that universalise these 'particular ways of seeing' (Storey 2018, 4). The political impact of texts, then, is heightened in proportion to their social reach.

This chapter focuses on the 'particular ways of seeing' encapsulated in popular artistic representations of state capture between 2012 and 2019. It explores how state capture was presented in paintings, non-fiction films and rap songs, and investigates how various South African publics responded to these artworks. It does this by highlighting work that gained heightened public attention.

Each section involves a close analysis of between two and five works, which are read against news articles and scholarly criticism in the state capture era. Through a combination of art, film and lyrical criticism, these sections trace links between popular art and the popular political imagination and investigate the relationship between the aesthetics of state capture and its politics.

To achieve this, I explore a single claim: popular art in South Africa narrowed the meanings of state capture between 2012 and 2019. It did this by confining the notion to a limited time period and restricting its actors to Jacob Zuma and the Gupta family, thereby obscuring state capture's structural and historical roots. As such, popular art suffered from – and simultaneously co-produced – a narrow conception of state capture, which oversimplified events of the late Zuma presidency and produced an ideology rather than an understanding of the notion. While these works seized unprecedented public attention, they also presented a binary conception of state capture.

THE DOMINANT NARRATIVE

Five features characterise what we will call the 'dominant narrative' of state capture. Firstly, it confines the notion of state capture to the late years of Zuma's administration (2012–2018). This tends to obscure state capture's deeper systemic – even structural – roots. It also disregards forms of state capture that preceded – and, indeed, have followed – the Zuma presidency. It treats these years as aberrant, even roguish, rather than a continuation of underlying trends in African National Congress (ANC) governance. It treats the Gupta era – as it might be called – as peculiar, rather than locating it in a long history of parasitic public-private bargains, which date back to the Dutch East India Company's settlement at the Cape in the mid-seventeenth century (Van der Merwe and Du Plessis 2004). Furthermore, the dominant narrative treats state capture as the product of evil intentions and grandiose premeditations rather than the product of public-private interdependence that is deeply embedded in contemporary debates around development.

Secondly, the dominant narrative relies on a strict separation between 'angels' and 'devils'. Broadly, this separation credits those who endorsed Cyril Ramaphosa for ANC president in 2017, and discredits those who supported Jacob Zuma's preferred successor, Nkosazana Dlamini-Zuma. This obscures the ever-shifting alliances within the ANC, the state and its various allies in the private realm. For instance, following the ANC's 2017 elective conference, Nkosazana Dlamini-Zuma assumed high governmental office as minister for cooperative governance and traditional affairs.

The narrative also shields various ANC politicians who abetted the state capture project through either silence or complicity. For instance, Cyril Ramaphosa became deputy president of the ANC in 2012, running on Jacob Zuma's electoral slate in that election. The narrative fails, therefore, to explore the multiple allegiances between those it paints as state capture's angels, and those it paints as its devils. Take a figure like Fikile Mbalula, the serving minister of transport. In 2007, he supported Zuma for the ANC presidency (Twala 2009); in 2012, he contested Zuma's slate in an unsuccessful bid to become ANC secretary general (Munusamy 2012); in 2017, he again supported Zuma's preferred candidate, Nkosazana Dlamini-Zuma, for the ANC presidency (Mbalula 2017); at the time of writing, he was a minister in Cyril Ramaphosa's cabinet.

It follows, then, that factional politics in the ANC is more fluid than the dominant narrative suggests. Political analyst Aubrey Matshiqi suggests that ANC factions comprise 'angels with horns and devils with halos' (2020). Like the first theme, which limits state capture to the latter years of the Zuma presidency, this strict separation between 'the captured' and 'the noble' fails to grasp the century-long sweep of ANC history.

Thirdly, the dominant narrative restricts the number of actors involved in resisting state capture. It places undue focus on the internal dynamics of the ANC and accords a triumphant role for investigative journalism, but it underplays the role played by activism and opposition politics. In this way, resistance to state capture is framed as a factional battle within the ANC, instead of a social, political, parliamentary and legal battle, in which various factions of the ANC were complicit, including those that presented themselves in opposition to Zuma. The effect of this narrative is to obscure a series of legal defeats suffered by the Zuma administration in the Constitutional Court, which were decisive in the fall of the Zuma presidency.

Restricting resistance to state capture to internal ANC dynamics and journalistic bravery also romanticises the role played by the South African media in state capture. As events at the Judicial Commission of Inquiry into Allegations of State Capture – known as the Zondo Commission – have shown, the role of the South African media was more ambiguous than the dominant narrative conveys. For instance, the evidence presented at the Zondo Commission suggests that some journalists were complicit in state capture, while certain media owners enjoyed relationships with Gupta-linked companies, and ANC factional politics influenced media framing and reporting before, during and after the late Zuma era.

Fourthly, the dominant narrative focuses on particular forms of corruption, to the exclusion of the wider privatisation of the South African state. This is evidenced by the pervasive role of law firms, accounting firms and management consultants in the core business of governmental administration (Gumede 2015). This is exacerbated by the relationship between private funders and political parties – or individual candidates within them – and the attempt by private actors to capture policy and champion ideological positions. Put into perspective, egregious corruption is a symptom of this broader process, and this is obscured by the dominant state capture narrative.

Finally, the dominant narrative conceals (what might be called) the globalisation of state capture. It confines these features of state capture to the subcontinental origins of the Gupta brothers and to the part played by a handful of American and European multinational companies. In so doing, it ignores the wider features of interrelated global capital markets or the interests of competing, external capital pools in defeating the state capture of the Guptas. Furthermore, it fails to show how the Guptas were themselves embedded within capital networks like those present in South Africa before and, indeed, after the late years of the Zuma presidency.

PAINTING

Having outlined the dominant state capture narrative, we now turn to illustrate these arguments in the context of various art forms. I analyse two popular paintings that very nearly bookend the state capture era – one that almost opened the moment, and one that came towards its end. Artist Brett Murray's painting *The Spear* was displayed at Johannesburg's Goodman Gallery in the artist's Hail to the Thief II exhibition in May 2012. It arrived at the dawn of discussions about state capture and prefigures much of the discourse that would follow in the ensuing decade.

The Spear is a work of both satire and irony. It alludes to Russian artist Viktor Ivanov's propaganda poster entitled Ленин—жил, Ленин—жив, Ленин—будет жить! (*Lenin Lived, Lenin Lives, Lenin Will Live Forever!*), which encapsulates the cult of Russian leader and communist theorist Vladmir Lenin (figure 8.1).

Like *Lenin Lived*, *The Spear* depicts Jacob Zuma – then president of both the ANC and South Africa – emblazoned in red, yellow and black, striking a heroic pose across a large portrait (figure 8.2). The canvas size, 185 cm by 140 cm, conveys an air of grandeur, which is later ridiculed by the work itself. The position of Zuma's body and the pose he strikes in *The Spear* mimics Lenin's body in *Lenin Lived*, and each figure wears the same three-piece suit.

One important difference between *The Spear* and *Lenin Lived* is that Zuma's head replaced Lenin's in *The Spear*. Another important difference is that *The Spear* depicts male genitalia hanging from the unzipped trousers of the body. The phallus

Figure 8.1: *Lenin Lived, Lenin Lives, Lenin Will Live Forever!* Soviet propaganda poster by Viktor Ivanov and inspiration for Brett Murray's *The Spear* (2010). Courtesy of Alamy.

Figure 8.2: *The Spear* by Brett Murray (2010). Image reproduced courtesy of Brett Murray/Everard Read Gallery.

jars with the rest of the image, symbolising at once sexual profligacy, a lack of political shame and a desire for power at all costs. Murray described the work as 'a metaphor for power, greed and patriarchy' (Murray 2012).

Arriving amid increasing resistance to the Zuma presidency, *The Spear* conveys multiple meanings. Murray compares the failed communist dream of the Soviet Union with that of national liberation in South Africa. Like Lenin's, the ANC's dream is illusory, he seems to suggest. The irony stems from Zuma's apparent obliviousness, in the picture, to his dangling phallus. Staring determinedly into the distance, the confident stance and sense of power are belied by the glaring ignorance that his genitals are exposed. Here, Murray introduced the ever-present trope of an emperor with no clothes, layering it simultaneously on both Lenin and Zuma.

In doing so, Murray subverts the propagandistic intention of *Lenin Lived*, twisting a mode of veneration into satire and ridicule: the observer can see what the emperor cannot see. The emperor plays a heroic character, while the artist and the observer engage in a silent game where each can see what the omniscient ruler cannot see, and so it is in South Africa's political sphere. This is the artist's message to the world.

The Spear inspired a torrent of opinion when the exhibition was launched. For two months, the painting invited praise and castigation from artists, scholars, politicians and pundits. The ANC and its Alliance partners, the Congress of South African Trade Unions and the South African Communist Party, campaigned against the image. This included an urgent application before a full bench of the South Gauteng High Court to remove the painting both from Johannesburg's Goodman Gallery and the website of weekly newspaper *City Press* (Hlongwane 2012).

Murray was criticised for exacerbating racial stereotypes and for a 'cruel lack of imagination' (Mbembe 2012). An ANC-led march to the Goodman Gallery involved approximately 4 000 supporters of President Zuma, and special laws were mooted to protect the dignity of the president (Ndenze 2012). The newspaper *City Press* eventually bowed to pressure, removing the image from its website, while the Goodman Gallery's director, Liza Essers, claimed, 'It is a sad day for South Africa when creative production is being threatened with censorship from our ruling party' (Abad-Santos 2012).

Twelve days after its initial display, *The Spear* was defaced by Limpopo taxi driver Louis Mabokela, who smeared black paint over the face and genitals depicted in the painting. Mabokela was later convicted of malicious damage to property and fired from his job. The gallery eventually removed the defaced work in a settlement announced in a press conference on 31 May 2012, which halted the court proceedings. In attracting public attention, *The Spear* sacrificed narrative nuance by centring on the body of Zuma and his right to dignity rather than the ANC or its private benefactors.

Four years later, another painter, Ayanda Mabulu, sparked equal controversy with a work entitled *State Capture*. This depicted a suited-out President Jacob Zuma gleefully licking the anus of a smiling, naked Atul Gupta inside the cockpit of an aeroplane. In the painting, the plane is airborne, yet its pilot and co-pilot – Zuma and Gupta – abdicate their seats in favour of an act of sexual congress. An ANC flag hangs from one of the plane's two yokes. In the distance, past the windscreen, another plane heads towards the Zuma-Gupta plane, threatening a head-on collision. Like Murray, Mabulu was criticised for the obscenity of his work, and the perpetuation of racial and homophobic stereotypes. Remarking on a series of controversial paintings, of which *State Capture* formed part, Mabulu said: 'What I'm trying to do with my paintings is look at the political realities of state capture and capital flight in democratic South Africa. The only thing I wanted to do with the painting is to show what people are already talking about, but I depicted it in a painting, as simple as that' (Feltham 2016).

It is rare that two paintings spark such public excitement, and rarer still that two such similar paintings do so: art forms like music and film are more popular and influential than fine arts such as painting, whose budgets and distribution capacities are limited by comparison. How did *The Spear* and *State Capture* generate such intense public interest, notoriety and fascination, and what do they say about state capture in the popular imagination? One important similarity between the works is their reliance on nudity, or what Brett Lunceford calls 'the rhetoric of the body' (2012: 125). Both the artists treat the bodies of Zuma and Gupta as symbolic of the body politic; both are artistic attempts at naked truth. Nudity functions as a metaphor for the vulgarity, brazenness and evil of state capture in both images.

Yet, while both works invoke nudity, they do so in different ways. For Murray, nudity represents what Zuma is trying to hide but the public can see; for Mabulu, it represents the shamelessness of the Zuma-Gupta corruption nexus. And, where Zuma's nakedness is the subject of *The Spear*, *State Capture* depicts Zuma clothed and Atul Gupta naked.

Nudity is a long-standing theme in political art in Africa, as it is elsewhere. As Achille Mbembe observes: 'In the ancient kingdom of Dahomey, the phallus was associated with Legba, a deity of trickery and deception. The meanings attached to an erect penis were always polysemic. Paradoxically, an enlarged penis might well allude to fears concerning infertility, sexual inadequacy, and even impotence' (2012).

By contrast, in sixteenth-century Rome, nudity reformed perceptions of sexuality and bodily expressiveness (Waddington 2004). In more recent times, grotesque nudity has been invoked in African satire to demythologise arbitrary power and debase despotism. In this regard, the carnivalesque – a form that upends social assumptions through humour and chaos – has become a constant theme of artistic satire (Veit-Wild 2005). Both *The Spear* and *State Capture* are examples of this model.

A common artistic strategy in piercing the public imagination, then, invokes the body of the president, especially 'those parts of the grotesque body, in which it conceives a new, second body: the bowels and the phallus', as Mikhail Bakhtin puts it. He continues, 'These two areas play the leading role in the grotesque image, and it is precisely for this reason they are predominantly subject to … hyperbolization' (Bakhtin 1984). Flora Veit-Wild develops this claim in the African context, averring that 'the figure of the fat, lecherous, imbecile dictator' uniquely epitomises the 'grotesque body' (2005, 228), while, in South Africa, Mbembe observes further that 'defacement, desecration, and profanation have become the dominant modes of expression in cartoons, humour, satire, parody or visual arts' (2012). In this way, Murray and Mabulu locate themselves in a long tradition of 'subversive jesters' (Marechera 1980, 13), poking fun at presidential protuberances to solicit public attention.

Yet, while *The Spear* and *State Capture* succeeded in attracting public passion by ridiculing officialdom, they also co-create the narrow definition of 'capture' in the process. By personifying state capture through Zuma (or Zuma and Gupta, in the second picture), they perpetuate the idea that Zuma was exceptional and unique. By depicting state capture through interpersonal erotic metaphors, Mabulu narrows the cast of characters involved in state capture to the detriment of a richer story.

By centring these works around the bodies of Zuma and Gupta, the two artists tacitly reinforce the notion that state capture is a game of evil personalities and nefarious intentions, rather than a manifestation of stubborn and long-standing structures. Murray and Mabulu distinguish Zuma's corruption from other forms of corruption by highlighting its unabashed nature. Sexual lust tokenises material greed and the unbridled desire for power. This further reinforces the notion that state capture in the Zuma era was deviant rather than a continuation of a long-established pattern of ANC behaviour.

Zuma is also rendered superficially in these works: his motives and desires, as depicted both by Murray and Mabulu, are confined to basic impulses, which derive irony from carnal metaphors. This, too, casts state capture as a function of individual impulse and avarice rather than a structural feature of the country's politics.

Interestingly, while both Mabulu and Murray introduce an international dimension to their work, this dimension is muted. As noted, Murray draws parallels between the ANC and the failure of Soviet-style communism, while Mabulu's representation of aeroplanes hints at flight, both capital and other. Yet, neither work seeks to link state capture to a deeper South African history of colonisation, nor do they interrogate any role for the US or Western Europe in state capture. This suppresses the neocolonial dimensions of state capture, particularly as the Gupta empire was centred around extractive mining practices (Njenje 2019; Shaik 2019). Hence, the international agents present in these images – Soviet Russia and present-day India – limit the global setting of South African corruption.

In this way, the two paintings frame state capture within a parochially centred conception of corruption, detached from global capital in the present, or from colonial patterns of exploitation in the past. These artworks depict a notion of state capture that conformed with and co-produced the dominant narrative, which conceived state capture as a time-bound and factional fight in the ANC. Because of this, these works gained peculiar popular attention in news publications that were invested in advancing the dominant narrative.

Admittedly, no single artwork – or even two – conveys infinite complexity. But all art makes choices about which complexities to depict, and which to omit. But, more importantly, these two works of many produced in the period struck a unique chord with South African audiences and generated media sensation. This, I contend, is precisely because they elide the complexities of state capture and accept standard journalistic interpretations – as contained in the dominant narrative – of the state capture moment. These works successfully demythologised Zuma but at the expense of illuminating underlying causes of which he was but a symptom.

NON-FICTION FILM

In a second cultural framing of state capture, we turn to films – two local and two international. *South Africa Corruption Inc.* (Zalk 2018) is a 2018 documentary that appeared on the Al Jazeera network, directed by Naashon Zalk; *How to Steal a Country* (Desai 2020) was released in 2020 and directed by Rehad Desai; and *South Africa's Gupta Scandal* is a non-feature length documentary produced by BBC Newsnight in 2017 (BBC 2017).

These films share important similarities. They fall squarely in the sub-genre of explicitly political documentary, in the category of journalistic investigation and under the techniques of 'new political film'. The latter rose to popularity in the early part of the twentieth century (Benson and Snee 2008). In this mould, the films rely heavily on compiled archival footage and curated interviews. In their selections of compilation footage, directors frame protagonists and antagonists;

in their selections of interviewees, they determine which voices to promote; and, in their choices of narrative style, they define the period that constitutes state capture. Each of these documentaries confines state capture to the latter years of the Zuma administration, although each considers a slightly different moment. *South Africa Corruption Inc.* typifies this in its opening words: 'Last month [February 2018], South African president Jacob Zuma was forced from office after a decade of fraud and corruption allegations. His former associates, the billionaire Gupta brothers, are fugitives from justice amid claims that they looted state assets' (Zalk 2018).

Furthermore, each documentary centres on the rise of Jacob Zuma in its opening sequences, and each ends with the closing of the Zuma presidency. 'South Africa has been plagued by grand corruption,' begins the documentary *How to Steal a Country*, 'with much of it connected to three ambitious brothers from India' (Desai 2020). One of its interviewees, journalist Thanduxolo Jika, describes the period as 'almost *ten years* [my emphasis] of unabated looting'. So, using these techniques of inclusion and exclusion, the narrative arcs of these respective documentaries position state capture within the heart of the Zuma presidency.

One exception to this rule is the documentary *Whispering Truth to Power* (Seedat 2018), which starts with a scene at the Constitutional Court. This documentary is directed by Shameela Seedat and takes the form of a biography of former Public Protector Thuli Madonsela. It is notable both for centring a woman in the narrative and for challenging some of the problems highlighted here with the dominant narrative.

In accordance with the dominant state capture narrative, these works rely on a strict dichotomy between the 'state capture faction' and the 'anti-state capture faction' – between angels and devils – within the ANC. So, for instance, towards the end of *How to Steal a Country*, Barbara Hogan – once Zuma's minister of energy – claims that the ANC elective conference of December 2017 comprised 'two factions, representing two forces: the Zuma faction, promoting state capture and corruption, and the Cyril Ramaphosa faction … [which was] …. trying to get the economy and South Africa back on track' (Desai 2020).

ANC politicians like Mcebisi Jonas and Pravin Gordhan feature prominently in stabilising the angelic setting of what we have called the dominant narrative. These individuals are cast as victims of a political conspiracy, and as staunch resisters of corruption. No mention is made of their support for Zuma in earlier periods, or their failure to speak out publicly before state capture became a national emergency. Consider the closing sequence to *South Africa Corruption Inc.* 'With the Zuma-Gupta era now over,' the narrator confidently avers, 'and a new president at South

Africa's helm, can corruption in the country be brought under control? … [Pravin] Gordhan thinks it can' (Zalk 2018). The film then cuts to Gordhan, who vows that '2018 is going to be about … demonstrating that South Africa is still Mandela's South Africa' (Zalk 2018). *South Africa's Gupta Scandal* closes on a similarly triumphant note, presaging a 'fightback against state capture, President Zuma and the Rainbow Nation's decline' (BBC 2017). The implication, in both cases, is that the Zuma era represented a deviation from the ANC's true (and pure) calling, and that this diversion can be corrected – and with dispatch, too.

Various mise en scène techniques create spectacles of nobility to draw these factional distinctions, including curating the settings of interviews in the 'talking heads' style and placing them in settings of authority like offices and boardrooms (Dirstaru 2020; Van Dijck 2006). On the contrary, Zuma, the Gupta brothers or their allies are never interviewed and only speak through short archival footage statements, which are used to confirm the averments of the narrator. Little attention is paid to how 'factions' evolve, split and co-produce one another. The election of Cyril Ramaphosa to the country's presidency in 2018 is called a 'watershed moment'. But this narrative avoids any consideration of the political pacting that brought Ramaphosa to power and involved compromises with Zuma loyalists such as Ace Magashule and David Mabuza, now respectively the secretary general and deputy president of the ANC. In all these ways, these films avoid the telling of a more dynamic story about the ANC.

At the end of *How to Steal a Country*, Zuma is forced to resign, the Gupta family compound in Saxonwold is raided and Zuma's son Duduzane is arrested for corruption. This suggests that a swift fight against corruption has ensued. Since the film, however, these moments have proved ambiguous. Although the Gupta compound was raided, the case that resulted from this raid was eventually dropped by the National Prosecuting Authority (Mjo 2019). Although Duduzane Zuma was arrested for corruption, this case, too, was eventually dropped. And, although Jacob Zuma was forced to resign, he continues to wield power within the ANC, even attending the party's National Executive Committee meeting in June 2018 (Phakgadi 2018).

The news media's role in exposing state capture is romanticised. Little attention is paid to the media's place in creating and sustaining the Zuma phenomenon. And no interest is paid to its narrow framing of state capture or its active participation in the corruption itself. For example, broadcast media company MultiChoice contracted with the Gupta brothers on a 24-hour news channel called Africa News Network 7. Further, at the state capture commission, Hawks officer Kobus Roelofse alleged that journalist Ranjeni Munusamy benefited unduly from crime intelligence funds (Matwadia 2019). Only *South Africa Corruption Inc.* mentions the role of the national newspaper, the *Sunday Times*, in promoting narratives designed, according to the narrator, to persecute Pravin Gordhan. Instead of subjecting them to critical reflection, journalists are framed as intrepid heroes and heroines, who are unquestioningly positioned alongside 'the good' faction of the ANC.

For example, *How to Steal a Country* opens with scenes of newspaper production and foregrounds various journalists in uncovering the so-called GuptaLeaks, which were a dump of emails that exposed the wrongdoing of the Guptas and their empire (Faull 2017). The film closes to the sound of triumphant music, with journalist Susan Comrie claiming, 'Journalism has gone through a rough time everywhere ... it held democracy together until the other parts of the state could be uncluttered' (Desai 2020).

Where the media's role is elevated, other players in the fight against state capture are plainly downplayed. Little attention is paid to opposition politics, legal strategists, the judiciary or activists. *South Africa Corruption Inc.* and *South Africa's Gupta Scandal* omit any mention of the various court judgments that challenged the Zuma administration and, in so doing, brought critical information to the surface. This included cases that sanctioned Zuma over spending state funds at his private residence in Nkandla; sanctioned a parliamentary vote to remove Zuma by secret ballot; and compelled parliament to develop rules for presidential impeachment. It also included a legal effort by various opposition parties to publish the Public Protector's report on state capture, which finally led to the Zondo Commission.

The international dimensions of state capture are also simplified. *South Africa Corruption Inc.* presents a handful of multinationals involved with the Guptas – McKinsey, SAP, KPMG – that the narrator claims 'should have known better' (Zalk 2018). *How to Steal a Country* ends with news that some companies have decided to pay back relatively minor sums and apologised. The primary role devoted to international complicity in state capture goes to Bell Pottinger, the London-based public relations firm, which contracted with the Guptas to sanitise their wrongdoing. Bell Pottinger's role in state capture occupies most of *South Africa's Gupta Scandal* and much of *How to Steal a Country*.

We can summarise the key challenges posed by these films in relation to my argument. The films fail to present alternative perspectives of state capture; they are, thus, as important for what they conceal as for what they convey. The dramatic narratives of the films – and the techniques within them – impinge on their informative capacities.

RAP MUSIC

Unlike the cases of non-fiction films and satirical painting, commercial rap music disrupts the dominant narrative.[1] Far from presenting a narrow critique, rap music often celebrates state capture as a legitimate route to enrichment and material progress.

The commercial and cultural ascendancy of rap music has been widely explored in both the South African and global perspective (Burkhalter and Thornton 2014; Hammett 2009; Podoshen, Andrzejewski and Hunt 2014; Sithole 2017). As Ntebaleng Mpetsi and Toks Oyedemi contend, 'The growth of [South African] hip-hop and a changing political environment … has given way to lyrics and culture that focus on individual advancement, sensuous pleasure, commercial-minded-ness, and boastful display of wealth' (2018, 93). Yet, commercial rap in the Zuma era is unique in mixing this crass materialism with a defence of political corruption.

In the late Zuma era, both rappers and politicians engaged in increasingly spectacular public displays of wealth – with flashy watches, exotic cars and fancy mansions. State capture was legitimised in popular rap as an accepted pathway to such symbols of financial status. The Guptas, President Zuma and his son Duduzane became regular totems for financial success and for economic advancement. The ANC co-opted the cultural appeal of rap music and, in turn, rap music fetishised the financial benefits of ANC patronage. In condoning corruption this way, commercial rap artists legitimated the Zuma presidency in the eyes of a crucial segment of the youth electorate, while younger ANC politicians, like Fikile Mbalula and Malusi Gigaba, both ministers during Zuma's presidency, traded their knowledge of rap music for cultural legitimacy.

So, for instance, when Malusi Gigaba delivered his first budget speech after controversially being appointed minister of finance in 2017, he quoted American rapper Kendrick Lamar's famous phrase, 'we gon' be alright'.[2] Similarly, as head of the ANC's 2016 local election campaign, Fikile Mbalula convened a celebrity endorsement event featuring several rap artists and celebrities clad in ANC regalia (Makhoba 2016). Kiernan 'AKA' Forbes, one of the country's biggest rap stars in the Zuma years, endorsed the ANC and Zuma on numerous occasions. He tweeted in 2017 that 'JZ [Jacob Zuma] is cleaning up the rot! He has two years left to show us what he can do for us! Today is a good day!' and 'I'll take a Gupta & a Zuma over a [Helen] Zille and an Oppenheimer … ANYDAY' (Independent Online 2020).

Moreover, in AKA's 2018 album titled *Touch My Blood*, various flattering references are made to Jacob Zuma and his son Duduzane. The song 'Mame' – a pop ballad based on simplistic commercial themes and featuring rapper JR – is another interesting case. Both artists reference the Zuma family in the context of materialistic aspiration. AKA (2018) raps:

> *Everybody under pressure/*
> *I'm in the mix like Duduzane/*
> *Spicy like Korobela/*

JR, for his part, sings:

> *Every time we link up Chardonnay/*
> *Celebrate my people/*
> *Just look how far we've come/*
> *Siyamkhumbula Jacob Zuma, Thabo Mbeki/*
> *FW de Klerk? No way!/*

Other AKA lyrics tie materialistic ambition to liberation nostalgia. In his popular 2018 single 'Fela in Versace',[3] AKA compares himself to 'Mandela in a Rari' (Ferrari sports car). 'Mandela' represents the allegiance to the ANC and its liberation history; the luxury sports car connotes spectacular displays of wealth, which are connected, in part, to the freedoms produced by the ANC. This image of Nelson Mandela in a Ferrari epitomises the tensions at play in rap music's subtle defence of the process of state capture.

Yet, while Mandela is the symbol of liberation in 'Fela in Versace', Jacob and Duduzane Zuma, and the Gupta brothers, feature prominently in other commercial rap songs of the period under examination. For example, in the song 'The Finesse' (2020), rap sensations Kwesta and the late Riky Rick extol their respective virtues in braggadocious boasts. Riky Rick typifies the glorification of state capture when he says:

> *Pretty nigga they love me like Duduzane/*
> *Get a verse and I promise you you'll be on/*
> *You know the saying a Venda man maak 'n plan/*
> *Act a fool cause, paper money rules us/*
> *Textbooks fooled us, lower-class school sucks/*

Reinforcing the theme is Cassper Nyovest, another of South Africa's prominent celebrity rappers in the Zuma era. His popular *Thuto* album was released in 2017 at the height of the state capture narrative. References to Zuma were again framed around the rapper's proximity to political power, rather than a criticism of corruption or misrule. For instance, in the song 'We Living Good' (2017b), Nyovest raps:

> *But dawg if you know me I got a letter from Zuma/*
> *And bought a Presidential Rolex like mama I made it/*
> *Really mama I made it/*
> *They won't say it in public but I'm the greatest/*

In an official presidential statement, Zuma congratulated Cassper Nyovest for filling up an arena in 2015: 'We congratulate Cassper Nyovest for his tremendous success which has demonstrated the rich talent that exists within our country's music industry, especially amongst our youth' (Independent Online 2020). In his song 'Touch the Sky' (2017a), Nyovest returned the favour, rapping:

> *We the new government/*
> *They treat us like Zuma 'n 'em/*

The song 'Vura' – by DJ Citi Lyts, featuring Sjava and Saudi (2016) – is a further illustration of how commercial rap music romanticised Zuma and the Guptas. The song, which has garnered over two million views on YouTube alone, refers to the Volkswagen Vura – a vehicle famous in township life as a symbol of status. In the song's opening lines, rapper Sjava compares himself to Zuma and the Guptas as he drives the car:

> *Ngena ngihamba nge-Vura [Get in, I drive a Vura]/*
> *Bafana eSoweto bayangvuma [The Soweto boys agree with me]/*
> *Ngiphetha imali ngiyiGupta [I have money, I'm a Gupta]/*
> *Ngihamba nengane kaZuma [I ride with Zuma's child]/*

These popular works stood in stark contrast to independent and underground rap songs. For instance, Cape Town rapper Ndlulamithi's 'Andivoti' (I am not voting) claims:

> *Lamnyala nimane niwaquma enziwa nguZuma [Covering disgraceful things done by Zuma]/*
> *Azawtyisa abantwana bethu kwimigqumo [Will have our children eating from dustbins]/* (Sithole 2017)

In a rap song of my own elsewhere, I observe (2017):

State Capture/
They shot thirty-four mineworkers for platinum/
We've got a state that gets paid to protect capital/
No more delaying, I say we march on the capital/

Despite these voices of resistance in the rap world, however, the dominant commercial narrative is the focus of this text. In this realm, little resistance is evident. Rather than contesting state capture, popular commercial rap music presented it as a legitimate path to material accumulation. In this way, rap became a key voice for state capture in the Zuma presidency. As such, rap artists developed a materialistic gaze, giving privileged insight into alternative conceptions of state capture in the popular imagination.

Rap music thus presents a contrasting perspective from which to view the lives of state capture in the popular imagination. In the context of South Africa's gross economic inequality, rap musicians framed state capture's actors as aspirational figures who had successfully found pathways to wealth, social mobility and fame. This exposes differences in state capture's conception across different audiences, especially across boundaries of age, race and class.

CORRESPONDING AND COMPETING NARRATIVES

For Roland Barthes, popular art can 'make legitimate and universal what is partial and particular' (Storey 2018, 4). I have contended that popular artworks in the state capture era co-authored a narrow conception of state capture – one that failed to depict its structural, historical, economic and political roots. In doing so, state capture was presented as an aberrant moment in the late Zuma presidency. In this way, popular art failed to examine the lesser-explored features and consequences of the state capture moment. This argument is supported through an analysis of art that uniquely captured public attention and rose to the level of popular cultural pre-eminence across three genres: painting, non-fiction films and rap music.

Events since Jacob Zuma's resignation underscore the problem identified in this chapter. When Cyril Ramaphosa prevailed as ANC president in December 2017, a new simplistic narrative encircled his presidency, drawing directly from the dominant state capture narrative. Heralded as a 'New Dawn', the narrative suggested that the ANC could return from the clutches of state capture, with the ascendancy of an angelic faction. This faction would swiftly uproot corruption and restore the ANC to its noble pre-Zuma path that was associated, in particular, with the Mandela years.

The correspondences between the new narrative and the state capture narrative were striking. First, the characters were aligned; second, the structural dimensions of corruption were ignored; third, the complicity of Cyril Ramaphosa and his supporters in state capture was eclipsed; and fourth, it masked the presence of Zuma allies in the ANC's new National Executive Committee.

Moreover, five years after Ramaphosa's election as ANC president, and more than seven years after many of the allegations of state capture emerged, little political accountability or economic recovery has materialised. Meanwhile, new allegations of ANC corruption have surfaced – many of these are associated with malfeasance around money earmarked for Covid-19 relief. In hindsight, the dangers of narrowing the state capture narrative to Zuma and the Gupta brothers have become evident. An updated, systemic account of the symbiotic relationship between private and public interest in twenty-first-century South Africa – which avoids the perils of the dominant state capture narrative – is long, long overdue.

In narrowing the state capture narrative to the bodies of men, popular paintings in particular conveyed subtle assumptions about gender. Yet, public debate over these paintings tended to ignore this dimension of state capture. Indeed, this reveals a further dimension of the dominant narrative: it is principally espoused by – and concerned with – men. With some exceptions, the filmmakers, painters and rap artists who achieved public attention for their work – and the subjects they considered in discussing state capture – were men. As Shireen Hassim argues, 'the babel of argument' that clouded *The Spear* 'made little dent on deepening debates on the gendered nature of power'. She states further, 'The limits of democracy are most clearly visible when bodies become present in the public sphere' (Hassim 2014, 168).

The arguments presented in this chapter open several opportunities for future scholarship. Future scholarship might test the claims advanced in the foregoing by reflecting on other artistic genres. One potential area of interest is the presentation of state capture in South African social media. Interestingly, little scholarship actively tracks this phenomenon (Mpofu 2019). Popular non-fiction is another potentially fruitful realm of inquiry. Here, works like Jacques Pauw's *The President's Keepers* (2017) – which broke multiple book sales records – and Pieter-Louis Myburgh's *Republic of Gupta* (2017) typify a genre of state capture literature consistent with my critique that the dominant narrative is unduly narrow. On the other hand,

Hennie van Vuuren's *Apartheid Guns and Money* avoids many of the criticisms I have levied here, while remaining popular. He locates prevailing examples of corruption such as the Arms Deal scandal in a wider history of apartheid corruption, which includes global financial intermediaries (Van Vuuren 2018). In doing so, Van Vuuren examines a broader historical canvas to reach similar conclusions about the pervasiveness of corruption in the present South African state. Other scholars may also interrogate other paintings, documentaries or rap songs, or explore artworks that challenge the dominant narrative of state capture, even if these works did not reach the same level of popularity as those presented in these pages.

NOTES

1 I distinguish rap music here from hip-hop culture. Rap music is one form within hip-hop culture, which includes graffiti, fashion, beat-boxing, music videos and a wide media network of podcasts and discussion forums.
2 Gigaba misquoted Lemar by saying 'we gon' be right' instead of 'we gon' be alright'.
3 'Fela' refers to Fela Kuti (1938–1997), the Nigerian musician and instrumentalist who became one of Africa's most notable musical figures in the twentieth century.

REFERENCES

Abad-Santos, Alexander. 2012. 'Surprisingly, Painting of South African President's Penis Creates Controversy'. *The Atlantic*, 18 May 2012. https://www.theatlantic.com/international/archive/2012/05/surprisingly-painting-south-african-presidents-penis-create-controversy/327938/.
AKA. 2018. *Touch My Blood*. Sony Music (compact disc).
Bakhtin, Mikhail. 1984. *Rabelais and His World*. Bloomington: Indiana University Press.
BBC. 2017. *South Africa's Gupta Scandal*. BBC Newsnight, 20 July 2017. https://www.youtube.com/watch?v=2KSHC6UPUgA&t=97s.
Benson, Thomas W. and Brian J. Snee, eds. 2008. *The Rhetoric of the New Political Documentary*. Carbondale, IL: Southern Illinois University Press.
Burkhalter, Janée N. and Corliss G. Thornton. 2014. 'Advertising to the Beat: An Analysis of Brand Placements in Hip-Hop Music Videos'. *Journal of Marketing Communications* 20, no. 5: 366–382. https://www.tandfonline.com/doi/abs/10.1080/13527266.2012.710643.
Desai, Rehad. 2020. *How to Steal a Country*. Johannesburg: Uhuru Films. https://www.showmax.com/eng/movie/ac4kolml-how-to-steal-a-country.
Dirstaru, Elena. 2020. 'Voices, Bodies, and Power in the Documentary Interview'. PhD diss., University of Essex.
DJ Citi Lyts. 2016. 'Vura Ft Sjava and Saudi'. Ambitiouz Entertainment, 12 August 2016. https://www.youtube.com/watch?v=E01NHBVO5R4&list=PLjLyN9azwAb9jCtoX-V0wAranwhteF8CeX.
Faull, Andrew. 2017. 'Who Can Stop the Rot?' *South African Crime Quarterly* 61: 3–6. https://journals.assaf.org.za/index.php/sacq/article/view/3065.

Feltham, Luke. 2016. 'Ayanda Mabulu Defends Zuma-Gupta Painting: We Must Expose the Naked Truth'. *Mail & Guardian*, 13 July 2016. https://mg.co.za/article/2016-07-13-ayanda-mabulu-defends-zuma-gupta-painting-we-must-expose-the-naked-truth/.

Gumede, William. 2015. 'Administrative Culture of the South African Public Service: A Finity of Transformation'. *Journal of Public Administration* 50, no. 3: 589–599. https://journals.co.za/doi/10.10520/EJC185663.

Hammett, Daniel. 2009. 'Local Beats to Global Rhythms: Coloured Student Identity and Negotiations of Global Cultural Imports in Cape Town, South Africa'. *Social & Cultural Geography* 10, no. 4: 403–419. https://www.tandfonline.com/doi/abs/10.1080/14649360902853270.

Hassim, Shireen. 2014. 'Violent Modernity: Gender, Race and Bodies in Contemporary South African Politics'. *Politikon* 41, no. 2: 167–182. https://www.tandfonline.com/doi/abs/10.1080/02589346.2013.865824.

Hlongwane, Sipho. 2012. 'The Spear: Two White-Hot Weeks Later, the Goodman Gallery, the ANC and Brett Murray Kiss and Make Up'. *Daily Maverick*, 31 May 2012. https://www.dailymaverick.co.za/article/2012-05-31-the-spear-two-white-hot-weeks-later-the-goodman-gallery-the-anc-and-brett-murray-kiss-and-make-up/.

Independent Online. 2020. 'AKA Admits to Missing Jacob Zuma amid Alcohol Ban Rant'. *IOL*, 22 July 2020. https://www.iol.co.za/entertainment/celebrity-news/local/aka-admits-to-missing-jacob-zuma-amid-alcohol-ban-rant-7c7e216b-1923-4d7a-beb9-6ca001931790.

Kwesta. 2020. 'The Finesse'. Sony Music Entertainment Africa. https://www.youtube.com/watch?v=qb2cBwZBavs.

Lunceford, Brett. 2012. *Naked Politics: Nudity, Political Action, and the Rhetoric of the Body*. Lanham, MD: Lexington Books.

Makhoba, Ntombizodwa. 2016. 'Celebs Join the ANC for a Mother of a Party'. *News24*, 7 July 2016. https://www.news24.com/citypress/Trending/celebs-join-the-anc-for-a-mother-of-a-party-20160716.

Marechera, Dambudzo. 1980. *Black Sunlight*. London: Heinemann.

Marechera, Dambudzo. 1992. *Cemetery of Mind*. Harare: Baobab Books.

Matshiqi, Aubrey. 2020. 'South Africa Needs a New Revolution'. Interview with Sizwe Mpofu-Walsh, 21 January 2020. https://www.youtube.com/watch?v=ApsL29r7JR4.

Matwadia, Eyaaz. 'Ranjeni Munusamy Implicated by Witness at Zondo Commission'. *Mail & Guardian*, 18 September 2019. https://mg.co.za/article/2019-09-18-ranjeni-munusamy-implicated-by-witness-at-zondo-commission/.

Mbalula, Fikile. 2017. 'Why I Support Dlamini-Zuma'. *Daily Maverick*, 13 December 2017. https://www.dailymaverick.co.za/opinionista/2017-12-13-sheisworthy-why-i-support-dlamini-zuma/.

Mbembe, Achille. 2012. 'The Spear That Divided a Nation'. *Amandla*, 26 May 2012. http://www.brettmurray.co.za/the-spear-opinions/26-may-2012-amandla-magazine-professor-mbembe-the-spear-that-divide-a-nation/.

Mjo, Odwa. 2019. 'NPA Drops Estina Dairy Charges and South Africans Want Answers'. *Timeslive*, 29 November 2019. https://www.timeslive.co.za/news/south-africa/2018-11-29-npa-drops-estina-dairy-charges-and-south-africans-want-answers/.

Mpetsi, Ntebaleng and Toks Oyedemi. 2018. 'Global Hip-Hop Culture and the Scopophilic Spectacle of Women in South African Hip-Hop Music Videos'. *Communicare: Journal for Communication Sciences in Africa* 37, no. 2: 92–106. https://journals.co.za/doi/10.10520/EJC-127f53d485.

Mpofu, Shepherd. 2019. 'Pornographic Intersections: Race and Genitalia in South African Political Art in the Age of Digital Media'. *Critical African Studies* 11, no. 2: 230–261. https://www.tandfonline.com/doi/abs/10.1080/21681392.2019.1663745.

Mpofu-Walsh, Sizwe. 2017. 'State Capture'. SeisMic Productions. https://www.youtube.com/watch?v=dnFTE0bitoA.

Munusamy, Ranjeni. 2012. 'Failure to Launch: Mbalula's Doomed Bid to Campaign for ANC Secretary-General'. *Daily Maverick*, 11 October 2012. https://www.dailymaverick.co.za/article/2012-10-11-failure-to-launch-mbalulas-doomed-campaign-for-anc-secretary-general/.

Murray, Brett. 2012. 'Artist Brett Murray's Affidavit'. *Brett Murray*, 25 May 2012. http://www.brettmurray.co.za/the-spear-press/25-may-2012-the-times-sa-brett-murrays-affidavit/.

Myburgh, Pieter-Louis. 2017. *The Republic of Gupta: A Story of State Capture*. Johannesburg: Penguin Books.

Ndenze, Babalo. 2012. 'Call for Zuma Insult Law'. *IOL*, 15 November 2012. https://www.iol.co.za/news/politics/call-for-zuma-insult-law-1423784.

Njenje, Gibson. 2019. Transcript of Testimony by Mr Gibson Njenje. State Capture Inquiry, 26 November 2019. https://www.youtube.com/watch?v=Gz_T6rnuynw.

Nyovest, Cassper. 2017a. 'Touch the Sky'. *Thuto*. Family Tree Records (compact disc).

Nyovest, Cassper. 2017b. 'We Living Good'. *Thuto*. Family Tree Records (compact disc).

Pauw, Jacques. 2017. *The President's Keepers: Those Keeping Zuma in Power and Out of Prison*. Cape Town: Tafelberg.

Phakgadi, Pelane. 2018. 'Corruption Charges against Duduzane Zuma Withdrawn'. *News24*, 24 January 2018. https://www.news24.com/news24/southafrica/news/corruption-charges-against-duduzane-zuma-withdrawn-20190124.

Podoshen, Jeffrey S., Susan A. Andrzejewski and James M. Hunt. 2014. 'Materialism, Conspicuous Consumption, and American Hip-Hop Subculture'. *Journal of International Consumer Marketing* 26, no. 4: 271–283. https://www.tandfonline.com/doi/abs/10.1080/08961530.2014.900469.

Seedat, Shameela. 2018. *Whispering Truth to Power*. Undercurrent Film and Television. https://www.showmax.com/eng/movie/3fn18c4y-whispering-truth-to-power.

Shaik, Rieaz 'Mo'. 2019. Transcript of Testimony by Mr Rieaz 'Mo' Shaik. State Capture Inquiry, 25 November 2019. https://www.youtube.com/watch?v=_Imu6R_byL0.

Sithole, Sipho. 2017. 'Triangular Relationships between Commerce, Politics and Hip-Hop: A Study of the Role of Hip-Hop in Influencing the Socio-Economic and Political Landscape in Contemporary Society'. PhD thesis, University of the Witwatersrand.

Storey, John. 2018. *Cultural Theory and Popular Culture: An Introduction*. London: Routledge.

Twala, Chitja. 2009. 'The African National Congress Youth League's (ANCYL's) Role as the "Kingmaker": A Moment of Post-Polokwane Blues?' *Journal for Contemporary History* 34 (3): 153–171. https://scholar.ufs.ac.za/handle/11660/9125.

Van der Merwe, Cornelius and Jacques du Plessis, eds. 2004. *Introduction to the Law of South Africa*. The Hague: Kluwer Law International.

Van Dijck, José. 2006. 'Picturizing Science: The Science Documentary as Multimedia Spectacle'. *International Journal of Cultural Studies* 9, no. 1: 5–24. https://journals.sagepub.com/doi/10.1177/1367877906061162.

Van Vuuren, Hennie. 2018. *Apartheid Guns and Money: A Tale of Profit*. London: Hurst & Co.

Veit-Wild, Flora. 2005. 'The Grotesque Body of the Postcolony: Sony Labou Tansi and Dambudzo Marechera'. *Revue de littérature comparée* 314, no. 2: 227–239. https://www.cairn.info/revue-de-litterature-comparee-2005-2-page-227.htm.

Waddington, Raymond. 2004. *Aretino's Satyr: Sexuality, Satire, and Self-Projection in Sixteenth-Century Literature and Art.* Toronto: University of Toronto Press.

Zalk, Naashon. 2018. *South Africa Corruption Inc. Al Jazeera,* 29 March 2018. https://www.youtube.com/watch?v=LD-o08xkK_k&t=544s.

9

Cycles of State Capture: Bringing Profiteers and Enablers to Account

Hennie van Vuuren and Michael Marchant

There is growing recognition that the challenge of corruption and state capture in South Africa is deep-rooted in the country's history. The early period of settler colonialism in South Africa is exemplary of state capture, given that Dutch rule was characterised by the use of state power to enable the Dutch East India Company to commercialise and draw significant profit from the then station. The Dutch East India Company was one of the world's first examples of a true multinational corporation. There are many alignments between South Africa's past and contemporary state capture. But using this history to score narrow points is not helpful. On all sides of the country's politics, there is a tendency to distract from a discussion of the malfeasance of one era by pointing to the other.

Consider the cases of F.W. de Klerk and Jacob Zuma. Both have wrought enormous suffering on many South Africans through their actions – the former as the last leader of apartheid South Africa and the latter as the fourth democratically elected president of the country, who is deeply implicated in the matter of state capture. Yet, when it suited De Klerk, he ignored the fact that the apartheid system was a crime against humanity, only conceding the point in 2020 (Kiewit 2020). At the same time, he, and the F.W. de Klerk Foundation, frequently passed judgement on the conduct of politicians like Jacob Zuma, while ignoring their complicity in serious crimes (Thale 2021).

Equally, when Zuma was facing arrest in late June 2021 for defying an order of the Zondo Commission, his supporters pointedly asked why Zuma was the target when De Klerk had never truly accounted for his role in the apartheid regime. As Jacob Zuma's brother Khanya is reported as stating, 'I am saying both [P.W.] Botha and De Klerk were above the law. How do they say this to my brother? They must first go wake Botha and call De Klerk, and then we'll see if my brother did really break the law. If they haven't brought these people up to answer, I, as a Zuma, say there is no such a law in South Africa' (Singh 2021).

This kind of thinking undermines the struggle for accountability for past and current criminality. It ignores the continuity in the networks that have profited from corruption in the country over decades. In any book, this form of amnesia and 'whataboutery' by elite political groupings operates against the interests of the most vulnerable people.

The apartheid state was captured by a powerful pro-Western network that profited from propping up the minority-ruled regime in the Cold War. We will show that the ending of apartheid did little to disrupt these same extractive networks, notwithstanding the promise of justice, both in the form of South Africa's celebrated transition and beyond that. These arms sales networks that have continued are best understood as representing (as is categorised in both academic and popular literature) the 'deep state' (The Economist 2017; Springborg 2018).

This chapter argues that the continuities between corruption under apartheid and post-apartheid 'state capture' are best understood by examining such 'deep state' networks.

Where these intersect, the social contract that underpins the understanding around (and of) the state is subverted for private gain. This happens because the 'trust' institutions tasked with oversight and accountability fail. In South Africa's case, the long complicity of the deep state in economic crime is illustrated by its role in facilitating illicit arms deals across several decades. Across time, a network of politicians, arms companies, spies, banks and intermediaries have collaborated to profit at the expense of South Africa's poor.

Within the context of this argument, state capture is best understood as a mechanism that is instrumentalised by deep state networks in order to capture the state and engage in criminal profit-taking. To be effective, such criminal profit-taking requires an element of political manipulation and control.

Present-day state capture, notably the looting of state enterprises by the Gupta network and their political accomplices, exhibits the continuities of an established system in two linked ways. First, those implicated in state capture have taken advantage of the corrosion of state institutions to commit economic crimes. Second, the system that subverted the state and its institutions was created and maintained with the assistance of domestic and multinational corporations, including banks, auditors, consultancies and law firms. These, the enablers of state capture, reflect the most recent manifestation of the deep state in South Africa but also mirror a global system of economic crime.

Despite the role of private actors, too much public discussion on accountability for state capture myopically fixes on politicians. In order to challenge state capture and corruption in South Africa, we cannot rely on prosecuting a small band of political operators alone. We argue that it is imperative to focus on the private actors within deep state networks and call for the investigation and prosecution of allegations of economic crime to finally disrupt those who have operated with impunity for so long.

UNDERSTANDING THE DEEP STATE

Like other terms in social science, the notion of the deep state is contested. In part, this is the product of naked politics. So it is that conservatively inclined political networks wilfully use the term 'deep state' to describe any challenges they face to their particular brand of politics. Former US president Donald Trump and his allies, for instance, used the term to describe career civil servants and bureaucrats, and it emerged, too, in the many public spats he had with US intelligence agencies (Sevastopulo 2018; Winter and Groll 2017).

Such reckless use of the term suggests how opportunistic its use has become. So, notwithstanding his antipathy towards the deep state, Trump's policies suggested a powerful influence of the military and corporate interests on his administration. In the form used by Trump and his supporters, the term deep state is prerogative and, at the edges, drives into that most seductive of all political theories, the conspiracy. In this case, the conspiracy theory is that there was a plot by liberal elites to thwart Trumpian politics and its plans for America's future. This is best described as a closed dialogue in which paranoia drives out the rationality afforded by constitutional politics (Stone 2020).

An alternative conceptual, less polemical account of the term 'deep state' comes from its loose association with the idea of both the 'shadow state' and/or the 'state within a state'. Its rooting here follows the Turkish equivalent of deep state: the phrase *derin devlet*, which has recently generated a small but lively literature. We will not use the populist, conspiratorial strain of the term 'deep state', but will focus instead on the Turkish form of the notion around which to test the evidence that follows.

In this form, the 'deep state arises in defective democracies that lack democratic civilian oversight: the military is either ... devoid of any control or it is under undemocratic civilian control' (Söyler 2013, 311). Predictably, these circumstances can service many masters, including global corporations, intelligence agencies, arms companies and compliant politicians. Where (and when) their individual interests intersect, the temptation to further bypass democratic processes is overwhelming. As a result, the rule of law is undermined, accountability is eroded, and public trust both in institutions and in democracy itself is further eroded. Understandably, too, the deep state (and the networks it draws upon) resists change to avoid accountability and calls for justice, even after moments of significant political upheaval. The latter was witnessed in Tunisia, when the 2014 Truth and Dignity Commission, which was tasked with addressing corruption and economic crimes since the mid-1950s (Maïzi 2021), was denied access to crucial state archives and faced public attacks from senior officials. Sihem Bensedrine – the commission's president – suggested that resistance to its work stems from the 'deep state' (Stephen 2015).

The latter strain of state capture has been defined as a 'network of individuals in different branches of government with links to retired generals and organised crime, that existed without the knowledge of high-ranking military officers and politicians' (The Economist 2017). But we should be aware that this limited definition is, at times, broadened to include a network of bureaucrats, politicians and organised criminals that acted as a backlash against secularism and democracy.

CORRUPTION AND CONTINUITY IN SOUTH AFRICA

The apartheid regime was rightly called 'a crime against humanity' by the General Assembly of the United Nations in 1966.[1] Accumulating resolutions of the United Nations General Assembly reflected its increasing isolation. Finally, in 1977, the UN instituted a mandatory arms embargo that aimed to cut off the regime's access to weapons and technology required to do the grunt work.

In many ways, these circumstances set up the perfect condition for a flourishing deep state needed to maintain the regime. Unsurprisingly, it was through access to arms that South Africa provided an opportunity for arms manufacturers, banks and opportunist middlemen to profit from the significant premiums the regime was willing to pay. Moreover, Cold War politicians in the West were interested in maintaining the strategic alliance with the country – but from an arm's length. To succeed, intelligence agencies and sanctions-busting operations became necessary in apartheid South Africa. As Mehtap Söyler points out: 'There is a robust relationship between "deep state" and the military-industrial complex, that is, a mode of capital accumulation that delivers political, economic, and industrial resources to military imperatives; hence decision making, defence spending, technical innovation, and academic research agendas serve national security and compromise democracy' (2013, 311).

Before we examine the murky pathway of its operation, it must be understood that a system of arms manufacture (and procurement) was anchored in the South African state from the 1950s onwards. The central player was the country's military and, closely linked with it, the state-owned arms company Armaments Corporation of South Africa, known as Armscor. This operation had its roots in the immediate post-Second World War years, when a wartime weapons-manufacturing industry was continued into the peace with the aim only of equipping the then Union Defence Force. As the struggle against apartheid quickened and external pressure over apartheid increased, and the country's industrial base grew, so did the sophistication of its armaments manufacturing. Military historian Ian van der Waag notes: 'Armscor grew rapidly from a producer of small arms and ammunition into a complex industry producing a range of sophisticated weaponry that was, at the time, equal or superior to comparable weaponry produced elsewhere' (2015, 264).

Its success was speeded up by both the arms embargo and greater state support for the armaments sector of industry. But there was more to it than this. Writing 'on the rise and fall of apartheid', David Welsh notes that Armscor was 'directed by law "to meet as effectively and economically as may be feasible the armaments requirements of the Republic"' (2009, 253). So it was that the flourishing of the military-industrial complex – to borrow Eisenhower's famous phrase – became increasingly tied to the fortunes of South Africa's largest private sector corporations. A submission to the country's Truth and Reconciliation Commission (TRC) confirmed:

> There was a high degree of integration between the public and private sectors ... Three industrial groups, namely Reunert, Altech, and Grintek, dominated the private sector defence industry. These groups were, in turn, owned or controlled by one of the six large financial, mining, and industrial conglomerates. Reunert was controlled by Old Mutual [a financial house], Altech by Anglo American [originally a mining house but at that time a complex agglomeration of interests], and Grintek by Anglovaal [then a mining house] (TRC Business Hearings 1997).

For the present purposes, it is necessary to point out that neither those involved in the management of these corporations nor the corporations themselves have been called to account for their support of the militarisation of the apartheid state.

The idea that the domestic arms industry in late apartheid South Africa was robust has fed the notion that the country was self-sufficient. This was confirmed in 1997 when Armscor's authorised history boasted that South Africa had 'not only to survive the stranglehold caused by the UN arms embargo but to become self-sufficient in many fields' (Van der Westhuizen and Le Roux 1997, 312). However, in 25 sites across seven countries, archival research suggests that this was not the case and detailed a worldwide clandestine network that supplied both weapons and associated technology to the minority government. Furthermore, the record shows that the five permanent members of the United Nations Security Council failed, at various stages, to enforce UN Security Council Resolution 418, the mandatory 1977 arms embargo. Even the Soviet Union and China, who were ostensibly anti-apartheid champions and supported the liberation forces that aimed to overthrow the state (Taylor 2000), violated the embargo, or encouraged their agents to do so (Pretorius 1983). Given this, it should be no surprise to learn that Pretoria could call on the support of some 30 states to buttress its weapons industry. Among the states called upon were other excluded – or 'pariah' – states such as Chile, Taiwan, Israel and Argentina.

The arms procurement programme was centralised, running its operations out of the South African embassy in Paris. Although located in Europe, evidence suggests that the reach of its Armscor officials was global (Van der Westhuizen and Le Roux 1997). Moreover, the nature of the operation changed over time: it grew more clandestine, more secretive, and more involved in sanctions-busting and money laundering. In total, the Paris office managed a network of around 130 front companies and some 800 bank accounts that hid the nature and origin of weapons trade with apartheid. So, for instance, 76 front companies identified in Liberia held a total of 198 bank accounts in Luxembourg and in that country's Kredit Bank, known by its initials, KBL (Open Secrets 2018).

How was it possible that apartheid agents could operate in Europe without being detected? The answer is that they were not under surveillance. Instead, thousands of pages of declassified documents from South Africa's Department of Defence archive reveal that French intelligence services were aware of the presence: indeed, they met regularly with South African military intelligence to manage secret weapons deals and promised other assistance to the regime. Allegedly, complicity in this went to the top of French politics (Report on Meeting between Director Intelligence Operations and Mr Roussin 1987). For example, a memorandum of a confidential

1987 meeting between the respective military intelligence agencies in Paris shows that French officials were willing to provide spare parts to South Africa's then ageing Mirage fighter jets and were not opposed to a plan to supply new aircraft to South Africa via Chile and Argentina. In fact, the then French prime minister's chief of staff, Michel Roussin, confirmed that he 'personally and the advisers to [the prime minister] would do their best to ensure the successful implementation of such a scheme should South Africa be interested' (Van Tonder 1987).

The same willingness explains why French companies were serial embargo-busters and identifies the channel through which this support for apartheid was delivered. None was closer to apartheid's military elite than the arms manufacturer Thomson-CSF. Indeed, the link was a long-established relationship: it commenced in the late 1960s, when apartheid's newly appointed minister of defence, P.W. Botha, visited Bordeaux to view a missile testing. A full itinerary of Botha's visit is available in his personal archival collection held at the University of the Free State Archive for Contemporary Affairs (Itinerary of P.W. Botha's Visit to Thomson-CSF in France 1969). Following this, Thomson-CSF was involved with the South African military in the co-production, development and update of the Cactus/Crotale missile system from the 1960s to the 1980s (Van Vuuren 2017, 226).

Records reveal that in 1987, Thomson-CSF's chief executive, Alain Gomez, visited South Africa to meet with then minister of economic affairs and technology D.W. (Danie) Steyn. In a letter following the visit, Gomez thanked Steyn and confirmed that Thomson-CSF was ready to accept a military delegation to France for a 'European high technology scanning mission' (Gomez 1987). It is clear from this that Thomson-CSF was a long-standing supplier of military materiel to apartheid South Africa, no doubt – as we have indicated – with the support of the French state. In return, the exchange would have yielded significant profits. Yet, as with most of the apartheid government's corporate accomplices, there is no evidence that Thomson was ever held to account, or even questioned, by French or South African authorities, for violating the arms embargo (Open Secrets 2018).

PLUS ÇA CHANGE, PLUS C'EST LA MÊME CHOSE

If apartheid's security legislation and the clandestine nature of the arms trade hid the name Thomson-CSF from public view, the name Thales is notorious in the annals of the post-apartheid state. But these two names are of a piece: the once clandestine Thomson-CSF continued operating in post-apartheid South Africa under the name Thales; continuing, too, its business as usual in South Africa notwithstanding the ending of apartheid. The company's notoriety is at the forefront of South Africa's imagination. In a long-drawn-out legal case involving corruption, it stands as co-accused, together with former president Jacob Zuma in the Durban High Court. The charges related to allegations of bribes paid to the former president by Thales during the course of the infamous 1999 Arms Deal. Proceedings in the case have faced interminable delays due to endless litigation brought by Zuma, and latterly by Thales itself, to have the decision to prosecute set aside (Maughan 2020).

The Arms Deal was the defining event of South Africa's early democracy, and its legacy was a weakening of the very institutions tasked with tackling corruption. One of the most damaging after-effects have been the bribes paid to Zuma: these were paid by an individual, Shabir Shaik, whose brother was the chief of acquisitions for the Arms Deal itself. The former was found guilty of a corrupt relationship with Zuma and sentenced to 15 years in prison. The evidence was so conclusive that the trial court spoke of a 'mutually beneficial symbiosis' between Shaik and Zuma (Pauw 2017, 72). The judgment, which was upheld by the Supreme Court of Appeal and the Constitutional Court, found Shabir Shaik guilty on two counts of corruption.[2] Thales won a R2.7-billion contract from the Arms Deal to provide equipment to be fitted to new navy frigates. This is arguably the most vivid display of the consequences of failing to challenge networks that facilitated and committed economic crimes during apartheid. As we have established, Thomson-CSF was tied to the supply of weapons to the apartheid government for three decades in defiance of the UN Arms Embargo, yet this posed no obstacle to doing business with democratic South Africa.

Thales is not the only arms merchant that was keen to work with both the apartheid regime and its democratic successor. In 1999, two state-owned German companies – Howaldtswerke-Deutsche Werft (HDW) and Ingenieurkontor Lübeck (IKL), today trading as a subsidiary of ThyssenKrupp– won the bid together with a fellow German company, Ferrostaal, to supply post-apartheid South Africa's navy with new submarines. The same companies, too, faced serious allegations of corruption in the ill-famed Arms Deal. A report by New York-based law firm Debevoise & Plimpton LLP, commissioned by Ferrostaal, reported several irregularities. These included the fact that Ferrostaal made some $40 million in payments to 'agents' in South Africa. The report further alleged that Ferrostaal employees had told investigators that much of the so-called 'offset program'[3] was a cover for paying bribes, rather than generating the promised economic benefits such as creating employment (Debevoise & Plimpton LLP 2011).

The backstory to this deal underlines the continuities of exchange between the old South Africa and the new. Both HDW and IKL were controversially linked to the sale of blueprints and technology, which was intended to equip apartheid's navy with new submarines during the mid-1980s (Open Secrets 2018). Ferrostaal's consultant, Jeremy Mathers, was tasked with securing a 'political connection' in the 1999 deal (Debevoise & Plimpton LLP 2011, 61). Mathers' expertise stemmed from his long career in the South African Navy, including as project manager in an earlier scheme to acquire submarine blueprints from (then West) Germany, in contravention of the UN arms embargo. The later deal was agreed at a meeting between then South African president P.W. Botha and West German chancellor Helmut Kohl in Bonn in 1984 (Report on the Meeting between P.W. Botha and Chancellor Helmut Kohl 1984).

While HDW and IKL were to provide the plans for the submarines, the German electronics companies Siemens and Zeiss were to supply additional expert equipment required by the vessels. In addition, two subsidiaries of the giant Krupp conglomerate would supply torpedoes and sonar equipment (Africa Confidential 1988). However, the immediate enterprise was scuppered when the Green Party publicly leaked information about the deal, to the embarrassment of the Kohl government. But the hopes for a revival of arms sales after apartheid ended were apparently never abandoned. Despite their histories of plotting to break UN sanctions and in doing so aiding and abetting the apartheid regime, there was little push-back for the corporations involved. Indeed, within a decade, they were again bidding for the sale of submarines to the ANC-led government, allegedly paying bribes to clear their pathway. As with the Thomson-CSF/Thales case, this is a case of unchecked destructive power, a lack of adequate investigation or accountability, which enabled networks engaged in illicit activity to survive and draw in new actors.

Another middleman who was implicated in the arms deal was Greek-British citizen Tony Georgiadis. The report alleged that Georgiadis was paid $20 million by Ferrostaal – around 2.5% of the contract value – to help ensure that key decision-makers supported the German submarine consortium's bid in the Arms Deal (Debevoise & Plimpton LLP 2011). Yet, Georgiadis had enjoyed access to the upper echelons of the National Party government during apartheid. His shipping company, Alandis, was linked to more than 50 crude oil shipments to the apartheid state in the 1980s in contravention of the UN oil embargo (Brümmer and Sole 2007). Like the others, Georgiadis was able to navigate the South African transition and build alliances with a new elite.

These examples provide a window into the continuity of practice across South Africa's history regarding the arms trade and corruption. In these cases, this represented a continuity in the failure to investigate and prosecute individuals and institutions complicit in the arms trade for their violations of the letter and the spirit of international understandings and, indeed, law. This allowed them to continue in the face of great change, showing that while the political elites can shift, corporate players prone to bribery often remain the same.

However, until grand corruption is understood as continuity, there is little hope of tackling it. In the form of state capture, the economic crime that today confronts the country primarily results from failure to dismantle the criminal networks that profited from apartheid. Not only have actors in these networks continued to profit, but they have undermined any attempts to hold them to account. Addressing this past remains 'a kind of "unfinished business" of [South Africa's] transition: the ghosts of our tortured past will continue to haunt [the country] until they are exorcised fully and publicly' (Van Vuuren 2017, 506).

THE CORPORATE ENABLERS OF STATE CAPTURE

While many of the actors implicated in state capture are different from those who profited from apartheid, the essential role of global private corporations in enabling the modern system bears striking similarities to Armscor's busting of the UN arms embargo. Those who have recently profited from the looting of state-owned enterprises (SOEs) took advantage of the same secretive global financial architecture that allows for hidden ownership and facilitates the seamless movement of money across borders. Moreover, this regime was established by professionals such as bankers, lawyers, accountants and consultants, despite the ethical responsibility to identify, first, and then halt such activities.

The so-called GuptaLeaks, a trove of emails between participants in the state capture network, exposed a web of companies and individuals in a closed network that was solely intent on pilfering from the South African state. In addition, testimony before the Zondo Commission has shown how procurement processes at SOEs were flagrantly undermined. This has exposed the ways in which private interests captured the boards of SOEs. The bribes, kickbacks and other profits from this theft rarely remained in South Africa, however. Instead, ghost corporations and phony bank accounts helped to siphon off the money. At the same time, lawyers, auditors and other professionals either looked the other way or helped legitimise illicit transactions, all the while taking a cut (Marchant et al. 2020; see also Thakur and Pillay in chapter 5 of this volume).

As we have established, Luxembourg was often used as a jurisdiction of choice. Sanctions-busting was enabled by KBL, which – again, as we have seen – managed hundreds of accounts for Armscor and its front companies. As is typical of contemporary international finance, most of these fronts were little more than shell companies, existing only on paper and for the purpose of hiding the beneficial owners (Serrao and Myburgh 2017).

The Gupta network took advantage of a worldwide system where jurisdictions deliberately claim the advantage of financial secrecy and celebrate their immunity from local laws, rules and taxes. These are located in powerful countries in the global North. Almost half of all international bank assets are held in tax havens concentrated in London, British Crown dependencies and countries with historical links to the UK, such as Hong Kong, Singapore and Dubai (Shaxson 2012). Accountants, lawyers and company formation agents specialise in setting up and selling front companies for their clients to guarantee anonymity – ready to 'quickly create, maintain, and dissolve offshore companies as needed' (Radu 2019).

The establishment of front companies across the globe allows local and international banks to move funds between one another without raising issues around money laundering. Many banks played this role in the development of the Gupta-driven financial network. The Indian state-owned Bank of Baroda, which until 2018 had a branch in Johannesburg, was involved in clearing multiple transactions, even when the bank's own employees had thought them suspicious (Marchant et al. 2020). The respected Organized Crime and Corruption Reporting Project (OCCRP) reviewed data from the GuptaLeaks email dump and discovered a staggering R4.5 billion was transferred between Gupta front companies that held accounts at Baroda between 2007 and 2017 (Sharife and Joseph 2018). To manage these transactions, Baroda required the services of a South African-registered bank. This service was provided by the banking giant Nedbank, which continued to provide this service to Baroda until 2018, two years after it closed its own Gupta accounts 'citing corruption and money laundering concerns' (Marchant et al. 2020, 70). It did so despite not having sufficient information to conduct due diligence on transactions between Bank of Baroda accounts (Sharife and Joseph 2018).

Some of the world's biggest banks facilitated the most brazen instances of this looting. One of the more egregious examples is the role of the giant HSBC in laundering the proceeds of the public funds from kickbacks linked to Transnet's locomotive procurement (Sharife 2017). In this instance, a Gupta associate, Salim Essa, set up two front companies, Tequesta and Regiments Asia, apparently for the purpose of laundering kickbacks. Banking data obtained by the OCCRP revealed that around R1.3 billion was paid by China South Rail in more than 40 transactions to HSBC accounts held by these fronts (Sharife 2017). Despite an obvious 'red flag' of two newly formed companies with no discernible infrastructure or operations receiving massive fees for ostensibly 'advisory services' and immediately transferring them elsewhere, HSBC failed to act (Marchant et al. 2020, 70).

The fact that banks enabled looting is not exceptional – indeed, it may well be the rule of global finance. Experts suggest that laundering money worldwide is an industry estimated to be worth $2 trillion annually (Katz 2019). In September 2020, the International Consortium of Investigative Journalists published the FinCEN files – a series of 'suspicious activity reports' filed by US banks to the US Treasury's Financial Crimes Enforcement Network. This showed that several banks, including HSBC, JP Morgan Chase, Standard Chartered, Deutsche Bank and the Bank of New York Mellon, knowingly facilitated trillions of dollars in suspicious transactions, despite flagging them as possibly criminal (ICIJ 2020). The role of the global banking sector in facilitating economic crime of this kind is not accidental but is, rather, systemic, purposeful and directed.

With so many banks facilitating illegality, law firms and audit firms who had sight of the deals in question should provide a check on criminal activity. But the record showed this did not happen in the case of the Guptas. Instead, many professionals were complicit in enabling state capture in South Africa. The most publicly ventilated example was the consultancy KPMG, which failed to report illicit activity while auditing multiple Gupta-linked companies. Their brief included Linkway Trading Pty Ltd, a company that is said to have diverted millions from a rural development scheme to pay for an extravagant Gupta family wedding at Sun City, a luxury South African pleasure resort (Le Cordeur 2017). Adding insult to this deliberate public injury, KPMG managers attended the event and were later found to have failed to disclose this as an obvious conflict of interest. The Independent Regulatory Board for Auditors eventually disbarred one KPMG auditor on the Linkway Trading account for 'egregious dishonesty' in providing inaccurate reports on Linkway's finances (Van der Merwe 2019), but others have gone uncensured.

THE SAME MISTAKES OVER AND OVER AGAIN

One striking difference between apartheid's corporate enablers and those who supported state capture is that the latter have not escaped media and public attention. This is an outcome of the ending of apartheid security legislation and the country's transition to democracy. It is also the result of the successful campaign by civil society – led by the Right2Know Campaign – that prevented the South African Protection of State Information Bill (more commonly known as the Secrecy Bill), which sought a return to a secretive state, from being signed into law.

Exposés by the media, mainly, have provided a unique opportunity to demand public accountability. This was not previously possible. Even during South Africa's transition, corporations, financial institutions and many professional institutions escaped the scrutiny of the TRC and law enforcement authorities. The prevailing openness offers a unique moment to uncover the origins and workings of all those involved in state capture in order to pursue accountability.

HOW CAN THIS BE ACHIEVED?

In February 2020, Open Secrets made a submission to the Zondo Commission, urging it to consider the mounting evidence that implicated corporations in state capture. It was argued that the commission was in a unique position to bring corporate crime to the forefront of public consciousness to disrupt the practices that enabled economic crime (Marchant et al. 2020). It was suggested that the responsibility of the commission is as much discursive as it is substantive. Choosing what to include and exclude from its hearings would make some issues visible and obscure others (Miller 2008). Regrettably, the commission did not act on these concerns, although it passed on essential evidence to the investigative and prosecuting authorities on a range of related cases. Despite being awarded several extensions, the commission failed to summon and question the corporations that were implicated in looting from the state. The consequences are that many have not accounted for their culpability in the state capture project, and the institutional framework and the networks that facilitated state capture have not been fully explored, let alone exposed (Marrian 2021).

TACKLING THE DEEP STATE

What is striking about economic crime in South Africa's case is the ease with which corporations and middlemen could work across regimes that are so ideologically opposed. This returns us to the issue of the deep state, and particularly to the role of the intelligence and security agencies that underpin state power. Under Zuma's presidency, the state security apparatus was used to protect the interests of a corrupt elite. The same had happened, of course, during apartheid when Cold War concerns masked the purchase of arms notwithstanding the UN arms embargo. These schemes show how the trap of 'state security' – and the institutions promoting it – are potent instruments in the hands of politicians with corrupt intent.

The extent to which the State Security Agency abused power by acting as a conduit for venality and corruption was laid bare in testimony to the Zondo Commission in January 2021. The acting Director General of Intelligence, Loyiso Jafta, detailed the sheer criminalisation of the country's security agencies (Tolsi 2021). However, Jafta was all but blocked from testifying by the responsible minister and was fired two months later with the approval of the president. The suggestion is that Jafta's evidence had been a step too far for some within the intelligence community (Hunter 2021). This echoes the hesitant approach to expose acts of criminality within state intelligence and military structures in the late apartheid period out of fear that exposure might reveal what was hidden behind the veil of state security, and compromise individual politicians and state functionaries.

The scale of abuse within the intelligence agencies in contemporary South Africa is dumbfounding. The evidence presented by Jafta suggests that R125 million was unaccounted for in the 2017/2018 financial year. He testified further that the intelligence agency involved itself directly in day-to-day politics. So, money was paid to sympathetic news outlets owned by scandal-ridden politically connected businesspeople. Alarmingly, too, Jafta revealed that 'upwards of R200 million was spent on … covert operations intended to co-opt members of the judiciary and bribe them to hand down judgments favourable to [President] Zuma' (Tolsi 2021). The scale and breadth of these revelations suggest that criminal elements within the State Security Agency enjoyed the upper hand. They spied on the opponents of Zuma by infiltrating trade unions, student organisations and social movements. This malfeasance, not to mention naked criminality, mirrors the excesses displayed by South African intelligence agencies in the waning years of apartheid.

So, to draw Lenin's famous question closer, what is to be done?

There are two fundamental ways in which to tackle the corrosive role of the deep state in South Africa. One, as already suggested, will be to widen public conversation and narrative on the issue of economic crime. Perpetrators can no longer simply be classified as the proverbial 'bad apples' of the commonsensical 'free market' system: perpetrators must be pursued to the full extent of the law to root out corruption. It is instructive to recall that the TRC focus on human rights abuses rendered invisible the role of economic crime in sustaining apartheid. As a result of the TRC's mandate, the world knows about police operative Eugene de Kock as the quintessential perpetrator of apartheid criminality. However, comparatively little is known of the corruption and sanctions-busting that funded the late apartheid state and permitted theft from the public purse. This suggests that truth commissions have the power to reveal but can also obscure. So, bringing the evidence of the economic crime – especially money laundering – into the public gaze is a vital first step in addressing it.

The second step is to institute prosecutions and – where this is possible – civil litigation against actors identified as complicit in committing severe economic crimes. Criminal and civil action should involve vigorous attempts to recover stolen assets, including where these assets are now in foreign jurisdictions. This form of asset recovery is essential in stripping the criminal proceeds from elites who inevitably use those resources to further entrench their impunity from prosecution (Carranza 2008).

In 2002, the Khulumani Support Group, a national membership organisation of victims and survivors of apartheid human rights violations, brought a class action lawsuit against 20 banks and corporations for aiding and abetting the crimes of the apartheid state (Gubbay 2014). The case had initially involved the Swiss banks UBS (Union Bank of Switzerland) and Credit Suisse, and a host of other multinationals from Ford and Daimler to IBM and Rheinmetall, for their alleged role in aiding and abetting gross human rights violations during apartheid. In the end, this was unsuccessful, with a New York Appeals Court dismissing the case in 2013 on the basis that US courts did not have jurisdiction to hear the case (Gubbay 2014, 340).

So it is that those who were responsible for apartheid's economic crimes have never faced prosecution or sanction within South Africa or abroad.

As we have seen, this impunity has allowed networks of corruption to survive and attract a new generation of politicians. And so, for individual and corporate interests, South Africa's much-celebrated 'transition' was continuity of purpose, not change – and certainly not prosecution or the fear of it.

The holding power of the deep state is an important reason why delivering justice at times of transition is so difficult. The long-term imperative is that all must account for their actions. Only this will end the exemption culture, which was seamlessly transferred from the 'old' South Africa to the 'new'. This is why when state lethargy has set in as it has in South Africa, civil society should provide the pressure for prosecutions. This approach explains the Open Secrets memorandum that was submitted to the National Prosecuting Authority (NPA) in September 2020. The memorandum provides detailed evidence of the conduct of European banks which aided and abetted the apartheid regime to break international sanctions (Open Secrets 2020). At the time of writing, the NPA has indicated an intention to lead an investigation into this matter, together with the Directorate for Priority Crime Investigation, although to date no concrete progress is apparent.

Although the investigation must still run its course, it should give hope that the passing of time does not preclude attempts at achieving justice. To fully succeed will require fiercely independent and principled institutions and effective investigative agencies. It is in large part due to the machinations of the deep state that these institutions were gutted of the capacity needed to investigate and prosecute the often complex financial and economic crimes that define state capture. This is why a resurgence in the capacity and determination of the NPA to pursue complex economic crimes is so significant. Any struggle against the deep state must start with empowering those institutions and fiercely guarding their independence. But it also requires a robust civil society, which South Africa thankfully enjoys.

THE LONG CHAIN OF CORRUPTION

As the Zondo Commission reached the end of its hearings, the sheer extent of state capture and the corrosion of good governance at corporations and within government has led to many asking, 'How did it get this bad?' This cannot be answered without a longer view of South Africa's history. An understanding of the networks that have operated at the core of its worst crimes during apartheid constituted what today is called the deep state. Over time, these networks have used their leverage to undermine the constitutional framework and institutions that aimed to keep them in check. The arms trade – and the corporations, individuals, banks and spies that support it – provides the clearest insight into not only the survival but also the continuity of these networks. This was affirmed by the first People's Tribunal on Economic Crime, which stated: 'State capture is ... also a result of the corrupt activities that had gone before it. Absent the violation of United Nations sanctions and the corrupt Arms Procurement Package, the kind of state capture described in the evidence would probably not have occurred. The examples of state capture mentioned here are the tip of the iceberg' (People's Tribunal on Economic Crime 2018).

The conditions that created state capture are deeply rooted in South African society. Zuma and his political allies simply ensured that the deep state thrived during his presidency, protecting him from any form of accountability and providing his network with a ready supply of stolen public funds. As we have seen, many corporations – and many professionals – benefited handsomely as enablers of state capture or through sanctioning corrupt business practices. At the same time, some honest corporate businesses no doubt also suffered the consequences of state capture – the burden of deep state-sanctioned crime.

Rather than the change promised by the ending of apartheid, networks of actors and networks of practice have continued, notwithstanding the emergence of a democratic order. This outcome favours deep state actors as it allows them to continue to wield power from the shadows. If South Africa is to rid the country of state capture, it will need to be tackled at root and branch. This will come at great political cost. However, the failure to do so will set the stage for the next generation of profiteers to optimise their links to deep state networks and their international corporate enablers.

NOTES

1   This was under Resolution 2202A (XXI) of 16 December 1966. In 1984, the Security Council endorsed this determination under Resolution 556 of 23 October 1984.
2   See full judgment: S v Shaik and Others (CCT 86/06) [2007] ZACC 19; 2008 (2) SA 208 (CC); 2007 (12) BCLR 1360 (CC); 2008 (1) SACR 1 (CC) (2 October 2007).
3   'Offsets' are provisions in an import agreement that incentivise the importing state to select the exporting country or company. They often include a commitment by the exporting company to directly invest in the country, thereby promoting new economic growth; or they could agree to purchase other goods from the importing state to balance the country's terms of trade. However, given their complex nature and the difficulty of monitoring such deliverables over many years, the record suggests that offsets are readily open to fraudulent conduct and non-delivery, with little consequences for the parties involved.

REFERENCES

Africa Confidential. 1988. 'West Germany/South Africa: Secret Ships Deal Goes Ahead'. *Africa Confidential* 29, no. 6.

Brümmer, Stefaans and Sam Sole. 2007. 'Tony Georgiadis: "A Kingmaker"'. *Mail & Guardian*, 9 February 2007. http://www.armsdeal-vpo.co.za/articles10/lobbyist.html.

Carranza, Ruben. 2008. 'Plunder and Pain: Should Transitional Justice Engage with Corruption and Economic Crimes?' *International Journal of Transitional Justice* 2, no. 3: 310–330. https://www.ictj.org/sites/default/files/IJTJ-Global-Justice-Corruption-2008-English.pdf.

Debevoise & Plimpton LLP. 2011. 'Ferrostaal Final Report: Compliance Investigation'. 13 April 2011. https://corruptiontribunal.org.za/wp-content/uploads/2018/03/Annex-M-Debevoise-and-Plimpton-Report-re-Ferrostaal.pdf.

The Economist. 2017. 'What is the "Deep State"? And Where Does It Come From?' *The Economist*, 9 March 2017. https://www.economist.com/the-economist-explains/2017/03/09/what-is-the-deep-state.

Gomez, Alain. 1987. Letter to D.W. Steyn. 10 February 1987. D.W. Steyn Private Papers.

Gubbay, Ingrid. 2014. 'Towards Making Blood Money Visible: Lessons Drawn from Apartheid Litigation'. In *Making Sovereign Financing and Human Rights Work*, edited by Juan Pablo Bohoslavsky and Jernej Letnar Černič, 337–356. London: Hart Publishing.

Hunter, Qaanitah. 2021. 'SSA Confirms Loyiso Jafta Replaced as Acting Director-General of the SSA'. *News24*, 27 March 2021. https://www.news24.com/news24/SouthAfrica/News/breaking-loyiso-jafta-replaced-as-acting-director-general-of-ssa-20210327.

ICIJ. 2020. 'Global Banks Defy US Crackdowns by Serving Oligarchs, Criminals and Terrorists'. *International Consortium of Investigative Journalists*, 20 September 2020. https://www.icij.org/investigations/fincen-files/global-banks-defy-u-s-crackdowns-by-serving-oligarchs-criminals-and-terrorists/.

Itinerary of P.W. Botha's Visit to Thomson-CSF in France. 1969. University of the Free State. Archive for Contemporary Affairs (PV 203, 1/W1/4, 1969 June, P.W. Botha). June 1969.

Katz, Alan. 2019. 'The Cost of Dirty Money'. *Bloomberg*, 28 January 2019. https://www.bloomberg.com/graphics/2019-dirty-money/.

Kiewit, Lester. 2020. 'De Klerk Now Admits Apartheid Was a Crime against Humanity'. *Mail & Guardian*, 17 February 2020. https://mg.co.za/article/2020-02-17-de-klerk-now-admits-apartheid-was-a-crime-against-humanity/.

Le Cordeur, Matthew. 2017. 'KPMG SA CEO, 7 Others Quit on #GuptaLeaks, SARS Rogue Unit Fallout'. *News24*, 15 September 2017. https://www.news24.com/Fin24/kpmg-sa-ceo-7-others-quit-on-guptaleaks-fallout-20170915.

Maïzi, Adel. 2021. 'Tunisia's Truth and Dignity Commission: Archives in the Pursuit of Truth'. In *Archives and Human Rights*, edited by Jens Boel, Perrine Canavaggio and Antonio González Quintana, 126–137. London: Routledge.

Marchant, Michael, Mamello Mosiana, Paul Holden and Hennie van Vuuren. 2020. 'The Enablers: The Bankers, Accountants and Lawyers That Cashed in on State Capture'. *Open Secrets*, February 2020. https://www.opensecrets.org.za/the-enablers/.

Marrian, Natasha. 2021. 'State Capture: Time for Corporates to Face the Music'. *Financial Mail*, 14 January 2021. https://www.businesslive.co.za/fm/fm-fox/2021-01-14-state-capture-time-for-corporates-to-face-the-music/.

Maughan, Karyn. 2020. 'Thales Insists It Was Ignorant of Shaik's Alleged Corrupt Relationship with Zuma'. *Business Day*, 26 October 2020. https://www.businesslive.co.za/bd/national/2020-10-26-thales-insists-it-was-ignorant-of-shaiks-alleged-corrupt-relationship-with-zuma/.

Miller, Zunaida. 2008. 'Effects of Invisibility: In Search of the "Economic" in Transitional Justice'. *International Journal of Transitional Justice* 2, no. 3: 266–291. https://academic.oup.com/ijtj/article-abstract/2/3/266/2356955?redirectedFrom=fulltext.

Open Secrets. 2018. 'Apartheid's Sanctions Busting Bank: The Arms Money Machine'. *The People's Tribunal on Economic Crime*, 3–7 February 2018. https://corruptiontribunal.org.za/evidence/apartheidbank/.

Open Secrets. 2020. 'Apartheid Banks: NPA Docket: National Prosecuting Authority Docket'. *Open Secrets*, 3 September 2020. https://www.opensecrets.org.za/apartheidbanksdocket/.

Pauw, Jacques. 2017. *The President's Keepers: Those Keeping Zuma in Power and Out of Prison*. Cape Town: Tafelberg.

People's Tribunal on Economic Crime. 2018. 'Final Report of the People's Tribunal on Economic Crime'. 20 September 2018. https://corruptiontribunal.org.za/wp-content/uploads/2018/09/Final-Report-of-the-Panel_Signed.pdf.

Pretorius. 1983. Memorandum from SADF Director of Foreign Relations to the Chief of Staff Intelligence. 2 March 1983. Department of Defence Archive (Intelligence Directorate, GP 31, Box 4, File DBB/SK/311/1/30, Ops Zaire, 1, 08/01/1980–11/05/1983).

Radu, Paul. 2019. 'Vast Offshore Network Moved Billions with Help from Major Russian Bank'. *OCCRP*, 4 March 2019. www.occrp.org/en/troikalaundromat/vast-offshore-network-moved-billions-with-help-from-major-russian-bank.

Report on Meeting between Director Intelligence Operations and Mr Roussin. 1987. Department of Defence Archive (DI Onder-Afdeling Inligting Operasies, Gp 26, Box

13, AMI/IO/311/1/69, Hulpverlening en samewerking met Ivoorkus, 1, 04/08/86–18/05/90). 22 July 1987.

Report on Meeting between P.W. Botha and Chancellor Helmut Kohl in Bonn. 1984. University of the Free State. Archive for Contemporary Affairs (File PV 203, PS 12/27/1, 1984, P.W. Botha). 5 June.

Serrao, Angelique and Pieter-Louis Myburgh. 2017. 'Dubai: The Guptas' City of Shells'. *GuptaLeaks*, 27 October 2017. www.gupta-leaks.com/atul-gupta/dubai-the-guptas-city-of-shells.

Sevastopulo, Demetri. 2018. 'Donald Trump Blames "Deep State" for Insider Attacks'. *Financial Times*, 6 September 2018. https://www.ft.com/content/114bdfe0-b1ec-11e8-8d14-6f049d06439c.

Sharife, Khadija. 2017. 'Guptas, Big Banks Linked to South African-Chinese Locomotive Deal'. *OCCRP*, 13 November 2017. https://www.occrp.org/en/investigations/7257-guptas-big-banks-linked-to-south-african-chinese-locomotive-deal.

Sharife, Khadija and Josy Joseph. 2018. 'India's Bank of Baroda Played a Key Role in South Africa's Gupta Scandal'. *OCCRP*, 27 February 2018. www.occrp.org/en/investigations/7696-india-s-bank-of-baroda-played-a-key-role-in-south-africa-s-gupta-scandal.

Shaxson, Nicholas. 2012. *Treasure Islands: Tax Havens and the Men Who Stole the World.* London: Vintage Books.

Singh, Kaveel. 2021. 'Zuma's Supporters Descend on Nkandla and Ask: "What Did He Do Wrong?"' *News24*, 30 June 2021. https://www.news24.com/news24/southafrica/news/see-zuma-supporters-descend-on-nkandla-and-ask-what-did-he-do-wrong-20210630.

Söyler, Mehtap. 2013. 'Informal Institutions, Forms of State and Democracy: The Turkish Deep State'. *Democratisation* 20, no. 2: 310–334. https://www.tandfonline.com/doi/abs/10.1080/13510347.2011.650915.

Springborg, Robert. 2018. 'Deep States in MENA'. *Middle East Policy* 15, no. 1: 136–157. https://onlinelibrary.wiley.com/doi/abs/10.1111/mepo.12330.

Stephen, Chris. 2015. 'Attacks by "Deep State" Leave Tunisia Truth Commission in Crisis'. *The Guardian*, 11 September 2015. http://www.theguardian.com/world/2015/sep/11/attacks-state-tunisia-truth-commission-crisis-democracy.

Stone, Peter. 2020. 'The Real Deep State Is Trump: How the President Used William Barr and Other Officials to Turn the Government into His Personal Fiefdom'. *New Republic*, 2 October 2020. https://newrepublic.com/article/159551/real-deep-state-trump.

Taylor, Ian. 2000. 'The Ambiguous Commitment: The People's Republic of China and the Anti-Apartheid Struggle in South Africa'. *Journal of Contemporary African Studies* 18, no. 1: 91–106. https://www.tandfonline.com/doi/abs/10.1080/025890000111986.

Thale, Neo. 2021. 'F.W. De Klerk Foundation Slams Zuma, "Race-Based Empowerment"'. *The Citizen*, 22 March 2021. https://citizen.co.za/news/south-africa/2459548/fw-de-klerk-foundation-slams-zuma-race-based-empowerment/.

Tolsi, Niren. 2021. 'A Despot's Time to Face Democracy'. *New Frame*, 1 February 2021. https://www.newframe.com/a-despots-time-to-face-democracy/.

TRC Business Hearings. 1997. Submission by the Centre for Conflict Resolution, University of Cape Town. October 1997. South African History Archive. FOIP Collection, AL2878, A2.2.14.4. Wits University.

Van der Merwe, Marelise. 2019. 'Gupta-Linked Ex-KPMG Auditor Struck from IRBA Register for "Egregious Dishonesty"'. *Fin24*, 28 March 2019. https://www.news24.com/Fin24/gupta-linked-ex-kpmg-auditor-struck-from-irba-register-for-egregious-dishonesty-20190328.

Van der Waag, Ian. 2015. *A Military History of Modern South Africa*. Johannesburg: Jonathan Ball.

Van der Westhuizen, L.J. and J.H. le Roux. 1997. 'Armscor: The Leading Edge'. Institute for Contemporary History, University of the Free State. https://corruptiontribunal.org.za/wp-content/uploads/2018/02/AC18_Armscor-History-Extract_The-Will-to-Win.pdf.

Van Tonder, C.J. 1987. 'Report on Meeting between Director Intelligence Operations and Mr Roussin'. 22 July 1987. Department of Defence Archive (DI Onder-Afdeling Inligting Operasies, Gp 26, Box 13, AMI/IO/311/1/69, Hulpverlening en samewerking met Ivoorkus, 1, 04/08/86–18/05/90).

Van Vuuren, Hennie. 2017. *Apartheid Guns and Money: A Tale of Profit*. Johannesburg: Jacana Media.

Welsh, David. 2009. *The Rise and Fall of Apartheid*. Johannesburg: Jonathan Ball.

Winter, Jana and Elias Groll. 2017. 'Here Is the Memo That Blew up the NSC'. *Foreign Policy*, 17 August 2017. https://foreignpolicy.com/2017/08/10/heres-the-memo-that-blew-up-the-nsc/.

10

Old Ways and New Days:
An Interview with Barney Pityana

This is an edited version of a conversation between Barney Pityana, Mbongiseni Buthelezi and Peter Vale that took place on 4 February 2020 at the Centre for the Advancement of Scholarship, University of Pretoria.

Buthelezi: Good morning, Professor Pityana, and thank you for agreeing to this interview. I would like to ask you to start by introducing yourself.

Pityana: Thank you very much, colleagues. My name is Barney Pityana, and I am the retired vice chancellor of the University of South Africa. I am also an emeritus professor of law at Unisa. I have an affiliation with Rhodes University's philosophy department, too.

I am very keen on this project you are doing, not just because this is a topical issue today, but more importantly because it goes to the heart of how states fail and how South Africa got to be where it is. And I hope ultimately that the wisdom that comes from scholarship of this nature will tell us how to avoid the pitfalls of democracy and bad politics. Unfortunately, in this country, we have failed to prevent this – indeed, we have failed in a very grotesque manner. And what is even more bothersome in failing to do that is our insistence that we were on the right track; we would not hear anybody saying anything different.

The general character of society and politics has been – to use a word that South Africans like to use – 'denialist'; and so this exercise has my enthusiastic support, and I hope it will open us up to new understandings of our politics.

Buthelezi: A helpful place to start is with the assertion that South Africans failed to prevent state capture. But in understanding how we failed, I would like to go back to how we got here. And I wonder if you could put this in a longer historical context for us, in the tradition or the history of South African politics?

Pityana: For me, there are two historical threads.

We know that for 50 years or so, South Africa was ruled by Afrikaner nationalists. This regime was very conscious of the perverse influence and power of the English colonial superstructure that had undermined Afrikaner consciousness and the possibilities for Afrikaner nationalism. So, the latter was a counter to the colonial power that was deeply complicit in the making of South Africa.

The response of the Afrikaner nationalists was to establish the Afrikaner Broederbond in 1918 (see Wilkins and Strydom 1978). In my view, this was the first expression of state capture under which we lived in this country over a long period of time. The Broederbond was a shadowy, informal 'brotherhood' that was founded to promote Afrikaner interests, even before the National Party victory in 1948; if one wanted to occupy certain positions in the church, in business, in politics, one had to be a member or enjoy the endorsement of the Broederbond. So secretive was this society that membership was strictly by nomination by members only. Of course, it was a prestigious society to many, but what attracted one to membership were the privileges of power and prestige.

It was never a political party. It never went to the polls. It never actually presented itself to the public for endorsement of a manifesto to govern. But it was the custodian, if you like, of the Afrikaans language, Afrikaner cultural values and the future of Afrikaans people. Until the revelations of the late 1970s, the only person who was known to be a Broederbonder was its chairman – and it was always a *man*. Its members were found in the universities, in the church and in business, but rarely in politics per se.

They were very powerful people, and I got this, if I may say so, from conversations with Beyers Naudé.[1] I asked Naudé about the Broederbond and what it is. And Naudé replied that you will never know because many Afrikaners do not know what the Broederbond is, except that they know that it determines what happens in public life, what happens in the state, who goes where and when – even who succeeds.

The interesting thing was that this idea was not just represented in the church, although the church was extremely strong; not just by business, although this was instrumental in the development of Afrikaner business; not just by education, although the Broederbond was central to the establishment of Afrikaner universities and their development and funding and what went on in the schools; not just in language, even though the Broederbond was key in supporting the Afrikaner language, their religion and even sport, especially rugby.

But it seems to me that all of those were not just because individuals were personally enriching themselves. It was about how they could control how the state was undertaking its functions, in whose interests and for whose benefit. Indeed, it was about how it was using public resources for the benefit of Afrikaners.

The power of the Broederbond started to diminish when there were contestations within Afrikaner nationalism and, indeed, in the National Party. In the mid- and late 1960s, talk began about the divide between the *verligtes* and the *verkramptes* (see De Klerk 1972).[2] The Broederbond at that time seemed to be moving towards the former position, but the others were trying to hold it back. Whatever the case, it was increasingly clear that the power of the Broederbond was not what it once was.

Against this backdrop, I want to suggest that South Africa has lived with the idea of 'a state under capture' for a long time. We almost always knew that certain values – and I am going to say this by acknowledging the difference of what we are talking about today – are championed by a need to gain and hold on to power. In the Afrikaner case, this was the idea of *die volk*, the nation. Frankly, the idea of *die volk* was not some benign conservative act of self-preservation. On the contrary, it was seeking domination of the political and economic structures of society. Such domination was the means by which self-preservation could be assured.

Let me turn to the African National Congress (ANC). Remember that my own political upbringing was in the ANC. The years that the ANC spent in exile were of necessity times that required forms of trust and dependence. These were especially needed during the Cold War. We need to recall that those were hostile times when Western countries were very close to the Afrikaners and the National Party regime under different administrations. This was a time, too, when the ANC, although it was distinctly not communist in ideology, needed the South African Communist Party (SACP) to build its relationships with the Eastern Bloc countries. These countries, it should be remembered, were needed to make headway in establishing the ANC in its military form and to further its international propaganda. I can even add that the ANC's liberatory credentials needed to be established if it was to gain the support of the African states and the Non-Aligned Movement. At the Morogoro conference, membership of the ANC, including election to office, was opened to compatriots who were not African. These compatriots could participate freely as equals, regardless of colour.

There was a justifiable fear that this would ignite the tensions between the African nationalist sentiment within the ANC and the communists, which had been latent since the establishment of the Pan Africanist Congress in 1959.

It has been said that the conditions under which the ANC was obliged to operate externally gave advantage and influence to the communists among its members in terms of ideological thinking. The political-military structure was success-fully established in order to balance the political and military strategies of 'the Movement'. However, it has been observed that large numbers of young cadres from the student movement since [the] Soweto [uprising], many of whom were single-minded in their determination to acquire military skills and be part of the armed struggle, were recruiting ground for the SACP. We learned that becoming a member of the SACP and being trained as a soldier were forms of prestige for them. Consequently, the SACP recruited the most militant cadres to its ranks. Therefore, there was a strong belief that influence and privilege went with becoming a member of the SACP, and promotion in the ANC's armed wing, uMkhonto we Sizwe (MK), went along with being a member of the SACP. The power of the SACP in the mili-tary side of things was actually very strong. For some, it was not just in the military where this power and hegemony expressed itself, but it was strongly believed that the SACP exercised superior political, strategic and radical ideas.

And yet, many of the ANC leaders were not members of the SACP, and in later years there was a contention as to the location of the ANC's critical and strategic brains trust.

But we lived with a culture where everybody in the ANC, in the camps and in exile, knew that the influence of the SACP and in some aspects of the ANC was with the Communist Party. It did not mean that people like Oliver Tambo and others had no mind of their own, which is the impression often created by the apartheid system and by the Western liberal and conservative anti-communist lobby. It is a fact that we lived for too long with the knowledge that power and influence were wielded not simply by those who held elected office. For now, one is not making the point that there was anything corrupt about this, but it is simply as matters were and, above all, many of us accepted it as such.

Then, towards the end of the struggle, there was much contestation about who controlled the ANC and who determined its intellectual capital. For a long time, of course, there was an acceptance that the guru of ANC thinking was Joe Slovo.[3] But the likes of Thabo Mbeki and Pallo Jordan contested this view, arguing that the ANC had to be separate from and distinct from the SACP. The demise of the communist states in the Eastern Bloc became an occasion for analysis and understanding what the implications were for South Africa's struggle for liberation. This was because it had its own mechanisms of decision-making and policy-making, and these had to be respected by everybody who was a member of the ANC.

In large measure, both Oliver Tambo and the ANC encouraged Thabo Mbeki to explore and understand what was happening on the ground and what the thinking about the way forward could be. Out of that exploration, those in exile came to understand that Nelson Mandela on his own was exploring similar tactics from behind bars. In addition, contacts between various social forces within South Africa, including the intelligence system, intellectuals, business and others, shifted the balance from the armed forces to the political. Understandably, all this brought about much debate as well as suspicions because not all these manoeuvres could be openly debated. Whether intended or not, the strategy of the armed struggle through MK for the first time seemed to lag behind the political-diplomatic approaches.

All that I am suggesting is that the role of the SACP in the ANC was what we might call a kind of 'family capture'. But if you accept that these were two partner organisations in an alliance and it was never the intention to be one organisation, but that somehow the dominance of one over the other had been allowed to take place, it may well be that these tensions were never resolved and hence may account for the contestations about strategy when the negotiations began.

Buthelezi: So, how does this translate into the state when the ANC comes to power?

Pityana: It needs to be pointed out that the way the ANC operated and functioned in exile could never be the same as the ANC's behaviour in a democratic state. The ANC discovered that it had other partners; of particular importance was the UDF – the United Democratic Front. The two sides sought the same thing, but they operated with different cultures. The fallback position for the ANC was to simply swallow the so-called Mass Democratic Movement, including the UDF. Not enough effort was made to try to understand how politics in a democratic society functioned. We are reaping today – with state capture – that these other cultures were never properly analysed and challenged; namely, the cultures of exile and the political culture of the internal forces of struggle. In fact, as Thabo Mbeki was saying not so long ago, when we started in the 1990s, the major – almost singular – focus was on the state, building the state and controlling the levers of power. In my view, this was a confession that the ANC had ignored the role of the political party. In a sense, then, the ANC was growing in new soil, in a new environment without much direction from Mandela – nor, indeed, with direction from anyone else. The inclination was to try to imagine the ANC in its pre-Rivonia manifestation and recreate in the ANC at home its exile persona.

How differently could the ANC function from the way in which it functioned during the years of exile? Or, indeed, in order to function in the new environment, should the ANC pick up from what it was before the bannings of the 1960s? However, these and other similar questions were never asked. Instead, the only thing that was done was to organise the ANC into branches and increase its membership. There certainly was a process to determine who exactly could become a member of the ANC, but this was never closely monitored.

People who had been Bantustan officials became members of the ANC; people who came from the 'colouredstans' held ANC cards; and chiefs, and others like them, were all incorporated into the ANC. In the process, many collaborators and ex-police found their way into favoured positions in the ANC. So – and very soon, too – nobody really understood any longer what and who exactly the ANC was. To the best of my knowledge, the issues around this were never examined – except from time to time, and in frustration more than anything else – by the likes of Nelson Mandela and Thabo Mbeki.

But all sorts of people had ANC membership cards until 2005. It was only when the National Executive Committee meeting was held at the University of Pretoria that there was a proposal that each member had to sign a declaration that states among other clauses, 'I am joining the organisation voluntarily and without motives of material advantage or personal gain.'

How did the ANC function at that time? It functioned in the same command-and-control culture that had characterised the period in exile. So, the new members of the ANC were swallowed up after returning home as if they were sitting in camps in Tanzania or elsewhere, where democratic values hardly characterised the way the organisation functioned, in contrast to the Mass Democratic Movement at home.

The ANC at the local level has collapsed today because it was easy for branches to be captured by individuals who had the authority to silence everybody else or quieten dissenting voices. Many are simply not prepared to tolerate alternative views or opinions. So, members who were constituting themselves into a branch found themselves under the power of an individual who dictated to everybody else what they should do and what they should not do. Thus, one got to the position where it was said that the movement's power is in the branches, while, in actual fact, the power lies with the individual who controls that branch. It is a quick step from this context to the buying of branches; if you have enough money, and every member must pay R12, you can make available R1 200 and sign up 100 people and thus constitute a branch that is, essentially, non-existent. That is what is happening right now.

So, branches across the country are not all bona fide 'branches'. Many are simply people who paid membership on behalf of others to own something they call a branch. If there were to be an honest audit, it would reveal that there is nothing like the number of ANC branches that are claimed to exist. There are a few genuine ones, of course, but almost all the branches are constituted on the basis of somebody paying the membership fees for 'captured' members and cannot genuinely be called branches because they owe their loyalty first and foremost to the one who has paid for the branch to exist. Now the leaders are trying to do something about it because they recognise that gatekeepers are capturing ANC branches.

So, I am saying that what the ANC is going through today happened because we never paused in the early 1990s to ask what kind of ANC was appropriate for the future. Was the ANC constitution – which was old – appropriate for the conditions of the South Africa that we seek to influence? These questions went beyond moralising about apartheid and why it was not right. They were positioned beyond thinking about why freedom was important and all that. The point is that we never paused to reflect on the vehicle that was carrying our hopes and dreams.

Indeed, I remember somebody said that maybe the first conference held back in the country should have been a conference to dissolve the ANC, close it, throw it away and start a new party.

Buthelezi: I have follow-up questions that move in two directions: the state itself, while the other links to the Bantustans, especially the way in which power was distributed in these pseudo-states. How have these influenced the kind of state that we have ended up with? What role have they played in the kind of capture of the state that we have experienced?

Pityana: In exile, there were robust support systems within the ANC; nowadays, its branches are controlled by one person, and, by this time, it was running the state.

The first ten to fifteen years after the ending of formal apartheid was consumed with building the state. I think a good job was done. After all, we set up the Constitution and its democratic institutions; we were working on a society based on reconciliation, fostering education, improving health, and all those things. We were trying to move society away from apartheid into a non-racial democracy. However, what did not happen was finding a way to protect the state from the ANC's power (or abuse of power).

As a result, it was easy for the state to be infiltrated by people because they had their own objectives and used the state for their own benefit instead of the high-minded objectives that we had set for ourselves.

And if, therefore, the people are incapable of stopping – or standing against – this intrusion into the national objectives, they are easily swept into being part of that which the state is not about.

One of the things that I have had a problem understanding is this: how is it possible for some of the most intelligent people that I know to have bought into Zuma's capture of the state to the extent that they did? For the life of me, I could never understand how such clever people did not see that what they were doing was not right.

This is something that I think psychologists will one day help us to understand. How did it happen? It happened, I think, because people who should have known better were not vigilant enough. To be under capture or to become beholden to the one who exercises the power of capture not only means that one is capable of suspending one's moral judgement, but rather that one does not have to exercise it or can do so with impunity because one believes that one is under protection.

The people who should have known better bought into an alternative and destructive ideology instead of the ideology that placed them in power; as a result, it encouraged them to do things they were not supposed to do. The new ideology was to destroy everything that they had, that they were there for, and what they claimed to believe in. What then transpired is that many people in the public service became agents of malfeasance and corruption and were also its beneficiaries. Sadly, very few did so ultimately for their own benefit but served the interests of the master.

My sense is that we lost it when we sought to make the civil servants into political operators, rather than empowering them with the ideology of state-making. Instead, we destroyed the public service systematically by stripping it of its independence.

Vale: Can I just stop you there and ask if you have a name for this other ideology?

Pityana: No, I don't.

Vale: Is it greed?

Pityana: No, it is the ideology that they were there to protect.

Vale: That I understand, but what is the corroding ideology called?

Pityana: Well, the corroding ideology was corruption, theft, greed and self-enrichment; there is a word that I want – materialism. Unfortunately, there is a materialistic culture that has set in among public servants in South Africa.

I have said this a couple of times before: because of that materialism, that is what made it difficult for people to say no.

Buthelezi: In the circumstances, how could we have hoped to build a capable bureaucracy if the members were absorbed from such different cultures and networks, especially those from the former Bantustans? I would like to hear your reflection on what were centralised, homeland bureaucracies. What do you think might have been their effect if they had been absorbed into the new state?

Pityana: There are two sides to that story. When we came into the new system, by and large, there was a strong, overriding desire to remove everything that was part of the apartheid system and imbued with Afrikaner nationalism. This culture was all over the civil service. Maybe that was the right thing to do, maybe not. But the real problem was how this was done. To be frank, capable and diligent decent public servants were eased out of the system and new ones introduced without adequate training in some cases. Bantustan civil servants were brought in, I think, with little hostility. The truth of the matter is that both the Bantustan and the apartheid people came with a semblance of understanding the ethos of public service that the ANC did not have because of the circumstances the movement was faced with.

It is helpful to understand how quickly former apartheid civil servants departed the system – it took about ten years to denude the system. And, it is important to note that not all of them were unprofessional. In other words, not all were ideological nationalists; some of them were diligent, dedicated public servants. But then, some of those who left returned to their departments as consultants; and when this happened, they had an even greater influence on policy and practice than they had wielded when they were sitting at a desk drawing a government salary.

So, as far as the Bantustan people were concerned, I have a little bit more sympathy with the country's interim government. But, on the other hand, I think most of the people who were there were in favour of ending apartheid and were accomplished civil servants. There was a necessity to bring them into the system and to help transform it.

I cannot speak authoritatively as to whether there was a process of rebuilding a new Public Service Commission. But we need to talk about training a new public service in the country from top to bottom. This is because one could not expect to develop a new public service without really running a public service school. This would enable the development of a different kind of public service than the one that previously existed. This we understand, but, with respect, there was no need to throw away all the Afrikaners. A solution was simply to move them away from where they were – to mix them up. This could have made them more receptive to new and different ideas. However, I still think that the parallelism of a Ministry of Public Service and Administration under which the Public Service Commission fell did mean that the professionalism of the public service was compromised.

Buthelezi: It was not really done until recent times with the formation of the National School of Government. Again, this was a big trick that we missed.

Vale: This is ironic because in the early 1990s every university in the country was offering to start schools of public management. There was money slopping around to support this and research in the field, with an eye to developing a new culture and rewriting the rule books.

Pityana: I suppose what you then did is you brought the liberation people into the public service, too. They were previously stuck in the camps – some of them with a decent education, some not; you brought them in, and they had their own rule book, and this was not being mediated effectively enough. A mix of different cultures, schools and influences could have surely produced a new dynamic public service.

Buthelezi: There was a suggestion in 1995 that a universal entrance exam into the public service should be introduced along the lines of the Indian system. But this was quickly shot down in flames because it was obvious that it would disadvantage people who came from poor educational backgrounds and advantage white people all over again. Recently, some folks have been trying to raise that idea again, because we need to train people on all the basic norms regarding the public service.

Pityana: Not only that, but just teach civil servants how to interface with customers and that kind of thing, and basic ethics.

So, I am trying to say that the capture of the state that we find exposed before the Zondo Commission could never have happened if we had public servants who actually knew their rights, knew their powers, knew where they should be going and resisted the temptation of being bought into corrupt mechanisms for their own benefit.

Vale: Taking a cue from Mbongiseni, could you sketch the same thing as a professor of law about the legal system? Surely, the law was the bulwark against corruption? And it should perhaps have been brought to work a lot earlier than it was.

Pityana: Two things helped in South Africa. The first was the media, the cheeky media in our country that comes from a liberal, anti-apartheid background. The media kind of set themselves as personae of eternal suspicion of government and the state, which irritated some of us. [*Laughs*]

The other was the judiciary. Actually, the judiciary was never subjected to any 'clean-up'; there was nothing like what happened in the public service. Judges were never encouraged to leave, to the best of my knowledge. It needs to be remembered that many of the judges who made strong pronouncements against apartheid were judges who had operated under the old system. One reason for this is that once you internalise the culture of being a judge, you value your independence – that is a number one reason. Therefore, it was never easy to instruct a judge how to behave even under apartheid because they relied on precedent. So, even though the law was bad, for the most part, the judiciary's performance was acceptable – in terms of procedurally, thinking in a judicial manner, this was mostly satisfactory.

But, in 1994, the country changed from a parliamentary democracy to a constitutional one. This helped to change the way in which judges thought. This is because there was a clear notion that there was a Constitution at the end of the day, and the final arbiter of this was the Constitutional Court.

One may disagree with individual judgments, but today I can think of very few judgments that are motivated by political malice, as they were under apartheid. Many of the judgments have been delivered by judges from the old order but have been perfectly correct. Take Justice Louis Harms, for example, who had a very nasty commission, and when he sat on the Supreme Court of Appeal, he produced fantastic judgments. The same individual in a new environment is seen differently because now, as a Constitutional Court judge, the institution ultimately determining the law is not parliament but the bench of judges interpreting the Constitution.

Buthelezi: You have made the point about the judiciary and the media being a kind of bulwark against state capture. I want to ask you further about what you think civil society did during the Zuma years or how you think it could have done better?

Pityana: I do hear this, Mbongiseni, but my view is that civil society is the same people in the political parties and who in the end vote these very people into power. So, I do not know what is 'civil' about society; I think it is the same society for me.

In other countries, people who were with us in the anti-apartheid struggle were asking why it took so long for South Africans – who were known to be strongly committed justice activists – for us as a nation to actually say that what happened under Zuma was wrong, that it was contrary to what we wanted and what we had fought for. But, unfortunately, we did not do so, at least not collectively enough.

Two factors explain it, I think. The first is that the political environment was contaminated by blind loyalty to the ANC. As a result, many were unable to see anything wrong if it was done in the name of the ANC, or, if they did, they were afraid to raise their voices for fear of falling out of favour. Those who did raise their voices were declared personae non gratae because people would not accept that the issue was not Zuma per se but that the ANC had enabled him to function in the way he was behaving. We got to learn something about the power of toxic leadership under Zuma.

The second thing is that society was becoming less and less conscious of moral, ethical conduct. People no longer blush when somebody does something wrong in this country, even if this is outrightly bad. In my language, we say, 'You don't do that; there are certain things that you don't do; you don't do that because it brings shame upon yourself and your family or organisation you are associated with.' It is just not done; it is not a done thing. But that particular understanding of both public and private behaviour is gone. Sadly, it has been substituted with this understanding: what are you going to get? You can do anything under the protection of the powerful whom you contract to serve. So, at the end of the day, anything is okay as long as you are going to get something out of it.

South African society has gone a long way in enabling an environment where the capture of the state took place and where politicians are not being held to account. So, for example, when Jacob Zuma was elected, I wrote a public letter saying that I really did not think that he should be the president of the ANC, certainly not of the country, because he was such a morally flawed individual (see Pityana 2013). He did not have what it took to be a leader. When I did so, many people were so angry with me; they would not talk to me for a long time. If they could have killed me, they probably would have. But there was no real sense that something wrong was happening. Take Mbeki's 2005 call for Zuma to resign as his deputy, which found no support in the ANC. President Mbeki was right but not because the judge had found Zuma guilty. He did not, of course. Rather, it was in order to point out that one could not be the president or deputy president of a country when there was a suggestive paragraph in the judgment that names you as implicated in a crime. That is not proper. But Mbeki was also saying that if you want to appeal the judgment, you have the right to; but as long as the judgment stands, it compromises one's integrity as a leader. While you have it on your record, you should not be in the Presidency.

From that moment onwards, there was a resurgence of sympathy for Zuma. But this sympathy – and what happened subsequently – irretrievably changed the politics of the ANC. Even with Zuma's rape trial, it was disturbing to see ministers and other highly placed people supporting him. Given this support, it is not surprising that the country faces such violence against women and experiences a rape culture that is so out of hand, because society, when it mattered most, seemed to be saying that it is okay to rape if you are a certain person, until the court finds you not guilty or finds you guilty.

Vale: But isn't this a global phenomenon?

Pityana: It is indeed at a global level. I mean, if you look at former US president Donald Trump, as somebody said, who tells a blatant lie with every other sentence he utters, there is no compunction about saying something that is just not true. And in one thing, they did a fact-check on a number of Trump statements, and 90 per cent of them were lies – but the people in the US do not seem to mind.

Boris Johnson is a buffoon, but Britons said he was protecting their interests because he was the champion of Brexit.

Then, there is Narendra Modi in India and Jair Bolsonaro in Brazil; sweeping the world today, there is a frightening extent of narrower and narrower forms of nationalism. So, yes, it is true. This is all the more reason that we should not allow this to happen when we can. People like that should not make it to this level of mainstream politics. Interestingly, they constitute a right-wing conservative revolt against the failed compromises of the state.

I do not think it has been a factor here, and I do not think it needs to be a factor here, especially after the removal of Zuma. Cyril Ramaphosa is not that kind of person.

Buthelezi: Moving towards the close, I would like us to reflect on the Zondo Commission. What are your thoughts on whether this is a good mechanism for dealing with state capture as we have experienced it in South Africa?

Pityana: No, it is not a good mechanism. For one thing, it is an overly expensive mechanism. It is also not a judicial exercise and, as such, it is not a court of law. Finally, by its nature, it is bound to take too long to help the government address the pernicious effects of years of rot in government.

But I always see the Zondo Commission as symbolic. Cyril Ramaphosa needed to do something to symbolise his determination and to get to the bottom of things. But the Zondo Commission is not a good option for other reasons, too; one is that by their very nature, commissions, because of the Act under which they are established, are never really going to resolve things because they are not criminal courts.

My own view is that Ramaphosa had to do this because, at the time that he did this, there was virtually no National Prosecuting Authority (NPA), there was no South African Police Service (SAPS), there was no Hawks, there was no Independent Police Investigative Directorate, South African Revenue Service ... all of these had been corroded by the Zuma years.

Buthelezi: But let's remember that Zuma established the Zondo Commission in his last months in office.

Pityana: But his hand was forced, of course. When Thuli Madonsela was doing the state capture report and it was coming to her last days in office, she could not conclude her investigation into state capture.[4] So, she decided that the best thing to do would be to have a commission of inquiry looking into these things in some depth. She knew that she could not leave it to Zuma to follow up on these things, nor could she leave it to anyone else who was going to succeed her. (I think at that point she did know who was going to succeed her.)

So, the best way to do that was to insist that there must be a 'state capture commission' and to insist, further, that the president should appoint its member/s on the advice of the Chief Justice. As we know, Zuma made a big issue of that particular remedial action that imposed a duty on him to act in a specific manner. He resisted this, asking why the president's powers were being subjected to the power of the Public Protector. But when the chips were down, Zuma was forced by the ANC to say we needed to get this thing out of the way. The ANC itself was obliged by public sentiment that was protesting against Zuma. By this time, too, there was significant civil society activism on the issue out in the streets.

So, Zuma had to do it in the end, but he did not want to do it. Not only that, but once it was done, Zuma would have preferred the NPA and the SAPS to investigate things. At the time, however, Cyril Ramaphosa could not have relied on those mechanisms, even though that would have been the correct approach.

Many people, myself included, are frustrated because the Zondo Commission is taking too long to finish its task [the commission ended formally on 1 January 2022]. In a sense, it was foreseen that the malfeasance unearthed by the commission is as extensive as it has turned out to be. As a result, there is reason to fear that evidence may be contaminated, and prosecutions may be hard to come by. Whether they are going to be able to prosecute some of the people who appear before the Zondo Commission will be a real challenge.

This said, all South Africans, I am sure, want to ensure that there are consequences to what is being done on this front. I think that there are changes – in the NPA, for example, with the new leadership that is there, and there are very, very good people in the Special Investigating Unit nowadays. So, I think there is a possibility that this thing can actually end up in the courts. But, more positively, in any event, Zondo has succeeded in shining the spotlight into hitherto hidden nooks and crannies of state institutions and how these were deliberately caused to malfunction.

When the final report is done, it should generate a new momentum of cleaning up the rot in the state. [The final report, divided into several parts and volumes, has been published through 2022.]

Vale: But doesn't the Zondo Commission have a public educational side to its work?

Pityana: It does, indeed. But my worry, though, is that unless the Zondo Commission leads to people being in court and tried and convicted, there will be a lot of cynicism setting in with the people of our country. That is the danger that it faces.

I think the judge is well meaning. He wants to do the right thing; the material that is being collected has to be handed over to the NPA and the Special Investigating Unit and people like that.

I am worried that Zondo is seeking an extension of the commission at the moment, because I think the commission has a symbolic value. [The commission held its first hearing in August 2018. After five extensions, public hearings concluded in September 2021.]

Buthelezi: Commissions have in the past served us poorly because we have wanted to see prosecutions coming out of those things. But beyond prosecutions, structural reforms are needed to insulate the state from corruption and to make sure that the state does not suffer what we see it has suffered. We see the judge asking a lot of questions about structural conditions: what enabled this to happen in the state? What possibility is there for the commission to have outcomes in terms of restructuring and reorganising the state to ensure that it is insulated from politics to some degree?

Pityana: That is one of the most important contributions that Zondo is going to make. But the challenge that Zondo (or anybody else) has is that ultimately the state is the people, you and me. And the destruction of the state was done with you and I watching, facilitating or enabling.

There has to be a way in which we can guard against this in the future. I have just done an investigation of the Vaal University of Technology, where the corruption has been absolutely shocking. We got to the point where we commissioners said if this university is going to move forward, the two top tiers of management have to go and new leadership will be needed in this institution, with authority and backing to clean it up – ruthlessly, if that is what it takes. This is because those who are now in control are never going to do it because they are part of the system that brought this all about.

I think that what you are talking about in our public service situations ... take a guy like Berning Ntlemeza.[5] He was never going to be the one to bring an end to high-level corruption.

So, it is only going to happen when the work that you talk about [and that the Public Affairs Research Institute is doing] of professionalising the state, removing politics from the public service and inaugurating a sort of arm's-length relationship in the public service, and garnering trust in the public service takes place. In my view, it also means an independent Public Service Commission to be the one that supervises, just like the Judicial Service Commission; exactly that, the judges are not under any politician's control.

When we took over the country, the Public Service Commission was independent; and we decided to make it part of the ministry, for reasons best known to the ANC. We need to get to a situation where we have an independent Public Service Commission, with commissioners who are protected, who have a mechanism of ensuring conditions and appointments and all of that. Appointments of directors general should not be political appointments; at the moment, they are political appointments, and they should not be.

Buthelezi: Thank you. That brings us to the end of our questions. Thank you very much for talking with us and, in so doing, supporting our work.

NOTES

1 Beyers Naudé (1915–2004) was a cleric and theologian who was a leading Afrikaner anti-apartheid activist (Melber 2015).
2 *Verligtes*, translated as the 'enlightened ones'; *verkramptes*, translated as the 'ultra-con-servative ones'.
3 Slovo (1926–1995) was an anti-apartheid leader and theorist who held senior positions in the SACP and ANC as well as in MK (Independent 1995).
4 Madonsela was South Africa's Public Protector from 2009 to 2016.

5   Ntlemeza was controversially appointed acting head of the elite crime investigation unit, the Hawks, by then president Jacob Zuma in 2014. He was eventually removed in 2017 after being found by a court to lack 'integrity and honour' (Meyer 2019).

REFERENCES

De Klerk, Willem. 1972. 'The Concepts "Verkramp" and "Verlig"'. In *South African Dialogue: Contrasts in South African Thinking on Basic Race Issues*, edited by Nicolas Johannes Rhoodie, 519–531. Johannesburg: McGraw-Hill.

Independent. 1995. 'Obituary: Joe Slovo'. *Independent*, 7 January 1995. https://www.independent.co.uk/news/people/obituary-joe-slovo-1566935.html.

Melber, Henning, ed. 2015. *Faith as Politics: Reflections in Commemoration of Beyers Naudé (1915–2004)*. Uppsala: Nordic Africa Institute.

Meyer, Dan. 2019. 'Daughter of Ousted Former Hawks Boss Berning Ntlemeza Quits Police'. *Timeslive*, 22 August 2019. https://www.timeslive.co.za/news/south-africa/2019-08-22-daughter-of-ousted-former-hawks-boss-berning-ntlemeza-quits-police/.

Pityana, Barney. 2013. 'Dear Mr Zuma: An Open Letter on the State of the Nation'. *Sunday Independent*, 12 December 2013. https://www.thesouthafrican.com/news/struggle-leaders-open-letter-to-zuma-resign/.

Wilkins, Ivor and Hans Strydom. 1978. *The Super-Afrikaners: Inside the Afrikaner Broederbond*. Johannesburg: Jonathan Ball.

11

Can Democracy Bind the State? Comparative Thoughts from Brazil, India and South Africa

Patrick Heller

The chapters in this book develop different approaches to understanding what is widely described as the phenomenon of state capture in Jacob Zuma's presidency. In 'Betrayal of the Promise', the authors argue that state capture goes well beyond corruption in two respects (PARI 2017). First, it is systemic, involving a wholesale and concerted effort by elites to repurpose state institutions to generate rents and subsidise patronage networks. Second, it is a political project that comes not only with its own ideology (populist radical economic transformation) but also with efforts to harness the juridical and security apparatuses of the state to its cause. As the authors say, 'it is akin to a silent coup' (PARI 2017, 4).

In its scale, audacity and brazenness, state capture in South Africa may have been unique. But the broader phenomenon of elites seizing or effectively securing control of the state and subverting democracy is not. Indeed, the rise of right-wing populism across the world has been driven in large part by popular anger at the perception that the state and the economy it is meant to govern have been captured by elites. Adam Przeworski, pointing to the ways in which neoliberalism has crippled the capacity of states to regulate economies and ensure a modicum of economic justice, pithily captures the logic of popular anger when he notes that the people have learned 'that they can vote, but not chose' (1992, 56).

Increasing pessimism about the state's capacity to serve the popular will finds support in two convergent, albeit theoretically and politically radically different, academic literatures. The first, following Przeworksi and other neo-Marxist theorists, argues that neoliberal globalisation necessarily undermines national economic sovereignty and democratic self-determination by ceding real decision-making powers to multilateral organisations, global capital and elite governance networks. The second and more traditional economistic vein of state pessimism treats the state as any other utility-maximising agent and points to its inevitable slide towards rent-seeking (Krueger 1974). This literature provided the intellectual ammunition for neoliberal prescriptions for rolling back the state in the 1980s and 1990s.

Ironically, as different as they are, the neo-Marxist and rent-seeking literatures on the capitalist state converge in their assumption that powerful, organised interests invariably capture the state. Both have limited faith in democracy, and specifically of democracy as a means to bind the state to the will of the people. If we limit our definition of democracy to the Schumpeterian idea of representative democracy, then they have a point. Regular elections, even under the definitionally ideal conditions of full associational freedoms and robust rule-of-law institutions, provide for, at best, a limited mechanism of accountability. Elections often merely reflect existing power distributions and, even when elections do roughly reflect the popular will (South Africa being a perfect example), the functioning of democratic institutions is readily subverted by organised power. Binding the state to the will of the people requires more than elections and strong institutions.

But for all its weaknesses, democracy is always contested; democracies travel complex and uneven paths. Most importantly, the introduction of formal, electoral democracy does open possibilities for new forms of mobilisation and new political coalitions that can, under some circumstances, deepen democracy and support binding forms of popular sovereignty. European social democracies represent the prototype of democratic deepening. Iterated cycles of working-class mobilisation supported the consolidation of a democratic state that enjoyed a high degree of autonomy from dominant class interests and was able to secure significant redistributive gains over an extended period. In my co-authored book with Richard Sandbrook and colleagues (2007), we showed moreover that even in the global South – despite sharp social inequalities and difficult colonial legacies – there have been successful trajectories of democratic deepening (Costa Rica, Mauritius, Chile and the Indian state of Kerala), in which the state's capacity to respond to lower-class demands has expanded significantly, even in the context of globalisation.

To put the South African case in comparative perspective, I argue that state capture is neither an inevitable outcome of some macro process of neoliberal globalisation nor the inevitable result of the institutional weakness of the state in the global South, but rather a problem best understood through the lens of political sociology, and more specifically through a comparative historical analysis of trajectories of democratic deepening. I make this argument by comparing South Africa to India and Brazil. Like South Africa's, these are two democracies that were built on the strength of long and vibrant social movements but have also, like South Africa, had to consolidate and expand democracy against the backdrop of deep social inequalities. The result has been contested processes of democratic deepening that have cycled through periods of elite domination and the revitalisation of popular sovereignty.

COMPARING BRAZIL, INDIA AND SOUTH AFRICA

Brazil, India and South Africa are arguably the most successful cases of democratic consolidation in the developing world (Heller 2019). Democracy has not only become the only game in town, but it has made a real difference. In India, it has helped forge a nation from the most heterogeneous social fabric in the world. In South Africa, democratic politics and constitutional rule have managed a transition from white minority to black majority rule with minimal conflict. And in Brazil the transition to democracy has not only neutralised the military, which was long the institutional basis for authoritarianism, but also saw a Workers' Party (Partido dos Trabalhadores or PT) come to power for more than a decade (2003–2016). That this has been achieved against a backdrop of extreme social exclusions (caste, religious and ethnic divisions in India) and what are arguably the most racially divided societies in the world, which also happen to have the worst maldistribution of wealth in the world (South Africa and Brazil), only underscores the achievements at hand.

But if all three have fared well in consolidating democratic institutions, including the rule of law, comparative analysis points to substantially different degrees of democratic deepening. I argue that in both India and South Africa civil society has become subordinated to the instrumental (power-aggregating) logic of political society. In India, this has led to a process that I describe as *involutionary*: associational life has become increasingly defensive and organised around narrow identities or interests. This has resulted in segmented and zero-sum political conflict, in which competitive rent-seeking has all but incapacitated the developmental state. This crisis of development has, in turn, set the stage for the Bharatiya Janata

Party's (BJP) ascendance. As an upper-caste, upper-class party, the BJP has ruthlessly played the Hindu nationalist card to assert its political dominance. Now in its second term in power, it has moved aggressively to impose its Hindutva (Hindu nationalist) agenda, demonising Muslims, actively repressing civil society and consolidating the dominance of its middle-class, corporate-sector base.

In South Africa, civil society formations born of the anti-apartheid struggle retain significant capacity but have little effective leverage over political society. This *containerisation* of civil society is, in turn, fuelling class polarisation and has triggered a decade-long upsurge of often-violent protest. The South African state, which inherited significant state capacity from the apartheid era and had all the institutional makings of a strong developmental state at the time of democratisation, has rapidly disintegrated during the Zuma presidency (2008–2018) into a captured state (PARI 2017). A resurgence of civil society in 2017 helped dislodge Zuma from power, but the new Ramaphosa government remains dependent on the elite-dominated, rent-seeking patronage networks that sustained Zuma and crippled the state's developmental capacity (see Von Holdt in chapter 1 of this volume).

In both India and South Africa, the democratic trajectory of the post-transition period has vacillated, but overall has been marked by the erosion of democratic practices and the disempowerment of subordinate groups. In India, the political opposition is prostrate, and civil society is under attack; there appears to be no effective countervailing force to BJP hegemony, other than some sub-national pushback (notably in South India). In South Africa, civil society has retained greater autonomy, and movements have marshalled significant organisational resources and a wide range of repertoires of contention (see Von Holdt in this volume). But power remains firmly entrenched in the African National Congress (ANC), with the future of South African democracy being largely played out in intra-party factional conflicts.

Brazil presents a different picture. In what I describe as a case of a *project* civil society, a wide range of associational forms and movements have developed autonomous organisational capacity in the wake of the pro-democracy movement of the 1980s and coalesced around a politics of deepening citizenship. Despite a political party system widely seen as dysfunctional, civil society demands have measurably impacted on the form of democratic governance (specifically through the expansion of participatory structures) and drove a significant expansion of the welfare state in the years of PT rule. The term 'project' carries a double connotation. Civil society in Brazil has been clearly marked by the specific project of building participatory democracy, and in the process has quite literally projected itself into the state. PT president Dilma Rousseff's deposal by a right-wing alliance in 2016 and Jair Bolsonaro's election in

2018 represent a dramatic reversal but should not obscure what has transpired in the 27 years since the new Constitution was inaugurated. The democratic legacy of that period includes a rights-based welfare state infrastructure, a sophisticated and diverse civil society sector that remains resourceful, and local governments (*municípios*) that are the most autonomous and capacitated in Latin America.

DEMOCRATIC DEEPENING

Much of the debate on democracy in the global South has focused on democratic consolidation and presumes a minimalist definition of democracy as representative democracy. Yet, democratic contestations in the global South have gone beyond representation to include demands for expanded participatory and substantive forms of democracy (Heller 2022). Kenneth Roberts has defined democratic deepening as 'intensifying popular sovereignty in the political sphere, that is moving from hierarchical forms of elitist or bureaucratic control to forms of popular self-determination by means of more direct participation in the decision-making process or more effective mechanisms for holding elected representatives and public officials accountable to their constituents' (1998, 30). This concept of democratic deepening can be subdivided into three dimensions.

The first dimension is *participatory democracy*, the process through which 'the people' are constructed as a political subject. Much of the political science literature treats interests as predefined, but normative theories of democracy have long emphasised that the formation of preferences and political subjects is inherently political. The democratic ideal in normative theory of what Jürgen Habermas calls 'opinion- and-will formation' (1996, 77) is tied to broad-based and capacitated participation. Amartya Sen's (1999) arguments about development as freedom have increasingly placed participation at the centre of debates about democracy in the global South. But Sen, and others who celebrate the virtues of participation, have little to say about the conditions under which participatory democracy might flourish. By definition, participation takes place in the spaces of civil society, which may be more or less autonomous and conducive to facilitating communicative practices or may be fully colonised by social or market power. Preconditions for meeting the participatory ideal include the classic Tocquevillian concern with a minimal level of social equality in which all citizens treat each other as rights-bearing, a degree of public legality (O'Donnell 1993), and the capacity of the state to protect basic rights of citizenship, including a level of fairness in relations between citizens.

The second dimension of democratic deepening is *representative democracy*, which consists of translating the people's preferences into actual political mandates. Elections are the classic mechanism of aggregation, with a plurality choosing the government and sanctioning a stated policy regime. The aggregative mechanism is, in practice, not limited to elections but includes other forms of formal influence on government policy, such as institutionalised arenas of bargaining (legally supported collective bargaining, corporatism, and so on), participatory structures and the judiciary.

The third dimension is *democratic stateness*. This takes its cue from the classic distinction between a government and a state. Evelyne Huber, Dietrich Rueschemeyer and John Stephens (1997) note that a key aspect of democracy must be that state institutions, the bureaucracy in general, but also key apparatuses such as the military, must answer to elected representatives. This distinction has been used to recognise cases in which a government has been democratically elected but 'the ongoing functioning of democratic procedures is not necessarily assured' (Collier and Levitsky 1997, 446). This, it should be emphasised, can be a problem at the national level, but it is a severe and endemic problem for the sub-national state in many developing democracies. Indeed, as I argue elsewhere (Heller 2019), the weakest link in the chain of popular sovereignty in much of the global South is local government. This third dimension of preserving the chain of sovereignty is critical for two reasons. First, if bureaucratic and coercive powers do not answer to democratic authorities, then the chain of popular sovereignty is clearly broken. Preference formation and aggregation may have been democratic, but the translation of those preferences into outcomes is not secured. Second, if stateness itself is not democratic, be it 'neo-feudalised' as in capture by powerful extra-democratic cliques or local strongmen, or 'governmentalised', as in driven by organisational or disciplinary powers that are constituted beyond democratic control, then the very foundations of democratic life – the effective protection and enforcement by the state of basic rights – are compromised. In his influential discussion of the problem of democratisation in Latin America, Guillermo O'Donnell (1993) couches his argument about the weaknesses of public legality (or what I am calling democratic stateness) almost entirely in terms of the day-to-day encounters of the state and its citizens. We then come full circle: the very foundation of democratic life – active participation that supports effective representation – is both predicated on and constitutive of democratic stateness. But how exactly and when exactly are these different dimensions of democracy mutually reinforcing?

BRINGING CIVIL SOCIETY IN

Political theorists have long argued that a democratic state is as much about civil society as it is about representative institutions. Although the definition of civil society has changed over time, it has always had the connotation of *authorising* the political, that is, as providing the normatively legitimating basis for organised political power. Following Habermas (1996) and Jean Cohen and Andrew Arato (1992), political society is governed by instrumental-strategic action and refers to the set of actors who compete for, and the institutions that regulate, the right to exercise legitimate political authority. Civil society refers to non-state and non-market forms of voluntary association, where the principal mode through which interactions are governed is communicative. These are ideal types and, in practice, the line between political and civil society is often blurred. But in institutional terms, political and civil society have distinctive modes of legitimation. The important distinction is that if the telos of politics is legitimate power and its logic the aggregation of interests, the telos of civil society is reaching new understanding by participating in the public sphere.

Whether civil society expands rights-based conceptions of democratic inclusion, serves as an extension of state power, or devolves into inward-looking and exclusionary forms of retrenchment (Castells 2003) is an empirical question, and one that is shaped by civil society's relation to the state and market (Burawoy 2003). Accordingly, we have to begin with the general recognition that civil society is fragile and contingent, constituted of multiple publics (Fraser 1992) that can vary dramatically in composition and activity level, as well as in their effects. This calls for carefully unveiling the contradictory relationships between the state and the civil sphere and the way in which these shifting relationships both reflect societal power and shape the functioning of the state and civil society. For reasons that I elaborate below, democratic deepening requires striking a delicate balance between the aggregative logic of political society and the participatory logic of civil society. A 'proper' balance, in turn, can deepen democratic stateness by strengthening the receptivity of the state to the demos and strengthening the legitimacy of state action.

Working within this frame, the comparative-historical argument I develop in this chapter is that, in South Africa and India, civil society is increasingly being subordinated to political society and communicative practices are being displaced by instrumental power. In South Africa civil society has largely been sidelined as a politically effective actor (containerisation), and in India much of civil society has been fragmented and instrumentalised by politicisation (involution). This is consequential for the sustainability of democracy because a weakened civil society cannot perform three critical democratic functions: (1) provide a space in which citizens can meaningfully practise democracy on a day-to-day basis; (2) anchor the legitimacy of political practices and state institutions in vigorous public debate; and (3) serve as a balancing force to the aggregative logic of political society. Viewed historically, this weakening of civil society is paradoxical, given that the democratic transition in both countries was driven by broad-based social movements whose communicative power was propelled by the moral force of arguments based on inclusive and modern claims to democratic citizenship (Gandhi's Indian National Congress and Mandela's African National Congress).

This paradox alerts us to the fact that civil and political society, though assumed to be in a mutually reinforcing relationship, are often in tension, and how this plays out has significant repercussions for trajectories of democratic deepening. Indeed, when one juxtaposes the robustness of representative democracy in South Africa and India to the ineffectiveness of civil society, it becomes clear that consolidation may well have come at the expense of democratic deepening. Narendra Modi's re-election in 2019 and the acceleration of his Hindu nationalist agenda and Zuma's state capture leadership mark unprecedented lows in each country's democratic history. In both cases, hegemonic political parties have demobilised civil society and severely compromised democratic stateness. Zuma's ousting and civil society opposition to the Hindu nationalist agenda are a reminder of the resilience of civil society. In contrast, the case of Brazil provides evidence of how civil society can transform politics and substantively impact on state actions. The particular pattern of political-civil society interactions that marked the process of democratisation in Brazil has allowed civil society to project itself into the state and to frame politics and policy-making in a rights-based logic.

PATHWAYS TO DEMOCRATIC DEEPENING

Any discussion of the history of democracy in Brazil, South Africa and India must begin with a foundational paradox. On the one hand, these are societies marked by extremes of categorically based and segmented inequality: slavery and race in Brazil, apartheid in South Africa and caste/religion in India. These have produced what Evelina Dagnino (1998) in the Brazilian context has called 'social authoritarianisms', deep-seated inequalities of income and property, as well as of cultural and social capital, that permeate social practices and govern social interactions.

On the other hand, and flying in the face of Tocquevillian assumptions that democracy can only take root where there is broad-based equality, in all three countries democratisation was driven by mass-based social movements. The foundational democratic movements in all three – the Indian National Congress, the ANC/United Democratic Front, and the 1980s civil society alliance in Brazil – were encompassing, self-consciously cutting across class, race and caste, and sustained high levels of mass mobilisation. They not only pushed for and secured representative democracy but also produced rights-based discourses and constitutions that were direct attacks on social inequality and domination.

This, moreover, was not merely a short-lived historical moment when national mobilisation created a sense of solidarity that aligned with ideas of democratic citizenship. In India, these norms of democratic equality have been sustained by a range of social movements and even sub-regional politics, most notably in the state of Kerala, where encompassing left movements have dominated politics since independence. Congress Party hegemony was challenged in the 1980s, with the emergence of new political formations driven by regional and lower-caste reform movements. In terms of social gains, a wide range of movement organisations played a critical role in shaping the expansion of rights-based welfare policies during the Congress-led United Progressive Front government of 2002–2014.

Similarly, in South Africa, despite the perverse inherited inequalities of apartheid, large segments of the black population were well organised, most notably the labour movement, and were able to secure significant redress such as labour protection and the deracialisation of formal labour markets. Moreover, a wide array of movements from local civics to 'single-issue' campaigns and HIV/Aids movements deployed a range of 'in-system' and 'extra-institutional' tactics to press both rights-based demands (HIV treatment) and counter-hegemonic challenges (such as opposition to neoliberalism) on the state (Ballard, Habib and Valodia 2006). More recently, new movements have explicitly challenged the ANCs hegemony (Von Holdt and Naidoo 2019).

The general point here is that in both India and South Africa, subordinate groups, despite pervasive social exclusions, have used the political space created by democratic institutions to make public claims. Thus, it is both possible to argue that democratic power in both countries continues to be concentrated in the hands of elites and intermediaries, while at the same time recognising that civil society continues to be a vibrant arena for democratic claim-making and participatory practices (Chipkin 2007; Jayal 2011; Mosoetsa 2005; Von Holdt and Naidoo 2019).

From this brief survey then, it becomes clear that the democratic deficit in India and South Africa lies neither in civil society per se nor in the formal character of the state. The state in both cases is a democratic one and, social inequalities notwithstanding, subordinate groups *have* organised in civil society. The intractable problem has been the vertical axis of democracy. Despite the conditions of highly consolidated democracies with legally guaranteed rights, citizens from subordinate groups find it difficult to engage the state effectively. There are two interrelated problems here. First, the institutional surface area of the state remains limited, especially when it comes to local government. In India, local governments, including those of its vast megacities, have limited powers of autonomous governance when compared with any other leading democracy in the world (Heller 2019). As a result, Indian citizens face significant constraints in exercising their rights at the local level. South African cities have additional resources and greater autonomy, but ANC dominance at the local level has made for insulated and patronage-driven local politics, including extensively documented cases of local state capture (Olver 2017). Popular discontent with the limits of local democracy has fuelled the service delivery protests of the past decade. Second, in both democracies, political parties not only monopolise the channels of influence but also exert near-absolute power in setting the agenda to determine which issues, claims and even identities enter the political domain. As a result, the public sphere is shaped primarily by forms of influence that flow directly from political or economic power (parties, lobbies, powerful brokers) rather than from the communicative practices of civil society actors. It is in this sense that I argue that the problem of democratisation lies less in the electoral institutions of democracy or the party system (which are dramatically different) than in the political practices and channels that link civil society to the state (which are similar).

Brazil's transition to democracy was, if anything, less fortuitous. Unlike India and South Africa, Brazil's initial period of electoral democracy (1946–1964) was based on a tightly limited franchise and politics entirely dominated by revolving pacts of elite coalitions. The extent of social inequality is probably better documented for Brazil than for any other developing country: from ethnographic studies (Scheper-Hughes 1992) that reveal the practices of 'cultural social authoritarianism' (Dagnino 1998) to demographic and econometric analyses (De Ferranti et al. 2004; Telles 2004) that lay bare some of the gravest material and racialised inequalities in the world. Social inequality, moreover, was directly enforced by state power. Guilherme Wanderley dos Santos (1979) has characterised this period as a system of 'regulated citizenship' (*cidadania regulada*), in which social rights were conferred only to categories of formal-sector urban workers recognised by the state.

Yet, since the mid-1980s, Brazil has travelled a different path from India and South Africa. Beginning with the democracy movements of the 1970s and extending into the post-transition period, subordinate groups actively occupied the spaces of civil society and transformed the public sphere, demanding new forms of

243

citizenship. Moreover, civil society groups have been able to link up with the state, sometimes *through* elements of political society (specifically through the PT, a party that was created by social movements) but more often *despite* political society.

Wendy Hunter summarises the findings of institutional analyses of Brazil's party system: 'high party-system fragmentation, low partisan identification, and strong orientation toward personalism and pork barrel' (2007, 448). No government in Brazil in the prevailing democratic period has ever enjoyed anything close to a working majority in the legislature. Yet, over the last two decades, Brazil has experienced notable reforms in areas as diverse as health care (Gibson 2018), urban governance (Wampler 2015), affirmative action (Paschel 2016), poverty programmes (Kerstenetzky 2014) and the environment (Hochstetler and Keck 2007); these reforms are impossible to explain without reference to changing civil society-state relationships.

In the rest of this chapter, I demonstrate how democratic deepening has been shaped by the balance of civil and political society. Elsewhere, I have made this argument by examining the local government as the crucible of democratic stateness (Heller 2019). Here I focus on social movements – that is, the contentious expressions of civil society – not only because democratic movements are a critical countervailing force to the oligarchic tendencies of political parties, but also because they can raise, define and politicise issues that political society is often deaf to (Cohen and Arato 1992; Habermas 1996).

SOCIAL MOVEMENTS AND DEMOCRATIC DEEPENING

In Brazil, India and South Africa, basic democratic structures can accommodate social movement formation, and contentious action is widespread. But in India and South Africa, social movements have run up against political party systems that have either been immune to social movement demands or have sought to instrumentalise them. By contrast, social movements in Brazil have profoundly impacted on the public sphere, problematising and politicising a wide range of social justice claims, engaging directly with the state to shape policy and, most importantly, redefining 'citizenship by challenging the existing definition of what constituted the political arena – its participants, its institutions, its processes, its agenda, and its scope' (Dagnino 2007: 550). There is no better example of this than Tianna Paschel's *Becoming Black Political Subjects* (2016), which documents the rise of the black movement that in a deeply racialised society has achieved significant reforms both in its access to the state and in securing equity-enhancing policies. Similarly,

Kathryn Hochstetler and Margaret Keck (2007) argue that the environmental movement in Brazil is by far the broadest and most successful in Latin America. The movement has self-consciously combined contention (*ecologia de denuncia*) with pragmatic engagement with the state (*ecologia de resultados*). This has been made possible by the dramatic expansion of the policy surface area through constitutional provisions that mandate engagement on environmental issues with community service organisations and through the proliferation of a range of councils that have given environmental groups direct access to policy-making. As Gay Seidman notes, 'Brazilian activists have learned to view the state as a site of struggle' (2010, 93).

That movements have played such a powerful role in so many different sectors in Brazil points to broader factors at work. In comparison with India and South Africa, it is the nature of civil society-political society relations that stands out. In Brazil, social movements emerged largely *in opposition* to political society. As Dagnino argues, movements acted against 'the control and tutelage of the political organization of the popular sectors by the state, political parties and politicians. Their conception of rights and citizenship embodied a reaction against previous notions of rights as favours and/or objects of bargain with the powerful (as in the case of citizenship by concession, *cidadania concedida*' (2007, 553). But even as movements sought to redefine the meaning and modalities of the political, they were also driven by practical demands for inclusion and determined to shape public policy. Brazilian scholars emphasise the extent to which movements effectively defined a new 'political-ethical field', generated a new public morality and exerted tremendous normative pressures on the state to redeem constitutional claims. The local state and the national state have had little choice but to respond to these demand-side pressures.

The immediate post-authoritarian period was marked by a ratcheting up of movement mobilisation, in no small part supported by the provisions of the new constitution (1988) that enshrined institutions of participatory democracy. Thus, despite being widely branded as 'neoliberal' by left critics, Fernando Henrique Cardoso's two administrations were noted for their openness to civil society. The party that succeeded Cardoso, the PT, was at the confluence of the social movements of the 1980s and claimed a patented model of governing (*o modo petista de governar*) that included a substantive commitment to redistribution and a procedural commitment to 'incorporating and even institutionalizing popular participation in decision-making' (Hochstetler 2004, 8).

This blurring of the traditional boundaries between state and civil society has, moreover, had substantive effects. One cannot account for changes in Brazil's health sector, including the response to HIV/Aids, the formalisation of labour markets, environmental reforms and the democratisation of urban governance, without reference to the role of movements. Finally, these movements have engaged with the state while preserving their autonomy. Even during the PT's 13 years in power, social movements have openly criticised the government's economic policies and continued to engage in contentious actions (Hochstetler 2004, 21). The mass street protests in the run-up to the 2014 FIFA World Cup were evidence that despite more than a decade of having the PT in power, civil society had hardly relinquished any of its autonomy. The protests critiqued the corruption and wasteful expenditures associated with the showpiece, and explicitly attacked political society. But they did so by affirming support for the public sector by demanding an expansion of health and education expenditures.

Social movements in India and South Africa have travelled a different path. In India, there is a long and rich post-independence history of social mobilisation, but, with the possible exception of the farmer movements that emerged in the 1980s, few social movements have been able to scale up and impact on the political arena. Other class-based movements have had even less success. Though landless labourers constitute by far the single largest class category in India and are overwhelmingly Dalit and lower caste, nothing even resembling a sustained movement has ever emerged, except in the state of Kerala. If anything, movements of the agrarian poor have taken place largely outside the democratic arena, in the form of various Maoist-inspired local insurrections. India's industrial labour movement has been especially weak. From the beginning of independence, India's labour federations were dominated by the state and, as Vivek Chibber (2005) has shown, were outmanoeuvred into accepting an industrial relations regime that subordinated labour's interests to the imperatives of promoting capital investment. Operating in a bureaucratic and quasi-corporatist environment, the federations have become instruments of political parties, and it is telling that they have not expanded their presence beyond the confines of the protected organised sector, which accounts for less than 9 per cent of the workforce.

Other movements, including those of Dalits, Adivasis, women and environmentalists, have developed innovative and effective forms of contention and built strategic ties with transnational advocacy networks, so it is difficult to downplay the richness and the vibrancy of the social movement sector. Yet, none of these movements have developed effective and sustainable ties to political society, and, indeed, many have taken an 'anti-politics' turn, embracing communities and rejecting engagement with the state (Corbridge and Harriss 2000). This reflects the degree to which civil society formations have come to distrust a political society increasingly characterised by corruption, personalism, and concentrated and insulated power.

This involutionary logic has paved the way over the past two decades to forces tied to the rise of Hindu nationalism, driven in large part by 'elite revolts' (Corbridge and Harriss 2000) against the new electoral power of the lower castes. Insofar as these movements seek to affirm traditional privileges of caste, male authority and the Hindu majority, they are deeply illiberal. And although they have proven effective in electoral politics – the Hindu-nationalist BJP won the national elections in a landslide in 2014 and 2019 – they have had a perverse effect on civil society by stoking inter-community violence, legitimising old and new exclusions, communalising schools, unions and associations, and in general reinforcing the involutionary logic of exclusionary identity politics.

In South Africa, social movements played such a critical role in the anti-apartheid struggle that they entered the democratic period with significant organisational capacity, enormous popular support and considerable momentum (Seidman 2010). Following a well-documented pattern (Hipsher 1998), some demobilisation was inevitable with the transition to democracy, especially considering the formal representation through various corporatist structures that the labour and civic movements were given. But the degree to which movements have been almost completely neutralised or sidelined requires some comment, especially given that such a demobilisation did not take place in Brazil.

First, one needs to address the most confounding case – organised labour. The Congress of South African Trade Union's (Cosatu's) strength and cohesiveness stands in sharp contrast to India's fragmented and marginalised labour movement and is testament to the depth and breadth of labour organising that took place under apartheid. Despite its alliance with the ANC, Cosatu has retained its organisational autonomy, often voicing criticism of the state and staging broad-based and well-organised strikes across sectors to leverage labour's bargaining capacity (Habib and Valodia 2006). Cosatu has, moreover, shown itself to be a powerful kingmaker, having played a critical role in Jacob Zuma's defeat of President Thabo Mbeki for control of the ANC at the party's December 2007 Polokwane conference (Pillay 2013). Yet, most assessments of labour's role in South Africa's corporatist structures, and specifically the National Economic Development and Labour Council, are critical, arguing that the ANC has largely set the agenda. Most notably, Cosatu failed to block or even modify the ANC's shift from the redistributive Reconstruction and Development Programme (RDP) to the orthodox, neoliberal Growth, Employment and Redistribution (GEAR) plan. Devan Pillay (2013) argues that the labour movement has vacillated between social movement unionism and political unionism, but on the whole has subordinated itself to the ANC. Cosatu itself recognises this political dependency. In a policy document, the federation complained that the

ANC National Executive Committee has no active trade unionists or social movement activists and goes on to complain that 'once elections are over we go back into the painful reality of being sidelined for another five years' (cited in Webster and Buhlungu 2004, 241).

For other social movements in South Africa, one can paint a much simpler picture. The South African National Civic Organisation, which was, next to labour, the most important component of the anti-apartheid movement – was defanged almost immediately after the transition, becoming little more than a compliant ANC mouthpiece. The transition from the RDP to GEAR in 1996 saw the dismantling of formal participatory structures at the local level and the marginalisation of community structures and non-governmental organisations (NGOs) from policy-making (Heller and Ntlokonkulu 2001). The resulting disconnect from politics and the extent of dissatisfaction about the quality of local government and persistent unemployment fuelled the rise of new social movements in urban areas, including anti-eviction campaigns and various forms of organised resistance to the commodification of public services. These movements had a programmatic thrust, namely opposition to neoliberalism and ANC hegemony, but they were never able to scale up politically. Since 2005, discontent has been demonstrated by a marked upsurge in what have been dubbed 'service delivery protests' (Atkinson 2007, 58). These community movements remain local and inchoate and have had little choice but to resort to contentious actions, many directed at elected ward councillors. On the whole, they have been met with silence or outright hostility by the ANC government.

COMPARING TRAJECTORIES OF DEMOCRATIC DEEPENING

I have argued that in South Africa and India, civil society has been subordinated to political society, whereas in Brazil, political and civil society have a more balanced relationship. In India and South Africa, the space for local democratic practices and encompassing social movements has contracted. While there is still plenty of room for vibrant associational forms and even contentious action, the nature of civil society's relationship to political society has severely restricted the impact that movements and subaltern claims can have on the political sphere and on the state. In India, local democratic government is extremely weak, almost non-existent in many states. For the urban and rural poor, sightings of the state (to borrow from Corbridge et al. 2005) are intermittent at best and, when they can or must engage with the local state, citizens work through intermediaries or powerful political brokers. Cities are controlled by growth cabals (Heller, Mukhopadhyay and Walton 2019). On a day-to-day basis then, the Indian citizen engages the state either as a client or as a member of a group, but not as a rights-bearing citizen.

The rise of the BJP and Hindutva and the proliferation of identity politics mark the involution of civil society. The BJP is in every respect a social movement party, having risen from the trenches of civil society through the activities of mass-based cultural and social associations to achieve electoral power. It is a direct response to the failures of the Nehruvian modernisation project. The resurgence of communalism and casteism in India is not as such the resurgence of deep, primordial loyalties but rather a failure of political society to link up with the democratic impulses of civil society. It is precisely this failure that has opened the space for the politicisation of identities with parties constantly seeking the electoral edge through the formation of new, but inherently unstable, ethnic alignments.

It may now have hardened into a new dominant bloc. The BJP government that came to power in May 2014, and was re-elected in 2019, is supported by a coalition that includes a pro-market urban middle class and mostly rural social conservatives from the upper castes. This unseemly but historically not uncommon marriage between economic liberalism and political illiberalism has two de-solidarising logics: rejecting the affirmative, equity-enhancing state, pithily captured in Modi's electoral slogan of 'more governance, less government'; and strengthening the role of the state as champion of a singular ethno-national identity.

South Africa's democracy is much younger, yet there are already troubling signs of a slide from civic to ethnic nationalism (Chipkin 2007; Hart 2014; Mangcu 2008). Subaltern civil society in South Africa has also become estranged from political society, but through a different process. Civil society has become deeply bifurcated between an organised civil society that effectively engages the state and a subaltern civil society that is institutionally disconnected from the state and political society. Business groups, professionalised NGOs, the middle-class beneficiaries of South Africa's Black Economic Empowerment policies and organised labour continue to be well positioned to engage the state. But subaltern civil society, and especially the urban poor, has virtually been sidelined from the political process in South Africa.

This containerisation has taken place through a complex set of institutional, political and discursive practices. In institutional terms, the surface area of the state in South Africa has dramatically shrunk over the past decade. Constitutionally mandated participatory spaces in local government have been hollowed out or altogether dismantled, and state-society relations increasingly bureaucratised and politicised. At the national level, corporatist structures are all but defunct. The state continues to transact significantly with civil society but does so in a selective and controlled manner. Across a wide range of sectors, the preferred mode of intermediation has become 'partnerships' with professionalised NGOs that carry out contracted services. Conditions for engagement with the state are increasingly set by complex standards for meeting performance targets and accounting practices that all but rule out community-based organisations. Generously paid consultants, often working for 'non-profits', now occupy much of the terrain between the state and society.

The political terms of engagement for civil society have eroded as a result of the ANC's increasingly centralised and dirigiste style of politics. Since coming to power, the ANC has sought to consolidate its electorally dominant position by asserting its right as the agent of the 'national democratic revolution' to demand political subordination of mass organisations. The ANC's relationship to civil society has shifted, moving from a democratic conception of the citizen to a nationalist conception anchored in an essentialised African identity.

To date, the dominant-party status of the ANC has pre-empted the type of involution that one sees in India. Yet, the problems of having containerised civil society are becoming progressively evident. On the one hand, the sidelining of civil society has shifted all political contention to the ANC itself. With the stakes of organisational control ratcheted up, violence has become endemic, both against those who would challenge party authority (such as the striking workers at Marikana) and among party factions fighting for control over local rents (Olver 2017). On the other hand, new social movements are giving way to 'movement beyond movements' in the form of increasingly disparate, angry and inchoate protests, including a wave of xenophobic murders in 2008 (Hart 2014, 3). Disillusionment and discontent, especially among unemployed youth, have fuelled the rise of demagogic, hyper-nationalistic and anti-democratic political leaders such as Julius Malema, leader of the Economic Freedom Fighters. The ousting of President Zuma in the aftermath of the state capture crisis that revealed the workings of a tightly knit cabal of ANC officials and private interests extracting substantial rents from the state, as reviewed in this book's chapters, underscores just how much the dominance of the ANC has led to the erosion of state institutions.

AT WHAT PRICE DEMOCRACY?

So, under what conditions can democracy actually bind the state and make the people sovereign? Democratic trajectories in India and South Africa point to the extent to which political consolidation can come at the expense of participatory democracy. Local spaces for citizen engagement have been subject to increasing control from above or simply shrunk, and social movements have had limited access to the state. In the absence of an effective civil society, mechanisms of accountability have been weakened and narrow, and sectoral or identity-based interests have largely displaced rights-based forms of claim-making. But what is more often treated as a problem of institutions (say, in the literature on good governance) must rather be viewed as a problem of how *politics is transacted*. Politics in India and South Africa has been increasingly instrumentalised, shorn of its normative and deliberative qualities, and reduced to little more than a competitive, mutually exclusive scramble for scarce resources (state capture in South Africa) or cultural hegemony (Hindutva in India). As a result, the democratic nature of the state, the third link in the chain of sovereignty, is compromised. In sum, even as representative democracy has gained tremendous traction and provides a critical baseline of inclusion in what are highly diverse and unequal societies – a tremendous achievement in its own right – the democratic trajectories of India and South Africa suggest that politics dominated by parties can come at the expense of developing effective forms of citizenship.

This interpretation should, however, not be read as a path-dependent argument, in which an initial imbalance of political and civil society, of elite and mass interests, has locked in a self-limiting form of democracy. In both cases, this lock-in should be treated as a conjunctural balance of power rather than as a stable equilibrium. At the time of writing in August 2022, the BJP had exploited the Covid-19 pandemic to double down on its repression of civil society. But just before the pandemic broke and a lockdown was declared in March 2020, the BJP had been confronted by the most open and direct challenge to its authority in six years of power. Responding to legislative changes passed by the government that undermined rights of citizenship for Muslims, a broad-based and pluralistic civil society coalition organised and sustained protests across the country. Most telling about the movement was that it was couched entirely in terms of preserving India's secular and pluralistic constitutional tradition, replete with street repertories that included public readings of the preamble to the constitution.

In South Africa, the political dominance of the ANC in the medium term seems assured. But the source of its ideological hegemony – its claim to represent the 'national democratic revolution' – sets a high bar. For large numbers of South Africans, the promise of a just and inclusive society continues to inflect the meaning of politics with a transformative thrust that by definition leaves much to be redeemed. As Karl van Holdt and Prishani Naidoo (2019) have argued, recent movements, including community protests, the worker protests at Marikana (and the formation of an oppositional miner union) and the student movement #FeesMustFall have challenged the ANC's monopoly claim to post-apartheid transformation, reinvigorated discursive claims that the ANC has suppressed (socialism, participation), and developed new organisational forms. The fact that Zuma's patrimonial monopolisation of the state was ultimately challenged by a broad coalition of formal civil society organisations building on the significant legal resources of South African democracy (see Klaaren in chapter 4 of this volume), and an array of movement actors within the Tripartite Alliance, is testament to the resilience of civil society.

The case of Brazil only underscores the historical contingency of the balance between political and civil society. Brazil was no less unequal at the time of transition than South Africa or India. If anything, its path to democracy has been more troubled and its political institutions were more fragile. Yet, the post-1988 constitution period witnessed not only the strengthening of an autonomous and combative civil society but also clear instances of civil society projecting itself into the state to shape policy. Most notably, civil society pressures have resulted in the institutionalisation of a wide range of participatory structures and the strengthening of local democratic government but can also be linked to the expansion of the social welfare state (Kerstenetzky 2014; Seidman 2010). Given such power and status shifts in a deeply hierarchical society, the Bolsonaro backlash, with is sharp class, racial and gender inflections, is hardly surprising and underscores just how transformative democratic deepening has been (Heller 2019). Bolsonaro's election is certainly a pointed reminder of the vagaries of representative democracy, especially in a democracy with a notoriously weak and fragmented party system. But this should not distract us from recognising the clear gains that Brazil had made in terms of participation and stateness and, in particular, the strengthening of rights culture and local government. The resilience of civil society and democratic stateness was in full evidence during the pandemic. Even as Bolsonaro refused to engage the crisis, civil society organisations and local officials mounted effective public health campaigns and successfully lobbied the National Congress for significant welfare measures. The presidential elections in October 2022 saw Bolsonaro lose to Lula, although by a much tighter margin than predicted. The reservoir of support for reaction in Brazil remains deep. But Lula was able to forge a winning coalition of the poor together with progressive elements of the middle class by emphasising the urgency of reinvigorating democratic institutions and expanding the welfare state.

Born as they were in the crucible of deep, categorical inequalities, Brazil, India and South Africa's democracies have cycled through periods of elite domination and revitalised popular sovereignty. The Brazilian case demonstrates that social movements and civil society can have transformative effects. At the other end of the spectrum, India points to the extreme dangers of illiberalism that can result from a hegemonic political party asserting itself over and against civil society. South Africa lies somewhere in between. The ANC has been able to contain but not completely dominate civil society. Zuma's capture of the state represented a period of extreme imbalance that was exposed and pulled back by a resurgent civil society.

Taken together, these three cases underscore that elite subversion of democracy is neither an inevitable outcome of some macro process of neoliberal globalisation nor the inevitable result of the institutional weakness of the state in the global South, but rather a problem best understood through the lens of political sociology, and more specifically through a comparative historical analysis of trajectories of democratic deepening.

REFERENCES

Atkinson, Doreen. 2007. 'Taking to the Streets: Has Developmental Local Government Failed in South Africa?' In *State of the Nation: South Africa 2007*, edited by Sakhela Buhlungu, John Daniel, Roger Southall and Jessica Lutchman, 53–77. Cape Town: HSRC Press.

Ballard, Richard, Adam Habib and Imraan Valodia, eds. 2006. *Voices of Protest: Social Movements in Post-Apartheid South Africa*. Pietermaritzburg: University of KwaZulu-Natal Press.

Burawoy, Michael. 2003. 'For a Sociological Marxism: The Complementary Convergence of Antonio Gramsci and Karl Polanyi'. *Politics & Society* 31, no. 2: 193–261. https://journals.sagepub.com/doi/10.1177/0032329203252270.

Castells, Manuel. 2003. *The Power of Identity*. Malden, MA: Blackwell.

Chibber, Vivek. 2005. 'From Class Compromise to Class Accommodation: Labor's Incorporation into the Indian Political Economy'. In *Social Movements in India: Poverty, Power, and Politics*, edited by Raka Ray and Mary Fainsod Katzenstein, 32–61. Lanham, MD: Rowman and Littlefield.

Chipkin, Ivor. 2007. *Do South Africans Exist? Nationalism, Democracy and the Identity of 'the People'*. Johannesburg: Wits University Press.

Cohen, Jean L. and Andrew Arato. 1992. *Civil Society and Political Theory*. Cambridge, MA: MIT Press.

Collier, David and Steven Levitsky. 1997. 'Democracy with Adjectives: Conceptual Innovation in Comparative Research'. *World Politics* 49, no. 3: 430–451. https://www.jstor.org/stable/25054009#metadata_info_tab_contents.

Corbridge, Stuart and John Harriss. 2000. *Reinventing India: Liberalization, Hindu Nationalism and Popular Democracy*. Cambridge: Polity Press.

Corbridge, Stuart, Glyn Williams, Manoj Srivastava and Rene Veron. 2005. *Seeing the State: Governance and Governmentality in India*. Cambridge: Cambridge University Press.

Dagnino, Evelina. 1998. 'Culture, Citizenship, and Democracy: Changing Discourses and Practices of the Latin American Left'. In *Cultures of Politics, Politics of Cultures: Re-Visioning Latin American Social Movements*, edited by Sonia E. Alvarez, Evelina Dagnino and Aturo Escobar, 33–63. Boulder, CO: Westview Press.

Dagnino, Evelina. 2007. 'Citizenship: A Perverse Confluence'. *Development and Practice* 17, no. 4/5: 549–556. https://www.jstor.org/stable/25548252#metadata_info_tab_contents.

De Ferranti, David, Guillermo E. Perry, Francisco H. Ferreira and Michael Walton. 2004. *Inequality in Latin America: Breaking with History?* Washington, DC: World Bank.

Fraser, Nancy. 1992. 'Rethinking the Public Sphere: A Contribution to the Critique of Actually Existing Democracy'. In *Habermas and the Public Sphere*, edited by Craig Calhoun, 109–143. Cambridge, MA: MIT Press.

Gibson, Christopher L. 2018. *Movement-Driven Development: The Politics of Health and Democracy in Brazil*. Stanford, CA: Stanford University Press.

Habermas, Jürgen. 1996. *Between Facts and Norms: Contributions to a Discourse Theory of Law and Democracy*. Cambridge, MA: MIT Press.

Habib, Adam and Imraan Valodia. 2006. 'Reconstructing a Social Movement in an Era of Globalisation: A Caste Study of COSATU'. In *Voices of Protest: Social Movements in Post-Apartheid South Africa*, edited by Richard Ballard, Adam Habib and Imraan Valodia, 225–254. Pietermaritzburg: University of KwaZulu-Natal Press.

Hart, Gillian. 2014. *Rethinking the South African Crisis: Nationalism, Populism, Hegemony*. Athens, GA: University of Georgia Press.

Heller, Patrick. 2019. 'Divergent Trajectories of Democratic Deepening: Comparing Brazil, India, and South Africa'. *Theory and Society* 48, no. 3: 351–382. https://link.springer.com/article/10.1007/s11186-019-09351-7.

Heller, Patrick. 2022. 'Democracy in the Global South'. *Annual Review of Sociology* 48: 463–484. https://www.annualreviews.org/doi/abs/10.1146/annurev-soc-030320-123449.

Heller, Patrick, Partha Mukhopadhyay and Michael Walton. 2019. 'Cabal City: India's Urban Regimes and Accumulation without Development'. In *Business and Politics in India*, edited by Christopher Jaffrelot, Atul Kohli and Kanta Murali, 151–182. Oxford: Oxford University Press.

Heller, Patrick and Libhongo Ntlokonkulu. 2001. 'A Civic Movement, or a Movement of Civics? The South African National Civic Organisation (SANCO) in the Post-Apartheid Period'. Research Report No. 84, Social Policy Series, Centre for Policy Studies, Johannesburg.

Hipsher, Patricia L. 1998. 'Democratic Transitions as Protest Cycles: Social Movement Dynamics in Democratizing Latin America'. In *The Social Movement Society: Contentious Politics for a New Century*, edited by David S. Meyer and Sidney Tarrow, 153–172. Lanham, MD: Rowman & Littlefield.

Hochstetler, Kathryn. 2004. 'Civil Society in Lula's Brazil'. Working Paper CBS-57-04, Centre for Brazilian Studies, University of Oxford. https://www.lac.ox.ac.uk/sites/default/files/lac/documents/media/kathryn20hochstedler2057.pdf.

Hochstetler, Kathryn and Margaret E. Keck. 2007. *Greening Brazil: Environmental Activism in State and Society*. Durham, NC: Duke University Press.

Huber, Evelyne, Dietrich Rueschemeyer and John D. Stephens. 1997. 'The Paradoxes of Contemporary Democracy: Formal, Participatory, and Social Dimensions'. *Comparative Politics* 29, no. 3: 323–342. https://www.jstor.org/stable/422124#metadata_info_tab_contents.

Hunter, Wendy. 2007. 'The Normalization of an Anomaly: The Workers' Party in Brazil'. *World Politics* 59, no. 3: 440–475. https://www.jstor.org/stable/40060165#metadata_info_tab_contents.

Jayal, Niraja Gopal. 2011. 'The Transformation of Citizenship in India in the 1990s and Beyond'. In *Understanding India's New Political Economy: A Great Transformation?* edited by Sanjay Ruparelia, Sanjay Reddy, John Harriss and Stuart Corbridge, 141–156. London: Routledge.

Kerstenetzky, Celia Lessa. 2014. 'The Brazilian Social Developmental State: A Progressive Agenda in a (Still) Conservative Political Society'. In *The End of the Developmental State?* edited by Michelle Williams, 172–198. New York: Routledge.

Krueger, Anne O. 1974. 'The Political Economy of Rent-Seeking'. *American Economic Review* 64, 3: 291–303. https://assets.aeaweb.org/asset-server/files/9452.pdf.

Mangcu, Xolela. 2008. *To the Brink: The State of Democracy in South Africa*. Pietermaritzburg: University of KwaZulu-Natal Press.

Mosoetsa, Sarah. 2005. 'Compromised Communities and Re-Emerging Civic Engagement in Mpumalanga Township, Durban, KwaZulu-Natal'. *Journal of Southern African Studies* 31, no. 4: 857–873. https://www.tandfonline.com/doi/abs/10.1080/03057070500370779.

O'Donnell, Guillermo. 1993. 'On the State, Democratization and Some Conceptual Problems: A Latin American View with Glances at Some Postcommunist Countries'. *World Development* 21, no. 8: 1355–1359. https://www.sciencedirect.com/science/article/abs/pii/0305750X9390048E.

Olver, Crispan. 2017. *How to Steal a City: The Battle for Nelson Mandela Bay*. Johannesburg: Jonathan Ball.

PARI. 2017. 'Betrayal of the Promise: How South Africa Is Being Stolen'. State Capacity Research Project Report, Public Affairs Research Institute, Johannesburg. https://pari.org.za/betrayal-promise-report/.

Paschel, Tianna S. 2016. *Becoming Black Political Subjects: Movements and Ethno-Racial Rights in Colombia and Brazil*. Princeton: Princeton University Press.

Pillay, Devan. 2013. 'Between Social Movements and Political Unionism: COSATU and Democratic Politics in South Africa'. *Rethinking Development and Inequality* 2: 10–27. https://www.researchgate.net/publication/304999996_Between_Social_Movement_and_Political_Unionism_COSATU_and_Democratic_Politics_in_South_Africa.

Przeworski, Adam. 1992. 'The Neoliberal Fallacy'. *Journal of Democracy* 3, no. 3: 45–59. https://www.journalofdemocracy.org/articles/the-neoliberal-fallacy/.

Roberts, Kenneth M. 1998. *Deepening Democracy? The Modern Left and Social Movements in Chile and Peru*. Stanford: Stanford University Press.

Sandbrook, Richard, Marc Edelman, Patrick Heller and Judith Teichman. 2007. *Social Democracy in the Global Periphery: Origins, Challenges, Prospects*. Cambridge: Cambridge University Press.

Santos, Guilherme Wanderley dos. 1979. *Cidadania e Justiça: A Política Social na Ordem Brasileira*. Rio de Janeiro: Editora Campus.

Scheper-Hughes, Nancy. 1992. *Death without Weeping: The Violence of Everyday Life in Brazil*. Berkeley: University of California Press.

Seidman, Gay. 2010. 'Brazil's "Pro-Poor" Strategies: What South Africa Could Learn'. *Transformation* 72: 86–103. https://www.researchgate.net/publication/241901399_Brazil's_'pro-poor'_strategies_what_South_Africa_could_learn.

Sen, Amartya. 1999. *Development as Freedom*. New York: Knopf.

Telles, Edward E. 2004. *Race in Another America: The Significance of Skin Color in Brazil*. Princeton: Princeton University Press.

Von Holdt, Karl and Prishani Naidoo. 2019. 'Mapping Movement Landscapes in South Africa'. *Globalizations* 16, no. 2: 170–185. https://www.tandfonline.com/doi/abs/10.1080/14747731.2018.1479019.

Wampler, Brian. 2015. *Activating Democracy in Brazil: Popular Participation, Social Justice, and Interlocking Institutions*. South Bend, IN: University of Notre Dame Press.

Webster, Edward and Sakhela Buhlungu. 2004. 'Between Marginalisation & Revitalisation? The State of the Trade Union Movement in South Africa'. *Review of African Political Economy* 31, no. 100: 229–245. https://www.jstor.org/stable/4006889#metadata_info_tab_contents.

CONTRIBUTORS

Ryan Brunette is a research associate at the Public Affairs Research Institute (PARI) in Johannesburg. He is a doctoral candidate at the Graduate Centre of the City University of New York.

Mbongiseni Buthelezi is the director of the Public Affairs Research Institute (PARI) and an associate professor in the Department of Anthropology and Development Studies at the University of Johannesburg. Prior to joining PARI, he was a researcher and a lecturer at the University of Cape Town, variously in the Research Initiative in Archive & Public Culture, the Land and Accountability Research Centre, the Department of English and the Centre for Popular Memory.

Robyn Foley is a researcher at the Centre for Sustainability Transitions at Stellenbosch University. Focusing on complexity in governance and the political economy, she has spent the past five years researching the phenomena of corruption and state capture in South Africa. She is co-editor of the *Anatomy of State Capture* (2021). Foley holds an MPhil in Sustainable Development from Stellenbosch University, a BSc in Physics and a BSc Honours in Technology Management from the University of Pretoria.

Patrick Heller is the Lyn Crost Professor of Social Sciences at Brown University. His main area of research is the comparative study of social inequality and democratic deepening. He is the author of *The Labor of Development: Workers in the Transformation of Capitalism in Kerala, India* (1999); co-author of *Social Democracy and the Global Periphery* (2006) and *Bootstrapping Democracy: Transforming Local Governance and Civil Society in Brazil* (2011); and co-editor of *Deliberation and Development: Rethinking the Role of Voice and Collective Action in Unequal Societies* (2015).

Jonathan Klaaren is a professor at the University of the Witwatersrand. He works in the areas of competition and regulation, the legal profession, migration and citizenship, and socio-legal studies. He is the author of *From Prohibited Immigrants to Citizens: The Origins of Citizenship and Nationality in South Africa* (2017). He holds a PhD in Sociology from Yale University and law degrees from Columbia (JD) and Wits (LLB). He was dean of the Wits Law School from 2010 to 2013 and director of the school's Mandela Institute from 2005 to 2007. In 2016, he served as an acting judge on the High Court of South Africa (South Gauteng).

Michael Marchant is the head of investigations at Open Secrets, where he works with a small team of investigators to expose the role of powerful private actors in corruption and economic crimes. An important focus of this work is the role of banks, auditing firms, consulting practices and law firms that enable economic crimes and profit from them. Marchant holds an MSc in International Development from the University of Edinburgh, a PPE (Honours) from the University of Cape Town and an LLB from the University of South Africa. He was the lead researcher on *Apartheid Guns and Money: A Tale of Profit* (2017).

Sizwe Mpofu-Walsh teaches at the University of the Witwatersrand. He was educated at the University of Cape Town and received a DPhil in International Relations from the University of Oxford, where he was a Weidenfeld Scholar. His 2017 book, *Democracy and Delusion: 10 Myths in South African Politics*, won the City Press Tafelberg Award. The book was accompanied by a rap album of the same name. His latest book, *The New Apartheid*, was published in 2021.

Devi Pillay is a researcher for the State Reform Programme at the Public Affairs Research Institute (PARI) in Johannesburg. She is an interdisciplinary social scientist, and her work has largely concerned the anthropology, history and historiography of the state, and its relationships with other institutions. She worked as a researcher and analyst for the Zondo Commission for the entirety of its lifespan, where she focused on developing a systematic understanding of state capture in the South African context, both within the legal framework and through a social scientific lens.

Barney Pityana ranks among the most respected public figures in South Africa. As an intellectual and human rights activist, he has a global following. Drawn to the Black Consciousness tradition at an early age, Pityana was harassed and detained by the apartheid state. In exile, he trained as an Anglican priest: he remains an exponent of liberation theology – the field in which he took a PhD. Pityana trained in law and is an admitted attorney. Between 1995 and 2001, he was chair of the South African Human Rights Commission. Subsequently, he was appointed vice chancellor of the University of South Africa – a post he held for nine years. At the behest of South Africa's president Cyril Ramaphosa, Professor Pityana serves as chair of the National Lotteries Commission.

Reg Rumney has worked as an economics, business and financial journalist in both broadcast and print media. He is a journalism teacher, economics and media researcher, and an editor. Rumney has written extensively on issues of transformation of the South African economy as the director of the research organisation BusinessMap. He founded the South African Reserve Bank Centre for Economics Journalism at Rhodes University, where he is now a research associate of the Department of Journalism and Media Studies. He has co-edited a literary magazine and is a published poet.

Luke Spiropoulos is a historian trained by and affiliated to the Wits History Workshop. He has worked in academic and civil society research spaces since 2011, covering a wide range of topics from migration histories to anti-racism strategy. He is currently undertaking doctoral research in the history of immigration governance in southern Africa.

Cherese Thakur graduated with an LLB from the University of KwaZulu-Natal, an LLM in Constitutional Litigation from the same institution, and a BCL from Oxford University. A qualified attorney, she has worked at the Helen Suzman Foundation and for the amaBhungane Centre for Investigative Journalism, where she was the advocacy director. Most recently, she has taken up a position at the German development agency GIZ. In 2022, Thakur was named one of the *Mail & Guardian*'s prestigious 200 Young South Africans.

Peter Vale is senior research fellow at the Centre for the Advancement of Scholarship at the University of Pretoria and senior fellow at the Public Affairs Research Institute (PARI). He is visiting professor in International Relations at the Universidade Federal de Santa Maria, Brazil, and an honorary professor in the Africa Earth Observatory Network, of which he was a founding member. Vale was the founding director of the Johannesburg Institute for Advanced Study and Nelson Mandela Professor of Politics at Rhodes University. He is co-author, with Vineet Thakur, of *South Africa, Race and the Making of International Relations* (2020).

Hennie van Vuuren is the founding director of Open Secrets. Educated at the University of the Witwatersrand, Johannesburg, and at the Free University, Berlin, he has more than 20 years' experience working on issues of economic crime and accountability from within civil society. Previous appointments include the Institute for Justice and Reconciliation, the Open Society Foundation for South Africa, the Institute for Security Studies and Transparency International. He is the author of the acclaimed *Apartheid Guns and Money: A Tale of Profit* (2017) and co-author of *The Devil in the Detail: How the Arms Deal Changed Everything* (2011).

Karl von Holdt is a professor at and former director of the Society, Work & Politics Institute at the University of the Witwatersrand. His books include *Transition from Below: Forging Trade Unionism and Workplace Change in South Africa* (2003); *Beyond the Apartheid Workplace: Studies in Transition* (2005), co-edited with Eddie Webster; *Conversations with Bourdieu: The Johannesburg Moment* (2012), co-authored with Michael Burawoy; and the co-edited volume *Critical Engagement with Public Sociology: A Perspective from the Global South* (2022).

A

Abrahams, Shaun 53, 93
accountability 3, 11
  evasion of 13, 51, 116, 118, 126, 198, 200, 205, 212
  weakening of 44, 50–51, 73
Achebe, Chinua
  A Man of the People 1–3, 8
African Bank 113–114
African National Congress *see* ANC
Afrikaner nationalism 218–219, 225
  ethnic 249
Ahmed Kathrada Foundation 12, 135, 139–140, 143, 146
AllPay Consolidated Investment Holdings (Pty) Ltd 95–96, 104, 138
AmaBhungani 113, 135, 154–155, 162–164
ANC 6, 25, 30, 131
  behaviour driving decay within 56
  electoral decline of 35–36
  Leninist organisational doctrine of 68, 71, 76
  moral regeneration movement 67
  people's expectations of 7–8
  see also factional politics within ANC
ANC economic policy 8, 22–23, 34
  Growth, Employment and Redistribution (GEAR) plan 70, 131, 247
  racial-nationalist approach 68, 72
  Reconstruction and Development Programme (RDP) 131, 148, 247–248
  see also South African economy: re-embedding of commodities in
ANC as mass liberation movement
  command and control culture of 222
  in exile 219–221, 223

and transition to democracy 14, 76, 221–226
ANC Tripartite Alliance 34, 68, 131–132, 221, 252
  conflict between partners within 5, 19, 23
ANN7 48*t*, 51, 152, 159–162, 167n4
anti-apartheid struggle 67, 232n1, 248 *see also* civil society: influence of anti-apartheid protest history on
anti-corruption discourse 20, 91
  Marxist-Fanonist 13, 65–66, 68–73, 81
  moralist 13, 65–68, 70–72, 81
  neoliberal 13, 36, 65–66, 68–73, 76, 81
anti-state capture litigation 13, 52–53, 93–96, 101, 130, 134, 139, 144, 187
  Glenister cases 98–99, 137
  role of public interest law organisations 93, 96–100, 102–103, 136–138
  rule-of-law agenda of 100, 103–104, 136–137
  see also civil society's role in curtailing state capture
Antonie, Francis 132, 135–137, 142–143
apartheid 3, 5, 7, 10, 12, 23, 220
  Bantustan system 8, 222–223, 225
  corruption/state capture continuities 8, 14, 56, 184, 193, 198, 200, 203–206
  military-industrial complex 201–203
  see also Armscor
Arms Deal 6, 25, 27–28, 31, 90, 193, 204–205
  civil society mobilisation around 98–99, 134
Armscor 201–202, 206 *see also* global/international corporations: support for apartheid arms procurement programme
Auditor-General 113–114

B

Bain & Company 31, 34, 48*t*, 50, 116–117, 121, 123, 125–126
Balton, Neeshan 133, 135, 139–142, 144–147, 148n4
Bank of Baroda 118, 207
BBC Newsnight
    South Africa's Gupta Scandal 184–187
Bell Pottinger 34, 51, 118, 122, 153, 187
Biebuyck, Brian 115–116
Bhardwaj, Vinayak 132–135
black bourgeoisie 23, 69–70
black capitalist class 24, 28, 33, 70, 72, 79–81
    see also class formation
black economic elite formation *see under* class formation
Black Economic Empowerment (BEE) 8, 25, 28, 48*t*, 68, 249
    Broad-Based (BBBEE) 24, 28, 47*f*
Black Sash Trust 53, 58n7, 95–96, 99, 103
Bolsonaro, Jair 229, 237
Bosasa 25, 55, 115–116, 126
Botha, P.W. 198, 203, 205
Brazil
    changing civil society-state relations in 243–246, 252
    local government in 238
    Partido dos Trabalhadores (PT) 236–237, 244–245
    see also democratic deepening; social movement formation in South Africa: comparison with Brazil and India
Brkic, Branko 54, 162
Broederbond 218–219

C

Cash Paymaster Services (CPS) 94–96
Centre for Accountability 98–99
Centre for Applied Legal Studies 95, 99–100, 103
China 19, 31, 66, 72, 202
China South Rail 50, 207
City Press 158, 163, 181
civil service *see* public service
civil society 212
    calls for institutional change 97–98
    influence of anti-apartheid protest history on 97–98, 103, 131, 142, 160, 227–228, 237, 247–248
    see also democracy in South Africa: and containerisation of civil society
civil society, balance of political society and 12, 146, 236–237, 240–243, 249–250
    repercussions for democratic deepening 241–242, 244, 248–249, 251–253
    see also Brazil: changing civil society-state relations in
civil society mass mobilisation 3, 11, 19, 41, 53, 68, 93, 98, 130, 139, 227–228, 237
    impact of court action on 144–145
    role of coalitions in 101, 103, 134, 140–141, 143–147
    see also Right2Know campaign; SAVE South Africa campaign; #ZumaMustFall movement
civil society's role in curtailing state capture
    approaches to Chapter Nine institutions 50, 53, 57n5, 91, 98, 138
    commissions of inquiry 12, 54, 145, 164, 230
    court challenges *see* anti-state capture litigation
    increased business participation 97–98, 103, 134
    investigative media *see* media's role in exposing state capture
    mass communication approach 130–131, 134–136
    public mobilisation *see* civil society mass mobilisation
    see also whistleblowers
class formation
    black economic elite 7, 9–10, 13, 20–21, 24, 26, 32
    link between patronage-dependent accumulation and 70, 79–81
    project of re-embedding 27–29
    see also patronage-violence networks: elite formation as intrinsic to
clientelism 3, 52 *see also* patronage
colonialism 5, 23
    legacies of 3, 10, 37, 70, 235
Congress for a Democratic South Africa 7, 9–10
Congress of South African Trade Unions (Cosatu) 5, 19, 23, 27, 68–69, 247
Constitution of South Africa 2–3, 7, 9, 24, 28, 43, 96, 227
    on public administration 123, 125
    and right to privacy 95–96, 155
constitutional dimension of state capture 90–91, 93, 102–103

Constitutional Court judgments 50, 53, 91, 93–96, 102, 137
corrupt syndicates 36, 80
    establishment of political machines by 13, 73, 77–79, 81
    participation of private businesses in 74–75
    see also 'Zupta syndicate'
corruption 1, 3–5, 13, 26, 41, 50, 56–57, 148n3
    civil society's anti-corruption efforts 132, 135–136, 139–144
    as counter move to colonial accumulation 13
    Covid-19 related 35, 192
    diverse conceptualisations of 12, 42, 66
    nexus between formal and structural moments of 70–71
    political economy of 20, 25, 33, 39
    private sector/corporate complicity in 34, 73–74, 91, 122, 124, 126, 163, 177–178, 199, 212
    provincial regimes of 9, 30, 32, 34
    at Vaal University of Technology 232
    see also anti-corruption discourse; Arms Deal; 'racket' society
Corruption Watch 53, 58n9, 93, 95–96, 99–101, 138, 146
Council for the Advancement of the South African Constitution 12, 53, 58n9, 93
Covid-19 pandemic 34–35, 165, 192, 251
Council for the Advancement of the South African Constitution (CASAC) 12, 53, 58n9, 93, 96, 99–100

D
Daily Maverick 158, 162–163, 166
De Klerk, F.W. 197–198
Debevoise & Plimpton LLP 204–205
decolonisation 21, 70, 72
deep state
    complicity in economic crimes 198–200, 212
    loose association with shadow state 199
    relationship between apartheid military-industrial complex and 201, 209
    role of intelligence and security agencies in 209–210
    see also economic crimes: deep state complicity in
Deloitte 51, 112–114, 119, 125
democracy in South Africa 2, 43, 236–237
    and containerisation of civil society 237, 240–241, 249–250

maintaining legitimacy of 51–52
democracy, Tocquevillian assumptions about 2, 238, 241
Democratic Alliance 20, 68, 99–100, 144
democratic deepening 14, 235–237
    democratic stateness dimension of 239
    participatory democracy dimension of 237–240, 242, 245
    representative democracy dimension of 235, 238–239, 241, 251–252
    see also civil society, balance of political society and: repercussions for democratic deepening
democratisation 239, 241–243, 245
developmental state 22–23, 27, 31, 70, 76, 123, 236–237
disembedding of marketisation processes
    global 13, 20–21, 33
    under Mbeki 22–23, 26
DJ Citi Lyts 190
Dlamini, Bathabile 48*t*, 53, 91, 95,
Dlamini-Zuma, Nkosazana 145, 151–152, 176–177
Dutch East India Company 176, 197

E
Earthlife Africa 53, 58n8
economic crimes
    during apartheid 90, 204, 206, 210–212
    People's Tribunal on 146, 212
    role of global banking system in 208
    submission to Zondo Commission on 209
    see also deep state: complicity in economic crimes
Economic Freedom Fighters (EFF) 19–20, 99, 138, 144–145, 250
Eskom 29, 31, 34, 134
    irregularities in procurement processes at 46, 49, 113, 117, 145
Estina dairy farm scandal 30, 49, 112

F
factional politics within ANC 9–10, 19, 35–36, 53, 158, 165, 176–177, 185–186, 237 *see also under* local government in South Africa
factionalism 68, 76–77, 152
Ferrostaal 204–205
FIFA World Cup 103, 246
Forbes, Kiernan 'AKA' 188–189
Frankfurt School of Critical Theory 13, 42, 57n1
Freedom Under Law 58, 93, 96, 99–100, 103

G

Gigaba, Malusi 49, 188, 193n2

global corporations *see* international corporations

globalisation 22, 24, 26, 178, 253
  neoliberal 234–236

Goodman Gallery, Johannesburg 178, 181

Gordhan, Pravin 19–20, 31, 55, 137, 147, 163, 185–186
  attacks on/firing of 40, 97, 113, 142, 187
  Operation Fiela 143

Gordhan-Ramaphosa campaign 33–34, 97, 152

Gupta, Atul 156, 159–160, 182

Gupta network 5, 39, 91, 109, 185
  see also Zuma-Gupta state capture project; Zupta syndicate

H

Harber, Anton 156–158, 160, 162–163, 165

Directorate for Priority Crime Investigation (the Hawks) 50, 98–99, 134–135, 211, 230

Helen Suzman Foundation 93, 99–100, 132, 136–138, 140

HIV/AIDS 97, 242, 245

Hogan Lovells 99, 115–116

Howaldtswerke-Deutsche Werft (HDW) 204–205

HSBC 118, 207–208

I

Independent News and Media Group 157, 160, 164, 166, 167n6

Independent Police Investigative Directorate 101, 135, 137, 230

Independent Regulatory Board for Auditors (IRBA) 112–115, 120121

India 19, 71, 226, 229
  Hindu nationalist BJP party 236–237, 247, 249, 251
  involution of civil society in 240–241, 246
  Kerala 242, 246
  limited powers of local government in 243, 248–249
  see also democratic deepening; social movement formation in South Africa: comparison with Brazil and India

Indian National Congress 241–242

inequality 9, 24, 34, 52, 235
  apartheid legacy of 36–37, 241–242
  economic 154, 164, 191
  endemic/deep-seated 9, 12, 241
  racial 10, 23

informal political-economic system 11, 24–26, 28–29, 32–33
  in Eastern Cape 25, 30–31
  see also patronage-violence complex

Ingenieurkontor Lübeck (IKL) 204–205

international corporations 22–23
  complicity in corruption 34, 114, 121, 123, 125–126, 163–164, 199
  as enablers of state capture 47f, 50–51, 112–113, 116–118, 153, 178, 187, 199, 206, 209, 212–213
  support for apartheid arms procurement programme 202–207
  see also professionals as enablers of corruption and state capture

Ivanov, Viktor 178–179f

J

Jonas, Mcebisi 40, 48t, 185

judiciary 27, 44f, 55, 101, 138, 187, 227, 239, 210

July 2021 uprising 34, 36, 166

K

Kathrada, Ahmed 139–140, 143 *see also* Ahmed Kathrada Foundation

KPMG 31, 34, 51, 112–113, 119, 121, 125, 187, 208

KwaZulu-Natal 9, 36, 77
  political killings in 56

L

Legal Practice Council 116, 119–121

local government
  hollowing out of participatory spaces in 249
  insulated, patronage-driven 5, 28–31, 32, 54, 56, 75, 77, 140, 143, 158, 222, 243
  as locus of factional politics 25, 104

M

Mabulu, Ayanda
  State Capture 182–183

Mabuza, David 54, 186

Madonsela, Thuli 3, 11, 55, 138, 185, 230, 232n4

Magashule, Ace 30, 32, 36, 53–54, 109, 186 *see also* Estina dairy farm scandal

Mail & Guardian 53–54, 121, 158, 164–165

malfeasance within government 4, 11, 75, 152, 192, 197, 210, 224, 230
role of professionals in facilitation of *see* professionals as enablers of corruption and state capture
see also corruption
Mandela, Nelson 2, 22, 24, 67, 133, 154, 186
Mani Pulite scandal, Italy 71, 74–75
Marechera, Dambudzo 175, 183
Marikana Massacre 140, 250–251
marketisation 12, 21–23, 29, 33–34
Mass Democratic Movement 221–222,
Mbalula, Fikile 177, 188
Mbeki, Thabo 5, 7, 28, 30, 133–134, 156, 189, 220–222, 228, 247
downfall/recall of 20, 27, 36
dynamics of renationalisation under 22–24
see also Arms Deal scandal
McKinsey & Company 31, 50, 117, 121–122, 125, 187
media capture 152–153, 162, 167, 177, 186
attacks on established press 156–157
New Age newspaper's role in 43, 48*t*, 51, 57n2, 135–136, 156–159, 161
RET campaign 153–155
state ownership as key part of 164–166
#WMCLeaks 153–155, 167n1
see also ANN7; social media; South African Broadcasting Corporation
media's role in exposing state capture 14, 29, 52–53, 111, 131, 135–136, 147, 209, 227
Gupta wedding scandal 165
#GuptaLeaks 4, 46, 49, 51, 162–164, 187, 206–207
romanticisation of 177, 186–187
through collaborative journalism 163
Modi, Narendra 229, 241, 249
Moeti, Koketso 132, 143–144
money laundering 112, 115, 118, 202, 207–208, 211
Moyane, Tom 48*t*, 54, 115–117
Multichoice 182, 186
Murray, Brett
The Spear 178–180&*f*, 181–183, 192

N
National Director of Public Prosecutions (NDPP) 53, 93–94
fight against partiality in 93
National Party regime 14, 218–219

National Prosecuting Authority (NPA) 4, 27, 31, 34, 50, 54, 135, 164, 186, 211–212, 230
disbanding of Scorpions within 98, 137
Mokgoro inquiry 49
Open Secrets memorandum to 211–212
Special Investigating Unit 231
Zuma's control of key positions in 28, 53, 93–94
National Treasury 20, 28, 94, 117
attempted capture of 33, 90
oversight role played by 50
Ndlulamithi 190
Nedbank 118, 207
Nelson Mandela Bay 25, 32–33
Nene, Nhlanhla 40, 91, 137, 139, 141
neoliberalism 19, 21–23, 28, 245, 247, 253
opposition of social movements to 132, 242, 248
see also anti-corruption discourse: neoliberal; globalisation: neoliberal
News24 116, 147, 153–154, 162–163, 166
Ntlemeza, Berning 232, 233n3
Nugent Commission of Inquiry *see under* South African Revenue Service
Nyovest, Cassper 189–190

O
Oakbay Resources and Energy Limited 112–113, 164
Office of the Public Protector 50–51, 102, 230
2016 'State of Capture' report 39, 41, 46, 91, 138
Open Secrets website 113–114, 117, 125, 145–146, 202–203, 205, 209
Open Society Foundation 89, 141
Opposition to Urban Tolling Alliance (OUTA) 136, 143
Organisation for Undoing Tax Abuse 99–100

P
patrimonialism 2, 8, 252
and rising neo-patrimonialism 10–11, 56
patronage 52, 56, 70, 77–78, 124, 188
role in community politics 79
see also clientelism
patronage networks 45*f*, 126, 234, 237, 243
deep state 212–213
patronage-violence complex 25–26, 29, 31, 35, 37, 79
destruction of SOEs by 27, 31, 34

patronage-violence complex (*continued*)
  elite formation as intrinsic to 32–33
  involvement of business in 25, 31–32
  and rent-seeking 50, 69, 92, 235–237
  as source of ANC funding 25, 30–32
  violence as integral to 32, 48*t*
  Zuma's expansion of 28–29
People's Tribunal on Economic Crimes 146, 212
Polokwane conference 5–6, 20, 132, 247
popular culture, narrowing of state capture
    narrative in 14, 176, 183, 191–192
  nudity as metaphor in 182–183
  see also BBC Newsnight; Desai, Rehad;
    Mabulu, Ayanda; Murray, Brett; rap music
    narratives on state capture; Zalk, Naashon
populism 27, 36, 51, 200, 234
Portfolio Committee on Public Enterprises
    46, 49
postcolonial African State 3, 8, 10–11
power elite 3, 46, 57n3
  Zuma-centred 7, 13, 30, 32–33, 42, 46–47, 52
power relations
  between corporate and political elite 14,
    39, 51, 55, 67
Prevention and Combating of Corrupt
    Activities Act 100, 122
Prevention of Organised Crime Act of 1998
    113, 122
PricewaterhouseCoopers (PwC) 51, 112,
    114–115, 119, 123
privatisation 22–23, 31, 177
professionalism
  contested meaning of 110–111
  ethics and independence as key facets of
    118–121
  rebuilding of public trust in 112, 125
professionals as enablers of corruption and
    state capture 13–14, 47*f*, 50–51, 99, 122,
    126, 212
  auditors and accountants 109, 111–115,
    118–119, 123, 208
  bankers and financial advisors 14, 47*f*, 51, 118
  lawyers 13–14, 47*f*, 51, 109, 111, 115–116, 118
  management consultants 13, 51, 109, 111,
    116–118
  reputational damage linked to 34, 112–113,
    115, 117–118
  sanctions against 121–122
  transparency as structural intervention
    124–125

propaganda 51–52, 154, 159, 178–179*f*, 219
Protection of State Information Bill 92, 135,
    208
public administration *see* public service
  see also corrupt syndicates
Public Affairs Research Institute (PARI)
    41–42, 52, 57, 92, 142, 146, 232, 237
  'Betrayal of the Promise' report 4, 28–30,
    32, 51, 90, 234
  state capture conferences 11–12
public procurement system
  need for reform of 119, 125
  manipulation/violation of 28, 44*f*, 48*t*,
    49–50, 92, 95, 113, 116–117, 126
Public Relations and Communications
    Association (PRCA) 118, 121–122
public service
  ANC's powers of appointment and
    dismissal in 76–78, 81
  compromised professionalism of 123–124,
    225–226, 232
  corroding ideology of 224–225
  importance of checks and balances within
    73–75, 125
  politically insulated 75–76, 79, 81
  politicisation of 126
Public Service Commission 226, 232

R
'racket' society
  concept of 13, 42–43, 57
  types of racketeering in 48*t*
radical economic transformation 28, 53
  as elite political project 6–7, 10, 26, 31, 52,
    153, 234
  Marxist-Fanonist 69
Ramaphosa, Cyril
  anti-state capture platform of 34–35,
    53–55, 67, 93–94, 185, 191, 229–230
  complicity in state capture of 34–35, 55,
    176–177, 186, 192
  media attacks on 153, 166
  'New Dawn' narrative of 20, 89, 191–192
  precarious presidency of 9, 29, 35–36, 89,
    97, 147, 154, 176
  see also Gordhan-Ramaphosa campaign
rap music narratives on state capture
  commercial endorsement of 188–191
  independent and underground criticism
    of 190–191

see also DJ Citi Lyts; Forbes, Kiernan
'AKA'; Ndlulamithi; Nyovest, Cassper
Regiments Capital 117, 122, 207
repurposing of state institutions/SOEs 2–4, 42,
52, 90, 134
to facilitate rent extraction 5, 7, 24, 39, 44*f*,
47*f*, 49–51, 55, 234, 250
#RhodesMustFall protests 10
Right2Know (R2K) campaign 135–136, 140
Roussos, Mike 131, 133, 135–136, 139–140,
142, 1144, 146–147
Russia 19, 31
Zuma-Gupta nuclear deal with 32, 40, 53

S

SAP 50, 121
SAVE South Africa campaign 97, 142, 144
Secrecy Bill *see* Protection of State
Information Bill
Section27 97, 136, 140
service delivery
impact of state capture on 56, 73, 140
protests 51, 243, 248
shadow state 92
deception and manipulation within 44*f*–45, 46
'fightback' campaign within 54–55
protection racket 52
relationship between constitutional state
and 6, 42, 92, 103
rent-seeking initiatives of 50
roles and functions within 47*f*
Shaik brothers 48*t*, 134, 184, 204
Sikwebu, Dinga 131–134, 140–142, 144–146, 148
Slovo, Joe 220, 232n3
social media 14, 100, 166
onslaught of 'fake news' in 34, 51–52, 153,
155
Zupta campaign 34, 152–155, 166
social movement formation in South Africa
19–20, 101–102, 132, 140, 210, 221
comparison with Brazil and India 236,
241–252
Sole, Sam 154–156, 163
South African Airways (SAA) 31, 49, 114, 123, 137
South African Broadcasting Corporation
(SABC) 51, 135, 138, 140, 161–162,
164–166
South African Communist Party (SACP) 5, 19,
23, 68, 70, 132, 145, 181, 219–221
South African economy

re-embedding of commodities in 13,
20–24, 26–28, 29, 33–34, 37
South African Federation of Trade Unions
(Saftu) 69, 142, 145
South African Institute of Chartered
Accountants 120–121
South African Police Services (SAPS) 4, 27, 230
South African Reserve Bank 28, 55
South African Revenue Service (SARS) 28, 31,
34, 112, 123, 137–138, 142, 148n5, 230
Nugent Commission of Inquiry into 48*t*,
49, 54, 115–117
'Rogue Unit' report 113, 137
South African Social Security Agency
(SASSA) 99, 138
legal mobilisation against state capture in
90–91, 94–96
Southern African Faith Communities'
Environment Institute 53, 58n8
Soviet Union 22, 72, 179*f*, 181, 183–184, 202
State Capacity Research Project (SCRP) report
28, 41, 89–92, 94
state-building 98
ANC focus on 223–224
state capture 29, 54
dominant narrative of 176–178, 184–185,
191–193
neocolonial dimensions of 13, 184
as outcome of predatory power 43, 44*f*–45,
52, 56
and questions of public/private division 92,
103, 122–123, 176–177, 192, 200–201
see also Zuma-Gupta state capture project
state capture, understandings of term 3–6, 15,
39, 72, 91, 132, 145–147, 152
as form of 'grand corruption' 41–42, 56, 90,
133–134, 145, 152, 154, 185, 206
see also popular culture, narrowing of state
capture narrative in
state institutions
apartheid legacy within 22
decimation/destruction of 2, 11, 13, 31, 66,
90, 109, 113, 118, 230
see also repurposing of state institutions/
SOEs
state-owned enterprises (SOEs) 34, 97, 119, 159
destruction/looting of 2, 11, 13, 31, 92,
123, 140, 206
lack of/destruction of expertise and
capacity in 34, 80, 102, 122–124, 212

state-owned enterprises (*continued*)
    see also Eskom; patronage-violence
      networks: destruction of SOEs by;
      Transnet; Zuma-Gupta state capture
      project: focus on state institutions/
      SOEs
State Security Agency 48*t*, 52, 210
    High-Level Review Panel 49
Steinhoff financial scandal 57n4, 114
Stofile, Makhenkesi 97, 139
Sunday Times 4, 162, 187
Survé, Iqbal 160, 164

T
Tambo, Oliver 220–221
Thomson-CF/Thales 203–205
Transnet 29, 31, 49, 122, 135, 163, 207
    locomotive procurement project 117
    investigations surrounding 46
Trillian 40, 122
Trump, Donald 155, 199, 229
Truth and Reconciliation Commission (TRC)
    12, 90, 201, 209–210
Twitter 152–154

U
unemployment 52, 78, 248, 250
United Democratic Front (UDF) 131, 141,
    145, 221

V
Van Rooyen, Des 40, 137, 139
VBS Mutual Bank scandal 25, 32, 54, 113–115

W
Washington Consensus 70, 131, 148n2
Watson brothers 25, 47, 109
whistleblowers 32, 40, 52, 73, 111, 118, 138,
    164
    and Protected Disclosures Act 125
white monopoly capital (WMC) 5, 28, 52,
working class 23, 27, 34, 69, 70, 132

Z
Zalk, Naashon
    South Africa Corruption Inc. 184–187
Zondo Commission 11, 35, 41, 43, 48*t*, 49,
    145, 187, 206, 230
    civil society support for 145, 230

on criminalisation of SSA 210
Gupta network as central focus of 46, 77
Open Secrets submission to 209
report 12, 40, 231
on role of South African media 177
symbolic value of 229, 231
testimony of professionals before 114, 117,
    123–124
Zuma, Duduzane 5–6, 40, 91, 161, 186,
    188–189
Zuma, Jacob
    appearances before Zondo Commission
      48*t*, 57n2, 198
    corruption charges against 6, 9, 11, 27
    forced resignation of 11, 20, 54, 89, 97, 139,
      147, 177, 185–186, 191, 228, 237
    lack of moral integrity of 228–229
    motions of no confidence against 3,
      20, 50
    Nkandla 'security upgrades' 50–51, 57n6,
      99, 134, 139, 165, 187
    patrimonial monopolisation of state by 252
    succession to presidency of 5–6, 10, 27, 132
    use of state security apparatus by 50, 52,
      92, 135, 138, 209–210
    see also Murray, Brett: *The Spear*
Zuma-Gupta state capture project 3, 5–6, 11,
    25, 224, 227
    corrosion of rule of law by 29, 50, 53, 56
    cost and broader impact of 55–56, 197
    deepening of informal patronage-violence
      network through 28, 33
    focus on state institutions/SOEs 7, 9, 13,
      27, 29–30, 49, 52, 54, 198–199, 230
    and Gupta-linked front companies 29–30,
      32–33, 40, 47, 112–113, 117, 163–164,
      177, 207
    private sector/corporate involvement
      in 47*f*, 50, 55, 92, 95, 132, 152, 166,
      198–199
    replication at provincial/local government
      level 5, 30, 35, 54, 77
    role of cabinet reshuffles in 6, 40, 50,
      134–135, 138
    see also global/international corporations:
      complicity in corruption and state
      capture; Mabulu, Ayanda
#ZumaMustFall movement 4, 14, 40, 141
Zupta syndicate 6–7, 9, 77, 151, 165–166
    see also social media: Zupta campaign